FAMILY VALUES

Family Values:
Between Neoliberalism and
the New Social Conservatism

Melinda Cooper

ZONE BOOKS

near futures

ZONE BOOKS
633 Vanderbilt Street, Brooklyn, New York 11218

First paperback edition 2019

Printed in the United States of America.
Distributed by The MIT Press,
Cambridge, Massachusetts, and London, England.

Library of Congress Cataloging-in-Publication Data
Names: Cooper, Melinda, author
Title: Family values: between neoliberalism and the new
    social conservatism /Melinda Cooper.
Description: New York: Zone Books [2017] | Includes
    bibliographical references and index.
Identifiers: LCCN 2016042842 | ISBN 9781935408840
    (hardcover: alk. paper)

CONTENTS

CHAPTER ONE

Between Neoliberalism and the New Social Conservatism

> The family in the Western world has been radically altered,
> some claim almost destroyed, by events of the last three decades.
> — Gary Becker, *Treatise on the Family*

The history of the family is one of perpetual crisis. Yet, this crisis presents itself in distinct, even contradictory fashion to different political constituencies. For social conservatives of the left and right—the inheritors of 1970s neoconservatism—the contours of family crisis appear to have changed very little over the past several decades. The American family still seems to be suffering from a general epidemic of "fatherlessness."[1] Young, impoverished women, particularly African Americans and Latinas, are still having children out of wedlock and still expecting the welfare state to take care of them. In the 1990s, social theorists complicated this story somewhat when they announced that the long-standing, quasi-mythical crisis of the African American family, infamously diagnosed by the neoconservative Daniel Patrick Moynihan in 1965, had now spread to the white middle class, encouraging generations of younger women to forsake the stability of marriage in favor of career-minded narcissism.[2] Even more recently, they have discovered that marriage itself has become a marker of class in American society—a privilege that appears to be reserved for the college-educated middle class—and inversely, perhaps, a practice that

should be encouraged as a shortcut to social mobility.[3] With all its variations and refinements, this discourse has shifted only slightly since it
was first fashioned in the 1970s. And although it has inspired four
decades of punitive welfare reform, its proponents continue to blame
the Great Society welfare state for what they see as the ongoing decline
of the American family.

Neoliberals have always entertained a more complex relationship
to the discourse of family crisis. It would not be an exaggeration to
say that the enormous political activism of American neoliberals in
the 1970s was inspired by the fact of changing family structures. Certainly Gary Becker, the Chicago school economist singled out as exemplary by Michel Foucault, understood the breakdown of the Fordist
family wage to be the critical event of his time, and one whose rever-
berations could be discerned in everything from shifting race relations
to the recomposition of the labor market and the changing imperatives
of social welfare.[4] In effect, while it lasted, the Fordist family wage
not only functioned as a mechanism for the normalization of gender
and sexual relationships, but it also stood at the heart of the midcentury organization of labor, race, and class, defining African American
men by their exclusion from the male breadwinner wage and African American women by their relegation to agricultural and domestic
labor in the service of white households. The neoliberal response to
the crisis of the Fordist family can be described, in the first instance,
as adaptive and accommodationist. Eschewing the overt moralism
of social conservatives, neoliberals are interested in subsuming the
newly liberated labor of former housewives within an expanded market for domestic services and are intent on devising new mechanisms
for pricing the risks of (for example) racial discrimination or unsafe
sex. There is no form of social liberation, it would seem, that the neoliberal economist cannot incorporate within a new market for contractual services or high-risk credit.

Yet it would be a mistake to think that neoliberalism is any less invested in the value of the family than are social conservatives. "Since the family is the foundation of all civil society," notes Gary Becker, we have good reason to be concerned about the "enormous changes in the stability and composition of families in recent decades."[5] Neo-⌐ liberals are particularly concerned about the enormous social costs that derive from the breakdown of the stable Fordist family: the costs that have been incurred, for example, by women who opt for no-fault divorce, women who have children out of wedlock or those who engage in unprotected sex without private insurance; and the fact that these costs accrue to the government and taxpayer rather than the private family.[6] Although they are much more prepared than are social con-⌐ servatives to accommodate changes in the nature and form of relationships within the family, neoliberal economists and legal theorists wish to reestablish the private family as the primary source of economic security and a comprehensive alternative to the welfare state. If American welfare reform has been singularly focused on the question of marriage promotion and responsible family formation in the past few decades, it is thanks to the ongoing collaboration between neoliberals and social conservatives on this point in particular.

In contrast to both neoliberals and social conservatives, and in spite of the prominence of family in contemporary social policy, a certain kind of left-wing critic has come to see neoliberal capitalism as itself destructive of family life. The idea that the flexible labor relations introduced by neoliberal reform have somehow disabled the long-term obligations of love and parenthood is pervasive among left-wing social theorists interested in the effects of late modernism on the structures of intimate life. Each in their own way, and with varying degrees of nostalgia, Anthony Giddens, Zygmunt Bauman, Ulrich Beck, Elizabeth Beck-Gernsheim, and Eva Illouz all point to the increasingly fleeting character of love in an era dominated by the short-term contract and employment at will.[7]

By far the most elaborate and sustained argument in this direction, however, is provided by the German political economist Wolfgang Streeck, whose recent work reflects at length on what he sees as the causal relationship between the flexible employment contract and the "flexible family."[8] Streeck is concerned here with the dismantling of the standard postwar employment relationship and its correlate, the so-called Fordist family consisting of a male worker, a stay-at-home wife and mother, and two or more children. As he notes, the economic security of the postwar era was premised on a tightly enforced sexual division of labor that relegated women to lower-paid, precarious forms of employment and indexed the wage of the Fordist worker to the costs of maintaining a wife and children at home. How and why did this particular architecture of economic security crumble so rapidly in the 1970s, Streeck asks, and why did its decline provoke so little opposition from those who benefited so much from it?

Searching for an answer to this question, he notes that "the social and family structure that the standard employment relationship had once underwritten has itself dissolved in a process of truly revolutionary change. In fact, it appears that the Fordist family was replaced by a flexible family in much the same way as Fordist employment was replaced by flexible employment, during the same period and also all across the Western world."[9] The destabilization of the long-term marital contract, Streeck wants to argue, occurred a short but significant time before the dismantling of the Fordist employment relationship and can be seen as having provoked the decline of the latter.[10] The revolution in family law and intimate relationships that occurred in the 1960s—from the introduction of no-fault divorce to the growing acceptance of cohabitation—destroyed the very raison d'être of the Fordist family wage and thereby led to its gradual phasing out over the following years. If women were no longer tied to men in long-term relationships of economic dependence, and if men were no longer obliged to look after a wife and children for life, then who would be left to defend that great Fordist institution of economic security, the family wage?

At this point, Streeck's antifeminism becomes overt. It was feminism, after all, that first challenged the legal and institutional forms of the Fordist family by encouraging women to seek an independent wage on a par with men and transforming marriage from a long-term, noncontractual obligation into a contract that could be dissolved at will. In so doing, feminists (whom he imagines as middle class) robbed women (whom he imagines as working class) of the economic security that came from marriage to a Fordist worker.[11] By undermining the idea that men should be paid wages high enough to care for a wife and children, feminism helped managers to generalize the norm of precarious employment and workplace flexibility, eventually compromising the security of all workers.

Without descending into the overt antifeminism of Wolfgang Streeck, Luc Boltanski and Eve Chiapello's *New Spirit of Capitalism* offers a conceptual critique of the countercultural left that leads ineluctably to the same conclusions. Their revisionist history of late Fordist social movements points to an incipient fracture between the productive left, focused on building and maintaining the economic security afforded by the postwar consensus, and what they refer to as the artistic left, more interested in critiquing the predictable securities and norms of Fordist life.[12] If the former can be more or less equated with the trade union movement and old socialist left, the latter consisted of the distinctly new components of the left—from feminism and gay liberation to the student movement and counterculture. Having thus distinguished between a good labor politics (focused on economic security and the permanence of social relations) and a bad sexual politics (focused on liberation from the same set of social relations), Boltanski and Chiapello identify the decline of the family as the most visible sign of neoliberalism's social insecurity. "During these years of social regression," they write, the family "became a much more fluid and fragile institution, compounding job insecurity and the general sense of insecurity.... The search for maximum flexibility in firms chimed with a depreciation of the family as a factor of temporal and geographical inflexibility, so that…similar ideological schemas are mobilized to justify adaptability in work relations and mobility in emotional life."[13] Like Streeck, Boltanski and Chiapello argue that the artistic left prepared the groundwork for the neoliberal assault on economic and social security by destroying its intimate foundations in the postwar family. By implication, their analysis posits the restoration of the Fordist family (or some revision thereof) as a necessary component of a renewed left agenda.

It is somewhat more surprising to find such reflections in the work of Nancy Fraser, who has done so much to uncover the role of the family wage in shaping the sexual divisions of labor constitutive of American Fordism. Yet, Fraser's longstanding commitment to the conceptual distinction between cultural recognition and economic redistribution places her in a similar bind to Boltanski and Chiapello when it comes to the sexual politics of capital.[14] In her most recent work, Fraser accuses second-wave feminism of having colluded with neoliberalism in its efforts to destroy the family wage. "Was it mere coincidence that second-wave feminism and neoliberalism prospered in tandem? Or was there some perverse, subterranean, elective affinity between them?"[15] Fraser goes on to answer in the affirmative: "Our critique of the family wage," she writes, "now supplies a good part of the romance that invests flexible capitalism with a higher meaning and moral point."[16] What she offers as an alternative is a renewed politics of economic security that would allow women (and, in the long run, men) to sustain the families that have been torn apart by the enforced flexibility of the neoliberal labor market. Without advocating the simple return to Fordism that Streeck seems to have in mind, Fraser seeks to imagine an improved family wage that would in the first instance recognize and valorize women's reproductive labor and perhaps ultimately disrupt the gendered division of labor itself.[17] But having identified the specific evil of neoliberalism as the destruction of the Fordist family wage, her analysis leads inescapably to the conclusion that resistance demands the restoration of family, albeit in a more progressive, egalitarian form.

Each of these theorists is clearly indebted to the work of Karl Polanyi,[18] whose thesis of the "double movement" is pervasive and well nigh uncontested in contemporary left-wing formulations of anti-capitalist critique.[19] In his signature work of historical sociology, *The Great Transformation* (1944), Polanyi distinguishes laissez-faire capitalism from all previous economies of exchange by virtue of the fact that it strives to include what was once inalienable within the ambit of exchange value.[20] Reaching its purest form in nineteenth-century England, Polanyi sees modern capitalism as inhabited by a relentless calculative drive that submits even foundational social values such as labor, land, and money to the metrics of commodity exchange. Under the conditions of modern capitalism, human labor itself loses any intrinsic value and sees its price fixed by the highest bidder; money is subject to the nominal measure of interest and exchange rates; and the price of land is determined by the fluctuations of speculative value. Thus, essential social properties that should by rights function as foundations and anchors to any stable system of exchange are set to circulate in the open market as "fictitious commodities." Having posited Aristotle's household economy of measured exchange as ethical reference point, Polanyi can only envisage these innovations as departures from a transcendant norm of economic justice. Polanyi understands modern capitalism as the generalization of Aristotle's "chrematistics"—an economic regime in which the perverse logic of self-multiplying value has overtaken and subsumed the measured reproduction of foundational social values.[21] As a twentieth-century social democrat, however, he also wants to argue that the disintegrative forces of the free market will inevitably provoke a "countermovement" bent on protecting the social order (indeed the free market itself) from the excesses of laissez-faire capitalism.

In a somewhat paradoxical manner, Polanyi imagines the countermovement as external to the dynamics of capitalism and yet historically inevitable and indeed necessitated by the free market itself. Reflecting on the history of nineteenth-century industrial capitalism, he observes that the laissez-faire utopia of the self-regulating market cannot survive in the long run without the intervention of some external form of social protectionism. When implemented as an economic ideal, the self-regulating market unleashes destructive forces that threaten the very existence of the market system. Pushed to the limit, then, the individualizing excesses of liberal contractualism will generate at some point a social countermovement intent on protecting workers from the stiff winds of the market. But while it must be understood as external to free-market capitalism, the countermovement is ultimately necessary to the continued functioning of the market itself, since its role will be to safeguard those essential "fictitious commodities"—money, land, and labor—that capital is incapable of protecting of its own accord.

What makes Polanyi's theory of the double movement so appealing to a certain kind of left is its tendency to conflate capitalism itself with the logic of the free market and thus to reduce its ideological expression to economic liberalism, understood as a force of social disintegration. Once one has accepted these premises, however, resistance can only be imagined as conservative. If capitalism as an ideological formation is reducible to the tenets of economic liberalism, and if market freedom tends inexorably to disintegrate, disembed, and homogenize social existence, then any viable countermovement must seek to reanchor value as a way of arresting these trends. This imperative applies not only to the "fictitious commodities" of land, labor, and money—which the social protectionist movement seeks to "decommodify" and restore to a position of fundamental value—but also to social life more widely, which ultimately demands to be stabilized and reembedded within the institution of the family.[22] If capitalism is theorized as uniquely and exclusively destructive of prior social solidarities, then the countermovement can be imagined only as an effort to restore, or at least reinvent, that which was allegedly destroyed by the advent of industrial capitalism. It is not by chance that Polanyi evinces an unmistakable nostalgia for the old territorial order of feudal England, where (he imagines) aristocrats and peasants shared a common attachment to land, family, and community.

Polanyi himself was well aware of the potential affinities between his theory of the countermovement and the social conservatisms of the right. Indeed, he saw the fascist movements of early twentieth-century Europe as one particularly destructive manifestation of the countermovement, and one that could be avoided only by implementing the alternative of a socially protectionist and politically democratic welfare state.[23] For Polanyi, the difference between a social democratic countermovement and the social conservatism of the right was decisive in its historical consequences—and yet it was a difference of methods and degree, not of kind. The Polanyian social democrat shares the conservative's nostalgia for community, land, and family but seeks to transform these institutions into conduits for state-based forms of social protection. Where the Burkean conservative strives to instill family values by force, the social democrat seeks to encourage them through the redistribution of social wealth. Polanyi, it might be said, replaces the private family values of the old Elizabethan poor-law tradition with the redistributive family values of a certain kind of social progressive left. In this respect, his philosophy of the double movement can be read as the ideological expression of the mid-twentieth-century welfare state, which perfectly combined social democracy and social conservatism in the form of the Fordist family wage.

This book assumes instead that what Polanyi calls the "double movement" would be better understood as fully internal to the dynamic of capital. This is to say that economic liberalism and political conservatism—even when the latter speaks the language of anticapitalist critique—are equally constitutive expressions of modern capitalism. We need not defer to a Hegelian reading of Marx to recognize that this double movement is central to his depiction of capital's "differential calculus," putting him radically at odds with Polanyi on the question of critique.[24] Most lucidly in the *Grundrisse*, Marx discerns two countervailing tendencies at work in the logic of capitalist valuation: on the one hand, a propensity to deflect from all external limits to the speculative generation of social wealth, and on the other hand, a drive to reestablish such limits as the internal condition of value's realization as private wealth.[25] In more suggestive, less austere mathematical terms, Marx recognized that the capitalist injunction to self-valorization "drives beyond national barriers and prejudices as much as beyond nature worship, as well as all traditional, confined, complacent, encrusted satisfactions of present needs, and reproductions of old ways of life,"[26] at the same time that it calls for the reaffirmation of such limits as a way of channeling and restricting the actual realization of wealth.

Yet, while Marx recognized that the restoration of fundamental value could be accomplished through any number of institutional and juridical means—from the gold standard to private property in land to vagrancy laws limiting the mobility of workers—his analysis does not extend to the intimate, reproductive dimensions of this process.[27] In its efforts to overcome all quantitative barriers to the generation of wealth, Marx observed, capital transgresses all established forms of reproduction—that is, all customary or religious strictures on the organization of gender, all status-like constraints on social mobility, and all national restrictions on the circulation of money.[28] But is it not also compelled to reassert the reproductive institutions of race, family, and nation as a way of ensuring the unequal distribution of wealth and income across time? Isn't it compelled, in the last instance, to reinstate the family as the elementary legal form of private wealth accumulation?

On this point, Marx's thinking must be radicalized.[29] The assertion of foundation is never merely "economic" in character since it must ultimately incorporate the "social and cultural" conditions under which value is to be reproduced and reappropriated in private form—kinship, lineage, and inheritance. If the history of modern capital appears on the one hand to regularly undermine and challenge existing orders of gender and sexuality, it also entails the periodic reinvention of the family as an instrument for distributing wealth and income. Thus, according to Reva Siegel, the legal history of the modern family can be understood as a process of "preservation through transformation" rather than one of progressive liberalization, where challenges to established gender and generational hierarchies are repeatedly recaptured within new, more democratic, but no less implacable legal structures.[30]

What Eric Hobsbawm refers to as the "reinvention of tradition" can usefully be understood as the expression of this double movement, provided that we accord no prior stability to tradition as such and recognize the very historicity of the term as an invention of nineteenth-century industrial capitalism.[31] Translating these insights into a general reflection on the philosophy of history, Peter Osborne argues that the peculiar temporality of modern capitalism is defined by the oscillation of tendencies that are alternatively self-revolutionizing and restorative, speculative and radically nostalgic. For Osborne, both these orientations "may be regarded as temporally integral political forms of capitalist societies, alternative political articulations of the social form of capitalist accumulation itself: that 'constant revolutionizing of production, uninterrupted disturbance of all social conditions, everlasting uncertainty and agitation,' which Marx and Engels identified as the distinguishing feature of the present epoch nearly one hundred and fifty years ago."[32] One consequence of this analysis is its neutralization of Polanyian critique. We cannot hope to counter the logic of capitalist exchange by seeking merely to reembed or stabilize its volatile signs, as Polanyi counsels, since this project is already a necessary component of capital's double movement. The tension between the adaptive forces of credit expansion and the appropriative drive to social foundation is constitutive of capital itself, although realized in widely different political forms in different historical moments.

Accordingly, this book takes neoliberalism and the new social conservatism as the contemporary expression of capital's double movement. In doing so, I follow Wendy Brown, whose seminal essay "American Nightmare" argues that neoliberalism and neoconservatism must be thought together—in their convergences, collisions, and symbioses—if we are to understand the political rationality of power in the United States today.[33] This thinking together, I would add, is necessary if we are to avoid the trap of mobilizing a left neoliberalism against the regressive forces of social conservatism or a left social conservatism against the disintegrating effects of the free market.

By neoliberalism, I refer in particular to the American schools of new economic liberalism that emerged at the University of Chicago, the University of Virginia, George Mason University, Virginia Polytechnic University, the UCLA Department of Economics, and various other institutional outposts in the early to mid–twentieth century. The historiography of American neoliberalism is vast.[34] Here I focus on a distinct phase in the evolution of this new economic liberalism, one that was defined by the social and economic upheavals of the 1960s and '70s and the intellectual response that it provoked among free-market economists of the Chicago and Virginia schools. During this period, American neoliberals refined and in some cases utterly revised their founding concepts in direct response to the changing gender and racial composition of the workforce, the civil rights and welfare rights movements, and the rise of student radicalism. Throughout the 1970s, leading neoliberal intellectuals such as Milton Friedman, Rose Friedman, George Stigler, Richard Epstein, Richard Posner, James M. Buchanan, Gordon Tullock, Richard Wagner, and Gary Becker helped redefine the intellectual and popular consensus on state deficit spending, the role of the central bank, inflation, taxation, consumer protection laws, tuition fees, and welfare. At no other moment before or after have the affiliates of the Chicago and Virginia schools been so directly involved in formulating and implementing government policy. A figure such as Milton Friedman, for instance, was remarkably involved in the policy decisions of the Nixon, Carter, and Reagan administrations: At various moments, he could be found lending his hand to proposals to introduce a basic guaranteed income, informing central bank policy on inflation, and calling for the introduction of tuition fees in the University of California system. If Milton Friedman went on to become more of a public intellectual than a political insider, and if neoliberalism itself later lost the clearly identifiable profile it once enjoyed in the 1970s, it was because it had become so widely accepted among policymakers of all political stripes and so thoroughly disseminated throughout mainstream economics.[35]

By new social conservatism, I refer to the spectrum of conservative movements that emerged in or after the late 1960s, often in response to the same set of concerns that mobilized neoliberals into action. Under this umbrella term, I include the neoconservative movement as such (which in its earliest incarnation was almost exclusively preoccupied with domestic social issues), the new religious right comprising conservative Catholics and evangelicals, the new paternalism of Lawrence Mead (the principal American architect of welfare-to-work programs), and the communitarian movement in social welfare. Although others have used the term "neoconservative" to refer to this broad coalition of conservative currents, I prefer to use the more generic term "new social conservatism" so as to address the specificity of the actual neoconservatives within this coalition. The "new" in "new social conservatism" serves to distinguish these various currents from the traditionalist or Burkean conservatism of the American paleoconservatives, whose antistatism, anti-Semitism, and aversion to racial democracy made them ill-suited to any compromise with the New Deal left.[36] Many if not most of the new generation of social conservatives, in fact, had traveled some part of the way with the political left and were opposed to the Great Society expansion of the New Deal, not the New Deal experiment itself. The representatives of these movements came from diverse political backgrounds. A small handful of them had been fellow travelers of right-wing figures such as Barry Goldwater or the *National Review*'s William F. Buckley Jr., key figures in the Cold War conservative-libertarian alliance.[37] Others had emerged out of the more fundamentalist, traditionally quietist currents within American Protestantism.[38] Many more came from the political left. Most of the first generation of neoconservatives were former Trotskyists and Cold War Democrats who remained fiercely committed to the New Deal welfare state and its conservative sexual order.[39] Although the more prominent among them—Irving Kristol and his son Bill Kristol most notably—would later join forces with the Republicans, others remained firmly attached to the Democratic Party. The communitarians who succeeded them on the political stage after the 1980s were closely aligned with "Third Way" New Democrats such as Bill Clinton and were always striving to bridge the divide between religious and secular conservatives, the partisan left and right.[40] For his part, the new paternalist Lawrence Mead never identified with any party in particular and in fact achieved his greatest policy success under President Clinton, who introduced sweeping workfare legislation in 1996.[41] Throughout this period, only white religious conservatives have remained overwhelmingly associated with the political right.

During the 1970s, American neoliberalism and the new social conservatism matured and came together in response to the same set of events and a convergent perception of crisis. It is almost always assumed that the neoliberal–new social conservative alliance was forged in response to Keynesianism itself, as exemplified in the New

Deal welfare state and radicalized under Johnson's Great Society. But this is to misunderstand the specificity of their critique. Emphatically, what prompted their reaction was not the New Deal welfare state itself (although neoliberals certainly had a long tradition of critique on this front) but rather the panoply of liberation movements that emerged out of and in excess of the postwar Keynesian order toward the end of the 1960s. At various moments between the 1960s and 1980s, poverty activists, welfare militants, feminists, AIDS activists, and public-interest lawyers articulated a novel politics of redistribution that delinked risk protection from the sexual division of labor and social insurance from sexual normativity.[42] These movements were historically unique in that they continued to fight for greater wealth and income redistribution while refusing the normative constraints of the Fordist family wage. While neoliberals and neoconservatives were surprisingly sympathetic to efforts to democratize the New Deal welfare state — most notably when it came to the inclusion of African American men within the family wage system — they balked when the Fordist family itself came into question.

In short, it was only when the liberation movements of the 1960s began to challenge the sexual normativity of the family wage as the linchpin and foundation of welfare capitalism that the neoliberal–new social conservative alliance came into being. What they proposed in response to this "crisis" was not a return to the Fordist family wage (this particular nostalgia would be the hallmark of the left), but rather the strategic reinvention of a much older, poor-law tradition of private family responsibility, using the combined instruments of welfare reform, changes to taxation, and monetary policy. Under their influence, welfare has been transformed from a redistributive program into an immense federal apparatus for policing the private family responsibilities of the poor, while deficit spending has been steadily transferred from the state to the private family. Through policies designed to democratize credit markets and inflate asset values, these reformers have sought to revive the tradition of private family responsibility in the idiom of household debt, while simultaneously accommodating and neutralizing the most ambitious political desires of the 1960s.

Despite its prominence in the political rhetoric of the Reagan revolution and beyond, most accounts of this era see the politics of family values as peripheral to structural economic battles waged over (for example) monetary policy, state-deficit spending, or the redistribution of wealth through taxation.[43] Thus, Ronald Reagan is said to have deployed family values rhetoric to cover for his macroeconomic policies and to seduce the working class into alliances that would ultimately work against them. The neoconservative culture wars are understood in retrospect as a useful distraction from the real business of cutting funding to public education and the arts, while Clinton's communitarianism is similarly understood as a ruse designed to soften the edges of his neoliberal economic policy and a useful instrument for healing the historical breach between New and Old Democrats. Typically emanating from the left, these accounts tend to dismiss the florid defense of family values as so much flotsam and jetsam floating above the real story of monumental wealth redistribution and class warfare.

The idea that economic processes can and should be separated from the merely cultural phenomena of gender, race, and sexuality has a long intellectual pedigree, expressed variously in the Marxist vocabulary of base and superstructure, the vernacular distinction between identity and class politics, and the late Frankfurt school language of recognition versus redistribution (although all are perhaps ultimately indebted to the contract versus status opposition deployed by nineteenth-century anthropologists such as Henry Sumner Maine).[44] As a methodological and political point of departure, such distinctions have always been suspect. The nineteenth-century anthropological language of status and contract, for example, served to obscure and sentimentalize the existence of women's unpaid labor in the home at precisely the historical moment when the boundaries between the labor market and the private family were being established. Women were thus relegated to the quasi-sacred space of kinship and the gift relation at a time when they were being actively excluded from the contractual labor market by an alliance of male trade unionists and conservative protectionists.[45] In general, leftist demands for the decommodification of social life or the protection of kinship relations all too readily lend themselves to the social conservative argument that certain forms of (domestic, feminized) labor should remain unpaid.

The distinction between recognition and redistribution performs a similar kind of revisionist work today, obscuring the actual historical intricacies of economic and sexual politics while actively quarantining the family from critique. We need only look at the historical example of the Fordist family wage to see that redistribution and recognition cannot be understood in isolation: As an instrument of redistribution, the standard Fordist wage actively policed the boundaries between women and men's work and white and black men's labor, and in its social-insurance dimensions, it was inseparable from the imperative of sexual normativity. The Fordist politics of class was itself a form of identity politics inasmuch as it established white, married masculinity as a point of access to full social protection.

Today the politics of distribution is no longer channeled through the instrument of the Fordist family wage and (as Thomas Piketty has shown) is much more heavily influenced by the wealth-transmitting mechanism of private inheritance than it was in the postwar era.[46] But here again, the distinction between recognition and redistribution proves unhelpful as a way of understanding the actual imbrication of sexual and economic politics. How after all are we to separate the wealth-distributive work of inheritance from the legal and cultural legitimation of family? In what sense can the regulation of sexuality be abstracted from a legal instrument of wealth appropriation that takes the form of family genealogy?

This book proceeds from the assumption that the history of economic formations cannot be prized apart from the operations of gender, race, and sexuality without obscuring the politics of wealth and income distribution itself. By revisiting and questioning established historical accounts of the stagflation crisis of the 1970s, I seek to show that the question of family was as central to the formation of a post-Keynesian capitalist order as it was to welfare state capitalism, and therefore it cannot be ignored without profoundly misrepresenting the political history of the era. Unlike many on the left, the key actors of the neoliberal–new social conservative alliance had no hesitation in recognizing the family as the locus of crisis. These actors were in no doubt that the grand macroeconomic issues of the time, from inflation to budget deficits to ballooning welfare budgets, reflected an ominous shift in the sexual and racial foundations of the Fordist family. Given this assessment, they could see only one possible solution: the wholesale reinvention of the American family itself. This book will be dedicated to the project of exploring how this process of reinvention was conceived and how it eventually overtook the intellectual ambitions of its authors.

The Moral Crisis of Inflation: Neoliberalism, Neoconservatism, and the Demise of the Family Wage

During every great inflation, there is a striking decline
in both public and private morality.
—Henry Hazlitt, *The Inflation Crisis and How to Resolve It*

In 1979, the incoming Chairman of the Federal Reserve, Paul Volcker, initiated a new era in American political life by taking decisive action on inflation. After years of increasingly polarized debate, Volcker deployed the technocratic instrument of covert interest-rate adjustment and the ideological cover of monetarism to plunge the American economy into its deepest period of recession since the Great Depression, thereby ending a long-drawn-out process of spiraling inflation. The so-called Volcker shock created the conditions for the Reagan revolution and profoundly reshaped the landscape of American and global politics over the following decades.

It is at this turning point that neoliberalism and neoconservatism (and their derivatives) emerged as fully fledged social philosophies and dominant forces on the political stage. But it was in the preceding decade, in response to the combined problems of inflation and rising unemployment, that neoliberals and neoconservatives first elaborated and perfected their signature critique of the Great Society welfare state. If we are to understand how a discourse of crisis was born and how neoliberalism and neoconservatism leveraged this discourse to redefine the terms of political power over the following years, it is imperative that we revisit the debates of this period and question the established historical accounts of their resolution.

The economic and political factors that contributed to the inflation of the 1970s are well known, although few would claim to calculate the precise weight of each contributing cause.[1] It is widely believed that President Lyndon Johnson precipitated the onset of inflation in the late 1960s by refusing to cut back on military expenditures even while he initiated an ambitious new program of health, welfare, and education spending under the aegis of the Great Society. Historically, periods of inflation have routinely followed the exceptional military expenditures of wartime: President Johnson launched a disastrous new war in Vietnam while at the same time pursuing an expansionary domestic politics at home—a double venture that may have been feasible if he had at the same time increased revenue from taxes.[2] Inflation also reflected a shift in the old balance of powers between former colonial states and the metropolitan centers. America's military venture in Vietnam came at a time when many former colonies were gaining independence and were able to demand higher prices for their export commodities, a shift that ultimately fed into the price of all consumer commodities, from food to oil. By the mid-1970s, America was importing a third of its oil from foreign sources, as compared to one-fifth in 1960.[3] This left the entire productive and consumer economy vulnerable to the oil embargoes imposed by OPEC in 1973 and 1979. These then were the key factors contributing to the economic phenomenon of consumer price inflation.

How and why inflation became a political crisis is less clear. Today, many if not most accounts of the economic predicament of the 1970s subscribe to the idea that inflation represented an unmitigated crisis for all social classes, a narrative that has hardened into orthodoxy in the wake of the Reagan revolution and which in itself represents the triumph of a certain kind of revisionist analysis. The historian Iwan

Morgan contends that the 1970s "represented the most miserable period for the United States economy since the Great Depression of the 1930s," bringing to an end "the perpetual increase in living standards that had marked the post-war era."[4] Drawing on the work of the neoconservative Daniel Bell, the economic sociologist Greta Krippner attributes the "bitter distributional struggles" of the 1970s to "increasingly severe limits on the nation's prosperity," without asking how and where wealth was being redistributed and how a marked trend toward downward redistribution might have precipitated a neoconservative discourse around limits to growth in the first place.[5]

Yet, more than one contemporary observer of these economic trends acknowledged that the redistributive consequences of inflation were far from transparent. The economist Edward N. Wolff, who conducted a study investigating the effects of inflation on household wealth between 1969 and 1974, went so far as to argue that inflation "acted like a progressive tax, leading to greater equality in the distribution of wealth."[6] The force of trade unionism at the time was such that wages continued to rise alongside the consumer price index, with the consequence that inflation actively benefited those who "depended on wages for their income, not on interests and dividends from financial assets."[7] The Brookings Institution economist Joseph J. Minarik found that the benefits were particularly clear for middle-class homeowners, but even the lowest-income groups were not as vulnerable to rising prices as was generally assumed, since most social insurance programs were indexed to the Consumer Price Index.[8] Inflation, moreover, had the curious effect of redistributing wealth from creditors to debtors by steadily eroding the price of debt. As long as wages kept rising, it made sense for workers to buy for the future on credit—giving rise to the popular perception that everyday workers were turning into investors and speculators, indulging in luxury consumer goods that had only recently been out of their reach.[9]

For those whose net worth derived from financial assets, however, the consequences of inflation were unremittingly negative. Institutional and personal investors, including the wealthiest ten percent of households, searched in vain for a safe avenue of investment throughout this period as inflation eroded the real rates of return on their long-term financial assets.[10] Uncertainty hovered over the future of investment for rich and poor alike; but whereas the unpredictability of the dollar's future price promised depreciating interest payments to everyday workers and debtors, it signified the exact opposite to the nation's creditors—ever-diminishing asset values and the futility of investment itself. By the late 1970s, this situation prompted a sensibility of outright antigovernment rebellion among free-market neoliberals such as Rose and Milton Friedman, who accused the Federal Reserve of defrauding investors of their wealth via the manipulation of the money supply.[11]

For the investment class, the sense of crisis was exacerbated by the fact that the labor unions of the 1970s were able to hold their own against any attempt to push down wages in response to inflation. Business owners lamented the fact that rising costs of production could not be offset by a corresponding rise in labor productivity, as they encountered an ever more militant and restive workforce. It was similarly impossible for American corporations to recoup losses by pushing up prices, because they were now confronted with rising competitive pressures from Europe and Japan. The growing political influence of organized labor was reflected in the fact that wages continued to rise against a background of high unemployment. This phenomenon, known as stagflation, confounded the predictions of postwar Keynesian economics, which in the form of the so-called Phillips curve, posited "a stable negative relation between the level of unemployment and the rate of change of wages."[12] For the business and investment class, stagflation was a sign that the Keynesian consensus between labor and capital had outlived its political usefulness. Simply put, what had looked like a consensus solution to all parties in the wake of the

Great Depression now appeared to be empowering the working class over investors.

Today, a number of scholars argue that the Volcker shock of 1979 must be understood as a concerted political response to the rising militancy of the Fordist working class. In their illuminating analyses of this period, the political economists Leo Panitch, Sam Gindin, and Edward Dickens remind us that Arthur Burns, chairman of the Federal Reserve between February 1970 and February 1978, openly ascribed the problem of stagflation to the overweening power of trade unions and the social welfare expenditures that, in his view, served to subsidize strikes.[13] These theorists perform the important task of restoring the question of class politics to the historiography of inflation. Yet they are less successful in accounting for the peculiar focus and moralizing tenor of attacks on social welfare during this period. Having assumed an already unified conception of the working class, they cannot tell us why contemporary diagnoses of crisis focused so insistently on one welfare program in particular—AFDC or Aid to Families with Dependent Children—and why that program came to be associated with a general crisis of the American family. Consequently, they are unable to explain how the problematic of family dysfunction became so central to popular understandings of inflation or why the Reagan-era response to inflation would propel family values to the forefront of American politics over the next several decades. For contemporary commentators, however, the stakes were clear enough: Stagflation was a problem not only because it skewed the Fordist social consensus in favor of the working class but also because it threatened to undermine the normative foundations of the Fordist family wage.

In effect, by the late 1970s, commentators from across the political spectrum agreed that inflation represented a threat to the moral fabric of American society. With a nod to the work of Friedrich Hayek, Federal Reserve Chairman Paul Volcker described inflation as a "moral issue."[14] "It corrodes trust, particularly trust in government.

It is a governmental responsibility to maintain the value of the currency that they issue. And when they fail to do that it is something that undermines an essential trust in government."

Others traced a direct line of causation between this erosion of political trust and the breakdown of traditional family structures. The monetarist Milton Friedman understood inflation as a dangerous distortion of money that undermined its intrinsic neutrality and imposed a fraudulent tax on investors. For Friedman, inflation was foremost a consequence of excessive growth in the money supply, and yet the money supply also became entangled with fiscal policy when the government paid for indulgent social welfare programs by monetizing debt rather than raising taxes or borrowing funds.[15] Inflation then was not only an evil in and of itself; it had also served to finance welfare programs "whose major evil [was] to undermine the fabric of society"—that is, the natural incentives of the "family" and the "market."[16]

The Virginia school public-choice economists James Buchanan and Richard Wagner discerned an even more direct relationship between inflation and moral crisis. Unlike the monetarist Friedman, the Virginia school economists expounded a fiscal theory of inflation that pointed to government deficits as the primary cause of monetary instability. Accordingly, Buchanan and Wagner did not hesitate to attribute inflation to the decline of the "old time fiscal religion" that had once upon a time committed both governments and households to balanced budgets and everyday austerity.[17] By creating uncertainty about the future value of money, they argued, inflation had the effect of shortening time horizons and inducing a desire for speculative indulgence among the consumer public. This in turn had led to a general breakdown in public morality whose effects were visible in everything from expanding welfare rolls to sexual promiscuity. "We do not need to become full-blown Hegelians," they wrote:

> to entertain the general notion of zeitgeist, a "spirit of the times." Such a spirit seems at work in the 1960s and 1970s, and is evidenced by what

appears as a generalized erosion in public and private manners, increasingly liberalized attitudes toward sexual activities, a declining vitality of the Puritan work ethic, deterioration in product quality, explosion of the welfare rolls, widespread corruption in both the private and the governmental sector, and, finally, observed increases in the alienation of voters from the political process.... Who can deny that inflation...plays some role in reinforcing several of the observed behavior patterns. Inflation destroys expectations and creates uncertainty; it increases the sense of felt injustice and causes alienation. It prompts behavioral responses that reflect a generalized shortening of time horizons. "Enjoy, enjoy"—the imperative of our time—becomes a rational response in a setting where tomorrow remains insecure and where the plans made yesterday seem to have been made in folly.[18]

The American Hayekian Henry Hazlitt was even more emphatic in his denunciation of the moral effects of inflation. "During every great inflation," he wrote, "there is a striking decline in both public and private morality."[19]

These theorists can all be classified as neoliberals of one kind or another, variously aligned with the competitive price theory of the Chicago school of economics, the Virginia school of public choice theory or a peculiar brand of Austrian economics derived from Friedrich von Hayek and Ludwig von Mises.[20] Each in his or her own way was associated with the resurgence and reinvention of radical free-market liberalism in American political and economic thought in the postwar era. For all their singularity, however, the neoliberals offered an understanding of inflation that in key respects converged with that of the neoconservatives, political theorists who were otherwise opposed to the fundamental precepts of economic liberalism.

The sociologist Daniel Bell, for instance, perhaps the most famous neoconservative commentator on inflation, thematized the moral and economic crisis of the 1970s in terms very close to those of the

Virginia school neoliberals in particular. His sociological classic *The Cultural Contradictions of Capital* indicted the welfare state for undermining the proper order of familial relations and expanding consumption beyond the limits prescribed by Protestant good sense.[21] Inflation, he believed, was intimately connected to this breakdown of moral values. Time and again, both neoliberals and neoconservatives focused their attention on one welfare program in particular, Aid to Families with Dependent Children (AFDC), a marginal public assistance program that consumed a very small proportion of federal social expenditures. How did the great inflation of the 1970s come to be associated with a breakdown of the family, and why did public concern focus so obsessively on this one social welfare program?

To answer this question, one must attend to the sinuous complexities of political debate around the Fordist family wage and social welfare through the late 1960s and 1970s. As noted by the historian Marisa Chappell, an initial effort to expand the family wage to African Americans in the early 1970s progressively gave way to a wholesale critique of the family wage itself—a critique that became more vocal as inflation impressed itself on the political agenda.[22] In effect, a bipartisan consensus on the basic premise of redistributive social welfare existed right up until the 1960s. Until this time, Democrats and Republicans alike were committed to the redistributive policies of the family wage, although they were divided on the question of whether or not it should be extended to African American men. Old Democrats (and future neoconservatives) such as Daniel Patrick Moynihan were convinced that the family wage should include African American men, a view they shared with many liberals and leftists in the welfare rights movement. A free-market economist such as Milton Friedman preferred the racially neutral solution of a basic guaranteed income, channeled through the tax system, although he too remained pragmatically committed to a minimal system of income redistribution.

By the late 1970s, however, this consensus had given way to a comprehensive critique of the welfare state tout court. Critics on the left and right now accused AFDC—and by extension the welfare state itself—of radically undermining the American family and contributing to the problem of inflation. In response to this crisis, they now called for a much more dramatic reform of welfare than they themselves had hitherto imagined. It was now agreed that the redistributive welfare programs of the New Deal and Great Society would need to be radically restricted, even while the private institution of the family was to be strengthened as an alternative to social welfare. Welfare reformers now looked back to a much older tradition of public relief—one embedded in the poor-law tradition with its attendant notions of family and personal responsibility—as an imagined alternative to the New Deal welfare state. It is in this shift that we can locate the simultaneous rise of neoliberalism and neoconservatism as mature political philosophies. Neoliberalism and neoconservatism may be diametrically opposed on many issues, but on the question of family values, they reveal a surprising affinity.

AFDC, WELFARE, AND THE AMERICAN FAMILY WAGE

The controversy surrounding AFDC is in many respects illuminated by the peculiar position it holds within the history of the American welfare state and family wage. Unlike many European welfare states and indeed unlike the welfare policies of the American Progressive Era, the American New Deal did not espouse an overtly gendered politics of the family, a fact that the Catholic Daniel Moynihan lamented.[23] In its administrative and institutional form, however, the New Deal set forth a series of abstract category distinctions that subtly served to reinforce the privilege of the white male breadwinner family. By sorting citizens according to the purportedly neutral category of employment status, the New Deal created a welfare system that was highly divided along the lines of gender and race. Its panoply of programs, moreover, came under the jurisdiction of different levels of government, with federal programs administering a far more impersonal, generous, and predictable system of benefits than the states, which were free to exercise considerable discretion in the distribution of welfare. The hierarchization of welfare benefits was further inscribed in the very design of welfare programs: Social insurance programs that targeted life-long workers and collected contributions from workers or their employers enjoyed a much higher social status than the public assistance programs reserved for the noncontributing poor.[24] Public assistance came under the rubric of relief programs and was highly dependent on prevailing public opinion about the deserving or undeserving character of the poor. ADC fell on the wrong side of each of these institutional divides.

Aid to Dependent Children, as AFDC was first called, was one of the many welfare programs created by the Social Security Act of 1935. Although it was a public assistance program and subject to a high level of public scrutiny and state discretion, it inherited its original structure from the earlier Mothers' Pensions program and therefore enjoyed a certain level of respect.[25] Mothers' Pensions had embodied the family wage ideal of the Progressive Era, which mandated that white women and their children should be supported by the state in the event of their husband's death. The Social Security Act nationalized this program and reproduced many of its normative ideals. Unlike social insurance programs, however, which were heavily regulated by the federal government, ADC allowed states considerable freedom to enact and appropriate funds, with the result that many states funded the program poorly and were highly restrictive in their allocation of benefits.[26] Many states replicated Progressive Era rules that favored widows over women who had divorced or had never married, and most Southern states excluded African American women on the grounds that their work was needed outside the home. The predictable result was that, at least in the first few years of the program, most ADC recipients were white.[27]

In 1939, however, the Social Security Act was changed to allow widows formerly covered by ADC to access the more respectable Old Age Insurance (OAI) if they had been married to men covered by the program.[28] This decision allowed deserving women to upgrade to a more respectable form of family wage allowance—one that was premised on a woman's attachment to an independent male worker in standard, long-term employment. But the elevation of a certain class of woman, mostly white and middle-class, to a more respectable social insurance program also led to the further devaluation of the status of ADC. By default, ADC was now primarily reserved for widows who had been married to poorer men and to unmarried, divorced, or separated mothers. Increasingly, it also became associated with African American women.

During the postwar era, the composition of ADC changed dramatically as the number of African American women signing up outpaced that of white women, and more divorced or never-married women joined the rolls.[29] These changes were linked to the transformation of the Southern plantation economy and the racial composition of the Fordist labor force: The mechanization of agriculture in the South compelled many African Americans to migrate to the Northern rustbelt cities where they filled nonunionized and noninsured positions in factories.[30] Few African American men enjoyed the family wage privileges of the unionized industrial labor force, and, as a surplus population of cheap workers, African Americans in general experienced a disproportionate level of unemployment even during the boom years of the 1960s. In the North, however, state rules governing the allocation of ADC benefits were often less restrictive than those in the South. By 1961, then, 48 percent of African American women were on ADC, and many of these were single mothers—although, as Premilla Nadesan notes, their numbers were far lower than one would expect given actual rates of poverty and out-of-wedlock birth.[31]

ADC had always been a restrictive program, but faced with what the public perceived as a flagrant affront to the ideals of white American motherhood, many states responded to the 1939 amendments by redoubling their efforts to police the morality of welfare recipients. By the late 1950s, even the Northern states, which previously had been more generous, reinforced old laws or invented new ones to limit ADC payments to deserving mothers. These laws functioned as a kind of negative of the white family wage ideal embodied in Mothers' Pensions, their multiple exclusions serving to define the boundaries of state-subsidized reproduction. "Man-in-the-house" rules allowed states to refuse benefits to women who lived with or were in a sexual relationship with a man, deeming him a proper substitute for the paternal function of the state; "suitable home" laws allowed welfare case workers to deny aid to unmarried or immoral women; "employable mother" laws, often invoked in the South, designated African American women as indispensable workers outside the home and therefore excluded them from the domestic ideal of white motherhood; while residence laws sought to discourage interstate migrants from applying for assistance.[32]

Despite the ostensible neutrality of federal welfare law then, in practice, public assistance programs were qualified by a panoply of state administrative laws that strictly policed the moral and racial boundaries of the Fordist family wage. These racial and sexual normativities were truly foundational to the social order of American Fordism, determining just who would be included and who would be excluded from the redistributive benefits of the social wage. By the 1960s, however, some of the more egregious forms of "police power" embodied in state administrative law were coming under challenge as welfare recipients became increasingly organized and civil rights lawyers transferred their judicial activism to the field of welfare.[33] During this period, the Supreme Court was receptive to plaintiffs who challenged the right of the states to deviate from the general terms of federal welfare law. In a series of test-cases initiated by welfare rights activists and public interest lawyers, the Supreme Court proceeded to limit the prerogative of state welfare agencies to make judgments about the perceived morality of welfare recipients. In one particularly significant case, *King v. Smith*, decided in 1968, the Supreme Court unanimously overturned the state of Alabama's "substitute father" rule, which denied benefits to women who were in a sexual relationship with a man.[34] The decision enraged conservative Republicans and Southern Democrats who believed that African American women on welfare were benefiting from a program that was not designed for them in the first place. But it also troubled a surprising number of liberals and leftists who thought that welfare activism should be focused on the task of restoring and promoting the African American male-breadwinner family rather than subsidizing the non-normative lifestyles of unattached African American women.

MOYNIHAN, THE LEFT, AND THE BLACK FAMILY WAGE

In June 1965, President Johnson delivered a remarkable speech before the graduating class of Howard University, a traditionally African American institution with strong ties to the civil rights movement. Reflecting on the progress of the Great Society reforms, Johnson acknowledged that neither opportunity liberalism nor the formal recognition of civil rights would be enough to overcome the enduring legacy of racial discrimination in the United States. The most important factor in the persistence of black disadvantage, he argued, "was the breakdown of the Negro family structure."[35] Accordingly, any effort to go beyond the Great Society agenda would require both affirmative action and a comprehensive program to strengthen the African American family.

The Howard University speech had been drafted by Richard N. Goodwin and Daniel Patrick Moynihan, advisors in the early Johnson administration, and reflected the content of a report, then unpublished, that Moynihan had recently written. The report, entitled *The Negro Family: The Case for National Action*, would prove much more divisive than Johnson's speech before an audience of African American graduating students. In this study, Moynihan reflected on postwar trends in the formation of black and white families, the changing composition of welfare rolls, and the rise in unemployment rates among young black men—all familiar themes to readers of the popular press—and offered a longue durée historical analysis to account for them. For Moynihan, the contemporary situation of African Americans living in the inner cities was unambiguously pathological. High rates of criminality, youth alienation, and unemployment were all signs that something was seriously wrong; and this malaise could ultimately be traced to the disintegration of the black family. Moynihan lingered over the details of this apparent disintegration—the rising rates of separation, divorce, unwedded childbearing, and female-headed families in which women had assumed an unnaturally dominant and overbearing role.

As many critics on the left would point out, the Moynihan Report subtly shifted the focus of attention away from the structural factors of urban segregation, discrimination, and educational disadvantage that might implicate contemporary white racism in the reproduction of poverty and pointed instead to the distant crime of slavery as a causal factor. By destroying the proper order of gender relations in the African American family, slavery had engendered a pathological kinship structure that was transmitted from generation to generation and was now quite "capable of perpetuating itself without assistance from the white world."[36] Yet, Moynihan did concede that New Deal social welfare policy had also played a key role in exacerbating the decline of the black family. In particular, he singled out AFDC as responsible for allowing this process of decline to proceed as far and as fast as it had done in the 1960s. "The steady expansion of this welfare program," he wrote, "can be taken as a measure of the steady disintegration of the Negro family structure over the past generation in the United States."[37]

In 1965, Daniel Patrick Moynihan was not yet a self-identified neoconservative. Although Irving Kristol points to 1965 as the year in which the neoconservative movement was born,[38] Moynihan was still very much a New Deal Democrat at this time, one with decidedly social-democratic leanings. An enthusiastic adherent of Johnson's Great Society agenda, Moynihan was in favor of extending the New Deal welfare state beyond its original constituencies by including African American men within the family wage. Moynihan's views on welfare were shaped by a Catholic social philosophy that had long seen the welfare state as the ideal conduit of family values.[39] He was concerned, however, that the abstract individualism favored by American liberalism had undermined the implicit familialism of the New Deal vision, allowing a program such as AFDC to subsidize frankly pathological forms of sexuality as its constituencies changed.[40] As a solution, he urged Johnson to adopt a "national family policy" on a par with the Employment Act of 1945 and to include all races within its provisions.[41]

The Moynihan Report met a hostile reception from many liberals and leftists who otherwise supported the goal of progressive welfare reform. By the mid-1960s, a coalition of middle-class liberals and radical leftists had united around the cause of pushing for a more generous and activist expansion of welfare than that envisaged by Johnson's rather tepid Great Society reforms. This coalition included established labor unions, welfare associations, religious charities, civil rights groups, social workers on the liberal spectrum, and, farther to the left, more radical groups such as the Black Nationalist movement, the emerging National Welfare Rights Organization, and feminist activists. Independently, these activists had developed an analysis of racial injustice that responded to precisely the kind of malaise identified by Moynihan, but whose causes they had carefully located outside of the African American community itself, in the enduring nature of structural discrimination. Many of these people responded angrily to the tone of Moynihan's report, accusing him of pandering to existing psychocultural explanations of African American oppression. It is this hostile reaction that is most often recalled in contemporary accounts of the Moynihan Report. And yet, as the historian Marisa Chappell has recently argued in some detail, the anathema surrounding Moynihan's name has tended to obscure the considerable affinity between Moynihan's family wage ideology and leftist and liberal conceptions of welfare reform at the time.[42] The liberal and left coalition for welfare reform may have quibbled with the causes of African American disadvantage adduced by Moynihan, yet they were in fundamental agreement on the point that this disadvantage undermined the family and that any long-term solution to racism would therefore require an effort to restore the African American family and the place of men within it.

This consensus reached across the spectrum of liberal and left participants in the welfare reform movement. Reformist civil rights leaders such as Martin Luther King were sympathetic to the findings of the report, while Black Muslim and Black Nationalist leaders were in frank agreement with its suggestions of pathological matriarchy and male castration.[43] But even those on the radical labor left were receptive to Moynihan's arguments. A few years after the publication of Moynihan's report, a new kind of labor activism would erupt on Detroit's auto plants as African American workers, both men and women, adopted strike tactics outside the wage bargaining framework of the New Deal labor unions. Brought together under the umbrella of the League of Revolutionary Black Workers in 1969, these unions openly repudiated the reformist and assimilationist methods of civil rights activism on the one hand and the white New Deal labor unions on the other. But they were by no means hostile to the family wage arguments proffered by Moynihan; indeed, even while the first wildcat strikes were initiated by women, the Revolutionary Unions saw the restoration of African American manhood, via an extension of the New Deal family wage to black men, as the ultimate aim of their extralegal activism.[44]

In the meantime, the sociologist Richard Cloward, who helped found the National Welfare Rights Organization in 1966, was as forceful as Moynihan in condemning AFDC.[45] Cloward could hardly be accused of New Deal reformism. Along with Frances Piven, Richard Cloward famously coauthored the 1966 call to arms, "The Weight of the Poor: A Strategy to End Poverty," which advocated a strategy of crisis for pushing through a radical overhaul of the American welfare system.[46] The article pointed to the fact that the actual numbers of poor people receiving benefits was much lower than it should have been due to the multiple institutional obstacles which prevented eligible citizens from recognizing and claiming their welfare dues. Piven and Cloward understood this discrepancy to be a constitutive feature of rights discourse: Their activism, then, was not based so much on an appeal to formal rights as a strategy of sabotage through excessive deference to the letter of the law. If all eligible poor people were to claim their welfare rights en masse, the welfare system would be overwhelmed and the state would be forced to institute a guaranteed income instead. This strategy rested on the idea that the formal equality promised by federal welfare law could, if taken at its word, force a more revolutionary change on the state. Despite their methodological radicalism, what Cloward and Piven meant by a basic guaranteed income was in fact a male breadwinner's wage. Thus, where Moynihan suggested that increasing enrolments in AFDC were a symptom of the disintegrating black family, Cloward and Piven went further and identified AFDC as a leading *cause* of family breakdown. Commenting on local programs to train welfare mothers for work in the *Nation*, they complained that:

> such measures reinforce the female as breadwinner in an already female-headed household. Men for whom there are no jobs will nevertheless mate like other men, but they are not so likely to marry. Our society has preferred to deal with the resulting female-headed families not by putting men to work but by placing the unwed mothers and dependent children

on public welfare—substituting check-writing machines for male wage earners. By this means, we have robbed men of manhood, women of husbands, and children of fathers. To create a stable monogamous family, we need to provide men (especially Negro men) with the opportunity to be men, and that involves enabling them to perform occupationally. Over the long term, women will then leave the welfare rolls, not to work but marry.[47]

This statement, published in the same year as the Moynihan Report, attests to the considerable political affinity between Moynihan and the founding members of the National Welfare Rights Organization. However loudly these leftists disavowed the details of the Moynihan report, there was very little of substance to distinguish their positions. To be sure, the family wage politics of welfare activists such as Piven and Cloward did not exhaust the spectrum of positions held within the National Welfare Rights Organization. In fact, many of the welfare mother activists who would later assume a more dominant position in the organization articulated a much more complex position on the intersections of race, sexuality, and gender and were critical of the family wage tout court.[48] Yet, it was the male breadwinner activism of leftists such as Cloward and Piven that resonated most strongly with the New Left and the Black Nationalist movement. The practical— if disavowed—proximity between the Democrat Moynihan and the welfare activists of the New Left would soon become even more pronounced when both came out in favor of a new family wage system based on a guaranteed basic income.

NIXON AND THE BLACK FAMILY WAGE: EXORCISING AFDC

In June 1969, the National Welfare Rights Organization officially launched a new campaign in favor of an annual guaranteed income of $5,500. This campaign was designed to phase out AFDC as a stigmatized, stand-alone program and to guarantee a living wage to all welfare recipients. In August 1969, on the advice of Moynihan, President Nixon announced a similar program to replace the state-based AFDC with a more secure federal program known as the Family Assistance Plan. Unlike AFDC, the latter targeted working families and promised to extend basic income guarantees to men; to two-parent families and those engaged in low-waged work.[49] Nixon, who adopted the plan against the advice of his more conservative colleagues, envisaged the reform as a way of extending the family wage to black men while catering to the resentment of the mostly white lower-income workers who felt excluded from existing public assistance programs.

In its broad conception, the Family Assistance Plan was inspired by Moynihan's arguments in favor of the black family wage. By extending welfare to men and two-parent households, the proposed reform was designed to eliminate what many saw as the perverse disincentives to family formation that were built into the AFDC program.[50] Its practical blueprint was based on the idea of a negative income tax first proposed by Milton Friedman in 1962.[51] Friedman conceived of the negative income tax as a way of channeling income redistribution through the federal tax system, thereby eliminating the excessive administrative costs associated with dedicated welfare programs. Those whose income fell below a certain threshold would receive a fraction of their unused tax exemptions and deductions in return, guaranteeing them an annual basic income. By replacing in-kind welfare with the most liquid form of benefit—cash—Friedman thought that the negative income tax would encourage the poor to behave as responsible free-market actors. He also specified that those in low-wage work should continue to receive subsidies in order to avoid the moral hazard of promoting nonwork. With its minimal but efficient system of redistribution, the negative income tax would bypass the disabling paternalism of the welfare state and undermine the entrenched power base of liberal welfare bureaucrats.[52]

The fact that Nixon's proposal for an expanded family wage attracted such a broad alliance of supporters—embracing the Republican president and moderate conservative Richard Nixon, the neoliberal Milton Friedman, the Democrat Moynihan, the liberals and leftists of the National Welfare Rights Movement, and liberal economists such as John Kenneth Galbraith and James Tobin—is testament to the very different political atmosphere of the 1960s. During this period of steady economic growth, Keynesian fiscal expansionism was an orthodoxy shared by left and right. In a reflection on federal welfare reform published in the *National Catholic Weekly Review* in 1966, Moynihan noted that the "United States is now in the 53rd month of unbroken economic expansion—the longest and strongest in peacetime history. During this brief, fleeting period...we have raised the Gross National Product by some $160 billion."[53] It was now the perfect time, he concluded, to supplement the founding moment of New Deal social reform with a second generation of family-based policies.

This remarkable consensus continued into the early years of the Nixon administration, even as inflation became a discernible problem. This is not to say that the various supporters of Nixon's black family wage shared exactly the same vision of reform. Among those who supported the plan, differences of opinion were already incipient—Friedman, for example, envisaged a more frugal form of welfare redistribution than that favored by liberals or leftists (in private correspondence, he conceded that he saw the negative income tax as a pragmatic step toward the elimination of all social welfare programs).[54] But with the exception of a few dissident, feminist voices in the National welfare rights movement, all agreed that welfare in its existing form undermined the traditional family. And all converged on the necessity of maintaining some kind of redistributive welfare system. In the 1960s, even Friedman recognized the need for a basic income redistribution program to ameliorate the inevitable market failures of private charity.

In 1970, the Democratic Party–controlled House of Representatives approved Nixon's recommendations by a large majority. Later that year, though, the Family Assistance Plan was roundly defeated by a coalition of Republicans and Democrats in the Senate, presaging a long-term reshuffling of left and right in the American political landscape. Designed to suit all stakeholders, the final version of the Family Assistance Plan ended up disappointing everyone. Welfare rights activists objected that the plan would reduce benefits to well below the poverty line for most welfare recipients, would eliminate the right to a fair hearing, and would reintroduce arbitrary powers of surveillance.[55] Free-market economists such as Friedman thought the plan ended up complicating rather than streamlining the current welfare bureaucracy and did not sufficiently remove disincentives to work.[56]

What defeated the plan, however, were not so much these specific objections as Nixon's own decision to abandon the politics of consensus on welfare in a context of rising inflation.[57] In the first year of his presidency, Nixon had surrounded himself with liberal policy advisors such as Moynihan and Robert Finch, who convinced him that an expansion of the family wage was the best way to placate racial tensions while simultaneously allowing him to wrest the white working class from its traditional allegiance to the Democratic party. By his second year in government, the economic outlook had soured and Nixon was less convinced that this strategy would work. Instead, he decided, behind closed doors, to abandon any attempt to reform AFDC while simultaneously overseeing some of the most generous expansions to Social Security in the program's history.[58] Social Security was (and still is) one of the New Deal's less contentious social insurance programs precisely because it remains relatively untouched by the normative issues of race, gender, and family formation that intersect in programs such as AFDC. When Nixon retreated from the agenda of reforming AFDC then, the extraordinary consensus that had formed around the project of the expanded family wage came apart and reshuffled into distinct political positions. As the expanding economy of the mid-1960s gave way to the soaring inflation of the 1970s, AFDC became the touchstone for increasingly acrimonious debates about the very feasibility of welfare redistribution. In this new economic context, liberal Democrats such as Moynihan and free-market neoliberals such as Friedman who had once converged on the necessity of the family wage began to formulate a distinct new political philosophy of non-redistributive family values. It is at this turning point that we can locate the emergence of both neoconservatism and American neoliberalism as mature political philosophies.

TURNING AGAINST THE FAMILY WAGE: NEOLIBERALISM AND NEOCONSERVATISM COME INTO THEIR OWN

Moynihan's trajectory from New Deal Democrat and supporter of the Great Society to new social conservative is in some sense emblematic of the birth of neoconservatism per se. In the optimistic atmosphere of the mid to late 1960s, Moynihan was willing to join forces with moderate conservatives such as Nixon in the hope of constructing a more inclusive family wage. Indeed the alliance between New Deal Democrats and moderate conservatives, under the early Nixon administration, appeared to him to represent the most effective means of formulating a social welfare program that combined the goals of income redistribution with those of familialism. It was only after the defeat of the Family Assistance Plan that Moynihan became a recognizable neoconservative.[59] Although the plan had been opposed from the left and the right and was defeated by Nixon himself, Moynihan placed the blame squarely on the shoulders of the countercultural New Left. More precisely, he excoriated the radicalism of black women in the welfare rights movement, whom he perceived to be hostile to the moral premises of the Fordist family wage. Prefiguring the use of the soon-to-be ubiquitous term "welfare queens," he dismissed the "militant black

mothers" of the National Welfare Rights Organization as the "aristocracy of welfare recipients" and accused them of sabotaging a plan that
would have benefitted working families.[60] Looking back on this period
from the vantage point of the early 1990s, Moynihan now conceded to
his critics on the right that the Great Society had contributed to the disintegration of the American family: "For a brief time, the Great Society gave great influence in social policy to viewpoints that rejected the
proposition that family structure might be a social issue. Accordingly,
even if social policy might have produced some effective responses, no
such policies were attempted. In that sense, the current crisis [of the
family] is indeed a 'grim harvest of the Great Society.' "[61]

The defeat of Nixon's black family wage, he concluded, sounded the
death knell of the expansionary welfare politics of the 1960s. Without completely renouncing the principle of income redistribution, the
neoconservatives now focused their energies on reviving the punitive
and pedagogical function of welfare. Under the austerity politics of
President Reagan, Moynihan abandoned his commitment to the Fordist family wage and instead campaigned for disciplinary reforms to
AFDC that would encourage work and family formation among welfare recipients.[62]

Milton Friedman's change in position was no less decisive as a
turning point in American neoliberalism. Throughout the 1960s,
Friedman operated as a pragmatist who was willing to compromise on
the shape of welfare reform for the sake of effecting some kind of positive change. By the end of the decade, his pragmatism was much less
in evidence. In 1970, he testified against Nixon's Family Assistance
Plan in Congress, even though he had consulted on its implementation and had devised the negative income tax on which it was modeled.
The negative income tax, he now argued, could only work if it completely replaced all other welfare—that is, social insurance and public
assistance—programs and as long as it did not undermine incentives
to work. Friedman saw Nixon's final version of the Family Assistance

Plan as a messy compromise.[63] In the meantime, Friedman was becoming increasingly disenchanted with Nixon himself, who had been elected on a platform of austerity and tight monetary policy, but proceeded to ignore the advice of monetarists once he came into office. In addition to the groundbreaking consumer and environmental protection laws introduced under his administration, Nixon also signed off on some of the most generous increases to Social Security in the program's history. Most galling of all, Nixon completely ignored Friedman's monetarist prescriptions for dealing with inflation and instead opted for a brief experiment in wage and price controls. All of this led Friedman to dismiss Nixon, in hindsight, as "the most socialist of the Presidents of the United States in the twentieth century."[64]

By 1980, Friedman's critique of welfare was much more vehement than it had been in the 1960s. In *Free to Choose*, he castigated welfare programs for destroying the moral fabric of the free-market society: "They weaken the family; reduce the incentive to work, save, and innovate; reduce the accumulation of capital; and limit our freedom."[65] More than one commentator on Friedman's intellectual trajectory has noted that he became increasingly libertarian in the 1970s.[66] This apparent shift testified as much if not more to the change in public mood than to any vacillation on Friedman's part—since Friedman had always qualified his support for redistributive welfare and acknowledged the pragmatism of his position. During the 1960s, Friedman went so far as to concede that "we are all Keynesians now."[67] By the early 1970s, Chicago school neoliberalism had come into its own and was willing to formulate an uncompromising argument against redistributive welfare per se.

It was during the 1970s, then, after the defeat of Nixon's family wage, that American neoliberalism and neoconservatism emerged as mature political philosophies with distinct positions on welfare reform. During this period, Chicago school neoliberals abandoned their pragmatic accommodation with the Keynesian welfare state and articulated a new and uncompromising position in favor of social spending cutbacks. Neoconservatism, for its part, emerged as a reaction against the New Left. Although it never fully abandoned its roots in New Deal liberalism, it was now prepared to promote "family values" without invoking the necessity of income redistribution. These positions were by no means equivalent: While neoliberals called for an ongoing reduction in budget allocations dedicated to welfare—intent on undercutting any possibility that the social wage might compete with the free-market wage—neoconservatives endorsed an expanding role for the state in the regulation of sexuality. Despite their differences, however, neoliberals and neoconservatives converged on the necessity of reinstating the family as the foundation of social and economic order. Their alliance would profoundly shape the direction of social policy over the following decades, culminating in Clinton's radical welfare reform of 1996.

THE RISE OF NEOCONSERVATISM: INFLATION, WELFARE, AND MORAL CRISIS

It is often forgotten today that the first wave of neoconservatives—those who grew up during the Cold War—were overwhelmingly concerned with domestic social welfare issues rather than foreign policy.[68] Among this generation, some had been associated with the anti-Stalinist Trotskyist left in the 1930s; almost all would later became anticommunist liberals and New Deal Democrats during the Cold War; all were vehemently opposed to the anti-welfare politics of Republican conservatives such as Barry Goldwater, whom the neoliberal Milton Friedman had supported, and none were as yet Republicans. Many of these figures were associated at one time or another with *The Public Interest*, a journal founded by Daniel Bell and Irving Kristol in 1965, and *Commentary Magazine*, first published in 1945 and edited by Norman Podhoretz in the 1960s. By the time Bell and Kristol founded *The*

Public Interest, they had long since renounced socialism and had by the 1950s morphed into New Deal liberals—critical of both the communist left and McCarthyism. In its first years of publication, *The Public Interest* presented itself as a venue for the perfection of nonpartisan social policy expertise. Its first few issues featured articles from across the policy spectrum and included contributions from scholars as diverse as Milton Friedman, James Tobin, and Daniel Patrick Moynihan. With few exceptions, these contributors accepted the premises of the New Deal and (to a large extent) the Great Society welfare programs and merely applied themselves to the task of better implementing such programs. The tone was one of cautious technocratic optimism.

By the late 1960s, however, the tone had become decidedly more pessimistic; its authors more attuned to the dangers of unintended consequences and perverse incentives than the task of neutral policy implementation. Irving Kristol locates the birth of neoconservatism as a coherent tendency in 1965, the year in which *The Public Interest* first came into circulation and Moynihan published his report on the African American family.[69] Certainly many of the names that would later be associated with neoconservatism appeared in the first few issues of *The Public Interest*. But Nathan Glazer is surely more accurate in locating the inflection point in the late 1960s, when these former Democrats and New Deal liberals turned decisively against the New Left and began to formulate a coherent politics of reaction from *within* the left. Reflecting on the evolution of *The Public Interest*, Glazer traces the subtle shift in mood among New Deal liberals as they moved from the optimism of the 1960s to the threat of looming inflation at the turn of the decade, and from a progressive consensus on welfare—embracing Democrats and moderate conservatives—to a growing sense of discomfort with the ideals of the New Left. "By the end of the 1960s," he writes:

> I was not alone in thinking that something had gone wrong, that we had been somewhat too optimistic. My insight, probably not original, derived

entirely from my experiences with social policy and not at all from reading any theorist or social philosopher, was that we seemed to be creating as many problems as we were solving and that the reasons were inherent in the way we—liberals, but also moderate conservatives of the day (recall that they were such people as Richard Nixon and Nelson Rockefeller) thought about social problems and social policy.[70]

Reflecting, it seems, on the fate of Nixon's black family wage, Glazer echoed the sentiments of many of his colleagues when he concluded that the social reform efforts of the left had done more to undermine the family than to save it. "In our social policies we are trying to deal with the breakdown of traditional ways of handling distress" such as the family, he remarked, but "in our efforts to deal with the breakdown of these traditional structures, our social policies are weakening them further and making matters in some important respects worse."[71]

By the late 1960s, even the most progressive of old Democrats and champions of the Great Society (a position exemplified by a figure such as Moynihan) were alarmed at the direction in which leftist welfare politics was heading. These future neoconservatives had supported the extension of the family wage to black men but recoiled from redistributive welfare reform as such when they found themselves outflanked by a new and countercultural left. In particular, they were alarmed by those elements at the margins of the New Left that questioned the very premise of the family wage—the notion, that is, that income redistribution should be linked to the normative policing of legitimate childbearing and sexual morality. As we have seen, this critique was extremely marginal even among the most countercultural tendencies within the New Left, and indeed within the welfare rights movement itself. Yet, it was in reaction to this countercultural and antinormative left—a left that challenged the sexual foundations of the Fordist consensus—that neoconservatism was born. Reflecting on the concept of counterculture, Kristol noted that "'Sexual liberation' is always very near the top of a countercultural agenda.... Women's liberation, likewise, is another consistent feature of all countercultural movements—liberation from husbands, liberation from children, liberation from family. Indeed, the real object of these various sexual heterodoxies is to disestablish the family as the central institution of human society, the citadel of orthodoxy."[72]

But what did the neoconservatives mean by "counterculture"? The historian of neoconservatism, Justin Vaïsse, describes the New Left counterculture as primarily a phenomenon of the white, educated, middle class who had "time and money to spare."[73] This new class of militants, composed for the most part of college students and antiwar protestors, reacted against the reformism of the civil rights movement and defined itself in opposition to both the blue-collar trade union movement and the lower-middle class whites who represented the core constituency of the Democratic Party. Yet Vaïsse's characterization of the countercultural left relies heavily on neoconservatism's own denunciations of the "new class" and conflicts with other accounts of the shifting power relations within the left during the 1960s. Far from being confined to the white, college-educated middle class, the anti-authoritarianism of the counterculture reached far into the blue-collar labor movement during this period, provoking the president of the United Automobile Workers' Walter Reuther to remark that official trade unionism would need to adapt itself to a very different kind of worker.[74] The irruption of extralegal, wildcat militancy within the ranks of the labor movement was particularly disturbing to the neoconservative Samuel Huntington. As Huntington recognized, the antireformist spirit of the "counterculture" extended well beyond the white middle class to embrace blue-collar labor activism, black liberation, and the welfare rights movement, where it found expression in a newfound willingness to question the authority of the family as an instrument of social discipline.[75] This perhaps explains why neoconservative denunciations of the counterculture tend to begin with general fulminations against the white, educated, and privileged student class—the "new class"—but just as insistently conclude with the figure of the black welfare recipient. In text after text, neoconservative critique of the counterculture somehow transmutes into a critique of AFDC, the welfare program that they perceived, no doubt correctly, as the linchpin of the Fordist social order, and a virulent attack on the activists whom they saw as most responsible for disestablishing this order.

AFDC recipients could hardly be characterized as the most privileged of social subjects, and yet the neoconservatives consistently describe welfare mothers as a nonproductive rentier class—a lumpenproletariat that has taken on the qualities of the idle aristocracy by virtue of its dependence on the "unearned income" of welfare benefits.[76] Neoconservative rhetoric caters to the resentment of Fordism's most protected workers by reversing the order of actual social hierarchy amongst the poor, presenting itself as the defender of the white blue-collar working class against the demands of an unproductive rentier class of welfare *queens*, a move that is characteristic of reactionary populism on both the left and right. If inflation had come to be associated in the popular imagination with the problem of sumptuary speculation—since everyday consumers had learnt that it was in their interests to buy on credit—the moral denunciations that accompanied this observation fell disproportionately on the shoulders of the nonworking poor.[77]

The neoconservatives perfected their rhetoric of social disorder throughout the 1970s. As the problem of rising consumer prices impressed itself on the political agenda, the neoconservatives offered a comprehensive social theory of inflation that linked it, through sheer repetition as much as anything else, to the expansion of welfare programs, the breakdown of traditional values and the crisis of the family. Samuel Huntington's 1975 contribution to the Trilateral Commission Report was one of the first to posit a causal relationship between rising public deficits, inflation, and welfare spending that would soon accrue the aura of incontrovertible truth. Huntington noted that the immediate postwar years had seen a rapid increase in the proportion of government expenditures devoted to the military, but this "defense shift" was later superseded by a "welfare shift" that saw health, education, and income transfers compete with and then outpace military spending after the Vietnam War.[78] Reprinted in a special issue of *The Public Interest*, Huntington's report established the spurious but enormously influential argument that inflation could be attributed to budget deficits[79]—although through sleight of hand, inflation seemed to derive only from deficits accrued through social welfare spending, not from the profligate defense spending of the Cold War. Huntington's argument, repeated in relentless detail by his neoconservative colleagues, would prove decisive in shaping the future of government responses to inflation, not only under Reagan but also under subsequent Democratic and Republican administrations.

The neoconservatives added something new to the neoliberal argument, outlined by Milton Friedman in his Nobel Prize lecture of 1973, that stagflation had upset the quantitative calculus of Keynesian demand management (as embodied in the so-called Phillips curve).[80] Huntington intimated that the crisis of inflation represented not only a quantitative shift in government social expenditures but also a qualitative shift in the nature of social expectations, which undermined the very sources of authority on which the Keynesian social order had rested. "The essence of the democratic surge of the 1960s," he wrote, "was a general challenge to existing systems of authority, public and private. In one form or another, this challenge manifested itself in the family, the university, business, public and private associations, politics, the government bureaucracy and the military services."[81]

It was Daniel Bell, reputed to be the most progressive of the neoconservatives, who would fully develop this argument in *The Cultural Contradictions of Capitalism*, first published in 1976.[82] Here he accuses the Keynesian revolution of undermining, through its very success, the principles of Protestant frugality upon which the modern fiscal state was originally based.[83] The historical novelty of the Protestant ethic, according to Weber, was to combine a chrematistics of the market with an austere philosophy of desire—one founded on abstinence, deferred gratification, and frugality. If early modern capitalism promoted limitless accumulation in the market, it simultaneously imposed restraint on consumption. The welfare state, Bell argued, had reversed this logic by freeing welfare expenditure from all economic and moral constraints and thereby unleashing a limitless drive to sumptuary accumulation in the private sphere. Little by little, the perverse logic of chrematistics had shifted from the market to the workplace to the household, generating limitless desires that challenged the traditional order of sexual relations—not to mention the fiscal viability of the state, which was now called upon to subsidize these nonnormative ways of living.[84] By pointing to the incompatibility between Keynesian deficit spending and sexual liberation, Daniel Bell elucidated what he saw as implicit within the American economics of public finance (tellingly dubbed the economics of the "public household" by the economist Richard Musgrave).[85] The calculus of postwar deficit spending was premised on the normative assumption of the family wage and therefore contained within limits that were simultaneously sexual and economic. If one could imagine an expansion of welfare state spending to include nonwhite men within the category of breadwinner, one could not question the normative premise of the male breadwinner family itself without completely defeating the arithmetic of the "public household"—and thus generating runaway inflation.

The thrust of Bell's argument—which in the last instance, attributes inflation to a breakdown of household order—helps to explain why the neoconservatives were almost exclusively preoccupied by a welfare program that consumed so little of the overall social welfare budget. Huntington may have identified the "welfare shift"—by which he meant the expansion of *all* social programs, from health and education to social insurance and public assistance programs—as the source of inflation, but time and again neoconservative attacks on welfare home in on AFDC in particular. Nathan Glazer recognizes the apparent contradiction here when he concedes that "welfare [AFDC] was far from the biggest of our social programs" and "no great drain on our financial resources…compared with other large social programs."[86] Yet, he goes on to argue, "it was seen, and with good reason, I would argue, as being closer to the heart of our social problems than larger programs such as social security, or aid to the disabled, or Medicare, or Medicaid."[87] Inflation could not reasonably be attributed to the *quantitative* increase in AFDC rolls, then, but it could well be associated with the *qualitative* shift in moral expectations that allowed AFDC recipients to flout the norms of the Fordist family. Having established that inflation was a problem of affective expectations rather than quantitative laws, the neoconservatives could confidently identify AFDC as symptom and cause of the crisis of inflation: Of all the New Deal and Great Society social initiatives, AFDC was the one program that contributed to the breakdown of the traditional family and therefore *the program that most directly expressed the moral malaise of inflation.*

NEOCONSERVATISM AND NEOLIBERALISM

How did neoliberals and neoconservatives manage to form an alliance on social welfare despite seemingly insurmountable political and epistemological differences? Irving Kristol candidly acknowledged these tensions when he was invited to deliver a paper at the twenty-fifth anniversary meeting of the Mont Pèlerin Society in 1972. The paper was written at the request of Milton Friedman, who was then presiding over the organization and hoped, by inviting Kristol, to rekindle some of its earlier pluralism.[88] Despite Friedman's overtures, however, Kristol was skeptical of any continued alliance between free market economics and neoconservatism, bluntly accusing the neoliberals of continuing to fight a battle they had already won.[89] As politicians contemplated the incapacity of orthodox Keynesian economics to cope with the novel economic conditions of the 1970s, the once marginal prescriptions of monetarists such as Friedman had now become increasingly respectable. In the meantime, however, the neoliberals were ignoring what to Kristol was the more pressing problem of the countercultural left, which he saw as hostile to the very values of "bourgeois society" on which a free market order depended. In Kristol's eyes, neoliberalism was incapable of countering the rising tide of the counterculture because it shared the New Left's essential amoralism. The neoliberal ethos propounded by a Friedman or a Becker (who at various moments would contemplate consumer markets in kidneys, babies, and drugs) was ultimately compatible with the antinormative desires of the New Left because it accepted no a priori notion of transcendent virtue. For neoconservatives such as Kristol, by contrast, the free market order propounded by neoliberals could not exist without the assumption of some fundamental moral value. In Kristol's words: "The idea of bourgeois virtue has been eliminated from Friedman's conception of bourgeois society, and has been replaced by the idea of individual liberty."[90]

Kristol's account of neoliberalism's amoralism is one that might be readily endorsed by commentators on the left.[91] But it fails to do justice to the nuance of the neoliberal position, which does not so much eliminate moral philosophy as posit an immanent ethics of virtue and a spontaneous order of family values that it expects to arise automatically from the mechanics of the free market system. Much like Kristol, critics of neoliberalism have failed to recognize that Friedman and his Chicago school colleagues posit the self-sufficient family as much as the individual as a basic manifestation of the free-market order.

Gary Becker makes this point explicitly when he argues that the familial incentive toward altruism is as central to the constitution of the free market as the utilitarian incentive of self-interested exchange.[92] The nature of family altruism in some sense represents an internal exception to the free market, an immanent order of non-contractual obligations and inalienable services without which the world of contract would cease to function.[93] This premise is so constitutive of economic liberalism, both classical and neoliberal, that it is rarely articulated as such. Yet it explains why, in Wendy Brown's words, private family values constitute the secret underside of liberal contractualism.[94]

Milton Friedman, for his part, assumes the nuclear family as a natural or spontaneous state of the uncorrupted social in much the same way as he posits an equilibrium state of money. In its free or equilibrium state, money appears so neutral as to exert no power at all on the actual workings of economic exchange—money is merely a veil that permits the proper unfolding of contractual relations.[95] But in the same way that the Federal Reserve may intervene to distort the natural rate of growth of the money supply, giving rise to such perverse consequences as inflation, excessive government spending on welfare upsets the equilibrium state of the family and undermines its natural incentives toward altruism and mutual dependence. Pointing to the example of Social Security—which Friedman would like to see privatized in its entirety—he notes that the natural obligations of kinship that once compelled children to look after their parents in old age have now been replaced by an impersonal system of social insurance whose long-term effect is to usurp the place of the family:

> The difference between Social Security and earlier arrangements is that Social Security is compulsory and impersonal—earlier arrangements were voluntary and personal. Moral responsibility is an individual matter, not a social matter. Children helped their parents out of love or duty. They now contribute to the support of someone else's parents out of compulsion and fear. The earlier transfers strengthened the bonds of the family; the compulsory transfers weakened them.[96]

In a true free-market order, Friedman argues, economic security would ideally derive from the familial transmission of property rather than state-based redistribution. The freedom to bequeath wealth to one's children should therefore be understood as a natural, spontaneous incentive of the free-market order and protected from any kind of state confiscation in the form of an estate tax:

> This is really a family society, not an individual society.... And the greatest incentives of all, the incentives that have really driven people on, have largely been the incentives of family creation. The thing that is amazing that people don't really recognize is the extent to which the free market system has in fact encouraged people and enabled people to work hard and sacrifice—in what I confess I often regard as an irrational way—for the benefit of their children. One of the most curious things to me in observation is that almost all people value the utility their children will get from consumption higher than their own.[97]

A similar intuition underlies and informs Becker's entire theory of human capital investment, which can be read as a systematic historical comparison of the effects of state versus family investment in the welfare of children. Becker begins his *Treatise on the Family* by noting that the "family in the Western world has been radically altered—some claim almost destroyed—by events of the last three decades."[98] He goes on to list a familiar series of ills: from the rapid rise in divorce rates and female-headed families to the decline in birth rates and the growing labor force participation of married women, which has "reduced the contact between children and their mothers and contributed to the conflict between the sexes in employment as well as in marriage."

These dramatic changes in the structure of the family, he argues, have more to do with the expansion of the welfare state in the postwar era than with feminism per se—which can be considered a consequence rather than an instigator of these dynamics. Predictably, Becker singles out AFDC—the "poor woman's alimony"—as one of the prime culprits in the breakdown of the family.[99] But like Friedman, he also credits more generic social insurance programs and public services such as state education with weakening the bonds of familial obligation. For Becker, the family in its equilibrium state can be understood as serving a kind of natural insurance function that is disturbed when the welfare state socializes insurance.[100] The fact that fathers "choose" to support wife and children and mothers "choose" to perform most of the unpaid reproductive work of care, thus relieving the state of any such responsibilities, represents the equilibrium state of the family in a free-market order, a state of mutual dependence and self-sufficiency that neoliberal welfare reform must strive to restore. If we can therefore derive a pragmatic policy lesson from neoliberalism's philosophy of the family, it is that the dismantling of welfare represents the most effective means of restoring the private bonds of familial obligation. Writing in the early 1980s, Becker credits the postwar welfare state with destroying the natural altruism of the family but surmises that the decline in welfare initiated by Reagan will ultimately compel the poor to restore the bonds of kinship as a source of privatized welfare.[101]

It is not that neoliberals completely reject the idea of virtue then, as Kristol wants to argue, but rather that they expect the strictest of virtue ethics to arise spontaneously from the immanent action of market forces. "Economic systems that rely on private behavior and competitive markets are more efficient than those with extensive government control," writes Becker. "However, the effects of a free-market system on self-reliance, initiative and other virtues may be of even greater importance in the long run."[102] This, he explains, is why nineteenth-century defenders of the free market "often emphasized the system's effect on values rather than on efficiency," predictably going on to quote Tocqueville on the mutually reinforcing relationship between self-interest and virtue. Thus if neoliberals can in one respect be described as laissez faire on the question of family—in the sense that they believe that cutbacks in government social spending will automatically restore the natural virtues of kinship obligations—this does not make them any less concerned with the necessity of family in a free-market order. It simply means that they theorize fundamental value itself as the emergent effect of market forces rather than its a priori foundation.

For the neoconservatives, by contrast, the ideal family is not the natural result of market forces but an institution that in some sense opposes the market and lies outside it. Its fundamental values must be actively protected by the state if it is to survive the corrosive force of contractual exchange. In this respect, neoconservatives appear much closer to left social Democrats such as Karl Polanyi than they do to neoliberals. Most of them, after all, continued to support the basic functions of the welfare state in an era when neoliberal arguments in favor of small government were otherwise on the ascendant. Even Irving Kristol—among neoconservatives, the most sympathetic to the free market ideas of Ronald Reagan—insisted that neoconservatism "feels no lingering hostility to the welfare state, nor does it accept it resignedly, as a necessary evil. Instead it seeks not to dismantle the welfare state in the name of free-market economics but rather to reshape it so as to attach to it the *conservative* predispositions of the people."[103]

Much to the chagrin of the libertarian and neoliberal right, neoconservatives such as Kristol were happy to endorse the expansion of Social Security (Friedman's bête noire) because it supported such a benign constituency, the elderly. Kristol even declared himself in favor of universal health insurance.[104] If the neoconservatives nevertheless directed so much of their critical energy toward AFDC, it was because it had abandoned the punitive and pedagogical function of the early Mother's Pensions programs and had instead come to subsidize immorality. Importantly, however, they never rejected AFDC outright but instead called for a new kind of public assistance program that would actively promote marriage and legitimate childbearing amongst the poor.

At first blush, then, neoconservatives and neoliberals would seem to endorse diametrically opposing positions on the role of the state in welfare reform. The neoconservatives are under no illusion that the traditional family will simply reassert itself of its own accord, absent government intrusion; rather, they see the primary function of the state as that of sustaining the family, the foundation of all social order, if necessary through the use of force. Social conservative policy practitioners such as the new paternalist Lawrence Mead thus develop an elaborate and explicit methodology of power that tells us just how the noncontractual virtues of work and family are to be imposed.[105] In the words of Nathan Glazer, the task of neoconservative welfare reform is to "reinvent tradition" by actively inculcating a culture of abstinence, monogamy, and marriage among the poor.[106]

Neoliberals instead envisage the private paternalism of the family as a spontaneous source of welfare in the free-market order; a state of equilibrium that may be disturbed by the perverse incentives of redistributive welfare but also restored through the diminution of state paternalism. In its mature articulation, the neoliberal agenda for welfare reform calls for the ongoing reduction of redistributive expenditures, the outright elimination of superfluous programs, the contracting out of social services to private providers, the replacement of dedicated government services by a "voucher" system that can be used to simulate private markets and consumer "choice," and the devolution of welfare provision from the federal government to the state and local levels.[107] In the long run, neoliberals hope that many of the functions formerly "usurped" by the welfare state will be returned to the private family, which they expect to automatically resume its "traditional" role in the provision of care. In the medium term, however, they readily acknowledge the reality of family failure (homologous to market failure) and the necessity of some kind of restorative intervention on the part of the state to correct such disorders. In these instances, their first impulse is to invoke "incentives" as the most efficient form of intervention.[108] Modeled on the price signaling mechanisms of the market, incentives such as fines, sanctions, and rewards are designed to correct the "perverse incentives" of voluntary unemployment and family dysfunction with as little effort as possible on the part of the state. Thus, Becker recommends the use of performance-linked benefits incentivizing parents to send their children to school, keep up with vaccinations, and stop them from taking drugs.[109]

When even the harshest of incentives fail to work, however, neoliberals have in practice relied on the much more overt forms of behavioral correction favored by social conservatives. Although they rarely acknowledge or theorize this imperative, neoliberals must ultimately delegate power to social conservatives in order to realize their vision of a naturally equilibrating free-market order and a spontaneously self-sufficient family. Neoliberalism and social conservatism are thus tethered together by a working relationship that is at once necessary and disavowed: as an ideology of power that only ever acknowledges its reliance on market mechanisms and their homologues, neoliberalism can only realize its objectives by proxy, that is by outsourcing the imposition of noncontractual obligations to social conservatives. In extremis, neoliberals must turn to the overt, neoconservative methodology of state-imposed, transcendant virtue to realize their dream of an immanent virtue ethics of the market.

TRANSITIONS

The inflation of the 1970s oversaw a profound reshuffling of political alignments. In the 1960s, New Deal Democrats and free-market neoliberals alike were contemplating the expansion of the family wage to include African American men, with the active support of a Republican president. Democrats and Republicans proclaimed themselves "all Keynesians now" as redistributive welfare imposed itself as the starting point and horizon of all social reform. By the mid-1970s, however, Nixon had secretly given up on the black family wage, and inflation now emerged as an overwhelming political concern. In this new context of diminished expectations, former New Deal Democrats such as Moynihan came out as recognizable neoconservatives, while free-market neoliberals such as Milton Friedman lost any pragmatic adherence to the precepts of income redistribution. These former champions of New Deal liberalism now accused AFDC—and by extension the welfare state itself—of radically undermining the family. And in response to what they perceived as the incorrigible perversion of the Great Society social state, they now called for a much more drastic reform of welfare than they themselves had hitherto imagined. It was now agreed that the welfare programs of the New Deal and Great Society would need to be radically restricted and qualified, even while the private institution of the family was to be strengthened as a general alternative to redistributive welfare. Family responsibility—a notion derived from the poor-law tradition of public relief—now became the watchword of neoliberal and neoconservative efforts to reform the welfare state.

One figure who was poised to benefit from this shifting political configuration was Ronald Reagan, who, as governor of California, had taken an active stance against Nixon's family wage. In 1975, the Governor's Office of California, under Reagan's influence, published the document, *California's Blueprint for National Welfare Reform*, which articulated a new, Republican-right agenda for social policy that stood in sharp contrast to Nixon's moderate liberalism.[110] The blueprint recommended the implementation of a comprehensive workfare program and was one of the first policy documents to weave together the neoliberal thematics of family self-sufficiency with a neoconservative agenda of moral reform. This combination of influences would come into its own under the impetus of the Volcker shock and prove decisive in shaping the future of welfare reform over the following decades.

Hoping to replicate his state experiment in welfare reform at the federal level, Reagan initiated his presidency by announcing his intention to cut spending across all social programs. The resulting budget plan, contained in the Omnibus Budget Reconciliation Act of 1981 (OBRA), "cut AFDC rolls by 400,000 individuals, reduced benefits for hundreds of thousands more, and cut federal AFDC costs by $1 billion, or 12 percent, in fiscal year 1982" but left much more costly programs such as Social Security, Medicare (for the elderly), and veterans' benefits virtually untouched.[111] As noted by Marisa Chappell, a purely economic perspective on Reagan's anti-inflationary politics cannot account for the disproportionate share of budget cuts inflicted on AFDC—a program that consumed a mere one percent of the federal budget.[112] The focus of these cuts can only be understood if we appreciate the sense of moral crisis that had accrued around the AFDC program in the preceding decade. In the eyes of both neoliberals and neoconservatives, AFDC had come to epitomize the specific moral malaise of inflation; it was hardly surprising then that it should be subject to such overwhelming firepower.

Throughout his terms as president, Reagan attempted to implement the California welfare blueprint at a federal level, but for various reasons he was never successful in pushing through the radical reforms he had envisaged. It was under President Clinton—the New Democrat who promised to "end welfare as we know it"—that the neoliberal-neoconservative alliance on welfare reform would ultimately come to fruition. The players that shaped Clinton's welfare reform were not necessarily the same. Among the neoconservatives, only Moynihan would continue to play a direct role in social policy. Their social conservative perspective on welfare reform would find new expression in the paternalism of Lawrence Mead, the leading exponent of workfare, and the communitarianism of the Institute for American Values, exponents of marriage promotion and family-law reform. And although Milton Friedman continued to play a role as a public intellectual, his early policy influence was now channeled through a dense network of policy think tanks ranging from the libertarian (the Cato Institute) to the neoliberal and social conservative (the American Enterprise Institute, the Manhattan Institute, the Heritage Foundation). Under Clinton, these figures would help shape a new era of social policy that unambiguously placed family values at the heart of welfare reform.

CHAPTER THREE

The Ethic of Family Responsibility:
Reinventing the Poor Laws

> If we are right that the tide is turning, that public opinion is shifting
> away from a belief in big government and away from the doctrine
> of social responsibility, then that change... will tend to restore
> a belief in individual responsibility by strengthening the family
> and reestablishing its traditional role.
> — Rose and Milton Friedman, *Tyranny of the Status Quo*

In 1996, President Bill Clinton enacted the single most dramatic overhaul of the federal welfare system since the New Deal. The Welfare
Reform Act, otherwise known as PRWORA (the Personal Responsibility and Work Opportunity Reconciliation Act) abolished the Aid to
Families with Dependent Children (AFDC) program, originally created as part of the 1935 Social Security Act, and replaced it with a time-
limited program known as Temporary Assistance for Needy Families
(TANF). Making good on his promise to "end welfare as we know it,"
Clinton's landmark legislation sought as far as possible to replace public responsibility for the welfare of poor women with a state-enforced
system of private family responsibility that actively revived and sometimes created kinship relations *ex nihilo*. States were now required to
increase their efforts to police, track down, and enforce paternity obligations, on the presumption that the biological father of a child on welfare should be forced to pay child support (to be deducted from state

welfare payments) whether or not the mother wished to maintain a relationship with him. And in what must be understood as a blurring of the boundaries between the free and unfree sexual contract, sanctions were to be imposed on mothers who did not sufficiently cooperate in helping welfare agencies to locate the biological father of their children. By diverting a substantial portion of the federal welfare budget to the task of extracting child support from fathers, welfare reform served to remind women that an individual man, not the state, was ultimately responsible for their economic security. Unless a woman could assume "personal responsibility" for her economic fate, she would have to accept her condition of economic dependence on an absent father or substitute husband.

Reflecting a new bipartisan consensus on the social value of monogamous, legally validated relationships, Clinton's welfare reform also created a series of initiatives to promote the moral obligations of family, including a special budget allocation to finance marriage promotion programs and millions of dollars in bonus funds for states that could demonstrate they had successfully reduced illegitimate births without increasing the abortion rate. These initiatives would be greatly expanded under the Bush and Obama administrations, where they flowered into elaborate healthy marriage and responsible fatherhood initiatives implicating multiple federal departments and consuming a growing portion of the federal welfare budget. The notion that private family obligations should ultimately take the place of welfare transfers was here supplemented by the idea that the state should take an active pedagogical role in cultivating proper family values among the welfare and non-welfare population alike.

Under the sign of family responsibility, Clinton's welfare reform sealed an effective institutional alliance between neoliberal and new social conservative perspectives on the family.[1] Their preoccupations were distinct: If neoliberals were adamant that the economic obligations of family should be enforced even when the legal and affective bonds of kinship had broken down, social conservatives were intent on actively rekindling the family as a moral institution based on the unpaid labor of love. Both agreed, however, that the private family (rather than the state) should serve as the primary source of economic security.

By making family responsibility the guiding principle of federal welfare law, Clinton brought to fruition a social reform agenda initiated by Ronald Reagan as far back as the 1970s. As governor of California, Reagan had vowed to "strengthen family responsibility" by transferring the legal burdens of public assistance onto parents, adult children, and relatives.[2] As president, he proclaimed that "intact, self-reliant families are the best anti-poverty insurance ever devised" and tried, with only partial success, to translate this insight into federal welfare law.[3] In the early 1970s, however, Governor Reagan stood well to the right of the political mainstream, proving too extreme for many of his more moderate Republican colleagues. At a time when Nixon was hoping to extend New Deal social protections to include black men within the ambit of the Fordist family wage, Reagan was busy reviving, or rather reinventing, a much older tradition of relief based on private family responsibility.

This tradition last flourished in the late nineteenth century, during the so-called Gilded Age of American capitalism, where both classical liberals and moral conservatives embraced it as the most appropriate way of managing the poor. Its origins can be traced back much further to the British and American poor-law tradition, whose provisions made no distinction between the emotional and financial bonds of kinship and "virtually equated the moral and the economic functions of the family."[4] In the 1970s, Ronald Reagan was nearly alone among Republicans in seeking to revive the discredited poor-law tradition of family responsibility as an alternative to the New Deal welfare state. By the 1980s, such ideas had entered the mainstream of social policy debate and were openly championed by right-wing think tanks such as the Heritage Foundation.[5] Ultimately, however, it fell to the New Democrat, President Clinton, to realize the reactionary pipe dreams that had once been shunned by more moderate Republicans.

The "family responsibility" tradition in American welfare originated in the Elizabethan and early colonial poor laws, and was reinvented in post–Civil War America, where it flourished as an elaborate and invasive methodology for policing the lives of the poor. When New Deal social reformers sought to import the principles of European social insurance to America in the mid–twentieth century, it was this tradition that they needed to overcome in order to impose their own vision of redistributive, yet nevertheless family-centered welfare.

Today, both neoliberals and new social conservatives see themselves as reversing this historical trajectory in order to recuperate a lost tradition of private family responsibility for the care of dependents.[6] It is no coincidence that contemporary scholars ranging from the Christian libertarian (Marvin Olasky) to the thoroughly neoconservative (Gertrude Himmelfarb) identify late nineteenth-century America as a misrecognized Golden Age of natural charity in which free-market capitalism happily coexisted with the most austere forms of moral conservatism.[7] The peculiar alliance of economic liberalism and moral conservatism that triumphed in the Gilded Age is one that they would like to revive today, while recognizing in their more lucid moments that history reinvents rather than repeats itself.

In practice, late twentieth-century welfare reformers could not simply revive the Gilded Age system of private-charity-based family responsibility; rather, they sought to absorb its imperatives into the existing institutional structures of the welfare state. Thus, the effect of Clinton's welfare reform of 1996 was to requisition a once redistributive welfare program and repurpose it as an immense federal apparatus for enforcing the "private" responsibilities of family and work. What we are witnessing here is not the outright dismantling of the welfare state envisaged by libertarian conservatives such as Charles

Murray or Marvin Olasky, but rather its reinvigoration as an instrument for imposing work and family obligations on the welfare poor. The family responsibility provisions that were once policed by charity workers and the courts are now incorporated into federal welfare law and imbued with all the institutional force of an elaborate national welfare infrastructure.

The role of the poor-law tradition in shaping recent welfare reform highlights some of the interpretive failures of popular accounts of neoliberalism. Most of these accounts focus on neoliberalism's overriding investment in the notion of personal responsibility. Jacob Hacker, for instance, denounces the neoliberal assault on social risk protections as a "personal responsibility crusade" and laments its destructive effects on public investment, job security and...the family.[8] But an exclusive focus on free-market individualism obscures the recurrent elision between the personal and the familial in neoliberal discourse and thereby renders unintelligible its historical compatibility with various complexions of moral conservatism. Yes, neoliberals persistently exhort individuals to take responsibility for their own fate, and yet the imperative of *personal responsibility* slides ineluctably into that of *family responsibility* when it comes to managing the inevitable problems of economic dependence (the care of children, the disabled, the elderly, or the unwaged). Wendy Brown speaks in this regard of a "persistent legal and political tension between the individual and the family in liberalism" — a tension which is clearly to be found in the poor-law tradition, where the individual responsibility of sustaining oneself through waged work has always implied a wider responsibility toward unwaged dependents within the family.[9] In the work of Milton and Rose Friedman, the slippage is presented as so self-evident it requires no further elucidation. "If we are right that the tide is turning, that public opinion is shifting away from a belief in big government and away from the doctrine of social responsibility," they write, "then that change...*will tend to restore a belief in individual responsibility by strengthening the family and reestablishing its traditional role.*"[10] The restoration of family responsibility is here presented as the natural consequence of the state's marginalization from the role of social welfare, as spontaneous and inexplicable as the freedom of the individual in a competitive market environment.

Social conservatives are typically much more conscious of the conceptual paradox at work here and much more mindful of the coercive force that must be harnessed to subordinate the free individual to the obligations of family. "It may appear a paradox," notes Gary Bauer, President Reagan's advisor on the family, "that American society, with its emphasis on rights of the individual, has placed great value on a strong family structure." To some, after all, "the nature of the family may seem opposed to freedom: a limitation on spouses bound by commitments to each other, a burden on parents obligated to care for children, and a restriction on children who live under parental authority." But Bauer, more than Milton and Rose Friedman, understands that it is precisely such family obligations that sustain the otherwise inexplicable freedom of the liberal individual:

> The experience of history...shows family and liberty to be natural companions, not enemies. The framers of our Constitution saw clearly that only those societies strong in certain civic virtues could sustain an experiment in representative democracy. The family is the primary training ground for individual responsibility, for self-sacrifice, for seeking a common goal rather than self-interest.... Conversely, only in a society that allows individual freedom can family members exercise the initiative and responsibility that makes for strong family life.[11]

Here we can see how neoliberalism and neoconservatism are ultimately able to reconcile their differences. Neoliberals such as Friedman begin with the self-evidence of individual responsibility but end up affirming the necessity of familial obligations when confronted with the social costs of unwaged dependents. Social conservatives begin with the foundational importance of the family and derive the liberty of the individual from here. Both, however, seize upon the necessity of family responsibility as the ideal source of economic security and an effective counterforce to the demoralizing powers of the welfare state.

FAMILY RESPONSIBILITY AND THE ELIZABETHAN POOR LAW

Dating from 1601, the Elizabethan Act for the Relief of the Poor, otherwise known as the Elizabethan Poor Law or the Old Poor Law, brought into being the first national system for the relief of paupers in England and Wales. Comprising a multitude of new and old statutes, the act was designed to replace earlier forms of church-based charity with a new, more comprehensive system of parish-administered relief to be funded by compulsory land taxes. The Poor Law is justly recognized as the first serious attempt to organize public relief on a national scale. It unambiguously acknowledged the vicissitudes of the labor market and the consequent need for some kind of permanent support structure, but it also placed strict conditions on the distribution of relief. Among these, the first to be enforced was that of family responsibility, the idea that relatives within certain degrees of kinship should be compelled to provide as much support as possible before the parish disbursed any funds. Thus, the text of the original 1601 act stipulated "that the father and grandfather, and the mother and grandmother, and the children of every poor, old, blind, lame and impotent person, or other poor person not able to work, being of a sufficient ability, shall, at their own charges, relieve and maintain every such poor person."[12]

The Elizabethan Poor Law thus introduced new filial obligation rules obliging adult children to care for their aging and impoverished parents, while also subsuming an earlier bastardy statute, enacted in 1576, making both parents liable for the support of illegitimate children and outlining criminal charges for illicit sex acts.[13] These statutory provisions supplemented the old common-law duty obliging a husband to support his wife and were most commonly invoked in cases involving the poorest members of the parish.[14] In each instance, the stated purpose of these rules was to relieve the local parish of the burden of public support by delegating primary responsibility to the family. Under certain circumstances, moreover, family obligations could be exchanged for work obligations, which were also provided for under the Elizabethan Poor Law: If a local parishioner failed to provide due support for an indigent family member, he or she could be forced to work for free to reimburse the local authorities for the costs of relief. From the very beginning, the Poor Law enforcement of labor and family obligations worked hand in hand.

When it came to adapting the laws and statutes of the Old World to the new American colonies, each of the thirteen states ended up replicating the Elizabethan Poor Law almost *in toto*, retaining many of the family responsibility provisions written into the original act.[15] Every one of the colonies enacted criminal penalties against unmarried sex and civil laws requiring putative fathers to support illegitimate children. These laws seem to have applied most rigorously to indentured servants, again with the express aim of relieving local authorities of the burden of support. Historian Mary Ann Mason notes that the colonial poor laws "were not simply prescriptive": Such laws were widely enforced, with courts frequently ordering fathers to post bonds with the local authorities and sentencing unmarried mothers to physical penalties such as whippings.[16] As in England, familial debts were readily monetized and transformed into work obligations: A female bonded servant who had conceived a child outside of wedlock might be required to extend her period of indenture to compensate for the costs of support, while a putative father could transmute criminal sanctions into a period of enforced work.

These laws survived the end of the colonial period and served as a regulatory backdrop to the lives of the poor into the Republican era and beyond. At various historical junctures, the poor law's family responsibility provisions were revised or enlarged to respond to the changing boundaries between work and household. As the private family unit separated off from the productive household in the course of the nineteenth century, and as the family became smaller, the network of kin included under family responsibility rules grew correspondingly larger to include sisters and brothers, and grandchildren as well as grandparents.[17] Likewise, as divorce became more common in the nineteenth century, new child support laws enforcing the responsibilities of estranged fathers were introduced both at common law and under new statutory provisions modeled on the original poor law.[18] When the Civil War ended and former slaves were declared free laborers, they, too, came under the purview of newly invented family responsibility laws. As this history demonstrates, the poor laws were not only imported intact from England but were subsequently reinvented many times over as a means of disciplining new kinds of sexual and economic freedom. As such, they have served to demarcate and police the outer bounds of the free labor market and consensual intimacy, enforcing the bonds of family and work as inescapable duties when the poor have failed to fulfill them of their own accord.

The reinvention of the poor laws played a particularly significant role in the shaping of modern industrial capitalism and its signature political philosophies, first in England in the 1830s and subsequently in post–Civil War America. When the Royal Commission into the Operation of the Poor Laws of 1832 investigated the state of pauper relief in industrial England, it found that the force of the original Poor Law had been hopelessly diluted by successive concessions on the part of local authorities. The Poor Law Commissioners were particularly alarmed by the fact that the generosity of relief measures appeared to be undermining not only the work ethic but also the traditional bonds of family dependency:

The worst results are still to be mentioned: in all ranks of society the great sources of happiness and virtue are the domestic affections, and this is particularly the case among those who have so few resources as the laboring classes. Now, pauperism seems to be an engine for the purpose of disconnecting each member of a family from all the others; of reducing all to the state of domesticated animals, fed, lodged and provided for by the parish, without mutual dependence or mutual interest.[19]

Work and family obligations, it concluded, should be reintroduced in the strictest of forms.[20] Within the classical liberal tradition, personal responsibility and family responsibility were held together in a metonymic relationship of mutual inclusion. When interpellated as an independent, free worker, the liberal subject was required to assume personal responsibility for his fate—failing which he would be subject to the workhouse or some other regime of unfree labor. When the care of nonworking dependents was at stake, however, personal responsibility was subsumed within the larger category of family responsibility and the ideal of the independent individual incorporated within the wider notion of the self-sufficient family. Family support duties could then be imposed with much the same rigor as unfree labor: Both were understood as noncontractual obligations that the state had every right to enforce in the service of the free-market contractual order.

The New Poor Law was closely informed by the thinking of Thomas Robert Malthus, whose Christian political economy reflected a peculiar combination of classical liberal and moral conservative concerns.[21] As the century progressed and the New Poor Law took shape as a comprehensive philosophy of charitable social reform, the ethic of family responsibility came to clearly reflect this double provenance in classical liberal and conservative philosophies of the social. The new "scientific charity" reformers of late nineteenth-century Britain and America saw themselves as the inheritors of the New Poor Law and sought to transform its sparse legislative dictums into an all-pervasive form of social regulation. These reformers understood the economic and moral obligations of family to be inseparable components of the law: It was not enough to protect public coffers by enforcing the economic duty of family support; one should also seek to rehabilitate the family itself in a form imagined to be "traditional." As the point of articulation between the economic and moral obligations of kinship, family responsibility served as a rallying cry for classical liberals and moral conservatives alike. While free-market liberals were concerned with enforcing the economic obligations of family, even when the moral and social bonds of kinship had broken down, conservatives were convinced that moral and legal foundations of the family needed to be shored up before the economic costs of marital breakdown could be properly attended to. In many cases, however, both philosophies were shared in some combination by one and the same person.

Two key moments in the history of the poor law's family responsibility provisions can be identified. First, family responsibility laws were extended to include newly enfranchised African Americans in the post–Civil War period; subsequently, such laws were revised and intensified in Gilded Age America, where they served to regulate the lives of the white American and migrant working class. In both instances, the ethic of family responsibility brought together classical liberal and moral conservative perspectives on the obligations of family and thus actively enabled the peculiar alliance between radical free-market economics and moral traditionalism that flourished in late nineteenth-century America. In the aftermath of the Civil War, family responsibility laws served to introduce former slaves into the rigors of the free labor market while also authorizing a new social conservative ethos of domestic life among African Americans themselves. And in Gilded Age America, such laws helped to reduce public welfare spending to a minimum but were also supplemented by a more ambitious campaign to rehabilitate the "traditional family" among the general population. It was this classical liberal-conservative ethic of family responsibility that needed to be defeated before the New Deal welfare state could come into being in the early twentieth century.

PROMOTING THE AFRICAN AMERICAN FAMILY:
REINVENTING THE POOR LAW AFTER EMANCIPATION

The creation of the Freedmen's Bureau in 1865, an institution designed to oversee the transition of former slaves from a state of bondage to freedom, is recognized as the first experiment in federal relief ever implemented by Congress. The welfare historian Walter Trattner goes so far as to characterize the Bureau as the "nation's first federal welfare agency": Its establishment "represented an unprecedented federal effort as the government took responsibility for the relief and sustenance of the emancipated slaves."[22] Despite its scale, however, the Bureau's experiment in federal relief was never imagined as anything more than a transitional project and was designed to be phased out within a few years. Even as the Bureau offered temporary relief then, helping former slaves to settle and find work, it also sought to transform African Americans into independent citizens and free laborers, appropriately schooled in the arts of contractual freedom and marital obligation.

As Amy Dru Stanley has argued, classical liberalism posited a reciprocal relationship between the freedom of contractual labor and the noncontractual obligations of marriage. Abolitionists had denounced slavery for stripping the black man of both his freedom to sell his own labor and his legal rights over the labor of wife and children.[23] They therefore imagined full emancipation as the moment in which black men would simultaneously be granted contractual freedom in the labor market and noncontractual rights vis-à-vis their dependents. True emancipation would not be secured until former slaves and incipient free laborers had been granted the same rights to marriage and paternity as white men.

Before the Emancipation Proclamation of 1863, slaves had no legal right to enter into commercial labor contracts and were precluded from the civil contract of marriage. Allowing legal marriage among slaves would have granted the male slave property rights in the labor of his wife and children and would therefore have threatened the absolute rights of the white slave master, who was considered the head of household and master of all his dependents—men, women, and children alike, free and unfree.[24] The effect of emancipation was to restrict the absolute power of the white head of household by limiting his property rights to his immediate wife and children, but in the process it also created a new gendered power relation between former slaves—elevating freed black men over women by endowing them, like white men, with rights and responsibilities toward their legal wives.

At the same time as the Freedmen's Bureau attempted to transform former male slaves into free wage laborers, then, it also taught them that freedom in the labor market came with the right to marry and the responsibility to support a wife and children. To drive home this lesson, Bureau agents set about overseeing wage contracts and formal marriages among emancipated slaves in the very first years of Reconstruction, ensuring that both were "enforceable by law."[25] In many cases, in fact, the civil marriage and labor contract were conjoined—since women were not considered to be free laborers on a par with men, Bureau agents routinely allowed men to contract for the labor of their wife and children as a means of sustaining a family wage.[26] Throughout the South, Freedmen's Bureau agents pursued a vigorous campaign to promote marriage among slaves, many of whom had previously been united in informal unions, had cohabited, or were involved in multiple relationships. Bureau agents were authorized to perform wedding ceremonies, to certify or dissolve informal unions that had begun before emancipation, and to track down spouses who had been forcibly separated by slave masters.[27] In all instances, they sought to regularize or dissolve what they perceived to be the illegitimate, immoral, and informal unions that had existed under slavery. Beyond these efforts at legal formalization, however, the Bureau also offered a sustained pedagogy of domestic life, schooling men in the notion that they were to become the breadwinners of the family and women in a new kind of economic dependence vis-à-vis free men.

The marriage promotion efforts of the Freedmen's Bureau were soon taken up and expanded by state legislatures. Almost immediately after emancipation, states across the South enacted legal reforms to transform the informal marriages initiated under slavery into properly formal unions.[28] Several methods were used. Some states simply conjured up legal marriages *ex nihilo*, declaring that cohabiting couples were henceforth to be considered husband and wife whether or not they wished to be married; others established a time limit of nine months within which former slaves were required to legitimize their informal unions or stop living together. As soon as they became applicable to African Americans, marriage laws were enforced ruthlessly: Former slaves who continued to cohabit without formalizing their unions or forcibly married slaves who moved on to a new partner without divorcing were subject to prosecution under adultery and fornication laws. Until the time of its dissolution in 1872, the Freedmen's Bureau continued to work closely with state legislatures to police these rules.[29]

The Bureau's interest in marriage promotion was motivated foremost by the fear that former slaves (particularly women and children) were likely to become a huge public burden if they were not taken care of within the context of the legal family unit. Here what prevailed was a classical liberal concern with the social costs of dependency and a desire to transfer these costs to the private sphere.[30] The Freedmen's Bureau and Southern legislatures had good reason to fear that the many thousands of women without husbands and children without legal fathers that had been created by the act of slave emancipation would become dependent on public relief if they were not immediately reinserted within the legal structures of the family. By creating family obligations where none had been possible before, the Freedmen's Bureau and Southern legislatures hoped to relieve the state of any responsibility toward this newly liberated population of free laborers and potential dependents. As if to underscore the point that marriage was to serve as a substitute for public relief, many states passed new statutes extending spousal maintenance and child support laws to African American men during this period, effectively updating the poor-law tradition of family responsibility to include former slaves.[31] When men were unable or unwilling to fulfill these obligations, they (and their children) could be sentenced to convict labor, often on the estates where they had once been slaves, while women could be forced into either convict labor or domestic servitude.

For most former slaves, then, the promise of free labor proved short-lived. The various Black Codes passed by Southern legislatures in the wake of Reconstruction comprised an elaborate array of criminal sanctions for everything from vagrancy to out-of-wedlock child-bearing and failure to support one's children.[32] Because it was nearly impossible for former slaves to attain self-sufficiency, most were very rapidly forced back into convict labor, debt peonage, or domestic servitude, in what marked a reinscription of the boundaries of unfree labor. In this way, African Americans were unceremoniously inducted into the poor-law tradition of legally enforceable family responsibility at the very moment they were welcomed into the world of contractual freedom. Here as in England under the New Poor Law of 1834, the radical implementation of classical liberal principles of freedom went hand in hand with the brutal assertion of family and work obligations.

At the same time, this punitive imposition of family obligations (most often directed at fathers and husbands) also served as the basis for new claims to patriarchal authority on the part of African American men and a new social conservative ethos of African American domesticity. By granting black men the right to sign contracts on behalf of wives and children, and assigning wage scales that penalized women, the Freedmen's Bureau not only made black men responsible for the support of their families, it also empowered them to assert their rights over women and children.[33] The law of paternal responsibility could be enforced by criminal sanctions, but it could also be celebrated as a moral virtue and mandate for patriarchal authority within the household. This vision of virtuous family life would be fully embraced by African American conservatives in the latter part of the nineteenth century, even as many of the other political victories of emancipation were reversed.[34]

THE GILDED AGE: FAMILY RESPONSIBILITY AND THE FREE MARKET

In many respects, the Freedmen's Bureau represented a unique episode in the history of American public relief. Not only was it the first attempt by the federal government to organize a large-scale relief effort, but it was also particularly ruthless in its application of new family responsibility laws. The Freedmen's Bureau was a demonstration project in the fullest sense of the term. Its primary objective was to induct former slaves into the rigors of legal marriage and to warn them of the dire consequences that would follow any attempt to elude the attendant responsibilities. Yet its lessons were also directed at the wider population. The Bureau's experiment in creating a market in free labor thus anticipated, in compressed form, some of the austere economic and social reforms that would also be extended to white domestic and migrant workers throughout the last decades of the nineteenth century, the Gilded Age of American capitalism.

The ethos of free labor emerged triumphant from the Civil War, seemingly vindicated by the defeat of America's old slave order. Inspired much more directly by the Social Darwinism of William Graham Sumner and the American Romantic tradition of Ralph Waldo Emerson than by professional political economists, the laissez faire credo of classical liberalism attained a popular, commonsense status in the United States that it always struggled to achieve in England.[35] In the wake of the Civil War, American workers and employers alike vied to position themselves as champions of "free labor"—although by the end of the century corporations had well and truly won the discursive war. During the Gilded Age, courts perfected what has come to be known as a jurisprudence of the free market, interpreting the Declaration of Independence and Fourteenth Amendment as defenses of corporate monopoly, and insisting that bosses and employees should be free to negotiate the terms of employment "at will," unfettered by legislative interference from the state.[36] And while the courts were busy imposing contractual freedom in the workplace, state legislatures oversaw a corresponding expansion of poor-law family obligations in the domestic sphere, with the ultimate aim of displacing the burden of relief from the public to the private realm.[37] As the Reconstruction experiment in free labor had demonstrated, the contractual freedom promised by classical liberal economics could not be implemented without at the same time enforcing the private, strictly noncontractual obligations of family. It is here, perhaps, that we can locate the historical and political origins of the slippage between individualism and family values that Wendy Brown identifies as intrinsic to classical liberalism.[38]

In the immediate post–Civil War years, however, the rigors of free market contractualism were yet to assert themselves in full. Faced with the multiple challenges of industrialization, the arrival of large numbers of economic migrants from Europe and a succession of economic downturns, many large cities actually expanded their public relief programs toward the end of the 1860s. Before long, this trend was met with the organized opposition of industrialists and social reformers who feared that any distortion of the "natural" price of labor would deprive them of a docile workforce. Over the following years, their campaign was so successful that by the early 1890s, many cities had withdrawn completely from the provision of outdoor relief and had instead shifted the burden onto a panoply of private charitable agencies and religious organizations. "Between 1874 and 1900," writes historian Stephen Pimpare, "one-fourth of the fifty largest American cities (and many smaller ones as well) abolished welfare ('outdoor relief' or 'out relief,' they called it); one third reduced their rolls and relief expenditures; and one-fifth offered only in-kind aid like food or coal, but no more cash. Most imposed a new 'work test' as a condition for relief, which even to the most 'deserving' was given sparingly, if at all."[39] As the states withdrew from the provision of public relief, they redoubled their efforts to enforce family and work obligations.

Despite its pretensions to laissez-faire spontaneity, economic liberalism has always relied in practice on the poor laws, which have always relied on the police powers of the American states to regulate everything from domestic relations, to morality, to vagrancy. The work of the legal historian William Novak serves to remind us that the so-called laissez-faire capitalism of the late nineteenth century was underwritten by extensive state police powers to regulate and punish the poor.[40] Family responsibility laws that compelled unmarried fathers to support illegitimate children or adult children to pay for the care of indigent parents fell under the police powers of the American states, which could use everything from local relief authorities to courts and private charities to enforce these obligations. In the late nineteenth century, the reinvigoration of the poor laws was aided and abetted by a new and flourishing enterprise in private charity, which supplemented the punitive power of the state with an intimate form of regulatory control extending into the homes of the urban poor.

Among the many private charities that sprang up during this period, the Charity Organization Societies (commonly referred to as the COS) were particularly influential in shaping commonsense ideas about the proper relationship between contractual freedom and family obligation. Gilded Age charity reformers sought to persuade state governments and private charities that a truly competitive market in free labor could only be achieved if the distorting and demoralizing effects of indiscriminate relief were reduced to a minimum.[41] The COS claimed to have perfected a method of "scientific charity" that could distinguish between the deserving and undeserving poor, and they preferred to err on the side of caution rather than corrupt the poor with undue benevolence. Public relief should only be dispensed as a last resort, after all other avenues of charity—chief among them the natural charity of the family—had been exhausted.

Like their British counterparts, American COS reformers understood themselves to be implementing the lessons of the New English Poor Law of 1834, which they saw in turn as a revival of the austere spirit of the original Elizabethan poor laws. The Royal Commission on the Poor Law of 1832 had condemned outdoor relief to the able-bodied poor as a violation of natural law that promoted improvident marriages and relieved the poor of their family responsibilities.[42] The English and American Charity Organization Societies reiterated this critique of public relief and argued that charity should seek above all to reinvigorate the natural support mechanisms of the family. In the words of the English COS reformer Charles Stewart Loch: "Social bonds must be maintained and utilized, family obligation—care for the aged, responsibility for the young—help in sickness or trouble—must be borne, to the extent of its capacity, by the family."[43]

If the poor-law tradition provided a legal framework within which to enforce the private obligations of family, one that was actively invoked by states when they deployed their extensive police powers over family life, the Charity Organization Societies went further than this to construct an elaborate social methodology for inciting and policing the ideal of family self-sufficiency. One of the chief innovations of late nineteenth-century COS reformers was the "friendly visitor," the usually female middle-class caseworker who was sent forth into the homes of the poor to educate them in the habits of appropriate gender difference and family responsibility. In a handbook written for other charity workers, the General Secretary of the Baltimore COS, Mary Richmond, instructed friendly visitors in the art of stimulating the charity of family members. Charity serves only to "weaken natural ties," she warned, "unless it is certain that relatives have done all that they can, or unless it has brought pressure to bear, at least, to induce them to do their part."[44] Friendly visitors were advised to pursue kin, friends, and neighbors as sources of support, before soliciting help from the local church, private charity, or, as a last resort, public relief.

The Charity Organization Societies were particularly concerned with the problem of "married vagabonds," men who had been legally married but had deserted or divorced their wives and no longer provided for their families.[45] Rates of separation and divorce increased dramatically in the final decades of the nineteenth century, confronting charity workers with a growing population of women and children without adequate means of support. In response to this problem, COS workers made strenuous efforts to update and administer a series of new poor-law provisions designed to enforce the responsibilities of absent fathers. In the early years of the nineteenth century, the American courts had invented a new common law duty of child support for parents who had separated or divorced, but no such duty existed in the poor-law tradition, which had hitherto concerned itself with illegitimate children only.[46] While the common law duty of child support sufficed for middle-class parents who had the means to initiate private actions in the courts and were not likely to create a burden on public relief, charity workers now sought to create a comparable body of statutory law that would allow them to take routine administrative action against working-class men. Having lobbied state legislatures throughout the 1870s, the COS reformers managed to convince a dozen states to pass new criminal statutes before the end of the century.[47] Under the terms of these statutes, fathers could be imprisoned for failing to provide child support; but prison sentences could also be transmuted into forced work.[48] As in the original Elizabethan poor laws, the legal duty of family responsibility was understood to be monetizable in the form of labor: Familial debts could be paid off in the guise of indentured labor if a father could not make enough money to satisfy the courts.

FAMILY CRISIS IN THE GILDED AGE

Although in the short term the COS reformers wished to enforce the economic obligations of family as an alternative to public relief, they also nursed a more ambitious, long-term vision of social reform. In the wake of the Civil War, charity reformers joined a growing chorus of social commentators, from evangelical Protestants to labor radicals and social scientists, to denounce the laxity of marriage laws and their disintegrating effects on social order. These critics feared that the traditional moral fabric of American life was being destroyed by a perfect storm of malign influences: the dispersion of households as young people migrated en masse to the industrial heartlands; the anonymity of urban life, which enabled young people to socialize without the burden of parental surveillance; interracial mixing; and the rise of a feminist movement intent on questioning male authority in the household.[49] Commenting on the profound demographic changes that took place in this era, the social historian David Wagner observes that "the post–Civil War period through the end of the 1870s may have been a period analogous to others in American history, most famously the 1920s and 1960s–70s, in which there was something of a sexual revolution."[50] This revolution in sexual mores appears to have triggered a full-blown discourse of family crisis and a heightened concern with the inadequacy of existing domestic relations law.

Such concerns had simmered throughout the antebellum period, but they emerged as a fully fledged movement for legal and social reform only in the last decades of the nineteenth century. In 1841, the

United States Supreme Court Justice Joseph Story challenged the then widely accepted practice of common-law or contractual marriage by calling for a clear distinction between the civil contract of marriage and the commercial contract of exchange: Although marriage was a contract "in the common sense definition of the word," it was also "something more than a mere contract. It [was] rather to be deemed an institution of society founded upon the consent and contract of the parties, and in this view has some peculiarities of its nature, character, operation and extent of obligation, different from what belongs to ordinary contracts."[51] Following the Civil War, the idea that the domestic sphere should be distinguished from and protected from the market became hegemonic. According to the modern will theory of contract, the commercial contract was by definition breachable by either party in exchange for compensation; marriage, by contrast, came to be understood as a special kind of contract—one that could not be breached at will. Thus, even while coverture was being undermined in favor of a contractual understanding of marriage, the marital contract was defined in exceptional terms—subject to irrevocable consent, as in rape in marriage laws, to fault-based breach, as in divorce laws, and to the imperative of inalienable labor, which gave rise to the expectation that wives would perform household labor for free.[52] Through the very exceptionalism of its terms, the sexual contract testified to what Durkheim would later describe as the noncontractual foundations of the contractual—"for everything in the contract is not contractual."[53]

In accordance with this view, the laws governing intimate relationships became considerably stricter in the last decades of the century. During this period, most states moved to restrict or outlaw common-law marriages, raised the age of consent, reestablished waiting periods for marriage, banned interracial unions, and criminalized abortion and contraception.[54] Thus, a social conservative view of the family as the foundation of moral order and the bastion of traditional, nonmarket values came into being alongside the laissez-faire individualism of the Gilded Age, not as its contradiction but as its necessary counterpart.[55]

Working at the boundaries of the labor market and the domestic sphere, Gilded Age charity reformers neatly articulated the concerns of classical laissez-faire liberalism with a moral conservatism focused on the private family. These reformers were convinced that the doctrine of family responsibility responded to the fiscal exigencies of the free market and the liberal state; but they also believed that the economic obligations of kin could not be properly enforced without a comprehensive effort to rebuild the family as the very foundation of social order. It was this classical liberal-conservative regime of private family responsibility that needed to be challenged before the progressive New Deal order of public responsibility could come into being.

FROM PRIVATE FAMILY RESPONSIBILITY
TO PUBLIC RESPONSIBILITY FOR THE FAMILY

The question of personal and, by extension, family responsibility was central to early twentieth-century debates surrounding the introduction of modern social welfare. The comprehensive forms of social insurance that had been implemented in Germany under Otto von Bismarck as early as the 1880s and in other European states throughout the following decades, were much slower to be accepted in the United States, where they had to overcome both elite and popular attachment to notions of free labor and family self-sufficiency.[56] Throughout the early twentieth century, opponents of social welfare, which included many associated with the scientific charity movement, argued that the socialization of risk would destroy the family as a moral institution by displacing economic solidarity among kin. Even public assistance to noncontributing dependents such as widows and the aged was attacked as a threat to the values of family responsibility and self-support.

One exemplary American critic of the European welfare state warned that the introduction of social insurance against old age, workplace accidents and illness would constitute "a most serious evil, moral as well as economic"; it would "exert an enervating and demoralizing influence upon character, lessening the sense of personal responsibility and self-reliance, and sapping the foundations of individual initiative and ambition."[57] In a similar fashion, it was argued, public assistance to single mothers and the aged "would weaken the bonds of family solidarity. It would take away, in part, the filial obligation for the support of aged parents, which is one of the main ties that holds the family together.... The assumption by the State of the obligation to support the aged in their homes would undermine filial responsibility, precisely as the guarantee of public maintenance of children would destroy parental responsibility."[58] Such views were shared by many in the trade union movement, who were equally invested in the idea that independent workingmen should be able to earn a breadwinner wage without help from the state.[59]

The progressive advocates of social insurance retorted that the old family responsibility laws were themselves destructive of the bonds of kinship.[60] Too often, they argued, the market price of labor and hence the actual wage earned by the male worker fell far below the level required to sustain a family. Both supporters and opponents of social insurance saw the family as the foundation of moral and economic life, differing only in their views on the proper relationship to be established between the family and the state. Opponents harked back to a Gilded Age conception of family self-sufficiency that made the independent male worker privately responsible for supporting his dependents. Supporters argued that the modern conditions of industrial life necessitated a much more sustained governmental effort to underwrite the risks of the male wage. If the former saw economic security as the private responsibility of the family, the latter wanted to transform the family into a public responsibility, indeed the prime welfare function of the state; by underwriting the unavoidable risks of the labor market, they argued, a fully fledged social welfare system would guarantee the male breadwinner wage and ensure that the wives of working class men would not have to go out to work themselves. Neither, however, questioned the centrality of the family within their vision of economic life, much less the dependence of women within this institution.

With the passage of the Social Security Act in 1935, the advocates of social insurance claimed a decisive victory. The New Deal introduced comprehensive forms of social insurance against workplace accidents, unemployment, and aging and definitively removed one class of workers (standard, white, male workers) from the poor-law system of family responsibility. Hoping to capitalize on this victory, federal administrators on the Social Security Board launched a vigorous assault on state poor laws over the following years and sought as far as possible to limit their use.[61] Yet, many states resisted these intrusions and continued to enforce family responsibility in public assistance programs for the nonworking and noncontributing poor. By all accounts, these provisions were enforced with greater frequency after World War II, as social welfare costs began to escalate.[62]

The dividing line between federal social insurance programs and state-governed public assistance became increasingly meaningful in this period. At a time when the government was assuming full social responsibility for standard male workers and their dependents, public assistance claimants were relegated to an older tradition of private (albeit state-enforced) family obligations. As noted by one contemporary legal scholar, "the inclusion of a family responsibility provision in general assistance law has given rise to the assumption that family responsibility for dependent persons is primary, that public responsibility is secondary, and that public assistance, therefore, cannot be given until all possibility of securing support under the family responsibility laws has been exhausted."[63] When single mothers, the blind, the disabled, the mentally ill, or the indigent claimed public assistance, state welfare departments were authorized to investigate and enforce private family obligations before disbursing any public funds. An adult child could be brought to court to pay for an elderly parent's nursing home costs; aunts and uncles held accountable for the costs of housing and educating a blind relative; and parents forced to contribute to the care of an insane child. In some states, the welfare department could claim retrospective compensation for benefits paid or seize the estate of a deceased claimant to reimburse the public purse. Although the maintenance of these laws was typically justified on fiscal grounds, most commentators agree that their effect was above all punitive and disciplinary.[64] The costs of administrative action meant that states saved little money by pursuing and extracting funds from relatives who were often poor themselves. Instead, the laws served to deter potential recipients from claiming welfare in the first place and reinforced the idea that for the undeserving poor, the private family unit was the first and only source of economic security.

By the 1960s, family responsibility laws were once again coming under attack, this time from organizations representing the disabled, the blind, and the aged. The case of California is particularly instructive in this regard, given the thoroughly progressive nature of the reforms it undertook in this era and their subsequent reversal under the governorship of Ronald Reagan. In 1961, the California state legislature completely abolished family responsibility clauses in its public assistance programs for the blind and disabled while restricting their use in programs for the mentally ill, the aged, and the indigent.[65] In a landmark decision handed down in 1964 (*Department of Mental Hygiene v. Kirchner*), the California Supreme Court prohibited the Department of Mental Hygiene from charging relatives of the mentally ill for state hospital costs. In defense of its position, the court argued that poor-law provisions constituted a form of unfair taxation and were not compatible with the redistributive principles of the

Social Security Act. The ruling was profoundly significant not only because it placed the "undeserving" beneficiaries of public assistance on the same legal footing as the "deserving" workers covered by the more respectable federal system of social insurance, but also because it challenged the very constitutionality of family responsibility laws (a challenge that could potentially be extended to *all* public assistance programs).[66] In 1965, Congress appeared to sound the death knell of family responsibility laws when it ruled that no state would be allowed to recoup costs from family members in the context of the new Medicaid program. Reiterating the arguments made by progressive advocates of social insurance in the first decades of the twentieth century, supporters of this decision contended that the inclusion of such clauses in the new Medicaid program would be "destructive of family relationships."[67]

During this period of rapid liberalization, only the much maligned AFDC program remained firmly embedded in the poor-law tradition. Far from phasing out the family responsibility provisions of AFDC, state legislatures continued to strengthen them after World War II, reinforcing the idea that impoverished women should look to individual men and not the state as sources of support. As we have seen, "substitute father" or "man-in-the-house" rules had been imposed on welfare mothers since the beginning of the program, serving to create a *de jure* relationship of paternal and marital responsibility where none had been consented to by the parties concerned. From the 1950s onward, many states, including California, extended their family responsibility laws to include "absent fathers"—the former husbands of women who had been separated or divorced or the biological fathers of children who had been born out of wedlock.[68] Now more than ever, women were reminded that their economic welfare depended primarily on their legal connection to a man.

Yet the fortunes of AFDC changed dramatically around 1965, thanks in large part to the rise of a new kind of public interest lawyer working in close collaboration with the nascent welfare rights movement. Beginning in 1965, President Johnson's Office of Economic Opportunity created and funded hundreds of legal service offices around the country with the express aim of providing free legal aid to the poor. These offices would become major players in the legal struggle for welfare reform, initiating most of the AFDC-related test cases that came to court over the next decade or so. Their signature strategy of test-case law reform was devised by a small group of scholars based at the Columbia Center for Social Welfare Policy and Law (CSWPL) who collaborated closely with activists in the welfare rights movement and soon became expert in the intricacies of welfare law.[69] In mounting their case against public assistance laws, these lawyers looked to recent changes in family law as a model of the kinds of freedoms that might also be extended to those on welfare.

Family law was effectively undergoing an extraordinary process of liberalization during this period: After more than a century of little change at all, laws that limited divorce, stigmatized nonmarital unions, and discriminated against illegitimate children were repealed or ceased to be enforced within the space of a decade or so.[70] Alongside the marginalization of older, status-based rules governing sexual relationships, a new jurisprudence came into being that explicitly recognized "sexual freedom" as a constitutionally protected right. In two landmark decisions, *Griswold v. Connecticut* (1965) and *Eisenstadt v. Baird* (1972), the Supreme Court fashioned a new "right to privacy" that limited the power of the state to police intimate, sexual relationships in the home. Yet none of these innovations extended to impoverished women on welfare who were regularly subject to salacious investigations into their sexual histories, unannounced home visits, and strict moral policing under state law. As the field of family law entered a new age of relative sexual freedoms, welfare law—aptly dubbed the "family law of the poor" by legal scholar Jacobus tenBroek[71]—continued to reflect the punitive moral conservatism of the poor-law tradition.

Relaying the most radical voices in the welfare rights movement, progressive public-interest lawyers questioned why recipients of public assistance and public housing were still subject to such intrusive forms of moral surveillance. If the Supreme Court now recognized a constitutional right to sexual privacy, why would this right not be extended to women on welfare? If middle-class women were now free to dissolve marriages at will and had increasing power to earn an independent wage in the labor market, why should poor women remain imprisoned within the private bonds of economic dependence? If marriage no longer counted in determining the legal status of middle-class children, why would the children of welfare mothers still be classified as illegitimate and punished for the sins of the parents?[72] In short, poverty lawyers were looking to the liberalization of family law to argue against the continuing enforcement of private familial obligations in the realm of welfare.

The institutional and judicial environment of the 1960s was extraordinarily conducive to such ambitious social reform agendas. Public interest litigators who sought to reform welfare found an unusually receptive audience in the progressive Warren Court and the even more liberal California Supreme Court. They also had numerous sympathizers among federal administrators in the Department of Health, Education, and Welfare (HEW), who sometimes initiated their own test cases against the punitive welfare laws imposed by state legislatures.[73] Their strategy of test-case litigation turned state public assistance into a federal issue, forcing the Supreme Court to pass judgment on matters it would rarely have encountered in the past. Having ignored AFDC during its first few decades of existence, the US Supreme Court presided over a full eighteen cases relating to the program between 1968 and 1975, while the lower federal courts issued hundreds of relevant decisions during the same period.[74] The outcome of these decisions was both to federalize (and thus liberalize) control of welfare and to align its provisions with recent changes in family law.

In the *King v. Smith* case of 1968, Chief Justice Earl Warren ruled that Alabama's substitute father rule violated the terms of the Social Security Act and was out of touch with family law, which no longer sought to punish extramarital relations and no longer recognized any valid status distinction between legitimate and illegitimate children.[75] In another decision, Justice Brennan opposed child support enforcement as an invasion of privacy.[76] The lower federal courts were especially aggressive in overturning the poor-law provisions of state welfare programs. In the wake of the *King v. Smith* (1968) decision to invalidate substitute father rules, the lower courts went on to outlaw all state rules compelling women to track down "absent fathers" as sources of support.[77] As a result of these rulings, the number of welfare applicants who refused to cooperate with district attorneys in child support matters rose dramatically.[78]

By themselves, these decisions might have remained at the level of formal change—an affirmation of juridical rights without substantive impact on the everyday lives of women on welfare. But combined with the significant presence of welfare rights groups in local communities, women were becoming increasingly educated in the intricacies of welfare law and emboldened to contest their treatment at the hand of social workers.[79] By placing welfare benefits on a more secure footing and ridding them of punitive behavioral rules, the federal court decisions of this era had the effect of liberating women from the confines of private family dependence. The overall message conveyed by these rulings was that the welfare of poor women was a public responsibility on a par with that of standard male workers. Whatever their marital status, sexual history, or race, impoverished women were just as deserving of a social wage as any other citizen. At a time when middle-class women were entering the work force in growing numbers and achieving some degree of economic independence from men, unmarried women on welfare also appeared to be in reach of a social wage that was no longer mediated through a "substitute husband."

For an all too brief moment, revised AFDC rules allowed divorced or never-married women and their children to live independently of a man while receiving a state-guaranteed income free of moral conditions. Public assistance benefits, however menial, were functioning like a social wage for unmarried women—a configuration that had not been envisaged in the Social Security Act, and one that many perceived as a perversion of its original intent. In a period when employment opportunities and access to higher education for both white and nonwhite women were expanding as never before, this was a profoundly liberating development.[80] It is this perhaps that accounts for the extreme violence of the anti-welfare backlash that unfolded over the following years. As Stephanie Coontz points out, it was not so much women's *dependence* on the state that provoked the outrage of neoliberals and neoconservatives (their alleged dependence, after all, was nothing compared to that of standard male workers); it was rather the growing realization that welfare was making women *independent* of individual men and freeing them from the obligations of the private family that turned a generation of social reformers against the welfare state tout court.[81]

Reflecting on the profound changes to family and welfare law that had taken place in the 1970s, one of President Reagan's closest advisors, the social conservative Gary Bauer, would look back and remark ruefully that the "cumulative message of these cases reverberates today." "Taken together," he observed, "these and other decisions by the Supreme Court [had] crippled the potential of public policy to enforce familial obligations, demand family responsibility, protect family rights, or enhance family identity."[82] The only logical response, he believed, was to attempt to revive the old family responsibility laws at both the state and federal level. Reagan himself appears to have reached the same conclusion a decade previously, during his term as governor of California.

If the welfare rights movement had been particularly successful in California, it was also here, under the governorship of Ronald Reagan, that it suffered its first substantial backlash. When Reagan was first elected governor in 1966, California had one of the most generous AFDC programs in the country and caseloads were rising rapidly. By the time of his second election campaign, Reagan, who was now among the most vocal Republican opponents of Nixon's expanded family wage, made revision of the state welfare program his overwhelming priority. At a time when the Supreme Court and Congress were attempting to federalize AFDC and wrest it from state control, Reagan aggressively asserted the rights of states to retain their police powers over the poor. Having first obtained a waiver from HEW, he sought to transform California into a laboratory for punitive welfare reform that could then be translated onto the national stage.[83]

In the midst of his second election campaign of 1970, Reagan quietly set up a special task force of conservative lawyers to review the state's public assistance programs and identify priorities for reform. After his resounding return to power, he promptly appointed one of the members of the task force as the new director of social welfare and undertook a systematic overhaul of the entire department. Anticipating later federal campaigns to defund the left by blocking the latter's access to bureaucratic power, Reagan was particularly keen to purge the department of what he called "professional welfarists," by which he meant state administrators with social work backgrounds. These positions were filled instead by professionals with fiscal or managerial experience who were not likely to sabotage the governor's plans for welfare austerity. Anticipating that any attempt at cutting back welfare would be challenged in the courts by California's various legal service offices, Reagan also appointed a cadre of conservative legal professionals to preempt possible test cases.[84] Having thus forestalled the possibility of any internal opposition, in 1971 Reagan presented a comprehensive Welfare Reform Act to the Democratic Party–controlled legislature, which, after extracting a few concessions, accepted it in August of that year.

At the beginning of the 1970s, Reagan was at odds with the political consensus on social policy. Nixon's efforts to extend the family wage to black men can be seen, in retrospect, as the high point of a New Deal vision of social welfare that sought to completely transcend the poor-law tradition of private family responsibility. In the expansionist and optimistic atmosphere of the late 1960s, moderate Republicans and Democrats agreed that the state should assume public responsibility for the families of all men, black and white (although very few were prepared to question the dependent role of women within this arrangement). There was also a widespread recognition that the invidious differences between social insurance and public assistance programs should be neutralized wherever possible. By contrast, Reagan's welfare reform agenda sought to revive and extend a much older poor-law tradition of public relief, with its attendant distinction between the deserving and undeserving poor. In the words of Alice O'Connor, "For all but the legitimately disabled, dependent, or otherwise 'deserving,' public assistance would be a tightly regulated, temporary, relatively inexpensive, locally controlled and heavily stigmatized—if not downright punitive—source of poor relief. Welfare, in Reagan's plan, would return to the old poor law tradition from which decades of reform, social policy, and (more recently) 'permissive' liberal governance had allowed it to stray."[85]

In particular, Reagan was intent on reviving the poor-law family responsibility provisions that had only recently been expunged from public assistance programs such as AFDC. In the words of Reagan's task force on welfare reform, one "important theme of welfare reform was the need to establish and enforce the principle that family members are responsible for the support of relatives. In its simplest form, the argument was that every dollar contributed by the relative of a person on the welfare rolls was a dollar saved the taxpayer. However, the welfare reform goals went further and identified the family as the basic unit in society, emphasizing increased dependence upon the family and eliminating aspects of the welfare system that constitute incentives to break up the family."[86] With recommendations extending to all of the state's public assistance programs, Reagan's welfare reform ended up reinstating family responsibility rules covering relationships between adult children and aged parents; grandparents, aunts, uncles, and impoverished children; parents and unwed minor mothers; as well as stepfathers and nonadoptive children.[87]

But in a move that anticipated the path of federal welfare reform over the following decades, Reagan's state-level reform was most concerned with the problem of enforcing the responsibility of absent fathers to support children born out of wedlock. Sensing perhaps that the old "substitute father" rules would have less chance of surviving in the more permissive environment of the 1970s, conservative welfare reformers now seized upon the obligations of biological but absent fathers as the best means of reviving family responsibility laws. The authors of *California's Blueprint for National Welfare Reform* observed, "A fundamental goal of the 1971 Welfare Reform Act was to strengthen the role of the family as the basic unit in society. The increasing occurrence of family dissolution has resulted in reliance on public assistance instead of parental support. Absent fathers frequently fail to assume their responsibility for supporting their children. Many AFDC mothers refuse to disclose the identities of the fathers of AFDC children."[88] The document singled out the War on Poverty's legal service offices, permissive social workers, and activist welfare mothers as behind-the-scene enablers of this newly recalcitrant class of welfare recipient. In an effort to obstruct this coalition of progressive forces, Reagan's welfare reform of 1971 introduced a number of new reward structures to incentivize the collection of child support by county welfare offices.

Ultimately, however, Reagan and his advisors were aware that only federal reform could permanently reverse the liberalizing trends in social welfare policy and thwart the endless court challenges by public-interest lawyers.

It would not take long for Congress to respond to Reagan's challenge. In 1974, it passed the Child Support Act, creating a federal Office of Child Support Enforcement and requiring states to establish their own child support offices as part of their AFDC programs.[89] Over the following years, successive amendments would seek to further strengthen this new federal system of child support enforcement.[90] By all accounts, however, child support remained discretionary, uneven, and haphazard. The law of family responsibility had been federalized by congressional edict, but it remained far from comprehensive on the ground. Governor Reagan's dream of a fully federalized system of family responsibility would need to await the election of the "New Democrat" President Clinton to be fully realized.

FEDERALIZING GOVERNOR REAGAN'S WELFARE REFORMS

In 1996, President Bill Clinton, in alliance with a Republican-dominated Congress, passed legislation promising to "end welfare as we know it." The Personal Responsibility and Work Opportunity Reconciliation Act (PRWORA) replaced the federal welfare program AFDC with the more punitive and conditional TANF (Temporary Assistance to Needy Families).[91] Under these new funding terms, the federal government was no longer required to provide open-ended, matching grants to fund state welfare programs; instead, it would provide a finite block grant that in any given year might fall well short of covering the benefit costs of all eligible welfare applicants. As an expression of federal devolution, PRWORA purported to give the states greater freedom to pursue the kinds of policy experiments that were once only possible under federal waiver. In reality, however, welfare block grants came with strict conditions and allowed the states only the limited freedom of imposing tougher rules than those required by the federal government.

Clinton's welfare reform is best known as the legislative intervention that abolished the federal entitlement to welfare benefits, introduced an absolute time limit of five years on welfare eligibility and required welfare recipients to engage in compulsory work programs. Most of this unfree labor took place in the low-wage service sector, a sector already dominated by African American, Latina, and migrant women.[92] The imposition of workfare requirements was bound to have a devastating effect not only on the lives of welfare recipients (who must fund their own childcare needs while they work, or more realistically, turn to the unpaid labor of female relatives), but also on service workers in general, since the state-subsidized supply of free or low-cost labor has inevitably worsened conditions for all service workers, especially those at the lower echelons of the labor market. As Collins and Mayer remind us, "the effects of welfare reform cannot be understood apart from the forces constituting demand for labor at the bottom of the labor market."[93] After a brief period of two decades during which the relative wages and working conditions of African American women appeared to be improving, the effect of workfare has been to brutally reinstate the historically racialized obligations of domestic servitude, in a form that responds to the imperatives of the post-Fordist service economy.[94] African American and other minority women may well have escaped the relations of personal dependence that characterized domestic labor in white homes well into the late Fordist era.[95] Welfare reform, however, has subjected them to new forms of unfree domestic labor *outside the home* and in the process places the labor of all other low-wage service workers under the shadow of workfare.

The parallels between Clinton's workfare laws and the labor history of the Reconstruction period are striking. Just as formal emancipation quickly gave way to convict leasing and domestic servitude mandated by the criminalization of former slaves, the formal victories of the civil rights movement have been rapidly qualified by the legitimation of various forms of unfree labor, again justified by the criminalization of impoverished minorities. The classical liberal doctrine of labor contractualism and at-will employment has never flourished without the simultaneous imposition of a poor-law regime of unfree labor, today exemplified by the expansion of both feminized workfare and prison labor.[96]

It is less often recognized, however, that the same symbiosis between contractual freedom and noncontractual obligation applies also to the question of domestic relations. Here again, Clinton's welfare reform closely replicates the relief efforts of the Reconstruction era. Much like the legal reforms that were mobilized to manage newly enfranchised slaves, PRWORA seeks to limit the potential social costs of sexual freedom among the post–Civil Rights poor by adapting and reinventing the family responsibility provisions of the poor law.[97] And like the Freedmen's Bureau, it envisages welfare reform as a kind of demonstration project in family formation that targets African Americans in particular but aspires in the long run to extend its lessons to the wider population.

After the piecemeal amendments of previous decades, Clinton's welfare reform radically overhauled the existing child support system, transforming it into the comprehensive federal enforcement regime that Reagan had dreamt of in the early 1970s: States were compelled to harmonize and strengthen their efforts to establish paternity for all children at the moment of birth, even if their mothers weren't on the welfare rolls; integrated databases for pursuing delinquent fathers across state lines were set up; the use of time-consuming judicial review was eliminated; and a cumbersome, fragmented and still discretionary system of case-by-case administration was replaced with a uniform and automatic enforcement process.[98] Each state was now required to demonstrate that it had increased paternity identifications on an annual, incremental basis until it had reached the overall goal of 90 percent. As under previous legislation, welfare applicants were required to cooperate with state welfare agencies in their efforts to identify and track down biological fathers, but the new rules also compelled states to sanction applicants who did not comply, either by reducing benefits or cutting them from the welfare rolls completely.[99] These and other petty sanctions led to a dramatic drop in welfare rolls within the first few years of its enactment.

PRWORA was no less punitive with respect to delinquent fathers. Under its terms, men who failed to pay child support could have their wages automatically garnished or could be ordered by a court to undertake workfare obligations, reproducing the Gilded Age practice of exchanging family for work obligations. In some states, delinquent fathers could have their passport, driver's license, or occupational license confiscated; in other states, they could be subject to criminal sanctions.[100] If child support orders had once been pursued on a discretionary and haphazard basis and were rarely enforced across state lines, they had now become virtually inescapable.[101]

With respect to fathers, however, the effects of welfare reform were never simply or unambiguously punitive since they also served to reinstate the authority of men within the family. In what marks a radical departure from standard family law, welfare law derives legal fatherhood from the mere fact of a biological relationship and proceeds to enforce the resulting obligations on this basis alone. Yet, even as this legal sleight of hand imposes obligations on men, it also authorizes them to claim certain exceptional rights. Once he has been named a legal father, a man can legitimately claim visitation and custody rights to his children, even if he previously had no relationship with them. This automatic accession to the status of legal fatherhood is peculiar to welfare law. Family law in general refuses to grant legal paternity to men on the simple basis of biological kinship, insisting that some more solid and long-lasting emotional relationship must be established before a man can be considered a father.[102] Only in welfare law can a man claim custody rights on biological grounds alone—an anomalous situation that clearly sanctions all kinds of abuse.[103]

The modern child support system serves to demonstrate that the state is willing to enforce—indeed create—legal relationships of familial obligation and dependence where none have been established by mutual consent.[104] Just as the Freedmen's Bureau created legal marriages *ex nihilo* without bothering to secure the consent of either partner, modern-day welfare law conjures family relationships into being as a way of enforcing the legal obligations of mutual dependence and support. The entire process is of little benefit to the applicant: if the old welfare law required states to allocate a $50 "pass through" portion of child support funds to the welfare claimant, this provision is now optional and states may use the funds for the sole purpose of covering their expenses. The administrative costs dedicated to the identification of fathers and collection of child support are enormous and consume a non-negligible portion of federal budget dedicated to welfare.[105] But in spite of this, the average amounts collected on behalf of each applicant are minimal—not surprisingly, given that "absent fathers" are often poor or unemployed themselves.[106] Why not disburse welfare funds directly to impoverished women? These laws appear to be motivated as much by a will to punish and deter as any concern with fiscal burdens: by detouring the payment of welfare benefits via legally designated fathers, the state reminds women that they cannot hope to find economic security without entering a relationship of personal dependence on a man. As noted by Laura Morgan, Clinton's welfare reform represents "the modern incarnation of the Elizabethan Poor Law," the most recent and most comprehensive attempt to date to substitute the private responsibility of family for the public responsibility of the state.[107] The federal welfare apparatus created by the New Deal and Great Society is here repurposed as an immense apparatus for enforcing the private family obligations of the welfare poor.

Thus, a Democratic President completed the experiment in radical welfare reform that had been initiated by a right-wing Republican as far back as the 1970s. In the words of Mark Neal Aaronson, "the basic features of today's provisions are not very different in premise and direction" from "the Reagan welfare reform legislation of fifteen and twenty-five years ago," although they are "harsher on the poor in the details." Like the Reagan reforms, he continues, Clinton's welfare reforms "largely reflect and give renewed vitality to principles of relief-giving dating back to the Elizabethan poor laws,"[108] or more proximately, the American post–Civil War era and Gilded Age.

In the meantime, the old terms of combat between the federal government and the states have completely shifted. Where federal administrators once sought to banish the poor-law tradition from state public assistance programs, hoping instead to upgrade all welfare programs to the higher standards of social insurance, now the federal government was itself taking the initiative in reinstating the poor laws. Where Reagan once needed a federal waiver to revive the poor-law tradition in California, Clinton's welfare reform now positively forced the states to implement family responsibility rules, under threat of sanction. Thus, PRWORA definitively upended the traditional relationship between the historically progressive federal government and the recalcitrant states. For the first time in American social history, the old poor-law tradition of family responsibility was fully integrated into federal policy.

Reporting on the progress of welfare reform in his monthly *Businessweek* column, Gary Becker enthusiastically commended the workfare and familial obligations written into Clinton's proposed legislation, finding fault with them only for being too lenient.[109] As Becker explains in a classic theoretical paper on the relationship between family and welfare, the freedom of contractual relations in the marketplace cannot be sustained without the existence of noncontractual obligations in the family.[110] Altruistic love may well be inefficient in the marketplace, but it is absolutely necessary in the family, where biological divisions of labor related to childbearing mean that mothers stand to gain from personal dependence on a man and fathers benefit from assuming personal responsibility for the welfare of mothers and children. The problem with social welfare, from this perspective, is that it undermines the natural incentives to family altruism and thus deprives the poor of their primary support system. Even as they celebrate freedom of contract in the public marketplace of love and money, neoliberals such as Becker just as insistently affirm the necessity of noncontractual obligation in the family and are more than willing to invoke the full power of the state to enforce it. It is here after all that they locate the proper locus of economic security and the ideal alternative to the social welfare state.

CLINTON'S WELFARE REFORM: BETWEEN NEOLIBERALISM AND THE NEW SOCIAL CONSERVATISM

It would be misleading, however, to assume that Clinton's welfare reform was informed exclusively by a neoliberal philosophy of private family welfare. As noted by Brenda Cossman, PRWORA represented a curious "hybrid of fiscal and social conservatism" — or what I would call neoliberalism and new social conservatism.[111] The opening preamble of PRWORA thus sets out the following extraordinary definition of public morality: "1) Marriage is the foundation of a successful society; 2) Marriage is an essential institution of a successful society, which promotes the interests of children"; and "3) Promotion of responsible fatherhood and motherhood is integral to successful child-rearing and the well-being of children."[112] In its findings section, the text of the legislation goes on to cite various statistics pointing to a correlation between out-of-wedlock births, rising rates of child poverty, poor health outcomes, child abuse, criminality, and drug addiction, although no attempt is made to establish a causal relationship. In light of these findings, the legislation outlines a number of conditions that must be met before a state receives a block grant. Each state must demonstrate that it has taken action to prevent and reduce out-of-wedlock pregnancies; it must also establish numerical goals for reducing rates of illegitimate childbirth, with a $100 million bonus fund set aside for states that manage to reduce illegitimate births without increasing abortion rates.[113]

Beyond these preventative measures, PRWORA also includes funds to actively promote heterosexual, procreative marriage in the wider, non-welfare population: It instructs the Secretary of Health and Human Services to disburse $50 a million a year in block grants for abstinence-only education in public schools and sets aside special budget allocations to finance marriage promotion initiatives undertaken by the states. In the words of Dorit Geva, "no previous American welfare legislation has so decisively positioned the ethic of 'strong families' and the importance of marriage as so fundamental to the prevention of 'welfare dependence.' "[114]

With its resounding affirmation of the social value of marriage, PRWORA reversed what had seemed to be an overwhelming trend toward the liberalization of family law. The distinction between legitimate and illegitimate children had been virtually invalidated in family law—and challenged in welfare law—since the 1960s. Clinton's welfare reform unequivocally reaffirmed the importance of legitimate childbearing as a goal of social policy. And if the states had long since tempered their efforts to police morality, at least in the private sphere, the federal government was now openly compelling the states to do just that, under threat of funding cuts. What had once looked like a slow but irreversible trend toward the liberalization of family law was abruptly suspended, as the federal government sought to bluntly reassert the noncontractual obligations of marriage and family.[115]

These impositions, of course, applied primarily to welfare recipients, who had only ever enjoyed a brief respite from state police powers. Yet, as outlined in detail by Tonya Brito, many of the practical measures invented to deal with unmarried mothers on welfare have subsequently been extended to single mothers in general—in a move designed to preempt any future claims to welfare benefits.[116] In a process that Brito refers to as the "welfarization of family law," the long-obsolete distinction between legitimate and illegitimate children is now being revived in family law in general—a shift that is perhaps best exemplified by the recent prominence of legitimacy arguments in same-sex marriage jurisprudence.[117]

THE NEW DEMOCRATS: BETWEEN NEOLIBERALISM
AND COMMUNITARIANISM

Here, once again, it was the Democratic president Bill Clinton who was able to fully implement a project first nourished by right-wing Republicans. As president, Ronald Reagan had struggled and failed to forge an effective political alliance between his neoliberal and social conservative constituencies. Despite the initial hopes of a lasting alliance, Reagan's social conservative supporters were just too closely aligned with the religious right and white populism to attract more than a small minority of the voting public. Accordingly, Reagan's presidential efforts to enact welfare reform were less spectacular than his achievements as governor of California.[118] Instead, it was Clinton who managed to form a broad bipartisan and cross-racial alliance between neoliberals and new conservatives, having first broken down the barriers to a social conservative politics within his own party.

Thus, although Clinton's welfare reform is commonly interpreted as an adaptation of Newt Gingrich's Contract with America (the platform with which the Republicans had campaigned for and won the 1994 Congressional elections), its passage also reflected a tectonic shift within the Democratic Party itself, as New Democrats came to exercise a growing influence on the formulation of the party's social policy goals. The New Democrats had emerged as an organized political faction in 1985 following the Republicans' resounding success in Reagan's second election campaign.[119] Organized under the umbrella of the Democratic Leadership Council and its think-tank, the Progressive Policy Institute, these new-wave Democrats sought to win back their old white, working-class base by actively dissociating themselves from the legacy of the 1960s New Left and instead promoting a centrist, moral conservative position on social welfare.

It was thanks largely to the Progressive Policy Institute that the Democratic Party came to embrace the "new paternalism" of Lawrence Mead, arguably the single most influential advocate of workfare and punitive child support reform in recent US welfare reform.[120] The New Democrats were also responsible for establishing the Institute for American Values and its associated think tank, the Council on Families in America, within the mainstream of social policy debate. Housing such prominent figures as William Galston (Clinton's chief domestic policy adviser until 1995), David Popenoe, Barbara Defoe Whitehead, Jean Bethke Elshtain, and James Q. Wilson and closely associated with the communitarian philosopher Amitai Etzioni, these organizations are committed to the project of bridging the political divide between social justice progressives and religious conservatives.[121] Much like their conservative Christian peers, the communitarian New Democrats are obsessed with the decline of marriage, rising rates of illegitimate childbearing, and the resultant epidemic of "fatherless families," but they deploy conventional social science methods to buttress their conclusions and carefully avoid the use of overtly antifeminist, homophobic language (indeed, some of them are recent converts to the cause of gay marriage). Hoping to wrest the discourse of family values from the religious right, these in-house scholars prefer the language of community disintegration to that of moral decline and present the loss of stable, monogamous marriage as a social justice issue rather than a symptom of cultural decadence.

The Institute for American Values and its affiliates have been instrumental in placing marriage promotion and responsible fatherhood at the center of US welfare reform.[122] Their rhetoric is capacious and nonpartisan enough to speak to religious and secular conservatives, neoliberal conservatives and those nostalgic for the New Deal family wage, as well as black and white advocates of family values. On the right, the Institute has worked closely with the National Fatherhood Initiative (NFI), a nonprofit organization cofounded by the evangelicals Wade Horn and Don Eberly in 1994 and now a clearinghouse for responsible fatherhood programs throughout the country.[123] The National Fatherhood Initiative is particularly focused on the alleged disintegration of the white family, a process they see as reproducing the black family crisis of the 1970s. Their defining moment was Dan Quayle's 1992 speech condemning the television depiction of the white single mother Murphy Brown and the subsequent debate it provoked in the liberal-progressive press.[124]

On the center left, the Institute for American Values also works in close collaboration with representatives of the Ford Foundation's various Strengthening Fragile Families initiatives, which focus on the problems facing low-waged African American and other minority fathers.[125] Fragile families advocates such as Ronald B. Mincy and Hillard Pouncy see themselves as heirs to Moynihan.[126] In contrast to the NFI, they are primarily concerned with the socioeconomic dynamics that have lessened the "marriageability" of minority men and prevented them from fulfilling their roles as fathers. Without descending into overt antifeminism, these scholars frame the problem of female and child poverty as stemming from the absence of economic and social opportunities for minority *men* and therefore envisage the restoration of proper gender hierarchies as a necessary first step in the project of social justice.[127] They claim that the decline of the industrial economy and secular expansion of the service sector have privileged minority women over men, once again creating the conditions in which black fathers are forcibly excluded from matriarchal families. Ultimately, as heirs to Moynihan, they envisage work creation and educational programs on a scale not seen since the Great Society as the ideal solution to the problem of fatherless families, but in the absence of any real political will in this direction, they have focused their efforts on making the child support system less punitive toward minority men.[128] Working in close association with state welfare offices, they have established "responsible fatherhood" programs within the child support system, allowing courts to send a delinquent parent to fatherhood classes in lieu of more severe sanctions. Thanks to the influence of the fragile families coalition, the connections between family responsibility, criminal sanction, and imprisonment have in recent years morphed into a more rehabilitative vision of responsible fatherhood while remaining firmly embedded in the criminal justice system.

These "left" and "right" incarnations of family-values politics came to fruition under the Bush and Obama administrations, as federal agencies began to fully implement the social conservative promise of Clinton's welfare reform. Shortly after arriving in office, George W. Bush appointed the right-wing evangelical Wade Horn, former president of the National Fatherhood Initiative, as director of the Administration for Children and Families, the bureau within the Department of Health and Human Services (HHS) that administers TANF. Under his direction, the Department of Health and Human Resources created the Healthy Marriage Initiative, a program designed to shape and finance marriage promotion efforts throughout the states, and persuaded the Republican-controlled Congress to fund the initiative for five years at a cost of $500 million. The HHS simultaneously diverted $100 million within existing programs (including child support) to marriage promotion efforts, in deference to the new common sense that welfare should go beyond the mere enforcement of economic obligations to actively promote the creation of traditional families.

Alongside this increase in federal funding to marriage promotion efforts, Congress also authorized $250 million to finance Wade Horn's Federal Fatherhood Initiative.[129]

It is under Obama, however, that responsible fatherhood programs have truly flourished. Within the first few years of his administration, President Obama more than doubled the funding for fatherhood initiatives, demoting marriage promotion to second place within the federal welfare agenda.[130] The HHS now collaborates closely with the Department of Justice and the White House Office of Faith-Based and Neighborhood Partnerships to design programs that are especially attuned to the experiences of low-income, minority men. As a consequence, fatherhood programs are now fully integrated into the legal system and may be assigned as alternatives to jail terms for low-risk offenders or included within a reentry program for former prisoners.

Father absence plays an extraordinary role in Obama's political persona, as both a biographical fact and a phenomenon he sees as defining the wider African American experience. His social welfare agenda is unmistakably shaped by the fragile fatherhood discourse of "left" social conservatives such as Ronald Mincy and Hillard Pouncy, but also testifies to the enduring influence of Moynihan in American social policy. In his political autobiography *The Audacity of Hope*, Obama defends Moynihan against charges of racism and praises what he sees as the instinctive conservatism of the black middle-classes.[131] "We should...acknowledge that conservatives—and Bill Clinton—were right about welfare as it was previously structured," he claims, but we also need to realize that work alone will not raise people out of poverty; what is also needed is a far-reaching campaign of moral and cultural rehabilitation of the kind envisaged by Moynihan.[132] "Our failure as progressives to tap into the moral underpinnings of the nation is not just rhetorical.... Our fear of getting 'preachy' may also lead us to discount the role that values and culture play in addressing some of our most urgent social problems."[133]

Yet, if Obama, like Moynihan, sees the renovation of fatherhood as key to solving the problem of racial and economic injustice, the imaginary of social welfare has utterly changed in the years since the publication of the Moynihan report. Moynihan, after all, was writing at the height of welfare expansionism and still hoping to extend the family wage to black men. His social conservatism was closely aligned with a social democratic vision of redistribution through the living wage. In the early twenty-first century, the redistributive promises of the postwar era have definitively faded into the distant past. Even while he invokes the name of Moynihan then, what Obama offers instead is an alliance of social conservatism and neoliberalism that is more strictly reminiscent of the Gilded Age politics of family responsibility, although now fully implemented by the administrative structures of the state.

RELEGITIMATING FAMILY LAW

Much like their Gilded Age predecessors, the communitarian scholars associated with the Institute for Family Values are deeply invested in the project of family law reform, identifying it as an essential pillar in their long-term strategy to rehabilitate moral values. The Council on Family Law, an affiliate organization, brings together conservative legal scholars such as Mary Ann Glendon, Milton C. Regan Jr., Margaret Brinig, and Carl E. Schneider, who are intent on reversing the trend toward the "privatization" of family law and have advocated such measures as the restoration of fault-based divorce or the introduction of religious alternatives to civil unions such as covenant marriage (an experiment carried out with only moderate success in the state of Louisiana).[134]

These scholars take direct aim at the neoliberal law and economics school of Richard Posner, which they see as enabling the dissolution of the family through the contractualization of family law.[135] Like many legal scholars, they describe the recent history of family law reform in terms of a distinct trend toward "privatization"—that is, the replacement of state-sanctioned obligations by a system of private, contractual ordering—a process they see as fully consonant with the aims of neoliberal legal theory. In the face of this trend, communitarian legal scholars assert the necessity of long-term, state-enforced obligations in marriage and parenthood. Without this guarantee, they argue, the family is deprived of its foundational role and the sexual disorder of "fatherless families" ensues.

Neoliberal legal scholars are indeed hostile to the premise of civic norms as regulative principles of intimate life and are in principle inclined to support the generalization of private, contractual ordering as a substitute for state-enforced "civil contracts" such as marriage. Yet, we misunderstand their argument in favor of contractualization if we do not also recognize its limiting conditions. Having declared themselves a priori favorable to private ordering, neoliberal scholars make a crucial exception for intimate relationship that are liable to generate social costs or externalities, for example, in the form of illegitimate children or uninsured STIs (a problematic we will explore in further detail in Chapter 5). Richard Posner and Gary Becker have long expressed their distaste for no-fault divorce—not out of any overt moral concern with the decline of family life (the rising divorce rates of the late twentieth century were an inevitable result of women's greater participation in the workforce, Becker insists) but because of the potential social costs involved in supporting dependent women and children.[136] When women and men fail to privatize the costs of their sexual behavior, instead transferring these costs to the state, neoliberals make an exceptional case for the imposition of noncontractual obligations. In cases of marital dissolution then, the legal responsibilities of marital and child support must take precedence over the wishes of the parties involved. And the state is more than justified in enforcing these responsibilities.

Here it becomes clear how profoundly the neoliberal philosophy of sexual freedom has been misrepresented in both scholarly and popular discourse. It is almost universally assumed, for instance, that neoliberal legal scholars must be sympathetic to—perhaps even ultimately responsible for—the jurisprudence of privacy that transformed sexual freedom into a (limited) constitutional right in the late 1960s and 1970s. Thus, a certain kind of left-wing critique of neoliberalism sees it as having inspired the individualist ethics of sexual choice informing such landmark cases as the *Roe v. Wade* decision of 1973 and by extension all other cases involving the recognition of a constitutional right to sexual liberty.[137] In fact, the opposite is true. A scholar such as Richard Posner is unequivocally hostile to the jurisprudence of sexual freedom, for the simple reason that a positive right to sexual liberty leads all too easily to the conclusion that the state must not only allow but also actively protect and enable the freedoms in question.[138] Arguably, it was just such a line of reasoning that led to the brief extension of privacy jurisprudence to welfare recipients in the 1970s—a scenario that neoliberals have always understood and decried as a form of state-subsidized personal irresponsibility. Instead, neoliberals support the more limited notion that private contractual freedom (as opposed to a constitutional right to freedom) should be extended to all arenas of social and intimate life, on the proviso that the associated costs are fully internalized by the contracting parties. Failing this, neoliberals are no less willing than communitarians to invoke the necessity of noncontractual obligations in marriage and parenthood and are more than prepared to call on their enforcement by the state. Despite their very real differences, then, communitarian and neoliberal legal scholars are united in their aversion to sexual rights discourse. Both are convinced that some limit must be imposed on sexual freedom, differing only on the question of whether these limits should be exceptional (the neoliberals) or foundational (the communitarians).

It is this convergence, no doubt, that explains why one of the most conservative scholars in the communitarian tradition, Margaret Brinig, also claims allegiance to the law and economics school,[139] and why one of the most libertarian of Chicago school legal scholars, Richard A. Epstein, is also the most radical in his commitment to the nonnegotiable nature of familial obligations. What Epstein recognizes perhaps more lucidly than any other law and economics scholar is that freedom of contract cannot exist without the ostensibly natural, noncontractual obligations of family. The rules of social welfare should therefore "follow the basic pattern of natural obligation as it is perceived to arise within families."[140] The task of neoliberal welfare reform is "to transform [this] inclination into duty" and thus to "derive an 'is' from an 'ought'"—a precise translation of the poor law philosophy of natural charity within the family.

CHAPTER FOUR

The Return of Inherited Wealth:
Asset Inflation and the Economic Family

> The inheritance of property can be interfered with more readily than
> the inheritance of talent. But from an ethical point of view, is there
> any difference between the two? Yet many people resent the inheritance
> of property and not the inheritance of talent.
> —Milton and Rose Friedman, *Free to Choose*

In 1979, the conservative legal scholar Mary Ann Glendon published
an influential and subtly alarmist article reflecting on the demise of
the family as an economic institution. Recent changes in both family and property law, she suggested, pointed to the "declining (but
not disappearing) importance of the family in the determination and
transmission of wealth, rank, and status in society," a change she saw
reflected in the diminishing impact of inheritance in shaping social
mobility.[1] In support of her thesis, Glendon drew heavily on the work
of Yale legal scholar Charles A. Reich, who famously argued that government largesse—in the form of social insurance, welfare, and public service contracts—was steadily taking the place of private property
in the allocation of income and assets.[2] With the postwar expansion
of government intervention into more and more areas of private life,
both citizens and corporations found themselves increasingly dependent on income and wealth transfers from the state. Translating
this thesis back into the idiom of family law, Glendon predicted the

inevitable demotion of private family wealth as a determining factor in social class. As Social Security and other forms of welfare distributed income from richer to poorer, the transmission of wealth through inheritance would inevitably lose its overriding significance in the shaping of social destinies.

Glendon's intuition was corroborated by contemporary property law scholars, who found that by the late 1970s traditional methods of family wealth transmission via the law of wills, trusts, and estates remained in relative use among the upper percentile of wealth holders but were of declining importance for the middle classes, whose economic security increasingly derived from noninheritable forms of income such as wages and social insurance.[3] It also appeared to find confirmation in empirical studies that showed that income and wealth inequalities had steadily declined for three consecutive decades following World War II, with a considerable intensification of these redistributive trends in the 1970s.[4]

For Glendon, however, what was at stake here was much more than a shift in forms of wealth and income distribution. Glendon understood the decline of inheritance to be intimately, and ominously, related to the rapid liberalization of family law that had taken place in the late 1960s—a veritable legal revolution that had in short order seen the introduction of no-fault divorce, the erosion of legal distinctions between legitimate and illegitimate children and the partial recognition of nonmarital relationships. Like many conservative commentators writing in the 1970s, a decade of tumultuous reform in both family and welfare law, Glendon believed that the enormous expansion of social welfare that had taken place after the New Deal was responsible for undermining both the economic and moral role of the private family. In this and other publications, she insisted that the waning importance of inherited wealth testified to the disintegration of the family itself.[5]

At first glance, Glendon's assertion that social welfare had contributed to the decline of the family appears counterintuitive. The American New Deal was inseparable from the racial and sexual normativity of the family wage. Its various actuarial programs identified the white, male industrial worker as the standard wage earner and demographic norm around which all income redistribution was to be statistically calibrated. In the words of Abraham Epstein, one of the early progressive architects of the New Deal, the "American standard assumes a normal family of man, wife, and two or three children, with the father fully able to provide for them out of his own income. This standard presupposes no supplementary earnings from either the wife or young children.... The wife is a home-maker rather than a wage-earner.... The needs of this family must be considered paramount."[6] The practical effect of the New Deal family wage system was the almost total exclusion of African American women and men from social welfare programs; the relative inclusion of white women as either dependents of a male breadwinner or beneficiaries of stigmatized public assistance; and a rigorous assertion of heteronormativity as the condition of inclusion in all state welfare programs.

Yet it is true that by the late 1960s, the link between the social wage and family normativity was becoming increasingly strained due to the changing profile of the workforce and the rise of new political movements combining feminism, civil rights, and welfare activism. By 1960, for example, Social Security had been extended to cover almost the entire workforce and now included farmers, domestic workers, nurses, and teachers—agricultural and service occupations whose original exclusion had heavily penalized women and African Americans.[7] In 1966, Johnson succeeded in significantly raising benefits as part of his efforts to wage a War on Poverty; and in the high-inflation period of the early 1970s, President Nixon introduced far-reaching and progressive reforms to Social Security when he indexed benefits to consumer prices.[8] It was the latter reform in particular which sustained the fortunes of the working and welfare classes in a period of spiraling price inflation. By the 1970s then, the New Deal's major social insurance program, Social Security, had expanded in quantitative terms to include both women and African Americans — Fordism's non-normative subjects — and to keep pace with rising wages.

But the reforms of the period were not merely quantitative in nature. As we saw in Chapter 3, a series of legal challenges mounted in this era steadily eroded the power of state welfare agencies to attach welfare benefits to particular family forms and police the morality of welfare recipients. In public-assistance programs ranging from AFDC to public housing, the Supreme Court repeatedly struck down the panoply of written and unwritten rules that had served to enforce sexual normativity throughout the Fordist era. Divorced or never married women could no longer be discriminated against in the allocation of welfare benefits. Unmarried women on welfare no longer had to abstain from sexual relationships in order to receive assistance. Public housing residents could no longer be expelled for allegations of immoral conduct. And for a very brief moment, the public housing lists were opened to cohabiting heterosexual and homosexual couples.[9]

In light of such radical reforms to the family wage, then, Glendon was perhaps justified in discerning a connection between the late Fordist expansion of welfare and the demise of traditional moral norms. When she spoke of the "declining (but not disappearing) importance of the family," what she had in mind, it seems, was not the classic Fordist family, whose sexual normativity was inscribed in the very form of the male breadwinner wage, but the challenge to normativity represented by late Fordist social movements. In a context where traditional configurations of family were being contested and income redistribution was rapidly undermining the importance of private wealth, it may well have seemed plausible to conclude that the family as a moral institution and conduit for wealth transmission was in terminal decline. Published in 1979, the tone of Glendon's argument is one of confident, if ominous, prediction. She writes as if she were discerning incipient trends that were destined to reveal themselves more fully in the long term.

More than three decades later, however, the scenario described by Glendon appears almost unrecognizable. Thomas Piketty is only the most prominent of theorists to have observed that private, inherited wealth has reemerged as a decisive factor in the shaping of social class, after a relative but significant period of decline in the postwar era.[10] Paradoxically, perhaps, the presumption of meritocracy has flourished in the neoliberal era where popular economics celebrates the virtues of individual risk-taking, the accumulation of fortunes from leveraged debt, and extravagant returns to investments in skilled labor or human capital. Yet the empirical data on wealth distribution suggests that inheritance is almost as decisive at the beginning of the twenty-first century as it was in the nineteenth.[11] This phenomenon also and inevitably entails the reassertion of the private family as a critical economic institution and a portal to social legitimacy. The fact that marriage and family formation have become the overriding concern of queer politics; the claim, axiomatic among American social policy theorists, that marriage is now a marker of class and a means to social mobility;[12] the fact that the recreation of the private family unit has become a key ambition of welfare policy — all of these trends point to the resurgence of the family as the essential vector for the distribution of wealth and status.

How and why did private family wealth acquire (or reclaim) such overwhelming importance in such a short period? And what is the relationship between neoliberalism and the legal institution of inheritance? The explanation I offer in this chapter differs from that of Piketty in that it attributes the reassertion of inherited wealth to political processes (that could have unfolded otherwise) rather than bioeconomic laws that, in the long run, can only ever be interrupted or forestalled.[13] At the time Glendon published her article — in 1979 — the United States was on the cusp of a regime change in monetary and fiscal affairs that would profoundly reshape the economic politics of the family. The so-called monetarist counterrevolution orchestrated by the incoming chairman of the Federal Reserve, Paul Volcker, brought to a halt the expansionary fiscal policies of the postwar Keynesian state and turned inflation targeting into the prime objective of central bank policy. Over the following years, the new monetary and fiscal policies adopted by the government and Federal Reserve would serve to rehabilitate the value of financial assets at the expense of wages and welfare, turning asset appreciation into a predictable feature of neoliberal economic life. In more or less overt ways, this paradigm shift was motivated by the sense that the interests of investors—along with the large family fortunes they amassed—were threatened by the expanding budgets of the welfare state. What I want to suggest here is that the question of family wealth—and its decline—was central to the political struggles of the period, although sometimes expressed in the most ambiguous of fashions.

It is now commonplace to characterize the neoliberal subject as one impelled to embody the qualities of the investor. Whether one actually owns any financial assets, it is argued, neoliberalism enlists the subject into an affective culture of investment that defines the "self" as an asset or "human capital." In the words of Gerald Davis, twenty-first-century America defines "investment...[as] the dominant metaphor to understand the individual's place in society and a guide to making one's way in the new economy. George Bush referred to this nascent system as an 'ownership society,' but its denizens were more like investors, or even speculators, than owners."[14] As financial returns take precedence over long-term industrial investment, it is further suggested, neoliberalism defines psychic reward in terms of asset appreciation rather than corporate profit or wages from labor. As Michel Feher puts it, "our main purpose is not so much to profit from our accumulated potential as to constantly value or appreciate ourselves—or at least prevent our own depreciation."[15]

Without wanting to contradict or abandon these arguments, I wish to highlight the equally important role of inheritance in channeling the investment politics of the neoliberal era. The monetary and fiscal interventions performed by the neoliberal state from Ronald Reagan onward have indeed rehabilitated the value of financial assets that were rapidly depreciating in the 1970s, but in so doing, they have also restored the economic role of the private family in the transmission of wealth. As the sociologist Yuval Elmelech reminds us, the distribution of financial assets is much more closely correlated to family background than are wages: Assets are inheritable in a way that professional status and wages are not.[16] When the price of assets appreciates against stagnant wages and welfare then, it is almost inevitable that family wealth will assume a decisive role in shaping and restricting social mobility. If there is a culture of asset appreciation, as political economist Jan Toporowski claims, it is one that is necessarily linked to the legal institution of inheritance.[17]

CLASS, INFLATION, AND THE EROSION OF INHERITED WEALTH

Mary Ann Glendon understood the decline of the private family to be linked in complex ways to the redistribution of wealth and income made possible by the welfare state.[18] These redistributive trends had been in train since the New Deal and had accelerated after World War II, as rising wages, social insurance benefits, and public investment in education steadily eroded income inequalities between rich and poor. Yet there is good reason why conservatives such as Glendon and others became obsessed with the moral dangers of wealth redistribution at the end the 1970s. The rising inflation of the 1970s—decried as a universal catastrophe for all social classes—had in fact greatly amplified the steady but not spectacular redistributive trends of the postwar era, compressing wealth and wage inequalities as never before in American history.

In an article exploring the effects of inflation on redistribution, the Brookings Institution economist, Joseph Minarik, found that since wages and welfare for the most part kept pace with the consumer price index, the poor and middle class did not lose much through inflation, and in some cases they made considerable gains.[19] Those who benefited most from inflation were the middle-income homeowners who had borrowed to purchase housing. With fixed mortgage repayments and interest rates, the indebted homeowner saw his mortgage debt depreciate in value as the price level, including that of housing, went up, meaning that the burden of debt seemed to vanish with time.[20] Even renters were not overly burdened by inflation as wages tended to keep up with rent increments. But Minarik also refuted the common assumption that low-income households, those that derived most of their income from government transfers, had been hardest hit by inflation. The effect of rising consumer prices on the welfare classes, he observed, was offset by the fact that most welfare programs were adjusted to inflation.[21] After Nixon's reforms, Social Security was indexed to inflation on an annual basis; in-kind transfer programs such as food stamps were recalculated every six months; and those that covered the price of existing services such as public housing, Medicaid and Medicare, were implicitly indexed to inflation.

By contrast, inflation seriously eroded the wealth of the top decile and centile of households, those whose wealth was invested in financial assets such as stocks, bonds, or real estate holdings and whose income derived primarily from interests, dividends, or rents. Throughout the 1970s, wealth holders were at a loss to find safe avenues of investment that would protect their assets from long-term depreciation. Wage and consumer price inflation translated into financial asset deflation and therefore posed a serious challenge to the forms of wealth accumulation traditionally favored by the rich. The real value of corporate stock had been falling steadily since the mid-1960s, while bondholders found themselves earning low, if not negative, real interest rates.[22] As inflation kept spiraling upward, a cloud of uncertainty hovered over the future of long-term investments such as Treasury bonds, while investors who moved into short-term Treasury Bills in the hope of finding a safer alternative discovered that their returns were intermittently negative.

By the end of the 1970s, bondholders were in revolt, demanding an inflation premium on interest rates to protect them from the depreciation of principal.[23] Free-market economists insinuated that inflation was a form of state-sanctioned fraud—a covert tax designed to extort wealth from investors and transfer it to the lower classes. Pointing to Minarik's findings, the Reagan-era ideologue George Gilder described the 1970s as the "Great Depression" of the upper classes and denounced Arthur Burns's Federal Reserve for conducting "a war against the rich."[24] The redistribution of wealth was real enough: The economist Edward Wolff found that wealth concentration fell sharply between 1972 and 1976, due primarily to the depreciating value of stocks and bonds owned by the top wealth holders.[25] Inflation, he concluded, had acted as a "redistributive tax" that greatly intensified the progressive tendencies of the postwar era.[26]

But if inflation was denounced as an extortion of private wealth, it was also widely perceived as an attack on the peculiarly familial forms of wealth transmission that had long sustained the reproduction of class. Alongside the highly racialized rhetoric of lower-class family crisis that flourished in the 1970s then, a parallel picture emerged of the rise and fall of the great American patrimonial family. "Trustees beware!" intoned one legal scholar, who went on to observe that if "times have been tough for investors generally," they "have been worse for trust beneficiaries" and other recipients of inherited wealth.[27] Another expert in estate law pointed to the growing disinclination of the rich to bequeath wealth to future generations in a context of general asset price depreciation: "Even a skilled acquirer and dedicated accumulator of wealth may find that his inclination to conserve wealth for his own retirement and for transmission to dependents and successors is affected by the inability of his investments to keep abreast of inflation."[28] But it was Gilder who offered the most extravagant picture of upper-class family decline. His Reagan-era bestseller *Wealth and Poverty* performed a rhetorical tour de force by linking the corruption of the wealthy American family with the amoral counterculture, and this in turn with the perceived crisis of family values among the welfare poor:

> The great secret of the American gentry is downward mobility.... Rich people who inherited and attempted to husband their wealth through the last five decades tended to see most of it wither away. Many who lived off of capital found their capital dwindling rapidly and their income from it shriveled by inflation and taxes. Many saw their children enter the professions and live moderately and well. But they then had to watch their grandsons grow hair to their shoulders, drop out of expensive schools financed by disappearing family wealth, and dabble in careers in art and carpentry, interspersed with unemployment checks, before they grabbed a briefly open slot in government bureaucracy from which to instruct the poor in the ways of upward mobility.[29]

At the beginning of the 1970s, fears that the wealthy American family might be under threat from inflation were accentuated by the simultaneous efforts of progressive tax reformers to increase the burden on large estates. During the 1972 presidential campaign, the left-wing Democrat George McGovern proposed to raise the estate tax to 100 percent on gifts or inheritances above half a million dollars. It was in response to this specific and credible threat that neoliberal economists first launched themselves into the estate tax debate, developing an elaborate account of the mutually beneficial relationship between private investment and the familial transmission of wealth.[30] Virginia school neoliberals Gordon Tullock and Richard Wagner argued that the ability to pass on one's wealth was a necessary stimulus to investment and therefore warned of the deadening effects of the estate tax on private enterprise.[31] And in a strange inversion of the argument from meritocracy, Milton and Rose Friedman classified inherited wealth as an "accident of birth"—comparable to musical talent—that should not be taxed at all.[32] Elsewhere, as we have seen, Milton Friedman characterized the family motive in wealth transmission as a mysterious force underlying and ultimately animating market freedom—a motive that he found "irrational" and "curious" but to which he nevertheless deferred.[33]

These arguments were notable not only because they prioritized the economic role of the family in free market economics—rendering explicit what for the most part remained unsaid or latent within their theoretical frameworks—but also because they represented a radical departure from the principled meritocratic values of early Chicago school neoliberalism. In the 1940s, after all, Milton Friedman's teacher, Henry Simons, held views on inherited wealth that were on a continuum with those of McGovern, going so far as to argue that inheritance and inter vivos gifts should be taxed progressively in the same way as income to ensure a fully meritocratic free-market system.[34] In the intervening years, Chicago school neoliberals radicalized their critique of the New Deal welfare state, casting welfare recipients as the true "rentiers" and parasites of the free-market system, and by the 1970s they had definitively aligned themselves with the interests of bond and stockholders under siege from inflation. Inherited wealth was now reconceived as a necessary spur to the investment energies of the free market.

Yet, if the Reagan revolution had presented itself solely as a movement to protect large fortunes, it would no doubt have failed. As Kevin Phillips notes, outright defense of the interests of the idle upper class has rarely managed to mobilize the passions of American populism: Reagan-era ideologues such as George Gilder were therefore "not trumpeting inherited wealth" but rather innovation, entrepreneurialism, and risk-taking, even while they waged a covert war on estate taxes and other levies on private fortunes.[35] This mixture of rhetorical meritocracy and political patrimonialism also fueled the conservative populism of the 1970s and radically shifted the class alliances of the late Fordist era.

The tax revolt of the 1970s had multiple points of origin, emerging in its early years from both left-wing and right-wing concerns with the redistributive politics of taxation at the local and state level.[36] As it matured, however, and as business interests joined forces with local activists, the movement acquired a distinctly nativist tone that was heavily coded by race. By the time of its first major ballot-box success—the passage of California's Proposition 13 in 1978—the movement was almost exclusively associated with white suburban homeowners in revolt against income transfers to the poor. It was this popular uprising against the redistributive welfare state, more than the machinations of wealthy investors, that ultimately made the Reagan revolution possible.

The vigor of the tax revolt was astounding, not least because its prime demographic—middle-class homeowners—had made outright gains from inflation. Yet, even as they saw the value of their homes double or triple in the space of a few years, many of these owner-occupiers experienced their recent windfalls of wealth as precarious. Most of them had been pushed into higher tax brackets as a result of inflation and progressive tax reform and resented the fact that their rising property taxes were being squandered on the nonworking, nonwhite poor. Their fears extended from local and state property taxes to the estate tax, which they denounced as a subterfuge serving to undermine the family itself. Johnson's Great Society programs had been successful as long as the working and welfare classes felt their interests to be somehow aligned; as unemployment increased and affirmative action programs continued to be rolled out, this fragile coalition broke down and white homeowners began to shift their allegiances toward the wealth-holding classes.[37] The latter, it is true, had objective cause to fear inflation. But it was middle-class homeowners, not investors or bondholders, who took the initiative in defending patrimonial wealth against the redistributive functions of the welfare state.

Thus, if neoliberals and supply-siders could express their defense of inherited wealth only in the most circuitous and coded of language, middle-class homeowners had no such reservations and launched an open assault on estate taxes, in what was to prove a long-term victory for the super-rich. As one spokesman of the tax revolt expressed it: "the estate tax has become increasingly traumatic to the family of modest means...we do not want an estate tax to behave as a punitive tax that destroys the average family's ability to retain a small family farm or business. We do not want an estate tax that destroys the continuity of the economic unit owned by persons of modest means who would like to pass that heritage to either their spouse or lineal descendants."[38] At a time when redistributive social welfare, rising public investment, and progressive taxation policies were attenuating the force of private familial wealth, white taxpayers recoiled in fear, preferring to claim their allegiance to a much older tradition of inherited wealth invested in the home.

In the latter part of the 1970s, then, the white middle class effectively refashioned itself in the image of the patrimonial, investment class and sought to exempt itself from forms of social redistribution that were now commonly denounced as subsidies to the family dysfunction of the poor. By articulating a defense of the private family as economic institution against the redistributive functions of the welfare state, the conservative populism of the 1970s provided the template for the fiscal and monetary politics of the Reagan era—and beyond. As the language of the taxpayer revolt makes clear, the neoliberal counterrevolution was intimately informed by a concern with private family wealth and its transmission.

FINANCIALIZATION: ASSET PRICE INFLATION
AND THE RETURN OF INHERITED WEALTH

Despite the gathering air of crisis, the 1970s was a decade in which political decisions remained in suspense, blocked by the sheer deadlock of social antagonisms and the still powerful influence of the progressive left. Throughout the decade, Federal Reserve chairman Arthur Burns continued to accommodate inflation with low interest rates, even as he recognized the threat it posed to investors. But as the interests of bondholders and homeowners began to converge in the late 1970s, the Federal Reserve was emboldened to intervene decisively in favor of the investor class. Thus, when Paul Volcker replaced Arthur Burns as chair of the Federal Reserve in 1978, he immediately set about implementing Milton Friedman's prescription for dealing with inflation by restricting the money supply and pushing up interest rates. Volcker's "monetarism" was more strategic than sincere.[39] Nevertheless, it had the desired effect of producing the deepest recession since the Great Depression, replete with double-digit rates of unemployment. Having thus broken the bargaining power of unionized labor, the Volcker shock laid the ground for a long-term restructuring of the US labor market. Manufacturers were now free to move production units offshore and cut wages to domestic workers, while the high interest rates that were maintained for the duration of Volcker's term brought cheap imports flooding into the country, putting an end to rising consumer prices. By 1982, the Federal Reserve appeared to have defeated wage and consumer price inflation; and more important perhaps, it had proven to bond holders that it was willing to do everything in its power to protect the value of financial assets.

The Volcker shock heralded a paradigm shift in American fiscal and monetary policy. Throughout the postwar period, the Federal Reserve adopted a monetary policy serving to indulge the expansionary fiscal stratagems of Keynesian demand management. Its remit, as outlined in the Employment Act of 1946, was to "promote maximum employment, production and purchasing power."[40] Within this policy regime, wage and price inflation were understood as signs of economic growth and benign trade-offs to full employment—a common sense understanding that was encapsulated in the so-called Phillips curve. The Volcker shock overturned this formula by turning inflation-targeting into the prime objective of monetary policy: henceforth the central bank would demonstrate its independence from potentially profligate governments by steadfastly disciplining wage and consumer price inflation, whatever the social costs. This signaled a complete turnaround with respect to the 1970s, when bond holders had seen the value of their assets depreciate as the Federal Reserve repeatedly deferred to the interests of unionized labor and welfare constituencies. Under the new monetary regime initiated by Volcker, the Federal Reserve spoke directly to the sensibilities of bondholders and sought to maintain their confidence by actively disciplining the policy choices of the state. If the government indulged in "excessive" social spending, interest rates would be raised. If it imposed fiscal austerity on wages and welfare, the central bank would accommodate with low interest rates. In short, if the Fed had once sacrificed the value of assets for wage inflation, it now strove to repress wages and consumer prices in the service of asset price appreciation.[41] The monetary priorities of the late Keynesian era had been completely reversed.

The macroeconomic consequences of this new monetary regime were quick to declare themselves. By the mid-1980s, when Volcker finally eased up on interest rates, bond and stock prices began a dizzying ascent.[42] Over the following years, bond prices would experience one of the longest bull markets in history, while the Dow Jones embarked on a fifteen-year boom, to be followed by the house price appreciation of the early twenty-first century. Together, these asset price booms generated enormous growth in capital gains and interest payments. The sustained appreciation of financial assets, sometimes glossed in the political economy literature as "financialization," led to a sharp turnaround in the distribution of national income. Epstein and Jayadev note that in many countries, the share of national income flowing to financial investors went from negative or stagnant in the 1970s to "substantially positive" in the 1980s. In the UK, the adjusted share was "–4.21% in the 1970s and 7.3% in the 1980s"; in the US, the share "was 3.99% in the 1970s and 22.11% in the 1980s, obviously a huge share," while labor's share of national income declined proportionately.[43]

Having entered office at a time when Volcker was remaking monetary policy at the Federal Reserve, Reagan set about work on the fiscal front, skillfully leveraging the passions of the antitax movement to push through with reforms that were much more comprehensive (and regressive) than those imagined by an unwitting coalition of middle-class homeowners. Under the influence of neoliberals and supply-siders, who argued that lower taxes on the rich would free up private investment, Reagan initiated a long-term Republican campaign against progressive taxation that would culminate with George W. Bush's attempt to phase out the estate tax in 2001. Under Reagan, the top personal tax bracket was slashed from 70 percent to 28 percent in seven years, yielding impressive gains for the top 1–5 percent of wage earners. The Economic Tax Recovery Act, passed by Congress in 1981, raised the exemption threshold on the estate tax, reducing the number of estates that owed any taxes at all to less than 1 percent by the end of the decade.[44] It also extended tax cuts to capital gains and the unearned income derived from financial assets (income, dividends, and rents).[45] These reforms were calculated to benefit the very top percentile of households and were enacted at a time when Congress was simultaneously letting Social Security taxes rise—a move that cancelled out the effect of income tax reductions for the middle class.[46] Households below the top decile were disproportionately burdened by Social Security contributions and therefore ended up paying higher overall tax rates, notwithstanding the much-celebrated cuts to their income taxes.[47] If Social Security had played a redistributive and equalizing role in the 1970s then, blunting the effects of inherited wealth on relative life chances, it now seemed to be accentuating class distinctions by increasing the burdens on the poor.

The Reagan-era revolution in fiscal and monetary policy had a dramatic effect on wealth and income inequality, effectively reversing the accelerated redistributive trends of the 1970s. It was at this point that average wages entered a long period of stagnation, a trend that was barely dented by the economic boom of the 1990s. A closer zoom reveals a more extreme picture of income divergence. Beginning in the 1980s, the real hourly wages of male workers fell at the bottom of the income scale, stagnated near the middle and rose near the top—precipitously so among the top 1 percent. Women's wages remained at an overall lower level than those of men but followed a similarly skewed pattern of distribution.[48] Even when productivity and corporate profits picked up in the latter part of the 1990s, prompting some economists to celebrate the arrival of a new economy based on human capital investment and knowledge work, average wages continued to stagnate.[49] These trends stand in stark contrast to the "Golden Age" of American capitalism, from 1947 to 1973, when wages (for white male workers) kept pace with productivity growth and wage and capital shares of national income remained stable.

The effects on wealth distribution, however, were even more striking. As asset prices began a vertiginous upward spiral around 1982, the super-rich experienced staggering increases in wealth, while the average wealth holding of the lower classes declined in real terms—with many households now reporting zero or negative assets.[50] By 1983, wealth concentration had reverted to its 1962 level and by the end of the decade had plummeted to levels comparable to 1929.[51] It has subsequently remained virtually unchanged.[52] The new monetary regime ushered in by Volcker (and perfected by Greenspan) favored those forms of wealth that were held disproportionately by the richest households—financial assets such as stocks, bonds, time deposits, and money-market funds—all of which saw substantial price appreciation during this period.[53] Wolff attributes much of the wealth concentration of the 1980s and beyond to the appreciation of existing stocks of wealth, that is, to capital gains on assets acquired in the past—observing that those who derived income from labor could not hope to accumulate comparable levels of wealth from stagnant or depreciating wages.[54] Promoting asset price inflation at the expense of wage growth, the Federal Reserve's new monetary policy placed a premium on established wealth and returned inheritance to a decisive position in the shaping of social class.

The overall effect of neoliberal monetary policy has been to reverse the relationship between wage and asset inflation that prevailed in the postwar era. Throughout the 1970s, wages and welfare kept pace with consumer price inflation as assets plummeted in value, tending to blunt (but not erase) the force of inherited wealth in shaping social inequality. After 1982, however, wages and welfare struggled to keep pace with anemic levels of consumer price inflation while the asset-based holdings of the richest households went up and up. Under these circumstances, it was inevitable that family wealth transmission (in which I include both transfers at death and so-called inter vivos transfers)[55] would once again assume a pivotal role in the production of social class. Far from a terminal decline of inheritance then, the last few decades have witnessed the phenomenal resurgence of large family fortunes—a fact that is confirmed by a newly thriving business in family trusts, a legal instrument traditionally favored by the wealthiest households.[56] More important, perhaps, the relative weight of wealth as opposed to wages in shaping social mobility has increased at all levels of the social scale. Today, it could be argued, traditional work-based definitions of class must be corrected for wealth holdings if one is to gain a precise sense of a person's net worth. In the words of Thomas Piketty, "inherited wealth comes close to being as decisive at the beginning of the twenty-first century as it was in the age of Balzac's *Père Goriot*."[57]

The effect, moreover, has been compounded by cutbacks to public education, health care, and other social services, which have progressively transferred costs back to the private family and compelled parents to take on debt on behalf of their children. The appreciation of house prices (itself a symptom of asset inflation) means that access to home ownership often depends on a loan or gift from parents; the de facto privatization of education and rise in student fees means that a student wanting to pursue a college education is now more directly dependent on the wealth of his or her parents than at any time in the recent past; while the absence of familial wealth can condemn a young person to a life of revolving debt. The shift from public spending to private deficit spending as a means of financing investments in "human capital" such as health and education has been well documented in the critical literature on neoliberal financialization.[58] Less noted, however, is the fact that private deficit spending or "privatized Keynesianism" as it is sometimes called, almost invariably takes the form of intergenerational, parental investment, where the family becomes the primary source of economic welfare for those born into a world of ever-diminishing public goods. It is in the specific form of spiraling household debt that neoliberal capitalism has revived the poor-law imperative of family responsibility.

It would be misleading, however, to suggest that this period has been completely devoid of social democratic interventions. In fact, the idea that the "wealth effect" could be democratized through the inclusion of middle- and low-income earners in the logic of financial asset inflation represents one of the central policy innovations of the neoliberal era and one that has been embraced by both sides of the political spectrum.[59] The idea finds inspiration in the tradition of property owning democracy, propounded variously by Thomas Paine and John

Rawls.[60] In mid–twentieth century Britain, it was embraced by early members of the neoliberal Mont-Pèlerin Society and the right wing of the Labor Party as an alternative to state investment in public assets.[61] Variations on the theme have been propounded by left and right and have gone under many names—from Drucker's pension fund socialism to stakeholder capitalism, from right-wing theories of "empowerment" to the Ford Foundation's asset-based welfare, and finally to George W. Bush's ownership society.[62]

The distribution of asset ownership did in fact change significantly after the Reagan revolution as workers were encouraged to entrust their pension savings to the investment strategies of mutual funds. Individual pension accounts such as 401(k)s exploded after 1982, the period of vertiginous stock price appreciation which followed the Volcker shock, when their promise of rising returns stood in stark contrast to the troubled state of the public pension program. Neoliberals and libertarians understood the migration from Social Security to individual investment accounts as the most effective way of neutralizing the divide between worker and investor, thereby preempting any possible opposition to neoliberal labor reform. After all, why would worker-investors continue to support public services and progressive income taxes if they too had a stake in the appreciation of financial assets?[63] But further than this, the champions of Social Security privatization explicitly sold these instruments as vehicles of familial wealth accumulation: unlike Social Security benefits, it was argued, the wealth invested in stocks was inheritable and would therefore serve to strengthen rather than undermine the bonds of family dependence.[64]

More recently, policymakers have called on home ownership to play a similar role in the generalization of private wealth accumulation. In a period when wages were barely stagnant, the prospect that low-income households might also benefit from the dynamics of asset price appreciation through expanded access to mortgages has been key to achieving a certain level of social consensus. A decade or so before it was embraced in the United States, social policy theorists in Britain were celebrating the genius of the Thatcher administration, whose strategies to push the working class toward private home ownership seemed to have undermined the entrenched class hostilities of a previous era. The British-Australian sociologist Peter Saunders depicted private home ownership as a form of "familial accumulation" that would teach the working class the value of inherited wealth and wean them off public services—in the long run perhaps completely altering their traditional political allegiances.[65] What had come to fruition under Thatcher, he argued, was a new form of property-owning democracy powered by asset appreciation and family bequests rather than savings: "The present generation will not simply leave a lot of money to its children, but many of them will themselves inherit substantial sums from their parents. Capital gains from the housing market are in this sense becoming cyclical, for each generation here on will benefit from its parents while in turn benefiting its children."[66] In the United States, similar ideas would be promoted by Third Way advocates of "asset-based welfare" under Clinton and Republican champions of the "ownership society" under George W. Bush.

The American experiment in neoliberal home ownership policy, however, was always haunted by the specific legacy of the tax revolt. If the tax resisters of the 1970s sought to opt out of the redistributive economics of the welfare state by turning to the resources of familial wealth accumulation, this pathway to economic security was later offered to America's minorities as a way of offsetting their steady decline in income. Where American minorities—both sexual and racial – were once denied the privileges of inheritable wealth, they were now exhorted to embrace the economic family as the only path toward social inclusion. The subsequent reshuffling of political allegiances has played out in sometimes unexpected ways in recent struggles around the "death tax," or tax on inheritance.

The Clinton administration was the first to actively promote the idea of minority home ownership as a long-term, structural response to the widening social inequalities of neoliberal America. This policy choice was influenced by the work of Third Way social reformers who in the 1990s put forward the idea of "asset-based welfare" as an alternative to traditional forms of social welfare. One of the most influential exponents of asset-based welfare was Michael Sherraden, an academic based at Washington University in St. Louis, who argued that traditional welfare programs focused unduly on the problem of income redistribution at the expense of asset ownership.[67] In an era where asset prices were moving ever upward and wages were stagnating, it no longer made sense to distribute welfare in the form of income transfers. Traditional welfare programs such as AFDC, Sherraden contended, disempowered the poor because they focused on the consumption of services, not the generation of private wealth through investment in assets. The means tests that had hitherto limited asset ownership among welfare recipients should therefore be lifted and replaced by active programs of asset democratization.

During the 1990s, asset-based welfare was embraced by both the Ford Foundation and the Democratic Leadership Council, the organization that represented centrist or Third Way New Democrats such as Bill Clinton.[68] Under Clinton, this preference flowered into a National Homeownership Strategy that identified private housing as the ideal vector of asset-based investment and general alternative to the diminishing returns of the welfare state.[69]

Launched in 1995, Clinton's Homeownership Strategy was informed by many of the same ideals as the welfare reform agenda he would implement in the following year. The newly appointed director of the Department of Housing and Urban Development (HUD),

Henry Cisneros, noted that Clinton was intent on "ending public housing as we know it," in much the same way as he had vowed to end welfare.[70] Both policy reforms rested on the premise that the welfare poor needed to be weaned off income transfers, with all their perverse and demoralizing effects, and instead made responsible for their own economic security. Both assumed that the private family would need to be rehabilitated as the proper legal and moral institution to achieve this goal. "You want to reinforce family values in America, encourage two-parent households, get people to stay home?" Clinton asked: "Make it easy for people to own their own homes and enjoy the rewards of family life and see their work rewarded."[71] Unlike Clinton's welfare reform, however, the National Homeownership Strategy outlined a comprehensive alternative pathway for achieving the poor-law imperative of family responsibility, one that relied on credit and asset appreciation rather than the traditional virtues of hard work and savings to render citizens independent of the state.

Having vowed to reduce the federal budget deficit to zero, Clinton followed the example of Reagan and George H. W. Bush in slashing federal outlays for public housing, limiting rent control and pushing for the voucherization of state-subsidized rentals.[72] During the first few years of his administration, federal spending on services for the homeless fell even further than it had under Reagan, with devastating consequences for the urban poor. But Clinton offered something the Republicans had not: a comprehensive new urban "empowerment" strategy that reinvigorated the much maligned HUD and shifted its focus from public housing to private home ownership. The Republicans had spent many years attacking HUD, the agency responsible for expanding public housing under Johnson's Great Society, and were threatening to eliminate it completely. Clinton managed to trump the Republicans by repopulating HUD with proponents of asset-based welfare and investing it with a new task: that of extending the benefits of private home ownership to those who were still excluded from the American dream.[73] Housing data collected in the 1980s showed that home ownership rates had stalled for the first time in over two decades and had declined among African American and Latino households.[74] Hoping to reverse these trends, HUD now enlisted the help of the Fannie Mae, Freddie Mac, and private mortgage brokers to expand credit options to "non-conforming borrowers," typically minorities, women, and the young, who frequently did not have the regular work history or credit profile required of standard borrowers.[75] Under Clinton's instruction, Fannie Mae and Freddie Mac were encouraged to relax their underwriting criteria, while the Community Reinvestment Act of 1977, originally introduced to police redlining, was vested with greater powers of enforcement.

Thus, Clinton promised to redeem America's most disadvantaged citizens—those who had fallen even farther behind in the cruel 1980s—by including them in the slipstream of ever appreciating asset prices. If Clinton had nursed any skepticism about pursuing such a policy at the beginning of his term in office, he was more or less forced there by the chairman of the Federal Reserve, Alan Greenspan, who counseled that any attempt to raise wages or expand public investment would set off fears of inflation and increase the long-term interest rates (or "inflation premium") demanded by bondholders.[76] In Greenspan's opinion, a better alternative was to scale back government spending, repress wages, and instead let long-term interest rates fall—a process that was sure to generate an abundance of cheap consumer credit.[77] As long as the government took advantage of this credit boom to push the income-poor to invest in housing, a virtuous circle would materialize whereby cheap credit would push up housing prices which would in turn provide ever-appreciating collateral for the extension of further credit. Rather than return to a discredited politics of social investment, an option that would in any case be blocked at every turn by the Federal Reserve, Greenspan urged Clinton to generalize the "wealth effect" of asset appreciation by relaxing the rules on credit.[78] The virtues of structured finance—including new, more risk-sensitive forms of securitization—would in the meantime enable mortgage brokers and investors to extract maximum profit while perfectly hedging the attendant default and liquidity risks of long-term lending.

Eugene Ludwig, Clinton's Comptroller of the Currency, hailed this strategy as the "democratization of credit" and described it as the final completion of a democratic process initiated under the New Deal but hitherto compromised by its normative exclusions. "Because of the democratization of credit," he observed, "yesterday's under-served have become today's core business customers."[79] The federal politics of postwar credit expansion that had enabled millions of middle class white Americans to purchase homes would now at last be extended to Fordism's non-normative subjects—minorities, women, and other dubious credit risks. Having been historically marginalized from accumulation of private wealth, they too would now be inducted into the logic of asset accumulation, if only in the prospective and aspirational form of revolving debt.

HOME OWNERSHIP, NORMATIVITY, AND THE NEW DEAL

The government promotion of consumer credit has long played a unique role in America's public-private welfare state, standing alongside social insurance as one of the key redistributive mechanisms developed under the New Deal. Federal policy makers from the mid-twentieth century onward have made strategic use of private credit markets to fulfill the so-called American dream of middle-class home ownership, inventing various kinds of administrative and legal guarantees to ensure that credit would be readily available to the suitably qualified borrower. These initiatives date back to the Great Depression, when President Franklin D. Roosevelt created a host of new federal institutions designed to protect borrowers from the risk of imminent foreclosure.[80] The Federal Housing Administration (FHA), created in 1934, encouraged banks to lend to qualified borrowers at low interest rates by insuring them against the risk of default, while the Federal National Mortgage Association (FNMA, or Fannie Mae, established in 1938) helped to relieve banks of long-term liquidity risk by buying up their mortgage portfolios and selling them on to investors. The Home Owners' Loan Corporation (HOLC), created in 1933, played an equally important role in facilitating consumer credit markets by inventing a new and safer form of mortgage contract—the long-term, fixed-rate, amortized loan (the so-called vanilla mortgage)—as a replacement for the short-term, interest-only mortgages that had hitherto dominated the market. Together, these initiatives allowed banks to expand their mortgage portfolios and lend at low-interest rates without incurring substantial financial risk.

The expansion of these New Deal housing programs after World War II led to a dramatic increase in home ownership rates: from 44 percent of male-headed families in 1934 to 63 percent in 1972.[81] By opening up mortgage insurance to unionized industrial workers, federal housing policies swelled the ranks of the American middle class and established suburban home ownership as a new, middle-class ideal. Yet, housing credit was always premised on the sexual and racial normativities of the Fordist family wage, which defined creditworthiness as a function of employment and marital status and therefore ended up favoring the standard white male worker over all other subject classes. The FHA imposed strict underwriting criteria on lenders, dictating everything from the acceptable payment structure of mortgages to housing models, location, and borrower profile, and banks needed to conform to these guidelines if they wished to receive federal guarantees. Ultimately, it was the FHA that decided who was creditworthy enough to receive a low-interest mortgage. The overall effect of such oversight was to restrict mortgage finance to the married, white man and to exclude Fordism's non-normative subjects from the forms of wealth accumulation that flowed from home ownership in the post-war era.

The very structure of the thirty-year, "vanilla" mortgage was closely modeled on the working life of the unionized industrial worker, making it almost impossible for non-standard workers to gain access to housing credit even in the absence of overt discrimination. The fact that unionized Fordist workers were also covered by generous forms of social insurance (from work-based health care to worker's compensation and unemployment coverage) made them doubly attractive to federal insurers; not only were they locked into long-term employment contracts, but they also had guaranteed wages and were therefore at very low risk of default. Borrowers who could not demonstrate such a stable attachment to the workplace were simply not able to qualify for a state-insured, low-interest mortgage, effectively excluding most African Americans and women of all races from the private housing market.

In the case of African Americans, these employment-based exclusions were exacerbated by the residential preferences of federal housing authorities, which consistently favored suburban, single-family homes over downtown tenements. As white, married families began their long postwar exodus to the suburban hinterlands, African Americans were left behind in increasingly impoverished inner cities. Those who may have wanted to purchase in the city center were further penalized by the HOLC's system of urban risk rating, which routinely assigned the color red—for "uninsurable"—to the inner-city ghettos (hence the term "redlining") and in the process made them especially vulnerable to the machinations of local slumlords.[82] Thus a series of seemingly innocuous bureaucratic choices, from urban risk ratings to insurable housing models, had a profound effect on the postwar landscape, largely confining African Americans to high-rent tenements in dilapidated inner cities while white Americans proceeded to accumulate state-insured housing wealth in the suburbs.[83]

Ira Katznelson aptly refers to federal housing policy in this era as a form of "affirmative action for whites."[84] Others refer to a "hidden welfare state" that allowed whites to accumulate what looked like private wealth but was in fact an alternative form of (asset-based) welfare multiply subsidized by federal guarantees, public insurance, and tax concessions.[85]

Federal housing policies, moreover, were not simply racializing but also tightly bound up with the normative regulation of gender and sexuality. The historian Clayton Howard has recently explored in some detail just how central these criteria were to the development of the postwar housing market.[86] Well into the 1960s, FHA guidelines instructed banks to check a borrower's "character" before issuing a loan and specifically identified marital status as a litmus test for creditworthiness. The 1952 edition of the FHA's Underwriting Manual counseled lenders: "The mortgagor who is married and has a family generally evidences more stability than a mortgagor who is single because, among other things, he has responsibilities holding him to his obligations."[87] Elsewhere in the Manual, banks were advised not to issue loans to people unrelated by blood, since the "probabilities of dissatisfaction...between members of the partnership are strong and seriously affect the desire for continuing ownership on the part of any one of the principals."[88] In an era where marriage was difficult to dissolve and no-fault divorce was still far off on the horizon, the marital contract between a workingman and his wife appeared to offer the same prospect of reliability as the long-term contract of employment. A white man tied to the responsibilities of work and family was considered the most creditworthy of borrowers and the most insurable of risks; a single white man might have enjoyed more financial independence but was less likely to respect his long term obligations; a single working woman was an uncertain credit risk at best; while a married woman was in general barred from receiving any form of consumer credit in her own name. The standardization of consumer risk profiles relegated borrowers to a continuum of more or less insurable risks—with women, homosexuals, and the nonwhite defined as outliers on the bell-curve of credit risks.

This premium placed on marital status within FHA lending criteria was supplemented by more overt forms of exclusion directed toward homosexuals. In the years immediately following World War II, political homophobia increased significantly as many states introduced new criminal penalties for non-heterosexual sex and stepped up their efforts to police and punish practicing homosexuals. FHA guidelines reflected this newly punitive environment by instructing lenders not to issue mortgages to people who had been convicted of sex-related offenses including "lewd vagrancy" or military discharge, automatically marginalizing many homosexual men who might have otherwise qualified.[89]

These policies very quickly impacted on the demographic profile of different neighborhoods, as census data reported a clear increase in married couples residing in outer suburban postcodes and a corresponding rise in unmarried, single residents in the inner cities. In Howard's words, postwar housing policies erected a "social and spatial closet around normative heterosexuality,"[90] creating suburban spaces in which homosexuality could only be lived in secret and by the same token urban spaces in which single homosexual whites congregated as an increasingly distinct social demographic alongside the nonwhite poor. Howard speaks in this regard of "parallel racial and sexual hierarchies" operating in the postwar housing market:

> By encouraging normative sexuality through mortgage regulation and by spurring the outward migration of married couples, the state facilitated the meeting of different groups of people in areas defined by marital status. This process never operated with the rigidity of racial segregation, since gay residents have always lived in the suburbs and many married residents continued to live in urban areas. Yet by the mid-1960s, the newest suburbs and oldest cities boasted unprecedented concentrations of

residents divided by marital status and newly built institutions like bars or churches that catered to different sexual communities.[91]

Depending on one's subject position, the hierarchies of the Fordist family wage could be seen as existing separately and side by side, creating strange urban proximities between sexual and racial outsiders, or (in the case of those who were both nonwhite and non-heterosexual) could intersect in the one person to create a concentration of uninsured risks.

The normative restrictions on consumer and housing credit persisted well into the 1960s, when they came under increasing attack from feminists, the civil rights movement, and gay liberation activists.[92] Over the following years, Congress passed a series of laws proscribing discrimination in consumer credit markets. The Fair Housing Act of 1968, followed by the Equal Credit Opportunity Act of 1974, extended racial antidiscrimination laws to housing and consumer credit markets respectively. These were followed by the Home Mortgage Disclosure Act (HMDA) of 1975 and the Community Reinvestment Act (CRA) of 1977, which explicitly outlawed redlining and introduced systematic procedures for monitoring the demographic distribution of bank loans. Regulation B of the 1974 Equal Credit Opportunity Act enabled married women to obtain full access to consumer credit in their own names. Only gay men, who had also protested their exclusion from mortgage finance, were not accorded any formal protection from bias in lending in this era.

In any event, these formal measures were only ever partially successful in redressing some of the normative exclusions of the Fordist credit regime. After all, no antidiscrimination law could reverse the fact that African Americans, Latinos, and women of all ethnicities were overrepresented among the ranks of the uninsured and precariously employed—classified as nonconforming by virtue of their distribution in the labor market rather than any personal prejudice on the part of bank managers.[93] Accordingly, the distribution of credit remained trapped in the normative limits of the family wage long after formal discrimination had been outlawed.

When credit was finally democratized, then, it was not primarily as a result of antidiscrimination laws, but rather thanks to the market-driven liberalization of consumer credit that began in the mid-1990s and accelerated thereafter.[94]

DEMOCRATIZING CREDIT: BEYOND THE NORM

The American mortgage market underwent a series of dramatic and highly consequential transformations in the decades preceding the subprime crisis. Throughout the 1970s, the government-sponsored entities Fannie Mae and Freddie Mac perfected a newer, more sophisticated method for helping banks to offload and sell on their loan portfolios. No longer did they simply purchase these loans and sell them on as is; they now repackaged and sold them on to investors as blended, risk-rated financial instruments known as mortgage-backed securities or MBS.[95] By the end of the 1970s, lenders had largely abandoned the marital-status-based criteria that informed lending decisions in the past and broadened their criteria for acceptable employment status. In an era where long-term employment contracts were becoming rare and marriage could be dissolved by no-fault divorce, it no longer made sense to base credit decisions on these considerations alone. Increasingly in this period, bank lenders began to use more granular, risk-based metrics to assess the creditworthiness of borrowers, basing their decisions on evolving credit scores rather than the status-like classifications of marriage and employment. Yet, for the most part, government-insured lending remained cautious, privileging standard or vanilla mortgage products and customers with minimal default risk—with the predictable result that mortgage decisions tended to marginalize minorities. Here again, the lending decisions of banks continued to replicate the normative exclusions of a previous era long after they had abandoned overt forms of discrimination.

By the mid-1990s, however, private lenders were entering the market en masse, and in a context of rising investor demand for MBSs, were increasingly willing to extend credit to those with riskier borrower profiles. Martha Poon notes that this new generation of nonbank lenders oversaw "a gradual shift away from traditional, exclusionary practices of credit control-by-screening and towards gradated practices of credit control-by risk."[96] Under control-by-risk, "managerial decision making was no longer confined to approving or withholding loans, but was extended to the exploitation of stabilized grades of credit quality accessed through scores to create multiple borrowing options tailored to accommodate varying levels of risk."[97] The standardization of credit (through the general adoption of commercial FICO scores) thus created the conditions for a destandardization of credit options, allowing even the most "nonconforming" of borrowers to be assigned a credit score and priced accordingly.

These techniques came into full effect at the height of the housing boom of the early 2000s, as mortgage brokers who had saturated the market for safe borrowers now turned their sights toward nonstandard credit risks. If banks had traditionally eschewed the asset-poor, the uninsured, and the precariously employed, private brokers were now scrambling to market credit to both subprime (low income) and Alt-A (credit blemished) borrowers, safe in the knowledge that the attendant risks could be rapidly securitized and sold on to investors.

In this way, the private mortgage sector broke through the normative barriers of the old Fordist credit regime. Well into the 1980s, notes Herman Schwartz, the vanilla loans favored by government-sponsored enterprises continued to operate within an actuarial calculus of risk established in the New Deal era: "vanilla MBSs in many ways are a classic product of the Bretton Woods or Fordist era welfare state. They socialized the risks attendant on providing housing finance, implicitly homogenized the returns to investors, favored debtors…and homogenized borrowers to a middle-class-family model buying single-family homes"[98] The new generation of private brokers replaced these traditional, actuarial models of risk standardization with a much more speculative strategy of risk-optimization through diversification into some of the more high-risk segments of the consumer credit market.[99]

In practice, such high-risk borrowers were disproportionately to be found among African Americans and Latinos in general, African American and Latino women in particular, and women of all ethnicities—precisely the demographic that was most likely to have recourse to welfare.[100] For the first time in the long history of American consumer credit, the subprime market allowed unprecedented numbers of marginal borrowers (women, African Americans, Latinos) and nonnormative households (single mothers in particular) to aspire to home ownership, although often at an exorbitant price. It was expected that a sizeable number of these borrowers would default, perhaps after rescheduling their loans several times. And yet as long as house prices continued to appreciate, these higher than average default rates would be more than compensated for by the higher than average returns to be gleaned from rescheduling fees and the punitive conditions of subprime loans.

In a certain sense, then, the democratization of credit did appear to resolve the enduring problems of race and gender-based exclusion that had long plagued America's hidden welfare state. For a brief moment, the private-sector expansion of credit embraced the nonstandard subjects who had once been summarily excluded from the New Deal social consensus, seeming to confirm the notion that financialization would usher in a superior form of social democracy—a social democracy beyond the norm. No longer would the poor need to rely on the degrading crutches of social welfare and income transfers to get by, since they, too, could now participate in forms of asset ownership once reserved for white married men and their families. Ultimately, what Clinton held out to minorities was a conduit into the avenues of private wealth accumulation long considered a privilege of the white middle class. The dividing line between America's hidden and overt welfare state—a line that was crudely exacerbated by the tax revolts of the 1970s—could now be closed, as all were shunted into the logic of familial wealth transmission. It is in this specific sense, no doubt, that Clinton discerned a secret alliance between asset-based welfare and the promotion of family values.

But it is here also that we can identify a latent contradiction within the Third Way strategy of asset-based welfare. How, after all, is it possible to overcome inequality by democratizing a legal instrument that is intended by its very nature to privatize wealth? Is social democracy achievable through the generalization of inheritance? Arguably, this tension is intrinsic to all forms of social democracy and has been at the heart of debates about the status of inheritance since the great wealth expropriations of the French Revolution and after.[101] By its very nature, social democracy can only ever partially resolve the tension between private wealth and the political ideal of equality; after all, if it were to completely abolish the institution of inheritance, it would become indistinguishable from socialism. At best, then, it can offer panaceas to the problems of maldistribution by seeking to increase earned income (wages) relative to unearned income (wealth) or by introducing some form of progressive taxation. But the tension becomes extreme in the contemporary policy agenda of asset-based welfare since the latter sets itself the impossible task of achieving equality through the generalization of inherited wealth. Here we find the perfect expression of capital's countervailing tendencies, as theorized by Marx: the coexistence, that is, of a democratizing impulse that appears to overcome the existing rigidities of inherited status with an equally forceful trend toward the reinvention and generalization of inheritance itself. Thus, primogeniture and entail were first abolished in the eighteenth century; in the late nineteenth century, married women were allowed to inherit property; and in the early twenty-first century, the rules of inheritance were changed to include same-sex couples and their children. At each conjuncture, the established form of inheritance is dissolved only in order to erect a new, more democratized, but no less implacable form in its place.

It is surely no coincidence, after all, that asset-based welfare's most celebrated policy experiment explicitly sought to school the income-poor in the art of managing a trust fund. Implemented in the form of pilot programs in the United States, but most comprehensively embraced in Britain under Tony Blair, the Child Trust Fund was designed to extend the benefits of familial asset accumulation to all children.[102] In his public pronouncements on the program, Blair presented the Child Trust Fund as an initiative to democratize inheritance itself:

> Overcoming the inequalities of wealth and income that hold people back is one of the greatest challenges facing Britain. We should aspire to be not just a democracy of property-owners, but a democracy in which ownership of wealth is open to all.... We are extending to everyone what the affluent take for granted. Our baby bond bestows to each child the advantages that come from reaching adulthood backed by a financial nest-egg, and extends the savings habit to all.[103]

In a similar vein, Bruce Ackerman and Anne Alstott, early proponents of the stakeholder society, hailed the Child Trust Fund as a form of "citizen inheritance" that would somehow neutralize the inequalities traditionally associated with private wealth accumulation:

> Young adults get the money regardless of whether their parents are stock-brokers or schoolteachers, computer geeks or construction workers. All have helped build Britain, and all may rightfully demand that their children share in the wealth they have helped create. Private inheritance proceeds on a very different premise—kids get their money on the basis of blood, not effort or common citizenship.... Citizen inheritance is not only

based on fundamental notions of fairness. It also provides a start-up fund to every Briton when he or she is beginning adult life and really needs it.[104]

Notwithstanding such grand ambitions, the aim of the Child Trust Fund, according to one commentator, was never that of comprehensive wealth redistribution, but rather the more modest one of fostering a culture of investment—and, I would add, a specifically familial culture of accumulation—among the asset-poor.[105] Short of implementing a radical reform of the tax system and a forcible redistribution of wealth, such projects have little chance of achieving the long-term democratic aims they claim to support. Here again we can point to the inherent contradiction at the heart of Third Way asset-based policies. The advocates of asset-based welfare may well proclaim their support for the progressive taxation of inherited wealth, but in practice their adherence to the logic of familial wealth works to undermine any popular investment in such a project.[106] It is this contradiction that has made asset-based welfare so vulnerable to recuperation by the right.

MINORITIES AGAINST THE ESTATE TAX: DEMOCRATIZING THE TAXPAYER REVOLT

Like so many other Third Way strategies, Clinton's project for the democratization of home ownership was something of a double-edged sword: after all, it could just as easily lend itself to the cause of Republican populism, with its rousing paranoia and much more radical opposition to redistributive taxes. This was precisely the intuition pursued by George W. Bush, who released his own *Blueprint for the American Dream* immediately after his ascension to power in 2001 and subsequently set about marketing the cause of expanded home ownership to traditional Democrat constituencies.[107] Bush pushed the liberalization of credit even further than his predecessor had, approving new legislation that preempted state efforts to regulate private mortgage brokers—the very institutions that were issuing the bulk of subprime loans to nonconforming borrowers. Most felicitous, however, was the fact that Bush's election coincided with the end of the dot-com boom and the transition from one period of asset inflation to another. As stock prices plummeted at the turn of the century, Greenspan sought to preempt a recession by cutting interest rates to historic lows while investors shifted funds from the Dow Jones into the residential housing market, with its high-yield mortgage-backed securities and collateralized debt obligations.[108] The progressive and still cautious liberalization of credit that had been initiated by Clinton now gave way to a veritable explosion of exotic and adjustable rate mortgages designed to price as many high-risk borrowers as possible into the market for consumer credit. And as cheap credit fueled ever-expanding house acquisition, house prices embarked on a dramatic upward spiral that seemed to include everyone in its aspirational promise.

During his election campaign, Bush's chief strategist, Karl Rove, advised him that the inclusion of minorities in the logic of inheritable wealth—even in the conditional and aspirational form of mortgage debt—would turn at least some traditional Democratic voters into allies of the Republican Party.[109] Nowhere was this intuition borne out more clearly than in the campaign to repeal the estate tax, which by the time of Bush's election in 2001 had managed to attract a surprising degree of support among minority voters. As far back as the early 1990s, at a time when Clinton was promoting the virtues of asset-based welfare, Republican tax reformers were targeting aspirational homeowners as new recruits in the campaign against the "death tax." These campaigners focused their energies on precisely those minorities that were now being actively courted by private mortgage brokers: African Americans and Latinos, single women, gays, and lesbians. Delegations were sent to the National Association of Women Business Owners, the National Black Chamber of Commerce, the National Indian Business Association, the US Hispanic Chamber of Commerce, the US Pan Asian

American Chamber of Commerce, the Texas Conference of Black Mayors, and various other minority associations, in the hope of convincing them that their newly acquired wealth was at risk of expropriation by the so-called death tax. By 2001, note Michael Graetz and Ian Shapiro, "a veritable rainbow coalition of minority groups were now actively urging repeal," convinced that their recent and conditional accession to familial wealth was threatened by a tax touching only the wealthiest 2 percent of households.[110] Arguably, it was this extraordinary wave of popular, bipartisan support that enabled Bush to push through with his temporary repeal of the estate tax.[111]

Bush's "ownership society" was almost identical in the details to Clinton-era "asset-based welfare," and yet its rhetoric insistently focused on the virtues of inheritance rather than redistribution, rendering explicit what remained unsaid and disavowed in Clinton's Third Way strategy. The anti–death tax campaign thus caught the Clinton administration off guard when it managed to recruit several members of the Congressional Black Caucus to its cause. When Congressman Sanford Bishop of Georgia spoke in favor of repeal, he used arguments eerily similar to those of the white antitax protesters of the 1970s: "The 'death tax' represents all that is unfair and unjust about the tax structure in America because it undermines the life work and life savings of Americans who want only to pass along to their children and their grandchildren the fruits of their labor and the realization of the American dream."[112]

Even though Republicans refused to support same-sex marriage, their allies in the tax repeal movement managed to convince an impressive number of gays and lesbians that their newly formed families were unfairly burdened by an estate tax that punished them twice over—once when a first partner died and a second time at the death of the surviving spouse. Because they were unmarried, gays and lesbians were not eligible for the estate tax "marital deduction" and were therefore penalized for the nonrecognition of their relationships.

This argument was so successful that by 2001 a full 61 percent of self-described lesbian and gay Democrat voters declared themselves in favor of estate tax repeal.[113]

The success of the Republican campaign against the estate tax suggests that the turning point marked by the late 1970s—when white middle-class owners turned their allegiance away from the welfare state—had now encompassed minority voters too. With their principled support of taxes on inherited wealth, the Ford Foundation proponents of asset-based welfare had grossly miscalculated the affective valence of private home ownership in a context of diminishing social welfare. As Karl Rove had intuited, the long-term effect of asset-based welfare was not so much to democratize wealth—this it did only temporarily and in the aspirational form of growing household indebtedness—but rather to enlist the political sympathies of the asset-impoverished on the side of inheritable wealth.

That wealth democratization through credit was in the long run an impossible feat was more than confirmed by the subprime crisis of 2007, which generated a net decline in American median wealth. Latino, African American, and female-headed households in particular experienced dramatic losses of wealth in this period as a result of falling house prices, underwater home loans, and foreclosures—an extraordinary step backward for those who were already among the most asset-impoverished.[114] This sudden and brutal negation of the aspirational promise of credit—neoliberalism's only policy response to growing inequality—has palpably reinforced the deep social divisions among Americans in the lingering postcrisis era. Once the mitigating effects of credit expansion were removed, it was inevitable that the actual polarization of American wages and wealth would reassert itself in the crudest of forms. Perhaps in the long run this crisis will enable a new cross-racial, cross-gendered alliance among America's poor. For the moment, however, it seems to have revived and radicalized the vicious nativism of the white tax revolt, in the guise of Donald Trump.

GAY MARRIAGE AND THE ESTATE TAX

If the relationship between neoliberal credit markets, race, and gender has been subject to intense commentary in recent years, the same politics has played out in distinct ways with respect to those who were (also or only) defined by their non-normative sexuality—in large part due to the fact that the non-heterosexual belong to no class, race, or gender in particular and inhabit all levels of the income and wealth scale. In effect, the political homophobia of the postwar era was remarkable in that it was perhaps the one form of state violence that could seriously disable the privileges of the white, male citizen. Aside from a criminal record, white men during this period could only be denied the right to credit and property for one reason—the fact that they were openly homosexual. This exclusion was enforced not only by legal means (for instance, the effective prohibition against lending to known homosexuals that was inscribed in federal housing guidelines) but also, and probably more often, by family homophobia. Its consequences became frighteningly real at the height of the AIDS crisis when gay men found themselves defined as "uninsurable risks" and deprived of health care, ousted from homes they had shared with a lover or unable to receive property from a deceased partner. As late as 1997, Judith Butler could plausibly conceptualize gays and lesbians as a distinct economic class defined by their simple exclusion from inheritance law and actuarial norms of insurable risk.[115]

With hindsight, however, it seems clear that the AIDS crisis also represented a turning point in the historical relationship between gay men and American capital. The invention of antiretrovirals and the subsequent conversion of HIV from a death sentence to a chronic illness coincided with a new expansionist moment in the market for consumer credit, as investor demand for consumer debt-backed securities persuaded lenders to aggressively market credit to new and previously untapped niche markets. At the same time that mortgage brokers and other lenders moved "down market" then, reaching out to the previously unbanked to market payday loans, subprime mortgages and other forms of nonstandard credit, the same class of lenders also moved "upmarket" into a high-end niche composed of putatively affluent, risk-taking yet loyal gay consumers.

Beginning in the early 1990s, financial service brokers and consumer lenders embarked on an extraordinary quest to capture the "gay market," offering everything from targeted credit cards, specialized mortgage products, and dedicated legal services in their efforts to lure this elusive and previously invisible demographic.[116] Coming at the end of the acute AIDS crisis of the 1980s, this exuberant induction into the world of consumer credit appeared to signal the demise of an older, cruder kind of homophobia—one shaped by the normativities of the family wage and its blunt forms of exclusion. Gay men who at the height of the AIDS crisis had been defined as uninsurable were now counted as exceptionally good credit risks and ideal consumers of financial services. Men who had been at risk of eviction in the 1980s were now celebrated as the agents of gentrification. Others who had seen their wills overridden by family members were courted by legal advisors offering to get their estates in order. Having been shunned for so long, white gay men—imagined to be uniformly high-earning, property-owning, and childless—were now fetishized as the perfect consumer niche market and taken to represent the "gay market" itself, an assumption that was apparently based on the very specific demographics of gay lifestyle magazines and later debunked.[117]

Market demographics notwithstanding, non-normative sexual practice is clearly not sufficient criterion to constitute a class. Queerness is rather transversal to class, cutting across the stratifications of race and gender and incorporating people from across the income and wealth spectrum. Yet, the expansion of credit into the market for non-normative lifestyles had the effect of obscuring these differences and making all gays and lesbians appear equally affluent. As long as the consumer credit market was willing to price all risk permutations, and as long as all could enjoy the benefits of immediate consumption, it was possible to believe that class, race, and gender differences no longer mattered. For credit brokers and cultural commentators alike, the rapid expansion of securitized credit appeared to affirm the infinite fungibility of identity markers and the perfect liquidity of risk profiles.

The creation of the "gay market" had a tangible impact on the kinds of activism that arose after the AIDS crisis of the 1980s. As advertisers, consumer bankers, and mortgage brokers seized upon the gay market as a source of untapped potential, much of the post–AIDS Coalition to Unleash Power (ACT UP) wave of activism refashioned itself in the image offered up by market demographics. With its performative reiteration of consumer spaces and semiotics, Queer Nation celebrated the liquefaction of identity in much the same way as the securitized consumer credit market affirmed the liquidity of diverse risk profiles and the profitability of the nonstandard risk.[118] Indeed, 1990s queer theory itself appears in retrospect to be suffused with the spirit of securitized credit markets. While much of this theoretical work—certainly Butler's *Gender Trouble*—was intended as a polemic against the residual biological essentialism of second-wave feminism, it was more commonly misread as a negation of actual inequalities and a utopian celebration of the willful mutability of identities.[119]

This utopianism had clear parallels in the literature on consumer finance. One of the more respectable celebrants of the consumer finance boom, the Princeton economist Robert Shiller, suggested that new techniques of credit-risk scoring, combined with securitization, had now made it possible to price and therefore hedge against any credit risk, including the most exotic or non-normative.[120] Borrower risks that in the past would have been considered too unsafe to be insured against could now be indefinitely deflected through the alternative means of credit derivatives. Uninsurable—or, in statistical terms, non-normalizable risks—could be hedged in a process that was proliferative or fractalizing rather than normative, thus opening up unheard of credit opportunities for the nontraditional borrower. It was precisely such a vision of democratic inclusion beyond the norm that was celebrated by Queer Nation and its affinity groups. If Clinton's legislative record on gay rights was ambiguous at best—presiding as he had over the Don't Ask, Don't Tell policy and the passage of the Defense of Marriage Act—he nevertheless ushered in a consumer credit boom that was more than willing to recognize the value of nonnormative lifestyles. As Queer Nation rightly insisted, its politics of performative consumerism was not about assimilation, but rather the credit-enabled investment in multiple lifestyle possibilities beyond the norm.[121]

Many commentators have noted the strange ambivalence of Queer Nation politics: the fact that it declared itself inassimilable within the profit motive while simultaneously confining its activism to the space of consumption; the fact that it celebrated the absolute liquidity of identity markers while relentlessly privileging white, gay men; above all, the fact that its spectacular performance of the non-normative gave way so rapidly to the most sober kinds of respectability politics.[122] Yet, it is hardly coincidental that the legal recognition of family became an explicit and overwhelming preoccupation of gay activism during this period, or that a performative activism held afloat by the dynamics of credit expansion should morph so quickly into a politics of marriage. The expansion of consumer credit did indeed cater to lifestyles and risk markets beyond the norm, seeming to banish the crude forms of invisibility that had reigned in the past, but the process of asset accumulation with which it was necessarily allied and the forms of collateral that it inevitably demanded, exerted an equally powerful stimulus to discipline oneself within the legal framework of inheritance.

The paradoxical relationship between collateral and credit is one that helps to illuminate the continued gravitational pull of the referent within the semiotics of performativity. If this relationship can be forgotten at the moment of greatest market euphoria, when all borrowers can enter the market with minimal or no collateral, it violently reasserts itself in periods of debt deflation when creditors "call in" their debts and demand the immediate materialization of assets. As soon as asset prices start plummeting, creditors start looking for some kind of "fundamental value" with which to take stock of their positions and recommence the process of accumulation: property valuations are reassessed (usually downward), bad risks are liquidated and ownership rights are clarified.[123] If the relationship between the foundational value of collateral and the aspirational promise of credit can seem tenuous, even infinitely elastic, in the throes of asset appreciation, it appears as slavishly referential when the bubble deflates, tethering credit back to the mooring points of "real values" and stable ownership rights. At stake here, however, is not so much a return to underlying fundamentals (as if the value of assets could be reliably ascertained outside the context of appreciating or depreciating expectations), as a positive reassertion of foundation on new and suitably purified terms. This dynamic helps to explain why the borrowers who survived the credit crunch were those who already held secure collateral in the form of actual housing assets not those who entered the market late in the game, relying on unpredictable wages to claim the virtual wealth of a mortgaged house; and why the housing boom ended up exacerbating the maldistribution of wealth rather than diminishing it.[124] If expanding credit at first seemed to free borrowers from the tyranny of family wealth, in the last instance it ended up reinforcing it, especially for those at the lower end of the income and wealth scale.

It is hardly surprising, then, that the demand for recognition of same-sex marriage—along with its legal forms of property transmission—asserted itself at the precise moment when queers were being welcomed into the market for consumer credit. How long, after all, can one sustain a lifestyle on credit without some long-term accumulation of wealth sufficient to provide collateral? And what use is the accumulation of wealth without some assurance that it will not be expropriated by strangers? If Butler could argue, in the wake of the AIDS crisis, that gay men as a "class" were defined by their exclusion from the family as the legal form of property transmission, these same men were now loudly demanding the recognition of their relationships as legitimate units of reproduction and inheritance. The question of legitimate reproduction—and inheritance more generally—has been central to campaigns in favor of same-sex marriage. Not only has the jurisprudence of same-sex marriage revived the old, discredited distinction between legitimate and illegitimate children (effectively reiterating the revival of such distinctions in recent welfare reform),[125] it has also placed the question of property transmission at the heart of its appeals for legal recognition.

As legal scholars have long noted, inheritance (particularly when it is enacted without the validation of a will) remains doggedly attached to traditional notions of the family and will almost invariably privilege legally recognized forms of kinship over partners of choice or affection.[126] If queer wealth holders are to secure some form of legal right to bequeath their assets, their relationships need to be validated as "family like" and endowed with the same degree of legitimacy as heterosexual marriage. It is far from coincidental, then, that when the Defense of Marriage Act (DOMA) was finally overturned it was in a case involving the unequal effects of the estate tax on gay and lesbian couples.[127] As we have seen, the estate tax is only likely to affect the wealthiest of couples and has no impact at all on the vast majority of gay and lesbian relationships. And yet the expansion of consumer credit has so thoroughly generalized the aspirational investment in inherited wealth that estate tax reform is increasingly popular among a wide swath of gay and lesbian voters, and has in recent years become central to efforts by the Human Rights Campaign and other advocacy groups to redefine "non-normative" citizens as legitimate credit risks and bearers of wealth.[128] Here we can see how the legal recognition of non-normative relationships demands the literal reinvention of tradition—that is, the inclusion of once criminalized relationships within the ambit of legitimate reproduction.

By any standard, the terrain traversed by queer politics over the last three decades has been extreme, moving as it has from the radical antinormativity of ACT UP and Queer Nation to the reproductive legitimacy of the same-sex marriage campaign. We live in an era where normativity itself no longer appears to play the overwhelmingly exclusionary—and hence central—role it once did in the regulation of sexuality in the mid- to late twentieth century, despite its prominence as a concept in contemporary queer studies. The fact of non-normative sexuality is no longer defined as criminal or pathological by the social sciences; nor is it likely to trigger a whole series of medical and psychiatric interventions on the part of the welfare state and its allied institutions (although these older forms of social stigmatization are now being rapidly replaced by new kinds of religiously inflected moral exclusion).

We live at a time where the public affirmation of one's status as a homosexual will no longer automatically exclude a person from employment, credit, or housing (which is not to say that homophobia no longer exists—far from it). In the spirit of Foucault's periodization of power, in fact, we might classify this period as postnormative—if we take normativity to refer to the precise forms of statistical exclusion that accompanied and shaped the Fordist family wage, along with their epistemological expression in the biological, psychological, and social sciences, where different kinds of sexuality were once overwhelmingly defined in terms of pathological deviance. In this sense, perhaps, Foucault was right to see the advent of neoliberalism as marking the passage toward a postnormative formation of power, where we find "an optimization of systems of difference" rather than their subordination to the norm.[129]

But this is also an era in which relationships of any kind are increasingly required to justify themselves within the framework of legitimate reproduction. In many but not all social contexts, non-normative sexuality is now much more likely to be accepted, as long as the attendant transmission of biological and economic assets—that is, children and wealth—is appropriately legitimated within the form of marriage. The socially meaningful dividing line, in other words, appears to have shifted from the normative and non-normative expression of sexuality to the legitimate or illegitimate relationship, as legally validated marriage fast becomes a prerequisite for the recognition of minimal social rights. At the same time, the most virulent new forms of homophobia are increasingly turning to the language of moral, divine law (rather than social scientific normativity) to contest the public expression of non-heterosexual desire, an issue we will return to in Chapter 7. Here again it is a question of legitimacy and its sources, divine or secular, rather than the distribution of norms. Perhaps then we need to question the continuing prominence of the term "normativity" within contemporary discussions of sexual politics. What is at stake in debates around same-sex marriage, after all, is not so much homonormativity as homolegitimacy—a demand for inclusion that is at once radically antinormative and relentlessly traditionalist[130]—and on the opposing side, not so much heteronormativity as a vision of morality grounded in the theological language of natural law.

CHAPTER FIVE

The Price of Promiscuity:
The Chicago School Confronts AIDS

From society's point of view, an unattached person is an accident
waiting to happen. The burdens of contingency are likely to fall,
immediately and sometimes crushingly, on people—relatives, friends,
neighbors—who have enough problems of their own, and then on
charities and welfare agencies.... All by itself, marriage is society's
first and, often, second and third line of support for the troubled
individual. A husband or wife is the social worker of first resort, the
psychiatrist of first resort, the cop and counselor and insurer and nurse
and 911 operate of first resort.
—Jonathan Rauch, *Gay Marriage*

What is the role of public intervention in the face of a health crisis
caused in large part by private actions between consenting adults?
This is the question posed by Richard Posner and Tomas Philipson,
two leading exponents of the Chicago law and economics school, in
a work on the AIDS epidemic published in 1993.[1] A prime example
of the strategic economics imperialism of the Chicago school, law
and economics is a methodology that sets out to apply the precepts of
rational economic behavior to all areas of social life, including that of
law. Its institutional success, first at Chicago, then at elite law schools
across the United States, and subsequently within the entire Anglo-
American legal curriculum, owes much to the background work

of Aaron Director, a key figure in the early development of Chicago school economics. Its epistemic and judicial impact owes more to the academic contributions of Ronald Coase, whose classic 1960 text on the problem of social cost served to undermine the commonsense acceptance of welfare state capitalism, and Richard Posner, a Reagan-era appointee to the United States Court of Appeals for the Seventh Circuit and prolific writer whose numerous books have done much to popularize law and economics among the general public.[2]

The law and economics approach proceeds on the assumption that all areas of social life—including sexuality—can be analyzed as a market in which "prices" are not only economic indicators but also measures of risk. "Such work is premised on the view that people do not leave off acting rationally—do not suddenly cease responding to incentives—when they leave the marketplace and go home, or for that matter (we would add), to a singles bar, a homosexual bathhouse, or a 'shooting gallery' where addicts inject themselves with needles shared among strangers."[3] Even "nonmarket markets" can be analyzed according to this model, if we consider that all transactions involve a calculation of the shadow price (or risk) associated with any given sexual act. "We shall, in short, be proceeding on the assumption that the market for risky sexual 'trades' (or, what is similar, for the sharing of hypodermic needles that have not been decontaminated) is, in its relevant features, much like other markets that economists study. The question is only to make clear that our analysis is not limited to prostitution; we refer to 'trade' in the standard economic sense of an activity perceived as mutually beneficial to the persons involved in it."[4] We must assume, for example, that individuals who engage in unprotected sex with full knowledge of the risks of HIV have done so after rationally calculating the costs and benefits involved: "The shadow price of engaging in unsafe sex is the expected cost, both pecuniary and nonpecuniary (with the latter dominant in this example) of becoming infected with the AIDS virus. It is another form of accident, or, like a disease caused by smoking, another form of avoidable illness."[5] Unsafe sex, in short, is a lifestyle choice, but one that responds perfectly to the mathematics of rational expectation.

Posner and Philipson begin by asking whether the AIDS epidemic is really the monumental public health catastrophe it is made out to be. "Most people who write about AIDS," they remark, "believe that it is the public health crisis of the twentieth century and requires massive public health intervention on both the regulatory and fiscal fronts."[6] At the time Posner and Philipson were writing, in the early 1990s, during the Republican administration of George H. W. Bush, many still believed that the United States had done far from enough to stem the spread of AIDS. The failure of the Reagan administration to respond to the epidemic with any kind of comprehensive prevention campaign was a scandal not only to progressives but also to more than a few conservatives within Reagan's inner circle. In October 1986, Surgeon General Everett Koop—an anti-choice Christian conservative who had been carefully selected for the task by the Reagan administration—delivered an unexpectedly scathing report on Reagan's public health record. Koop concluded his report by urging the government to fund a sexually explicit AIDS prevention campaign and to abandon punitive interventions such as mandatory testing and the use of quarantine. In June 1988, a presidential commission on AIDS headed by the social conservative Admiral James D. Watkins released a further report calling on the government to dramatically increase the public resources it devoted to AIDS and blaming underfunding of the health-care system as a whole for the current state of the crisis.[7] Both reports were promptly buried at the instigation of Christian conservatives and supply-siders within the Reagan administration.

As neoliberals, Posner and Philipson stood in a complex relationship to Reagan's political circles. Unlike several of Reagan's social conservative advisors, Posner and Philipson were vehemently opposed to any revival of the old public health tradition and its paternalist measures. In their view, normative judgments about sexual deviance or perversion were counterproductive to the smooth functioning of markets: as a quasi-market replete with shadow prices, the arena of sexual trades functioned most efficiently when it was free from the state regulations of quarantine or mandatory testing.[8] Michel Foucault was one of the first to point to the radical antinormativity of the Chicago school neoliberals; just as they rejected the disciplinary and regulatory institutions of the twentieth-century welfare state as so many barriers to the efficient functioning of market logics, neoliberal theorists such as Friedman, Becker, and Posner were methodologically indifferent to the normative categories of the twentieth-century social sciences and their allied disciplines. They thus found themselves somewhat unexpectedly aligned with the New Left.[9]

Yet Posner and Philipson were in complete agreement with Reagan that the social costs, and therefore the urgency of a concerted, federal-level public health response to the AIDS epidemic, had been greatly exaggerated. Taking into account the limited life expectancy of AIDS patients in the early 1990s and the correspondingly foreshortened burden on public welfare programs such as Medicaid, they calculated that the AIDS crisis might in fact have saved the state money in terms of long-term Social Security payments. Those who were dying of AIDS in the greatest numbers tended on average to be young but poor and relatively unproductive (aside from being ill, many of them were drug users); the state therefore would have lost relatively little in terms of productive working years from their premature deaths.[10] According to Posner and Philipson, the costs of the disease were likely to be self-limiting. "Despite the great suffering that AIDS has engendered, the net external costs of the disease—the focus of the *economic* case for public intervention—might be relatively modest were the disease left to run its course without public intervention."[11]

More important, for Posner and Philipson, was the fact that the peculiar mode of transmission of the HIV virus tended to limit, by its very nature, the kinds of external social costs commonly associated with communicable disease in the public health tradition. "Unlike most communicable diseases, AIDS is spread primarily by voluntary intimate contact between human beings."[12] Apart from the limit cases of rape and contaminated blood transfusion, the HIV virus is the result of voluntary sexual contact between consenting adults and thus represents the very prototype of the rational transaction and the freely assumed risk. Public health economists, Posner and Philipson observed, "have tended to regard communicable disease as a textbook case of negative externality,"[13] that is, an exchange of pathogens that generates social costs beyond the strict bounds of the consensual transaction, and have therefore tended to advocate state intervention as a necessary response. The social costs of tuberculosis, for example, cannot be internalized by the use of private contracts that would limit the effects of sneezing in public to freely consenting parties. Nor can waterborne disease that flows through public waterways and pipes be confined within the limits of the contract. Even by the admission of Posner and Philipson, the classical public health externalities of involuntary infection necessitate some kind of collective response, however limited.

Yet HIV is different, they argue, in the sense that it is most often transmitted through voluntary acts of unprotected sex or needle exchange. At least since 1984, when the virus and its mode of transmission was first ascertained, we can assume that most of those who have contracted AIDS have done so as the result of a freely assumed cost-benefit calculus. The HIV-infected have no doubt calculated "that the cost of reducing the risk of the disease to zero through a change in behavior [is] greater than the expected cost in disease, disability and death of the risk itself."[14] We may marvel at the fact that some place so low a price on the risk of infection (that African American women and drug users, for example, seem to "have above average discount rates or derive little utility from living")[15] but in no way should we be so paternalistic as to limit their freedom to assume risks. Clearly, such risk-takers have reasoned that the immediate rewards of pleasure maximization are greater than the long-term costs of infection and have acted accordingly. Why then should the state be expected to insure their choices? Why should the intimate and personal costs of private transactions between freely consenting adults be redistributed among the public? For Posner and Philipson, the risks of HIV transmission are fully internal to the markets in unsafe sex or intravenous drug use and should therefore be privately assumed by those who participate in them. As long as it poses no substantial social costs, the freedom to take sexual risks should never be limited or regulated by state paternalism, but nor should it be reinsured by the state in the form of subsidized health care, public education programs, or federally funded research. We are all of us free to assume—or shun—the risks of sexual pleasure and each of us is individually responsible for the risks we have chosen to bear.

But having rejected the paternalism of the old public health model, Posner and Philipson somewhat surprisingly go on to outline a specifically utilitarian argument against promiscuity and in favor of monogamy. The public health response to the AIDS epidemic is not only unwarranted, they argue, it is also likely to generate "perverse incentives" of its own. While individual preferences are always "rational" and never "perverse" within a law and economic perspective, incentives themselves can sometimes be considered "perverse," particularly when they approximate those of the welfare state.[16] The problem is posed as one of "moral hazard": When the state subsidizes health care for those who have voluntarily assumed the risks of infection, it ends up lowering the price of high-risk behavior and endorsing irresponsible lifestyle choices such as promiscuity or addiction. The law of large numbers dictates that any public health intervention that fails to condemn promiscuity will increase the probability of unsafe sex acts or accidents (broken condoms for example) and hence lead to an increase in HIV infection. "Anything that lowers the costs of sex will increase the amount of it, and an increase in the amount of sexual activity will increase the incidence of AIDS, provided that at least some of the activity is unsafe."[17] This is where Posner and Philipson identify a problem with publicly funded safe sex campaigns. Since the promotion of safe sex implicitly condones promiscuity, this in turn will tend to generate higher rates of seroprevalence through the sheer statistical likelihood of accidental contamination. At least on this issue, Posner and Philipson concede, the moral conservatives have a point, although they insist that their own aversion to promiscuity derives entirely from a utilitarian concern with minimizing state healthcare expenditures.[18] The regulatory response to public health externalities is ultimately counterproductive; in its efforts to insure social risks, whether through direct social insurance or the state funding of prevention programs, the state creates more social costs than would otherwise exist under competitive free market conditions. Insuring irresponsible lifestyle choices begets more of the same.

How then should the state intervene, if at all, to counter such perverse incentives? What should the government do to counter the undesirable effects of its own interventions? Here Posner and Philipson come up with a regulatory response to externalities that is axiomatic within the neoliberal literature but rarely acknowledged or analyzed as part of its economic discourse on market failure: To counteract the social costs of unsafe sex, they argue, the state would do well to limit its interventions to *promoting marriage*. While skeptical about the utility of using tax money to subsidize safe sex and prevention campaigns then, Posner and Philipson are enthusiastic about the prospects of marriage as a way of limiting the health and economic costs of HIV. And they are some of the earliest to advocate the legalization of same-sex marriage as a way of reducing the exorbitant costs of promiscuity in the gay male community.[19] While at present the social costs of AIDS are borne by the public in the form of Medicaid and other health services, they note, the recognition of same-sex marriage would return at least some of these externalities to the private household, forcing individual risk-takers to internalize the costs of their own actions and transforming public risks into private responsibilities.

Posner and Philipson anticipate that the legal recognition of same-sex marriage would help to internalize the costs of AIDS on two fronts: biomedical and economic. First, by placing a premium on monogamy, marriage would increase the psychological costs of promiscuous sex and thus decrease the average rate of infection. But it would also internalize economic costs by transferring at least some of the burdens of care onto a spouse. In an earlier text, Posner refers to the "insurance function of marriage," pointing to the fact that marriage is expected to serve as a form of risk protection in those social contexts "where kinship has receded but market and social insurance is not yet common" (or, we might add, has significantly diminished). This "insurance function" of marriage, he writes, "arises from the fact that the correlation of spouses' health and other welfare factors is less than one, so given a mutual obligation of support and assistance, marriage serves as a form of health, hunger, and life insurance."[20] Ultimately, then, Posner and Philipson identify the legal institution of marriage as a substitute for social insurance and the most efficient means of minimizing the social costs of health care. In this way, the neoliberal critique of normativity ends up endorsing an alternative form of moral philosophy—one that restores the private family and its legal obligations of care to a foundational role in the free-market order.

Here we encounter an aspect of neoliberalism that eludes the terms of Foucault's now classic analysis. Neoliberals may well be in favor of the decriminalization of drugs, sodomy, bathhouses, and prostitution and are adamantly opposed to the kind of normative police powers that regulated or outlawed such practices under the mid-twentieth century welfare state. Yet, their apparent moral indifference comes with the proviso that the costs of such behavior must be fully borne in private. Posner himself is at pains to make clear that "libertarian" is not the same thing as "libertine" or "free love" (interestingly enough, referring to Foucault's late work on the *Use of Pleasure* as the perfect example of such a non-normative, yet non-libertarian ethics).[21] The antinormativity of Chicago school neoliberalism is contingent upon a moral philosophy of prudential risk management that leaves no excess costs to the state. This double allegiance finds expression in the idea that non-normative sexual relationships must ultimately be channeled into the legal form of marriage.

NEOLIBERALISM AGAINST SOCIAL INSURANCE

Idiosyncratic as the views of Posner and Philipson might at first appear, they are strictly consonant with the wider critique of social insurance that has been developed and refined by Chicago school neo-liberals since the late 1960s. In a public conversation now dominated by the assumptions of neoliberal reason, it is disconcerting to recall the very different forms of common sense shared by orthodox economists of a previous generation. For many of the leading economists of the mid-twentieth century, however, the idea that social insurance repre-sented the most efficient means of addressing social risks was a given. Together, neoclassical welfare economists such as A. C. Pigou and neo-Keynesians such as Kenneth Arrow and Paul Samuelson helped to popularize the idea that certain kinds of "externalities," whether posi-tive or negative, were best managed by the state via regulation, state licensing laws, or taxation.[22] These representatives of pre- and postwar economic orthodoxy articulated their defense of the welfare state in the neoclassical language of social utility and efficiency, a compromise that allowed them to "formally justify the economic legitimacy of gov-ernment intervention while still pledging allegiance to the iconic neo-classical model of free markets."[23] In the face of market failure, they argued, public goods such as airwaves, transport infrastructure, or health care were best distributed by the state, while social harms such as pollution, car accidents, or illness were most efficiently dealt with by state regulation or taxation. The simplest solution to the unavoidable accidents of industrial life was the collectivization and redistribution of these risks via social insurance.

Neoclassical welfare economists were slow to address the specific question of health insurance, but when they did so, provided crucial arguments for the expansion of collective health care (in the form of Medicaid and Medicare) in the postwar era. In 1963, Kenneth Arrow was commissioned by the Ford Foundation to provide an economist's perspective on the problem of uncertainty in medical markets. After reviewing the peculiar characteristics of healthcare risks and noting the persistent failure of commercial markets to insure them, Arrow concluded that the "welfare case for insurance policies of all kinds [was] overwhelming"; the American government should therefore assume a much greater role in underwriting the healthcare risks of its citizens.[24] By redistributing the costs of unpredictable illness events among a broad group of people, he argued, the law of large numbers tended to diminish the average individual burden of health care, allowing even the poorest and sickest of citizens to access care they might otherwise have forgone. In so doing, social insurance resulted in "a net social gain which [might] be of considerable magnitude."[25]

Neoclassical theories of market failure were well established, even hegemonic, by the 1960s. The dominant paradigm in postwar American economics, the so-called neoclassical synthesis combining neoclassical microeconomics with Keynesian macroeconomic theory, articulated a powerful defense of government intervention in the face of market failure. But it is also during this decade that a concerted offensive against neoclassical welfare economics began to take shape. What we now refer to as American neoliberalism emerged out of the Chicago school of law and economics, the Virginia school of public choice theory, their various satellite schools throughout the United

States, and the more institutionally marginal American Hayekians, all of whom, despite their differences, evinced a common aversion to the expanding reach of New Deal social insurance.[26] Much like their neo-Keynesian counterparts, neoliberal economists and legal theorists spoke the idiom of neoclassical economics, but they combined this with a return to classical liberal principles of competitive markets, freedom of contract, and private tort law, which they sought to mobilize against the growing influence of welfare economics and public interest law in American political life. Even as they adopted the same formal language as postwar neo-Keynesians then, neoliberals sought to reinsert the analytics of risk within "the punitive and contractual framework that characterized nineteenth century [tort] law," with its related notions of strict personal responsibility, retribution, and fault.[27]

In 1968, the public-choice economist Mark Pauly published a brief response to Kenneth Arrow that would redefine the conversation around health insurance over the following decades.[28] Written in a deceptively unassuming style, Pauly's article simply and bluntly reversed Arrow's conclusions by invoking the now ubiquitous concept of "moral hazard."[29] Much like other consumer products, Pauly insisted, demand for health care is not a constant that can be calculated with reference to social justice or public health principles but a variable that responds haphazardly to the fluctuations of supply. Public health insurance distorts the true—that is, equilibrium- or competitive-market—price of health care by shifting the costs from the risk-prone to the risk-averse. When the costs of health care are redistributed across a large risk pool, it is in the interest of each individual to consume as much medical care as possible, with the paradoxical result that healthcare premiums are raised for all subscribers. Public health insurance, Pauly concluded, generates a problem of moral hazard that fatally compromises its aims, resulting in a net welfare loss rather than a gain.

The problem of moral hazard, moreover, extends also to the psychological effects of social insurance, as Posner pointed out in an influential review of the work of legal theorist, Guido Calabresi, on the social costs of accidents. Here Posner argued that social insurance shields the individual from the true costs of his or her behavior and thus distorts the otherwise bracing psychological effects of risk in a competitive free-market environment.[30] The classical liberal solution for managing the costs of accidents—private tort law and common law litigation—may well appear inefficient by the technocratic standards of the modern welfare state, but it at least has the virtue of inspiring personal responsibility. Social insurance, on the other hand, actively discourages the classical liberal virtues of prudence and self-care by subsidizing the costs of high-risk behavior.

Given what he saw as the overwhelming problem of moral hazard, Pauly concluded that the government should play a limited role in underwriting risk and instead delegate this role to private insurers, who in turn should be allowed to price each customer individually, on the basis of his or her risk profile. Far from suffering from an underdeveloped welfare state, Americans were *overinsured*.[31] Taking this argument to its logical conclusion, Pauly suggested that commercial failure to insure certain risks must be accepted as the final and irrevocable judgment of the market: some risks are simply *uninsurable* and should be left in the residual actuarial category of the "act of God."[32] In the medium term, however, he recommended a number of practical reforms to the insurance market. Insurers, for instance, should be allowed to transfer the true costs of risk-taking back to the consumer: subscribers with preexisting conditions should be asked to pay higher premiums; user fees such as deductibles and copayments should be implemented to give consumers an incentive to modify their behavior; and consumers considered to be high-risk (as gay men would later be) should be priced accordingly or excluded as uninsurable.[33] To do otherwise would be to unfairly burden the risk-averse with the costs of others' irresponsible behavior. If public welfare and insurance schemes such as Medicaid and Medicare were to be maintained at all, they should be designed to act only as insurers of last resort for emergency health care and "catastrophic risk" (that is, risk deemed unprofitable and thus uninsurable by private interests).[34]

The economic problem of "moral hazard," Pauly insisted, has "little to do with morality" as it is conventionally understood. It simply represents the logical expression of "rational economic behavior" in the face of perverse incentives: When the consequences of risk-taking are insured by the state, it is in the rational interest of the consumer to engage in irresponsible behavior.[35] Yet the neoliberal argument against social insurance does not so easily escape the charge of moralism, since it returns us, inescapably, to the logic of nineteenth-century tort law, with its attendant moral categories of personal responsibility, fault, and desert.[36] Indeed, neoliberal legal theorists explicitly revive the notion, foundational to classical tort law, that freedom of contract implies the voluntary assumption of risk. *Volenti non fit injuria*—to he who has consented no wrong can be done—is the legal translation of the idea that risk, once consented to, must be borne entirely by the individual, unless one can prove fraud or duress in the performance of a contract.[37] Crucially, this optic interprets self-inflicted harm as equivalent to consensual harm and thus without hope of redress. One must assume the price of one's own choices: Unless one can prove explicit fault or negligence by a contractual counterparty, the "fault" of irresponsible behavior is all one's own and thus deserved.

It is in deference to this principle that Posner and Philipson formulate their policy response to the AIDS epidemic, a response that draws a sharp distinction between those who were unknowingly exposed to the risks of HIV infection prior to the discovery of the virus and those who assumed the risks with full knowledge of its mode of transmission. If Posner and Philipson are willing to allow a case for state intervention on behalf of the unwitting victims of AIDS infection, they are adamant that most AIDS patients must assume full responsibility for their own choices. In any case, they muse, with each passing year "the fraction of AIDS victims who became infected before enough was known about the disease to enable avoidance by behavioral changes—the victims whose plight makes the strongest case for publicly financed AIDS research as a form of social insurance—declines."[38] Involuntary exposure may well justify government intervention against the market failures of private healthcare markets, but when risk is consented to, the costs are all one's own. Private insurers are well within their rights to exclude the HIV-infected from their healthcare policies, since exposure to HIV through consensual sex or drug use is a voluntary risk whose costs must be assumed by the individual.[39] From the point of view of competitive healthcare markets, those who have willingly submitted to the risks of HIV infection lie outside the bounds of the insurable.

DEINSTITUTIONALIZATION:
HOW NEOLIBERALISM ASSIMILATED THE NEW LEFT

AIDS was first observed, although not officially named or identified as stemming from a virus, in 1981, a time of profound upheaval in the American healthcare system.[40] President Reagan was elected in 1980, vowing to control rapidly inflating healthcare costs, rationalize healthcare delivery, and drastically cut federal budgets to welfare and social insurance programs such as Medicare and Medicaid. From the vantage point of the early 1980s, it must have been difficult to recall that barely a decade previously, President Nixon had been on the verge of implementing a national health insurance program.[41] The political force of the labor movement was so strong at this point that Nixon was perpetually waging a "rearguard action" to assimilate and moderate the more radical plans of his opponents to the left, while even traditional opponents of social insurance such as the American Medical

Association (AMA) and private insurers were so resigned to the idea that they sponsored proposals of their own.[42]

The 1970s witnessed a profusion of parastate healthcare experiments ranging from the women's healthcare movement to the Black Panther free healthcare clinics and various countercultural initiatives providing everything from sexual health services to recreational drug care. These experiments were contiguous to and in some cases directly enabled by Johnson's Great Society agenda—itself an exercise in federal deinstitutionalization that sought to undercut the entrenched power structures of municipal and state government by delegating power to "local communities." In 1965, the United States Office of Economic Opportunity or OEO, the body responsible for administering Great Society poverty programs, began distributing grants to hospitals, health departments, and nonprofits to create "neighborhood health centers" in low-income areas throughout the country. Inspired by the most progressive currents in the American public health tradition, these health centers "embodied ideas that had been espoused by healthcare reformers since the early twentieth century, including concepts of comprehensive health care, social medicine and community participation" and sought to deliver high-quality health care to the most impoverished sections of the population.[43] The federal government had never before invested so much money in the progressive tradition of American social medicine. Yet as valuable and enabling as these federal programs were, the New Left's healthcare movement very quickly outran the strictures of Great Society liberalism, generating a plethora of initiatives that had a much more antagonistic relationship to the state.

The Black Panther healthcare movement, for instance, evolved out of a critique of the War on Poverty and its failure to deliver anything other than token reform, even though many of those who helped set up the Black Panther clinics had been and indeed remained actively involved in the Great Society's neighborhood health centers.[44] Drawing on the professional and sometimes material resources provided by the institutional healthcare sector, the Black Panthers sought to distinguish their efforts from Johnson's neighborhood health centers by locating their clinics outside the walls of the public teaching hospital, a space associated with endemic racism, and combining political mobilization with the provision of health care. The relationship between these clinics and the state was a subject of intense debate within and outside the movement. Most Black Panther clinics refused to apply for federal or state funding and instead relied on skill sharing by medical professionals and regular donations of discarded medical supplies. But this also limited the scope of their services to primary and preventative care and obliged them to refer more difficult cases back to the institutional healthcare sector (a fate avoided by at least one Black Panther clinic, based in Portland, which broke ranks by successfully applying for a mix of state, federal, and private funding).[45] At the same time, federal administrators were variously alarmed by a movement that seemed to be siphoning government resources toward overtly militant initiatives and impressed by the ability of the Black Panthers to actually deliver the kind of self-managed services envisaged by the War on Poverty. The Black Panthers were kept under intense surveillance by the FBI, even while federal administrators sometimes tried to persuade them to contract their healthcare services to the state.[46]

Although its politics were at times diametrically opposed to those of the Black Panthers—notably on the issue of abortion[47]—the women's health movement practiced a similar ethic of political disobedience vis-à-vis the state. Feminist healthcare activists challenged the paternalism of a medical profession dominated by men and the inordinate power of the medical sector to define and limit women's sexual and reproductive experiences.[48] These activists came into open conflict with the authority of the AMA when they advocated home birth and lay midwifery as alternatives to the medicalized experience of childbirth. They were forced to work beyond the limits of the law when they challenged the power of the state to regulate women's sexuality though anti-abortion laws. In the late 1960s, activists involved in the Chicago Women's Liberation Union learned how to perform abortions and were reportedly carrying out up to fifty procedures a week by the time of the *Roe vs. Wade* decision in 1973.[49]

Less well known but no less consequential in light of the subsequent history of AIDS service activism was the network of gay healthcare clinics set up in major cities throughout the 1970s.[50] In Chicago, gay medical students opened up the Howard Brown Health Center in 1974 and used it as a base from which to send a mobile STD-testing van around to bars and bathhouses. And in Boston, with its well-established feminist health movement, gay and lesbian health activists took over the Fenway community healthcare center in 1975 where they provided various classes and services including a free once-a-week VD clinic. Such initiatives were notable not only for their commitment to "self-care" outside the boundaries of the medical institution but also because they refused to valorize sexual health over sexual desire. The publications produced by these early gay health initiatives offer some of the earliest articulations of "safe sex" education, where the goal is to minimize harm without sacrificing pleasure.

Together, these heterogeneous liberation fronts spearheaded a general movement of insurrection against the "total institutions" (Goffman) and "disciplinary powers" (Foucault) of the twentieth-century social sciences—the mental hospitals, prisons, homes for the disabled, the delinquent and deviant that were responsible for defining and policing notions of sexual and racial variance.[51] With gathering momentum, these movements challenged the epistemic power of professional elites to pathologize non-normative experience and called for the radical deinstitutionalization of care. Their critique had a lasting impact on the landscape of social welfare, forcing professional monopolies to retreat, regroup, and in the last instance, reinvent themselves. Where Cold War interest groups such as the homophile movement merely sought to neutralize the stigma of deviance, the new liberation movements challenged the very legitimating function of the norm and its status within the social and clinical sciences. It was in this spirit of radical critique that the gay liberation movement launched a successful campaign to remove homosexuality from the American Psychiatric Association's list of mental illnesses in the early 1970s. For these activists, homosexuality was no longer a psychopathology or deviation from the medical norm but simply a different practice of sexuality—a style of life among others.[52]

It is important to stress, however, that the antinormativity of these movements never implied a rejection of social insurance as such. Indeed, the new liberation movements were in a very direct sense enabled and invigorated by the democratization of social insurance that had occurred in the mid-1960s, when Social Security was extended to Fordism's nonstandard workers and public health care reached the indigent, the disabled, and the aged. The health activists of the New Left remained committed to the expansion of government-funded care and universal health insurance, even while they fought to dismantle the disciplinary forms in which these services were delivered.[53] If they were intent on banishing the taxonomic function of the norm—the norm as a statistical means of cataloguing the standard human subject and his deviations in morphological and psychopathological terms—they simultaneously sought to extend social insurance beyond the limits of the family wage—that is, to incorporate the non-normal risk within the calculative logic of social protections. Ultimately, perhaps, such a project was not possible or practicable within the limits of the Keynesian administrative state and in the long run would have required a complete rethinking of the forms and practices of social risk protection. Yet we misrepresent the historical specificity of these movements if we focus exclusively on their anti-institutional critique and fail to recognize their efforts to radicalize the imaginary of social redistribution.[54] It was this combination of redistributive and antinormative objectives, after all, that made these movements so threatening to the New Deal consensus, ultimately catalyzing the formation of the neoliberal–social conservative alliance.

In 1970, the combined political force of trade union and New Left advocates of universal health insurance held Nixon in its grip, forcing him to the left on almost all social welfare issues. Nixon looked poised to usher in a long-awaited and much-needed program of universal health insurance. Yet, only a few years into his tenure, these reforms were looking decidedly less certain, as the prospect of spiraling inflation brought Nixon's conservative advisers to the fore and the Nixon presidency itself descended into scandal. President Ford, who had entered office proclaiming his intention to push forward with universal health insurance, ended up shelving the project indefinitely as employers complained of impossible healthcare costs.[55] Ford's abdication proved to be the final blow, definitively banishing universal health insurance from the political agenda for many years to come.

In this newly austere context, the neoliberal critique of social insurance moved beyond the walls of academia to find a receptive audience among policymakers and public health specialists. And over the next few years, the muted ethic of moral hazard, fault, and responsibility that informed neoliberalism's academic critiques of the welfare state found more fulsome expression in a new public health rhetoric focused on irresponsible lifestyle choices and rising healthcare costs. In 1976, the Task Force on Health Promotion and Consumer Health Education (sponsored by the very respectable National Institutes of Health and American College of Preventive Medicine) stressed the "overriding importance of individual behavior and lifestyle as major factors in the nation's unsatisfactory health status and ever-rising health care bill."[56] Writing in the neoconservative *Public Interest*, the bioethicist Leon Kass went so far as to blame the inflation of healthcare costs on the unintended consequences of no-fault insurance. "All the proposals for National Health Insurance," he remarked, "embrace, without qualification, the no-fault principle. They therefore choose to ignore, or to treat as irrelevant, the importance of personal responsibility for the state of one's health. As a result, they pass up an opportunity to build both positive and negative inducements into the insurance payment plan, by measures such as refusing or reducing benefits for chronic respiratory disease care to persons who continue to smoke."[57] By blaming irresponsible lifestyle choices on the existence of social insurance, Kass, like other neoconservatives, implied that health-care inflation was foremost a moral affliction that would be best overcome by reintroducing notions of fault into the everyday practice of risk management.

Having emerged from the margins of economic and public health orthodoxy at the beginning of the 1970s, the neoliberal critique of social insurance had acquired something akin to common-sense status by the end of the decade. The plausibility of the neoliberal healthcare reform agenda can be credited, at least in part, to its willingness to accommodate the leftist critique of institutional health care while simultaneously neutralizing leftist arguments in favor of social redistribution.[58] Thus, the New Left challenge to the authority of the medical profession was translated by neoliberal reformers into an unrelenting attack on the "monopoly powers" of the AMA and private practice physicians. Deinstitutionalization now appeared as an excellent method for outsourcing care to the home and a perfect rationale for substituting the unpaid labor of the private carer for the waged labor of the medical professional. Even prepaid group practice, once considered a slightly subversive experiment in cooperative health care and bitterly challenged by the AMA, was now embraced as an organizational model capable of rationalizing healthcare costs—in the guise of the HMO or Health Maintenance Organization—and touted as the most efficient means of introducing competitive forces into the healthcare market. The cooperative, antihierarchical healthcare practices once envisaged by the left were now to be managed by for-profit companies that saw them as an ideal method for reducing expenditures.

The field of public health, once inseparable from the theory of social medicine, was not immune to the influence of neoliberal health economics, and in the 1970s it began to revise many of its founding assumptions. By this time, it was becoming clear to epidemiologists that in wealthier societies infectious diseases were giving way to noncommunicable diseases as the leading cause of illness and that many of these could be linked to avoidable behavior such as overeating, smoking, or lack of exercise. Moreover, it seemed that many of the residual infectious diseases that continued to affect wealthier populations (in particular, asymptomatic and undetected STDs) were linked to unprotected sex. In much the same way that neoliberal critiques of public health focused on the limit case of the self-induced harm, public health policies began to orient themselves around the problem of "lifestyle choice" and its presumed social costs. The president of the Rockefeller Foundation, once the leading philanthropic player in international public health, complained that "the cost of sloth, gluttony, alcoholic intemperance, reckless driving, sexual frenzy, and smoking is now a national, and not an individual responsibility. This is justified as individual freedom—but one man's freedom in health is another man's shackle in taxes and insurance premiums."[59] Even long-time advocates of universal health insurance began to wonder out loud if inflating healthcare costs could be attributed to the "prevailing hedonistic lifestyle" of affluent Americans and if responsible taxpayers should be expected to bear the cost of such lifestyle choices.[60] In Canada (1974), the United Kingdom (1976), and the United States (1979), health authorities called for the expansion of public health interventions beyond traditional medical and surgical care to encompass preventative measures targeting personal behavior and unhealthy lifestyles.[61] No longer should these interventions focus on the statistical risk—the risk that could be abstracted from will or fault or negligence—but on self-inflicted harms that could be attributed entirely to the volition of the individual. Daniel Wikler, a critic of this shift in public health priorities, summarizes the consequences of this new ethic: "If we become sick or disabled as a result of neglecting to take care of ourselves, or by having taken undue risks, then dealing with these health needs should be seen as personal rather than social responsibilities and as such should not be considered on a par with other, unavoidable, health needs."[62]

The question of whether or not one has voluntarily assumed and thus consented to risk becomes decisive within this optic. Social insurance, if it is to become economically sustainable, should be limited to covering illness events that occur independently of the will of the insured; one should not expect the public health system to redistribute the costs of voluntary risks. Without abolishing social insurance altogether then, the neoliberal critique of public health eats away at the edges of redistributive health care by introducing the distinction between the deserving and the undeserving ill, the faultless victim and the self-harming risk-taker, into the calculus of social harms. The person who has inflicted harm on himself by engaging in an imprudent lifestyle must be assumed to have taken this risk knowingly and is by definition unworthy of compensation.

THE POLITICS OF SELF-CARE: AIDS IN THE REAGAN ERA

The AIDS epidemic could hardly have emerged at a less propitious time in the recent history of public health. In the early 1980s, municipal governments had endured more than a decade of inflating social service costs and were in the full throes of a fiscal crisis induced by the Volcker shock. The mass redundancies brought about by recession meant that the number of people without private insurance was growing at a vertiginous rate. The Reagan administration's first major budgetary intervention, the Omnibus Budget Reconciliation Act or

OBRA, passed in 1981, exacerbated the already growing pressure on the public healthcare system by slashing the federal contribution to Medicaid and allowing states to implement further restrictions of their own.[63] Reagan's "New Federalism" called on the federal government to decrease its role in social service funding: in practice, it delegated the responsibility for implementing budget cutbacks onto state and local levels of government, leaving them with the "freedom" to decide where the ax should fall. Following OBRA, the states and cities that had been hardest hit by budget crisis, such as the recently bankrupt New York, took the opportunity to drastically reduce the Medicaid reimbursements they paid to hospitals. This had an immediate effect on the hospital emergency rooms that were often the first port of call for impoverished patients. Private hospitals had long been reluctant to accept the indigent but now saw Medicaid patients as an outright threat to their profits and responded by transferring them en masse to the overcrowded emergency rooms of public hospitals. At a time when freely accessible health care was more urgently needed than ever, the so-called emergency room dumping crisis was the most visible symptom of a public health sector under severe budgetary strain.

The neoliberal project to reform social services involved several mutually reinforcing processes of political and institutional devolution. While Reagan's New Federalism transferred authority to enact budget restrictions from federal to state and municipal levels of government, the transfer of social service costs also occurred at the level of the healthcare institution itself, as the managed care movement sought to outsource the labor of care from the hospital to the nonprofit sector to the home. In 1983, the Reagan administration introduced a new system for reimbursing costs under Medicare and Medicaid that set limits on the length of time a patient could be hospitalized.[64] In the past, a fee-for-service system had allowed medical practitioners to charge as many services as they liked to public insurance; the new system attached spending decisions to diagnosis and placed an absolute limit on the recoverable costs for each diagnosed condition. Hospitals would lose money if they let patients overstay this limit but make a profit if they managed to discharge patients earlier. In an environment where healthcare budgets were already strained, this decision had the effect of encouraging hospitals to discharge patients as early as possible, even when they still required highly skilled forms of care.

Hospital-based care was replaced, if at all, with intermittent healthcare visits at home as the burden of care shifted from the expensive labor of securely employed professionals to a feminized work force of home health workers, often employed as independent contractors.[65] But for the most part, health care simply shifted from the institution to the home and from the healthcare professional to the unpaid labor of family members—overwhelmingly sisters, mothers, and daughters.[66] Reports of the "death of the family have been greatly exaggerated," Reagan proclaimed as he announced the creation of an official Home Care Week: "The home should be the setting of first choice for care and treatment, because it is conducive to healing; in the home, family members can supply caring and love."[67]

Alongside his encomiums to home-based care, Reagan saw the revitalization of voluntarism as central to his welfare reform agenda. If the New Federalism called on federal government to devolve its responsibilities to the state and municipal levels, Reagan envisaged volunteer labor performing a similar transformative role in the nonprofit sector. "What federalism is to the public sector," he asserted, "voluntarism and private initiative are to the private sector. The country is bursting with ideas and creativity, but a government run by decree has no way to respond.... Voluntarism is an essential part of our plan to give the government back to the people."[68] As social service budgets were whittled back, neoliberals and neoconservatives loudly touted the virtues of community empowerment through "self-care." In a report sponsored by the American Enterprise Institute in 1981, the public health theorists and former New Left activists Lowell S. Levin and Ellen L. Idler identified "self-care" as an ideal alternative to the welfare state.[69] For these perhaps unwitting messengers of the New Right, the burdens of care engendered by the deinstitutionalization of public hospital patients called for a simultaneous reinstitutionalization of the private family, church, and charity as natural conduits for "self-care." Their prescriptions in many ways anticipated the actual contours of policy change over the next few decades, where filial obligation laws, faith-based welfare reform, and the selective mobilization of the nonprofit sector would reinvent family, church, and charity as the prime mediating institutions of social policy.

The effects of neoliberal healthcare reform were felt acutely in New York, the epicenter of the US AIDS epidemic in the 1980s. As noted by Charles Perrow and Mauro F. Guillén, "AIDS came to a city particularly ill prepared to cope with it."[70] New York City had been declared officially bankrupt during the recession of 1975, when bankers refused to purchase its municipal bonds and roll over its debts. The city was subsequently subjected to a prolonged austerity regime, conducted under the vigilant eyes of its business elites, that sought to restructure the economy around financial services and real estate while purging the poor from the city center, using a combined strategy of regressive tax concessions and cuts to social services. Well before the sea-change of the Reagan revolution, New York served as a laboratory for neoliberal reform: The crisis regime that was imposed in the wake of its bankruptcy prefigured the impact of the Volcker shock at a national level and served as prelude to the wave of structural adjustment programs that would be rolled out across the world during the 1980s.[71]

Health care was a prime target of Mayor Ed Koch's budget cuts. According to one study, the city's hospitals closed up to 1800 beds in the first half of the 1980s, at a time when AIDS infections were increasing at an alarming pace.[72] Even by the end of the decade, state and city officials remained seemingly oblivious to the urgency of the situation. As late as 1989, President George H. W. Bush was proposing to cut funds to New York City hospitals while the governor refused to spend funds that had been appropriated by the legislature (fewer than a third of the five hundred new AIDS beds that had been repeatedly promised became available before the end of the decade, and many of these remained unused because of a shortage of qualified nursing staff).[73]

As a result of this institutional inertia, grassroots AIDS service organizations were almost alone in mounting any kind of response during the first five years of the epidemic. In the cities hardest hit by HIV—New York, San Francisco, Washington, and Los Angeles—gay men, lesbians, transgender women, and their allies marshaled vast amounts of unpaid labor to confront the urgent healthcare, housing, and social service needs of the HIV-infected while also initiating the first prevention campaigns. In New York, Gay Men's Health Crisis (GMHC) provided the only substantial services to people living with AIDS until 1985, when Reagan finally broke his silence and small levels of federal and state support began to trickle through to nonprofits. Set up by a small group of activists with no outside support in early 1982 and operating out of a few rooms in a boarding house, the organization had, by the end of the year amassed "a volunteer force of over three hundred individuals and was training up to fifty new volunteers a month."[74]

The early AIDS service organizations were well aware of the catch-22 in which they found themselves.[75] The decision to set up healthcare and other services within the gay community was a political one: The early AIDS service organizations were the inheritors of the self-care movement of the 1970s and were reluctant to cede control to a public health sector perceived as punitive and imbued with normative ideas about sexuality. In the early 1980s, the pathologization of sexual deviance was far from a distant memory; homosexuality was still illegal in many states, while Reagan's key advisors on AIDS (the cultural conservatives William Bennett and Gary Bauer) were threatening to resurrect old public health methods such as quarantine, the closure of bathhouses, and compulsory testing.[76] But in a context where Reagan was touting the virtues of voluntarism as a solution to the failures of the social state, self-care also represented a practical capitulation to neoliberal social policy. In the early years of the epidemic, AIDS activists had no other choice than to take care of themselves, short of doing nothing, and so ended up assuming responsibilities that might otherwise have been taken on by the state. The political influence that the New Left healthcare initiatives of the 1970s had been able to exert from the margins at a time of proliferating welfare services was severely diminished in a context where these initiatives were simply substituting for state welfare. The effect of the expanding welfare agenda of the Great Society and its aftermath was to push the frontier of care services provided by the state beyond the racial and sexual limits of the Fordist family wage. The countereffect of neoliberal budget cuts was to shrink this space but also, as if accidentally, to reinscribe limits to care along the familiar lines of racial, gender, and sexual difference. Beyond the charmed circle of the privately insured family, health care was not readily available unless one took care of oneself. Personal responsibility was invoked nowhere more forcefully than at the margins.

FAMILY, CHURCH, AND CHARITY

Reagan's position on voluntarism was willfully equivocal, variously seeking to exploit and disable the energies of a nonprofit sector that had first become a target of government funding under the Great Society agenda. Even while he endlessly exhorted nonprofits to pick up the slack from failing public services then, Reagan did everything in his power to undercut the nonprofit infrastructure that had grown out of, and beyond, the Great Society community action programs. With their proximity to the civil rights movement and the New Left, these evidently were not the kinds of voluntary initiative that Reagan wished to foster. Reflecting on the legacy of Reagan's first few years in government, Lester Salamon calculates that Reagan ended up cutting "the equivalent of $115 billion in real terms" to the nonprofit sector between 1982 and 1985.[77] The Omnibus Budget and Reconciliation Act of 1981 led to huge cuts for grant-in-aid programs to state and local government, the first such cuts in almost a quarter of a century, and transformed a wide variety of categorical grants (that is, grants with budgets allocated to fixed programs) into block grants that gave states less money but more discretion in how to spend it.[78] These reforms eviscerated the smaller, more militant, nonprofits that had benefited from Great Society funding largesse[79] and had a particularly devastating effect on healthcare services for the poor. During Reagan's first term, it is estimated that cuts to healthcare block grants averaged from 20 to 35 percent nationwide; grants-in-aid to state and local governments for preventive health programs declined by 22 percent; for health resources by 42 percent; for health services by 22 percent; for alcohol, drug abuse, and mental health by 34 percent; and for Medicaid by 7 percent.[80]

At stake here was something more than a deference to limited government: Reagan was profligate in other areas of federal spending and indifferent to the soaring budget deficit, squandering billions on the military and tax concessions, much to the dismay of some of his closest advisers.[81] More than a testament to fiscal conservatism, Reagan's cuts to the nonprofit sector were motivated, foremost, by a political animus against the legacy of Great Society welfare programs. Upon entering office, Reagan quickly moved to shut down the Community Service Administration (which had begun life as the Great Society's Office of Economic Opportunity, the body responsible for funding Community Action Programs) and replaced it with a new voluntary sector agency named ACTION. He then appointed a "particularly ardent conservative" as head of the agency, who made a special effort to stop funds going to left-leaning activist organizations.[82] According to new rules issued by ACTION, organizations could not use federal funds to engage in the ill-defined activity of "political advocacy" and would have to isolate funds that they used toward that purpose if they received as little as 5 percent of their operating budget from the government. This stipulation was evidently aimed at the kind of public interest litigation that had grown out of and alongside the radical welfare activism of the 1960s and '70s—in particular, the various Supreme Court challenges that had undermined the power of state welfare agencies to police morality.[83] It was designed to stifle precisely the kinds of public policy activism that AIDS service organizations would engage in, despite all the odds, throughout the 1980s.

Alongside this general prohibition on "political advocacy," the Reagan administration outlined a number of specific limits to the kinds of nonprofit initiative the government was willing to finance. In 1988, Senator Jesse Helms convinced Congress to pass an amendment designed to prevent the federal government from funding any AIDS education or prevention resource that would "promote or encourage, directly or indirectly, homosexual activities."[84] The amendment, which was approved with overwhelming majorities by the Senate and the House, applied to the HHS—the major funder of AIDS prevention material at federal, state, and local levels. Without prompting from the federal government, the Center for Disease Control (CDC) responded to this decision by adopting its own guidelines restricting the appearance of sexually explicit content in any of the publications it funded.[85] Henceforth, all CDC prevention materials were expected to include warnings about the dangers of promiscuity and IV drug use and propound the virtues of abstinence, while safe sex messages somehow had to be conveyed without depicting an anus, a vagina, or a penis. Federal and state government generally refused to fund explicit safe sex material, obliging AIDS service organizations to create separate accounts for all AIDS prevention initiatives they might engage in.

These restrictions on the funding of AIDS prevention material were introduced alongside a prohibition on the use of federal tax dollars to fund free needle exchange programs, also sponsored by Helms, and a gag rule preventing federally funded health professionals from providing information and referrals relating to abortion.[86] Together, these rules carefully delineated the nature of the nonprofit services that the government was willing to fund and progressively narrowed the space of maneuver in which they could operate, particularly around questions of sexuality.

The equivocations of Reagan's position on the nonprofit sector become legible if we understand them as part of a more ambitious maneuver to refashion the very shape of social welfare. The Helms amendment and other restrictions on federal funding were designed to counter the perceived antifamily bias of Great Society social programs and to channel the flow of social-service contracts back into programs that promoted the family, heterosexual monogamy, and abstinence outside marriage. Not incidentally, the imposition of various moral restrictions on nonprofits occurred at a time when the religious right was itself claiming a growing share of social-service contracts, while actively seeking and achieving exemptions from federal laws relating to sexual freedom (a theme I will explore further in Chapter 7). In the late 1980s, for example, the Catholic hospitals of New York applied for government funds to provide care for AIDS patients but refused outright to comply with state guidelines to counsel patients on safer sex. Although strictly illegal, this refusal to comply with state guidelines did not prevent the church from receiving funds, and Governor Mario Cuomo tacitly overlooked it.[87] Such claims to religious exceptionalism would later be celebrated as expressions of religious freedom and institutionalized by Clinton's Charitable Choice act of 1996, which formally exempted religious organizations from federal antidiscrimination laws with respect to employment. In retrospect, it appears evident that the widening of the space of religious freedom has been contemporaneous with the growing number of restrictions placed on a dissident sexual politics. Religious freedom to impose moral law is asserted at the same time as sexual freedom from moral law is diminished: The one implies the other.

The proliferation of moral exclusion zones designed to channel nonprofit services toward the promotion of monogamous heterosexuality was strictly consonant with the Reagan administration's efforts to reinstitutionalize the private family as the primary locus of care. As noted by Jennifer Parks, "the de-institutionalization movement—the glorifying of home or 'community-based' care as the answer to hospital or nursing home care—is a 'homecoming' in more than one sense of the word. While patients are, indeed, coming home sooner, home care is also a return to a way of care-taking that is part of our social history," a return to a household economy of service that was always rigorously structured along the lines of gender and race.[88] The valorization of home-based care, one might add, is more than a little reminiscent of the American poor-law tradition of family responsibility, which, we have seen, was actively invoked to enforce the provision of care by family members well into the early twentieth century. It is no coincidence that at the very moment Reagan was pushing through legislation to shorten the length of hospital stays and return care work to the home, he also made it legal for states to revive and enforce centuries-old filial obligation laws as a way of recouping Medicaid and Medicare costs.[89] As we saw in Chapter 3, family responsibility statutes fell into relative disuse after the passage of the Social Security Act of 1935 and were explicitly overridden by the Medicaid statute of 1965, which forbade recourse to family support in lieu of public welfare. As governor of California and a vocal critic of Great Society welfare programs, Reagan had fulminated against the repeal of these laws. As president, he turned family responsibility into a watchword of social welfare reform and encouraged the states to enforce such laws wherever possible. The budgetary savings made possible by Reagan's revival of filial obligation laws appear to have been symbolic at best (it turns out that extracting money from the indigent families of indigent patients is easier said than done) but in any event the reinstitutionalization of the private family took place in large part by default, through the negative impact of dwindling social service and foreshortened hospital stays, not to mention the inertia of gender roles that in the throes of economic crisis seemed to slot back effortlessly into place.

These then were the boundaries in which nonprofits were forced to operate in the early years of the AIDS epidemic. If devolution to the nonprofit sector had become the guiding principle of Reagan-era social service provision, such expressions of empowerment were to be strictly channeled into the reinvigorated institutional forms of family, church, and charity. The relationship of the early AIDS service organizations to this governmental agenda was equivocal at best. While on the one hand organizations such as GMHC seemed to have perfectly internalized the injunction to self-care, they also transgressed the moral limits to service provision prescribed by the state and to this extent resisted assimilation. At a time when the neoliberal-religious conservative coalition was seeking to reassert the private responsibilities of the family, AIDS activists invented relations of care beyond the boundaries of family or kinship and promoted forms of "safe sex" that refused the alternative between abstinence or heterosexual monogamy. These practices of self-care often brought them into direct conflict with the church and the state. Most notable in this regard was ACT UP's Stop the Church action, in which activists staged a die-in in the pews of St. Patrick's Cathedral in New York to protest Cardinal O'Connor's vocal public stance against homosexuality and abortion.[90] The action was controversial even within the ranks of ACT UP and today appears unthinkable.[91] But it was offensive only because it so precisely targeted the nexus of theological and neoliberal forms of government that was to take shape over the following years.

At its most incisive, the AIDS activism of the 1980s asked what the familial connotations of "home" might mean to those who both refused reproductive, monogamous heterosexuality and were threatened with actual homelessness. It was more than ironic that "home-based care" was being promoted as an official alternative to the public hospital system at a time when affordable housing was becoming increasingly inaccessible. Deinstitutionalization itself was partially responsible for the sharp increase in homelessness that was recorded in the early 1980s, as patients who had been under long-term state care were offloaded onto the streets. But to this was added the pressure from tax-subsidized real estate investment and a strategy of planned obsolescence with regard to public housing. Again the tensions were felt acutely in New York, the city that most precociously and ruthlessly embraced asset inflation as a new model of economic growth. New York's homelessness problem had "a very prosaic source," note Perrow and Guillén: "mental patients were turned out into the streets... funds for subsidized housing for the poor were cut, even while financial benefits were available for housing for the well-to-do; in New York City developers of commercial office space and expensive condominiums benefitted from handsome tax breaks."[92] In Chapter 4, we saw how the focus of neoliberal monetary policy on stimulating asset inflation lent itself to the reassertion of the private family as a vector of wealth transmission. Gentrification as urban strategy went hand in hand with the revalorization of inheritance; and this confluence of factors proved doubly marginalizing to those who both resisted the family as a sexual institution and were deprived of family wealth.

In the early years of the epidemic, homelessness was a very real problem for AIDS patients of all classes, as many found themselves unable to pay rent after leaving their jobs or evicted from long-term rentals by homophobic landlords. AIDS service organizations such as GMHC successfully confronted the problem of middle-class homelessness in the early years of the epidemic by creating collective home-based care services for the dying, but were much slower to address the endemic problems of housing precarity facing the HIV-infected poor.[93] This task would be taken up by the Housing Committee of ACT UP, which saw the decline of public housing and social services in general as key issues for AIDS activism. In one of its first actions, the Housing Committee occupied the lobby of the New York Trump Tower (a monument to the investment magnate Donald Trump) in order to expose the contradiction between tax-subsidized real estate development and homelessness in the city. But the committee quickly sensed the limitations of such punctual, theatrical interventions when it came to issues of social provision, and in the space of a few short years morphed from a direct action group to an independent housing service provider for impoverished AIDS patients.[94] As a response to the public housing crisis, the initiative was small and no doubt inadequate to the scale of the problem, but by drawing the connections between homelessness, familial homophobia, and poverty, the Housing Committee refused to reprivatize the politics of care—and in so doing challenged the very rationale of home-based care.

VOLENTI NON FIT INJURIA: AIDS AND THE UNINSURED RISK

Beyond the issues of home and homelessness, the HIV-infected body appeared almost to somatize the peculiar risk exposures of Reagan-era health reform, as the neoliberal attack on welfare economics progressively undermined existing forms of health insurance. The percentage of Americans who were covered by private, work-based health insurance peaked in 1982, at the height of the Volcker recession, and then progressively declined as a result of the long-term restructuring of the workforce. In the new economic environment created by recession, corporate downsizing, and the relocation of mass manufacture offshore, employers who in the past had done everything in their power to retain a permanent workforce were now no longer convinced of the economic benefits of offering generous health insurance. In response to new competitive pressures, employers resorted to various strategies to decrease their inflating medical care costs. Some shifted costs to older employees and retirees, some dropped their coverage of dependents or sought to rationalize existing programs by delegating them to health maintenance organizations (HMOs). Some employers vetted new personnel for preexisting medical conditions while many others simply divested themselves of healthcare costs by employing uninsured workers on short-term contracts.[95] The historical exceptionalism of the American health insurance system—that is, its heavy reliance on a work-based system of private insurance under public auspices—made it particularly vulnerable to the changing nature of employment in the post-Fordist era. As long-term industrial labor steadily declined in favor of short-term, temporary employment in both the professional and low-wage service sectors, the American public-private system of healthcare insurance also steadily diminished, affecting all levels of the income scale.[96]

In the meantime, private insurers who in the past had been willing to act like state-guaranteed substitutes for public health care began to abandon their commitment to social insurance principles. The large Fordist corporations that had once subscribed to the redistributive tenets of risk pooling and community rating now began introducing specific premiums for different age groups and occupations while smaller insurance companies began "cherry picking" younger, healthier employees by offering them cheaper premiums.[97] The inevitable effect of such market fragmentation was to undermine the very logic of social insurance (which works best across large populations) and to narrow the pool of people able to afford insurance in the first place. By the 1980s, notes public health historian Dorothy Porter, "fewer Americans were insured at an ever increasing cost. The numbers of uninsured grew to dramatic proportions. Furthermore, as white-collar unemployment grew with recession at the end of the decade, a much broader band of Americans experienced 'episodes' of being without insurance."[98]

Beyond structural changes to the employment contract, however, private insurers were also introducing new kinds of exemption into their policies. Emboldened by neoliberal critiques of moral hazard and a public health discourse that was increasingly focused on the ill effects of lifestyle choice, private insurers began to reintroduce notions of fault into their policies, reserving special caps or exclusions for accidents that could be construed as the result of self-inflicted harm. This new attention to lifestyle choice was bound to have a particularly heavy impact on the HIV-infected, given the overwhelming association between the AIDS epidemic and irresponsible lifestyle choice. As late as 1982, in fact, scientists were still debating whether the strange new immune condition afflicting young gay men could be attributed to the repeated lifestyle stresses of dancing, poppers, and sodomy,[99] and even after the virus was officially identified, in 1984, its privileged mode of transmission through sex or drug use continued to attract a special kind of moral opprobrium. It is hardly surprising then that in the early 1980s, many private insurers introduced special "AIDS caps" into their group policies, placing absolute limits on recoverable costs for AIDS care, while others created *volenti* exclusions that reserved coverage only for the innocent victims of "involuntary infection" through blood transfusion.[100] In an era where public health experts saw behavioral risk as a form of self-inflicted harm, it seemed that AIDS infection through drug use or sexual contact represented the ultimate lifestyle choice—and the ultimate confirmation of the maxim *volenti non fit injuria.*

As the full extent of the AIDS epidemic became clear then, many employed gay men found themselves outright excluded from health insurance coverage or lost available coverage when they could no longer work. These men could only then become eligible for Medicaid after they had spent down all their assets on out-of-pocket medical care. The refusal of the competitive private market to insure the "voluntary" risk of AIDS infection—a refusal that neoliberal legal theorists such as Richard Posner and Tomas Philipson would qualify as a rational market failure—meant that the public welfare system became the de facto insurer of last resort for HIV/AIDS patients. By 1993, Medicaid, which covers approximately 10 percent of all US health expenditures, accounted for fully 25 percent of all AIDS-related costs—and Medicaid itself was supplemented by a specific emergency healthcare program (the Ryan White CARE Act of 1990) designed to provide a last-resort backstop for uninsured AIDS sufferers.[101] Increasingly, private insurers saw AIDS patients as uninsurable risks and ceded their costs to the public sector—a division of labor that reserved the most profitable risks for private insurance markets and inevitably exacerbated the inflation of healthcare costs in the public sector.

At a time when the ranks of the workplace uninsured were swelling, then, the social insurance system was itself entering a period of crisis. Reagan's 1981 cuts to social services allowed states to tighten their eligibility criteria for Medicaid, meaning that many more Americans were left with no insurance at all, and placed intolerable pressures on the already overcrowded emergency rooms of public hospitals. Television and newspaper reports in the early 1990s regaled their audience with stories of private hospitals unceremoniously dumping uninsured patients onto the nearest public hospital, of seriously ill patients being discharged without care from emergency rooms or transferred across state lines. Again, the particular impact of this crisis on AIDS patients was exacerbated by the fact that HIV-infected drug users, nonheterosexuals and sex workers had come to represent the undeserving ill in the eyes of the general public. With or without health insurance coverage, patients suspected of being infected with the HIV virus were routinely escorted out of emergency rooms and refused care by primary physicians.[102]

But the impact of institutional risk-protection on the unfolding of the AIDS epidemic went far beyond the question of insurance coverage. The growing fragmentation and restriction of health insurance shaped the very profile of the epidemic in the United States, deciding in advance who would be visible to CDC epidemiologists and who would remain uncounted. For AIDS to be recognized as an identifiable illness in the first place, it was necessary for a sufficient number of people of a certain demographic to have access to premium medical practitioners in direct contact with the highest levels of public health surveillance. In the words of Cindy Patton: "It is a devastating historical accident that HIV was first noticed among well-cared-for gay men; AIDS, a diagnosis of early death in the previously healthy, could only be recognized in a group on the verge of achieving the social status of 'healthy.'"[103] The CDC was first notified of the disease that would later be called AIDS when an immunologist working at UCLA's medical research center treated a number of young, white, gay men who appeared to be suffering from a similar kind of immune deficiency.[104] The immunologist was sufficiently apprised of the official channels of public health surveillance to know that he should contact the local health department and inform a colleague working at the CDC. The most immediate evidence of some common denominator linking the men was the fact that they were young, white, previously healthy, and gay. But these men also shared something else in common: Their health insurance was generous enough to cover consultations with a well-connected specialist in an elite medical center. It was this detail above all else that made them visible to the official public health system. In retrospect, it is clear that these men, although certainly at high risk, were not representative of the AIDS epidemic as a whole (which also included many intravenous drug users and their partners) and were far from representative of the "gay" community most affected by AIDS (which also included many nonwhite, non-middle-class, uninsured, and publicly insured people, bisexuals, and transgender men and women).

The effect of this differential access to privately insured health care was to distort the epidemiological profile of the HIV crisis at the very moment it became visible to public consciousness in the 1980s. The public health specialists D.C. Des Jarlais, S.R. Friedman, and J.L. Sotheran have found evidence that HIV/AIDS was widespread among intravenous drug users during the 1970s, well before the first cases were detected among white gay men.[105] Their research indicates that seroprevalence among injecting drug users hovered somewhere around 20 percent between 1975 and 1977, increasing to 50 percent between 1978 and 1982. This "shadow" epidemic disproportionately affected lower-income black and Hispanic drug users—those who were least likely to be employed or have a permanent residence, disposable income, and thus access to clean injecting materials. Their deaths were invisible to the private physicians who reported AIDS cases to state health departments because they rarely had access to continuous medical care in the first place; already suffered from a high rate of infections unrelated to HIV; and often only reached a hospital emergency room in the final stages of illness, where they appeared to be suffering from complications from pneumonia. As noted by Cathy Cohen, "this population most often received their care from 'Medicaid mills' or the emergency rooms of teaching hospitals that were so critical in identifying this disease among referred and formally admitted gay patients."[106]

For the women who contracted HIV in the early years of the epidemic, a disproportionate number of whom were low-income black and Latina, access to medical care was complicated by the fact that the opportunistic infections that accompanied AIDS in women were not recognized by the CDC. As the nation's premier public health institution, the CDC constructed the epidemiological facts of the disease and in so doing provided both public and private insurers with the classifications they needed to design coverage. AIDS is a syndrome that can manifest itself in a number of symptoms that differ widely by class, gender, access to preventative care such as vaccinations, environmental factors, and contact with animals. Up until 1992, AIDS was officially defined as the presence of antibodies to HIV, combined with a number of indicator diseases that had originally been observed in young, white gay men. This restrictive definition meant that the numbers of women infected with HIV were grossly underreported well into the 1990s: Many women were never sent to be tested in the first place because they did not suffer from the same kinds of opportunistic infections as men.[107]

A retrospective look at medical records, however, seems to indicate that significant numbers of low-income women died of AIDS in the 1970s and '80s, without provoking any alarm on the part of public health officials. Reports of unexplained spikes in mortality from pneumonia, tuberculosis, rare parasitic infections, nephritis, and chronic obstructive pulmonary disease were recorded among low-income women in New York City, Newark, Hartford, and Washington—precisely those cities that would come to be recognized as epicenters of the epidemic—from the late 1970s into the 1980s.[108] It is plausible that these cases did not come to light in the 1970s for the same reason that "junkie pneumonia" was not recognized as the sign of an emerging infectious disease: The people in question had such precarious access to health care that news of their death was never communicated to public health authorities. But in the 1980s these women remained invisible to public health surveillance because the CDC's own definition of the syndrome excluded them from consideration. The gender bias of CDC epidemiology had immediate, material and self-reinforcing effects: In many states, eligibility for health care and other benefits depended on an official diagnosis of AIDS, so women who were gravely ill but not recognized as HIV-positive were routinely excluded from Medicaid, Social Security Disability Insurance, and other support services for people with AIDS. These low-income women were thus defined as "uninsurable risks" twice over: Their marginalization from a healthcare system that provided only last-resort, emergency care for the underinsured and uninsured meant that their illnesses were barely visible to federal epidemiologists, and this marginalization was in turn exacerbated by the illegibility of their symptoms within the official risk classifications published by the CDC.

It was perhaps inevitable, given this context, that the politics of insurance should become a major focus of AIDS activism by the end of the decade, as the first antiretrovirals became available and people began to live longer. In the late 1980s, ACT UP in New York and San Francisco formed subcommittees specifically devoted to insurance actions, and were soon joined in this endeavor by ACT UP chapters around the country. ACT UP is routinely caricatured as an organization composed of wealthy white men, but one member of the New York subcommittee recalls that fully one-third of the gay men involved in meetings were uninsured—a fact she attributes to the kinds of feminized labor (hairdressing, waiting, temping) in which many gay men were employed.[109] Relative to their heterosexual peers then, even middle-income white men in ACT UP were at the avant-garde of changes in the post-Fordist employment relation—subject to forms of middle-class insecurity that had long been experienced by white women and that would become endemic to all classes of workers over the following decades. The work of these committees focused in the first instance on the exclusionary practices of private insurers but soon moved on to a much wider and more ambitious critique of the problems associated with Medicaid and the uninsured. In 1990, the ACT UP New York subcommittee achieved its first resounding victory when it forced the National Air Traffic Controllers Association to drop *volenti* clauses excluding from coverage those who had acquired HIV "voluntarily" through sexual contact or drug use.[110] It went on to pursue similar actions against other private insurers across the country. In San Francisco, the Golden Gate insurance committee pressured the state to monitor redlining practices in the private insurance sector and to put an end to disease specific exclusions and spending caps.[111]

After these first interventions against private insurers, the women's and minority caucuses within ACT UP pushed the organization to take its actions much farther and focus on the systemic exclusion of low-income HIV-infected women from all forms of social insurance. In the late 1980s, activists from ACT UP, the American Civil Liberties Union (ACLU), Women's Health Action Mobilization (WHAM), and legal aid lawyers put pressure on the CDC to revise its definition of AIDS so as to take account of the indicator diseases affecting women.[112] The CDC was reluctant to introduce these changes, complaining that any revision along the lines proposed by ACT UP would double the official caseload of AIDS patients and dramatically increase the burden on public services. After the failure of negotiations, activists from ACT UP and WHAM staged a mass action against the CDC in early 1990 in which they blockaded the entrance to its headquarters in Atlanta and unfurled a banner on the roof with the words "CDC AIDS definition kills women."[113] In October of that year, Terry McGovern, a lesbian legal aid lawyer working with women prisoners, filed a lawsuit against the HHS accusing it of knowingly using the CDC's definition of AIDS to restrict the benefits it had to pay.[114] To coincide with the event, ACT UP activists, including many low-income women with AIDS, staged a protest outside the Department of Health and Human Resources office that distributed these benefits. In 1991, the CDC finally offered to compromise, agreeing to add some but not all female-specific opportunistic infections to its official definition of AIDS. Although only a partial victory, the CDC's change of heart had the more important side-effect of convincing the Social Security Administration to change its definition of recognizable AIDS—a decision that at last made Medicare, disability benefits, and other services available to women with symptomatic HIV infection and persuaded many other social service programs to follow suit.[115]

By the early 1990s, ACT UP had moved beyond punctual actions against private insurers designed to win benefits for specific classes of employees to articulate a more radical agenda for health insurance reform, one that revived the expansive reform agenda of the early 1970s. In 1991, ACT UP joined a coalition of progressive organizations campaigning for universal, single-payer health insurance in the United States—a coalition that helped push health care to the forefront of the Democratic Party agenda during the 1992 presidential campaign.[116] In a brochure distributed at a demonstration in favor of universal health insurance in 1991, one ACT UP member reflected on the political evolution of the group: "We have had to fight battle after battle for immediate, stopgap measures just to keep people alive. Our targets sometimes seemed scattered.... We have not taken the time nor devoted the energy to long-term goals or broad-based solutions."[117]

Under pressure from its women's and minority committees, ACT UP had been forced to look beyond the issue of private insurance—an issue of most immediate importance to those who would otherwise have access to the middle-class privileges of full-time employment with benefits—to the systemic failures of the public insurance system. But this widening of political horizons to encompass the gendered and racialized dynamics of economic inequality in the US healthcare system remained controversial within ACT UP itself and ultimately led to its dissolution.[118] For those who saw exclusion from health care as a result of their sexuality alone, the most immediate issues were those of sexual discrimination and access to rights that would otherwise have been their due. Others experienced their outright exclusion from the healthcare system as a much more complex collusion of sexual, race, and class factors—and it was this more expansive vision that was captured in ACT UP's campaign for universal health insurance.

SAME-SEX MARRIAGE AND THE ETHIC OF FAMILY RESPONSIBILITY

Following in the footsteps of the welfare rights movement of the 1970s, the AIDS activism of the early 1990s articulated a radical welfare politics that called for the expansion of social insurance while simultaneously refusing the exclusions of sexual normativity. This pathway was in some sense made necessary by the peculiar history of the American welfare state. The New Deal's never-completed reform agenda had left the United States with a fragmented healthcare system, one that reserved privileged workplace benefits to the full-time, unionized worker, most often a white man, and his wife, while reserving an inadequate and expensive public health insurance system for the indigent and disabled. Good quality health insurance was contingent on full-time employment in a large, unionized workplace—or failing that, marriage to a man who enjoyed these conditions. Reviving the agenda of radical healthcare reform that had flourished in the early 1970s, health activists in ACT UP and allied groups sought to imagine a universal system of health insurance that was no longer tied to the old normative restrictions of the family wage—a system that divorced healthcare coverage from employment and marital status. Yet these activists were operating in an historical context that was much more inimical to such ambitious horizons of change. After trying (and failing) to push through with national healthcare reform in the first years of his administration, Clinton went on to "reform welfare as we know it"—an intervention that drastically restricted public assistance to impoverished single-mothers and made "marriage promotion" and "family responsibility" the centerpiece of social policy for the poor. The AIDS activists who campaigned for universal health care therefore found themselves working on two fronts simultaneously: Even as they sought to revive the reform agenda of the 1970s left, they also had to confront the increasingly influential ethic of personal and family responsibility associated with neoliberalism.

After the defeat of Clinton's healthcare reform and the subsequent success of his promise to "end welfare as we know it," the campaign for same-sex marriage rose to the fore of LGBT activism. The leftist healthcare coalition of the early 1990s had sought to detach collective health insurance from its residual reference to the family wage. The LGBT movement has subsequently moved in the opposite direction: Rather than challenge the limitations intrinsic to the public-private welfare state, it has instead fought for inclusion within an already exclusive system of private, work-based health insurance. At a point in time when access to healthcare coverage through full-time, secure employment (and by extension) marriage, has become an increasingly rare proposition, the LGBT movement has devoted much of its energies to attaining this shrinking privilege. The notion that same-sex marriage would ensure access to private healthcare insurance has thus become a key plank in the reform agenda of LGBT rights advocates. Similar arguments have been made with respect to Social Security, which in the event of premature death provides survivor's benefits for widowed spouses and children. At a time of shrinking political horizons, same-sex marriage proponents look to the surviving remnants of the family wage — social insurance benefits premised on marital and familial status — to argue *that they too should be included in this last vestige of Fordist normativity.* The call to recognize same-sex marriage thus becomes a demand for inclusion within a family wage system that is itself in terminal decline.

But beyond this, many of the same voices in the same-sex marriage debate simultaneously adopt the neoliberal argument that legal recognition of their unions will ultimately allow same-sex couples to take care of themselves and thus renounce their rights to state welfare altogether. In this optic, the campaign for same-sex marriage no longer entails a demand for inclusion in the family wage system of social insurance but rather an affirmation of one's ability to live independently of the state.[119] By allowing lesbians and gay men to enter into legally enforceable and long-term obligations of care and mutual support, it is suggested, the recognition of gay marriage will induct same-sex couples into a neoliberal ethic of family responsibility. The economist M. V. Lee Badgett, a prominent contributor to legal debates around same-sex marriage, cites the work of neoliberal economist Robert A. Pollak to buttress her argument that marriage performs a welfare function comparable to social insurance: "Robert Pollak...argues that family structures serve other important economic purposes by reducing what economists call 'transaction costs' involved in creating all sorts of agreements between individuals. The 'preexisting, ongoing, significant personal relationships'...present in families give the family some advantages in fulfilling social insurance functions in case of old age, divorce, economic hardship, or illness, for example."[120] Badgett's argument in favor of same-sex marriage rests on the idea—pervasive in the neoliberal literature and ultimately indebted to the poor law tradition of family responsibility—that the legal obligations of marriage should function as a primary source of welfare and the first-line of defense against the social risks of ill health, aging and unemployment:

> Economies of scale in household production increase the resources available for provisioning within a family. Within this economic context, particular forms of family arrangements and their accompanying legal arrangements seem likely to promote taking advantage of economies of scale more clearly. The promises inherent in marriage... include an obligation of mutual support between two individuals, giving individuals in those relationships a higher degree of security in their claims on their partner's resources. With both an explicit personal commitment and a legal obligation, one spouse cannot refuse to help meet the basic needs of the other.[121]

The legal theorist William Eskridge similarly identifies the "social insurance" function of marriage as one of the prime arguments in its favor:

> the third goal of marriage [is] social insurance. Each spouse promises to marry the other 'for better or for worse, for rich or for poor, in sickness

and in health.' So long as everything is for better, for rich, and in health, neither the law nor marriage has to do any heavy work. The work starts when something happens for worse, for poor, or in sickness. Marriage is a form of insurance against bad times; to the extent possible, the spouse is required to provide financial and emotional support when things are going badly. In the event of mental or physical breakdown (the nightmare people begin to have when they reach middle age), the unimpaired spouse is trusted to be both caretaker and surrogate decision maker.[122]

These arguments are not confined to the realm of theoretical debate but have been pervasive in same-sex marriage campaigns. Badgett, for example, has testified in numerous state high court decisions relating to the legalization of same-sex marriage. Her testimonies focus on both the social insurance and tax advantages that will be opened up to same-sex couples as a result of marriage and, more emphatically, on the fiscal savings that will be made available to the state once same-sex couples are authorized to take care of themselves. Ultimately, she concludes, the legalization of same-sex marriage will save the state more money than it loses in increased Social Security payments.[123] The impact of the neoliberal "family responsibility" argument in favor of same-sex marriage is clearly legible in the following remarks made by Chief Justice Ronald M. George of the California State Supreme Court, when asked to rule on the state's interest in excluding same-sex couples from marriage: "The legal obligations of support that are an integral part of the marital and family relationships relieve society of the obligation of caring for individuals who may become incapacitated or who are otherwise unable to support themselves."[124]

The AIDS epidemic plays a curious role—both catastrophic and redemptive—in the narratives of social progression offered here. William Eskridge merely reiterates a sentiment to be found in the work of many other gay commentators (the Catholic libertarian Andrew Sullivan or the communitarian neoliberal Jonathan Rauch, for instance) when he identifies AIDS as the moment of epiphany that turned gay men away from the uninsured risks of promiscuity toward the privatized risk protections of monogamy: "The AIDS epidemic that ripped through the eighties not only cast a pall over the sexual freedom of the seventies but, more important, illustrated the value of interpersonal commitment for gay people generally—and not just for safety's sake. To the person with AIDS the value of a committed partner is incalculable.... The social insurance feature of marriage has never been so relevant as it has been for people with AIDS."[125] For Jonathan Rauch, AIDS is what made gay men realize that the "absence of family structures was literally deadly"[126]—an uninsured risk that could only be hedged by claiming the economic and public health protections of married monogamy.

So an epidemic that prompted the rigorously antinormative welfare politics of ACT UP is here rewritten as a traumatic but necessary rite of passage into the world of family responsibility. In the wake of the Reagan revolution and its attempts to revive the poor-law tradition of family support, in the wake of Clinton's welfare reforms inscribing marriage promotion at the heart of social policy, the proponents of same-sex marriage seek to include non-heterosexuals in this same ethic. In the last instance, what is so striking about these narratives is how closely they hew to the neoliberal logic of Richard Posner and Tomas Philipson, for whom legalized gay marriage represented the ultimate form of privatized risk protection and the perfect solution to moral hazard. If AIDS was the price to pay for irresponsible lifestyle choice, same-sex marriage is now presented as the route to personal (and hence familial) responsibility.

CHAPTER SIX

In Loco Parentis: Human Capital, Student Debt, and the Logic of Family Investment

> Where does human capital come from? What constitutes a successful investment in human capital, either at the individual or national level? One has to start with the family.
>
> — Gary Becker, "Human Capital and Poverty"

The Federal Reserve has not traditionally been interested in the intimate dynamics of households, but as household debt has grown to historically unprecedented levels and the same debt has come to play a pivotal role in the economies of the United States and the world, acting as both stimulus and Achilles heel of the global market in asset-backed securities, central bankers have acquired a new, almost obsessive interest in the living arrangements of young adults. In surveys carried out by the New York Federal Reserve and the Pew Center, researchers have uncovered some striking but not entirely surprising results.[1] Since about the year 2000, many more young people have been lingering at home until late in their twenties, and the numbers have been increasing in a steady, almost linear fashion. The proportion of those under thirty who moved back home to live with their parents or simply opted to stay there increased sharply with the Great Recession of 2007. But while many assumed that the same people would set out on their own once the labor market picked up, the overall trend appears to be impervious to the business cycle. With each passing year, more young people are living at home, irrespective of job prospects. The one overwhelming constant here, according to the Federal Reserve of New York, is the extraordinary burden of student debt held by this generation of under-thirties. The total outstanding balance on student debt almost tripled between 2004 and 2012, climbing from $364 billion to $966 billion in less than a decade and proving remarkably resistant to the deflationary effects of financial crisis.[2] While outstanding balances on all other forms of consumer credit, from credit cards to car loans and mortgages, contracted during and after the Great Recession, student debt alone continued to rise at an astonishing rate.[3]

These trends are worrying, even from the point of view of the Federal Reserve. Student debt may well constitute a lucrative interest-bearing asset in global securities markets, and it has undoubtedly earned the federal government extraordinary profits in recent years,[4] but its effects on household consumption have serious knock-on effects for the overall economy. Until now, much of the momentum behind the consumer credit boom has derived from the expectation that each generation would leave home at roughly the same rate and in doing so, take out mortgages and consumer credit loans to purchase household goods. By keeping people at home, student debt is having a depressing effect on the entire consumer economy. There is reason to believe that short of decisive political action, the problem will not be resolved any time soon.

After all, student debt is in many ways unique. Not only is it excluded from the usual consumer protection laws that would make it dischargeable in bankruptcy, but it is also much more likely to assume a distinctly intergenerational form. As tuition fees have skyrocketed and safer loan options fail to keep up, many more students have been compelled to share their debt burden with parents and other family members. The federal PLUS loan, which allows parents to take out loans on behalf of students, is one of the fastest growing options in the federal loan program and one that is disproportionately used by low-income students who have exhausted all other sources of funding. Private student loans have also expanded at a rapid pace and almost invariably require a parent as cosigner. Wealthier parents often find it cheaper to remortgage their homes to pay for their children's college costs rather than take out actual student loans. Increasingly, then, student debt is a family affair, binding generations together in webs of mutual obligation and dependence that are quite literally unforgiving. The demographic trends uncovered by the Federal Reserve are but one expression of a new, debt-based temporal bind that radically reaffirms the economic function of the private family.

The situation could not have been more different in the 1960s, when rising federal investment in higher education made college newly accessible to large numbers of women, low-income students, and minorities. The creation of a generous federal grant and loan system, along with a system of public universities offering tuition-free education, made it possible for a generation of students to enter college without relying on family support. This was also a period in which rising wages and expanding public services allowed young adults to attain financial independence earlier than any other time before or after in American history.[5]

Neoliberal and neoconservative observers of the 1960s were convinced that these unheard of economic conditions were responsible for the peculiar kinds of radicalism bubbling up on college campuses around the country. Reporting on conditions in the United States for the Trilateral Commission, the neoconservative Samuel Huntington infamously denounced the "democratic surge of the 1960s" with its "general challenge to existing systems of authority, public and private."[6] In one form or another, he observed, "this challenge manifested itself in the family, the university, business, public and private associations, politics, the governmental bureaucracy, and the military services. People no longer felt the same compulsion to obey those whom they had previously considered superior to themselves in age, rank, status, expertise, character, or talents." It was particularly visible on college campuses. "The single most important variable" shaping this dynamic, he ventured, was the democratization of higher education.[7]

For their part, neoliberal economists such as Milton Friedman and James M. Buchanan also suspected some kind of causal connection between free public education and rising militantism of the student movement. Drawing on the pragmatic insights of rational choice economics, which understands the most antisocial behavior as a rational response to market signals, they sought to show how the creation of free public goods such as education could act as a perverse incentive toward destructive anarchism and, conversely, how the pricing of these same goods could reverse such alarming trends.

The question of family was central to neoliberal arguments against public investment in education and key to their proposals for a new economic order powered by private investment and household debt. Both Chicago school human capital theorists and the public choice economists of the Virginia school justified their opposition to public deficit spending by pointing to its role in inciting the anti-authoritarianism of the student movement. Although their arguments often meshed with the overtly moralizing rhetoric of neoconservatives such as Samuel Huntington, the neoliberals offered a much more adaptive and flexible solution to what they perceived as a threat to inherited wealth and a decline in family responsibility. Neoconservatives would spend the next few decades railing against affirmative action and fighting a cultural war against the new minority disciplines of black, ethnic, and women's studies. Neoliberal economists also opposed affirmative action as a distortion of the allocative virtues of the free market. But unlike the neoconservatives, they were more interested in the positive task of developing an entirely new model of education funding—one that would replace public with private deficit spending and in so doing reinstate the economic obligations of family. Milton Friedman and Gary Becker could not have foreseen how dramatically consumer credit markets would expand in the following decades, nor could they anticipate how closely the student loan market would approximate their policy prescriptions, but they did understand how private credit markets could perform democratic inclusion without disturbing the economic structures of private family wealth. To fully grasp the novelty of their position, we need to turn to the early history of neoliberal human capital theory, which for many years was overshadowed by its more successful neo-Keynesian rival.

VICISSITUDES OF HUMAN CAPITAL THEORY

Today, human capital theory is almost synonymous with Chicago school neoliberalism, thanks in large part to the publication of Foucault's seminars at the Collège de France.[8] In the late 1950s and 1960s, however, the concept of human capital was much more closely associated with the name of Theodore Schultz, an economist who worked alongside Milton Friedman and Gary Becker at the University of Chicago but who would be more accurately described as a neo-Keynesian of the likes of Paul Samuelson, Robert Solow, and Richard Musgrave.[9] It was Schultz who first popularized the idea that spending on human services such as education should be considered an investment rather than an act of consumption — and therefore that education itself should be considered a form of capital or interest-bearing asset. Specifically, Schultz believed that investment in education could help explain a hitherto perplexing problem in the calculation of national economic growth, one that had been identified by the founding figure of neoclassical growth economics, Robert Solow. In two seminal articles in the field, Solow reported that only a small part of the rapid economic growth of the United States in the early twentieth century could be attributed to increases in the size of the labor force or physical capital — the sources of investment traditionally thought to account for GDP growth.[10] Solow concluded that the part of economic growth not accounted for by investments in labor or physical capital could be described as the "residual" and explained by the efficiency with which labor and physical capital were used. He surmised that the "residual" was primarily a function of technological progress, although his model could not explain where this progress came from or how it could be improved.

Theodore Schultz, for his part, thought that he had a much more plausible explanation for the discrepancies uncovered by Solow. The "residual" gave "a name to our ignorance, but [could] not dispel it."[11] The problem could be resolved, however, if one took into account the sustained increase in private and public investments in education that had occurred over this period, an increase that was not the result of any conscious policy decision but that nevertheless had had the desirable effect of greatly improving GDP. Human capital investment, then, was the missing production factor in growth economics.

Schultz's insights led him to a number of practical conclusions regarding the role of public investment in education. First, he reasoned that if haphazard investment in higher education had been responsible for such a large portion of national economic growth, then the federal government would be well advised to adopt an active policy of sustained investment in the sector. Second, he argued that selective underinvestment in the education of the working class, African Americans, and women could account for the labor market discrimination experienced by these demographics.[12] Underinvestment in education was not only a source of economic, racial, and gender inequality; it was also a waste of national human resources that could have greatly increased GDP had they been deployed. Unlike his colleagues Friedman and Becker, Schultz was convinced that the federal government had a vital role to play in the field of higher education. When Friedman, commenting on one of Schultz's drafts, asked him the critical question of whether returns to investment in education accrued primarily to the individual or the collective, Schultz replied that such investment raised national income and was therefore in the interests of the public as a whole. The public provision of free education, more-over, enabled rich and poor to attend college, independently of family wealth; the corresponding increase in wages for poor students could be justified in the same way as progressive taxation.[13]

As an academic economist, Theodore Schultz exerted an unusual influence on government policy, thanks largely to the enthusiastic translational work of Walter Heller, a public finance economist who served as Chairman of the Council of Economic Advisers under Kennedy and Johnson.[14] Heller had been instrumental in persuading Eisenhower that increased investment in higher education was a necessary weapon in the Cold War struggle against the Soviet Union. In a consultation paper on fiscal policy delivered a few weeks after the launch of Sputnik II, Heller famously argued that only a sustained commitment to public education could generate the "quantity of brain-power" needed to compete with the Soviet Union; invoking what were then mainstream ideas about the economic role of the state, he identified military prowess and national security as "positive externalities" that only public investment could hope to provide.[15] After his nomination to the Council of Economic Advisers in 1960, and having encountered the work of Theodore Schultz, Heller modified his security-focused arguments in favor of higher education, now pushing for further public investment as a means of stimulating economic growth and overcoming inequality.

Thanks to Heller's advocacy, the idea that the federal government should play a much more direct and generous role in financing higher education became a mainstay of neo-Keynesian public finance economics. Richard Musgrave, the founder of modern public finance and a close associate of Heller, integrated Schultz's ideas into his theory of public investment to argue that "adequate provision for educational services is of prime importance to the nation's safety and welfare."[16] In Musgrave's work, the imperatives of national security, economic competitiveness, and democratic inclusion converged in apparently seamless fashion to render federal investment in education an urgent task of public policy. "The events of recent years," he remarked:

> have shown that the maintenance and strengthening of educational standards is of greatest importance for the future of our country. These educational services are needed not only as a means toward obtaining a fuller life, but as a condition of national survival. For one thing, the revolution of weapons technology over the last decades has rendered scientific advance and training a crucial, perhaps the most crucial element in national defense. For another, our leadership in the Western world requires that our economy continue to grow at an adequate rate so as to maintain our position of relative economic strength in the world. Investment in human capital through education is a most important and direct way of accomplishing these objectives. Moreover, among all policies to stimulate growth, that of advancing education is most in line with the social objectives and ideals of our society.[17]

By 1960, then, some combination of Schultz's human capital theory and Musgravian public finance economics had become the received wisdom among representatives of the Council of Economic Advisers, and it was this institution in particular that can be credited with inspiring President Johnson's astonishing commitment to public education. During his term in office, Johnson presided over the most dramatic expansion in higher education in the nation's history, overseeing dozens of laws designed to increase federal spending and democratize access. The centerpiece of Johnson's reform efforts, the Higher Education Act (HEA) of 1965, gave the federal government authority over almost every aspect of the nation's higher education system, doubled the federal budget for higher education, and imparted a coherent vision of democratic inclusion to the sector as a whole.[18] The HEA pumped federal aid into impoverished black colleges, oversaw the creation of student recruitment programs and bridging courses for disadvantaged students, increased the number of grants available to low-income students, and created a program of guaranteed student loans to be subsidized by the federal government. In a final bid to ensure the redistributive objectives of federal aid, in 1972 Senator Claiborne Pell convinced Congress to approve a program of low-income grants (renamed Pell grants in 1980), which would be administered directly by the federal government rather than allocated by colleges. These policies had the effect of welcoming unprecedented numbers of low-income, black, Latino/a, and women students into colleges and universities, a demographic shift that would soon be reflected in the political and pedagogical demands of the student movement. As Schultz had foreseen, sustained federal investment in higher education functioned much like an "inheritance tax."[19] By redistributing the costs of education through the tax base, Johnson had made it possible for students without family wealth to access an institution that had once been a major conduit of class reproduction. During the 1970s, Pell grants were generous enough to cover both tuition fees and living costs, liberating students from the need to rely on the contributions of their parents.[20] For a brief moment, the expansion of public investment in education replaced private, family investment as a means of access to education.

From the beginning, Schultz had his critics. Milton Friedman and Gary Becker in particular developed a perspective on human capital that highlighted the value of private as opposed to public returns to investment and led to policy recommendations at complete variance with those of Schultz. As early as 1945, Milton Friedman and Simon Kuznets were weighing up the costs and benefits of higher education by seeking to measure the precise returns to workers who had invested in some form of professional training.[21] Their study found evidence of significant wage differentials between college-educated and non-educated workers that more than justified the "opportunity costs" incurred by students who did not earn a wage during their college years. Although the article excluded a discussion of publicly funded education, the authors did raise two questions that have since become critical to policy debates around human capital funding: "First, how much public investment is needed? Second, should the returns from public investment accrue to the individuals in whose training the investment was made?"[22] Without offering an explicit response to the first question, Friedman and Kuznets suggested that in an ideal world, existing inequalities in education and wages could be resolved entirely through the private capital markets: With a few changes to corporate law, students could be persuaded to sell "stock" in themselves and obligated to pay a portion of their future wages as "dividends" to their public of stockholders.[23] In this remarkable passage, Friedman and Kuznets see students not so much as investors in their own human capital as corporations selling a stake in their human capital to outside investors—a vision that has now in large part been realized, albeit in the form of debt- rather than equity-based finance, and crucially without the usual corporate protections of limited liability or bankruptcy laws.[24]

In their 1962 book *Capitalism and Freedom,* Rose and Milton Friedman came out even more decisively in favor of private investment in human capital. Here they argued that the returns to investment in education accrued entirely to the individual student and that any ostensible social benefits were merely the summation of private wage gains.[25] The individual student should therefore be held responsible for the costs of his education. The Friedmans concurred with Schultz that there had been massive underinvestment in higher education, but unlike Schultz, they believed that this failure could best be remedied through the liberalization of credit. The fact that low-income students were unable to pay for a degree and thus discriminated against in the labor market could be attributed to "imperfections in the capital market," that is, the absence of a liquid market in private student loans.[26] At best, the Friedmans conceded that the state might play a minimal role in remedying this state of affairs by providing loans repayable through the tax system and contingent on future earnings.[27] But they clearly saw the private credit market as the most efficient source of funding for student loans and thought that government incentives to banks were the best way of stimulating this market.[28]

Gary Becker, who was always especially attentive to the micropolitical dimensions of public policy, developed an elaborate argument as to why private, familial investment in the education of children was more efficient than public investment. Free public education, he argued, could be critiqued on the same grounds as the progressive income tax, which "initially narrows inequality by reducing the variability in after-tax incomes" but ends up raising the "equilibrium level of inequality...because families reduce their investments in descendants."[29] The argument was improbable and at odds with the empirical evidence, but it enabled Becker to identify private credit markets as a logical and (he insisted) equally redistributive alternative.[30] In Becker's ideal world, students would once again need to look to the family as a source of economic support, and yet the old, once implacable stratifications of family wealth would simultaneously be deferred and elasticized by expanding opportunities for private debt. Becker's micropolitical perspective on human capital investment was a mirror image of the more familiar theories of the Chicago and Virginia school neoliberals, who famously argued that public deficit spending and the resulting national debt had the unfortunate effect of "crowding out" private credit markets and discouraging private investment. But whereas Milton Friedman and James M. Buchanan were primarily referring to business investment, what Becker meant by private investment was intergenerational, family investment. If the government would only scale back on its investments in public goods, Becker surmised, then the family would resume its proper role of investing in children.[31] Further than this, the family's traditional economic responsibility in ensuring the welfare of its members would be greatly expanded by the stimulation of appropriate credit markets. With a little help from government, the old poor-law tradition of family responsibility could be reinvented in the form of an infinitely elastic intergenerational debt.

Although well respected within the empirical literature, Friedman and Becker's theories of human capital had little political traction in the 1960s, when Johnson was ratcheting up federal investment in the nation's human capital and opening up public universities to a new generation of disadvantaged students. Throughout the 1960s, Schultz's ideas radiated outward. At the Washington OECD conference of 1961, member countries issued a resounding endorsement of Schultzian human capital theory.[32] Throughout the decade, UN agencies promoted his ideas as models of sound economic growth and encouraged postcolonial states to put them into practice. By 1970, however, this consensus was already faltering as governments began to feel the effects of rising inflation and dwindling economic confidence. At the Paris OECD conference of 1970s, representatives expressed a more cautious outlook on the slower returns from higher education. In the United States, a handful of economists reported that wage growth among college graduates had actually slowed, seeming to contradict the self-evidence of Schultz's predictions.[33] Alongside the growing militancy of the student movement, these economic trends troubled the once stable consensus that free public education was an unmitigated social good. As noted by Simon Marginson, public education in this period "faced the conflation of a resource crisis and a legitimation crisis."[34]

In the very different, recessionary environment of the 1970s, the ideas of Friedman and Becker came out of the cold and found increasing resonance among policymakers. The election of Ronald Reagan in 1980 marked the final triumph of Chicago school human capital theory, the moment when neoliberal ideas about the financing of higher education were first enacted on a federal scale and student debt became central to the experience of college life. But long before he became president, Reagan had experimented with these ideas in the policy laboratory of California, when he first encountered the Berkeley student movement of the 1960s.

THE STUDENT MOVEMENT: PROTESTING HUMAN CAPITAL AND *IN LOCO PARENTIS*

In the fall of 1964, a new kind of student radicalism flared up at the University of California at Berkeley, its aftershocks reverberating across other state campuses over the following months and years. The concentration of student protest at Berkeley was significant given its widely recognized status as a model of the new knowledge-based university and an exemplar of Johnson-era federal investment in human capital. In the late 1950s, the University of California was beholden to the institutional vision of Clark Kerr, a former labor economist and champion of Schultzian human capital theory who was appointed chancellor of Berkeley in 1952 and president of the entire University of California (UC) system in 1958.[35] As president, Kerr famously endorsed the landmark 1960 *Master Plan for Higher Education in California,* which preserved the UC institutions as the state's preeminent public research universities and affirmed the principle of free college access for residents of the state, who were to be charged only minimal administrative fees.[36] As a labor economist, Kerr had specialized in the resolution of industrial conflicts through collective bargaining; by the time of his appointment as chancellor of Berkeley in 1952, his attention had shifted to the importance of knowledge in modern economic growth. Throughout his tenure at the University of California, he worked on a series of large Ford Foundation grants exploring the transition from an economy of mass production to a knowledge economy, in which human resources would be the driving force of economic growth.[37] The consummate mediator, Kerr predicted that as the university replaced the factory as the prime locus of postindustrial accumulation, the antinomies between capital and labor would dissolve of their own accord. Taking stock of the new generation of intellectual workers represented by the students of the University of California, Kerr saw no reason to fear any possibility of conflict.[38]

Kerr published his most iconic statement on the knowledge economy, *The Uses of the University*, in 1963, just one year before the Free Speech Movement erupted on the Berkeley campus. Written at a time when student numbers were skyrocketing and the federal government was promising to dramatically increase its investments in the sector, Kerr's blueprint for the public research university succinctly distilled the lessons of Schultzian human capital theory. "The University is being called upon to educate previously unimagined numbers of students," he noted:

> Today, more than ever, education is inextricably involved in the quality of a nation. It has been estimated that over the last thirty years nearly half of our national growth can be explained by the greater education of our people and by better technology, which is also largely a product of the educational system.... Basic to this transformation is the growth of the "knowledge industry," which is coming to permeate government and business and to draw into it more and more people raised to higher and higher levels of skill. The production, distribution, and consumption of "knowledge" in all its forms is said to account for 29 percent of gross national product, according to Fritz Machlup's calculations; and "knowledge production" is growing at about twice the rate of the rest of the economy. Knowledge has certainly never in history been so central to the conduct of an entire society. What the railroads did for the second half of the last century and the automobile for the first half of this century may be done for the second half of this century by the knowledge industry; that is, to serve as the focal point for national growth. And the university is at the center of the knowledge process.[39]

Although Kerr was determined to include low-income, minority and female students within the new knowledge-based university, his social progressivism was allied with a highly instrumental, nationalist vision of academic knowledge production. There was no doubt in his mind that the emerging generation of knowledge workers would primarily be of service to the petrochemical, agrochemical, and defense industries, the agents of America's neocolonial wars in Southeast Asia. In keeping with the double vision of the Johnson administration, which had launched the War on Poverty at the same time it embarked on a disastrous war in Vietnam, Kerr saw public investment in human capital as serving the dual ends of domestic social justice and national security. When the student revolt erupted in the following year, it was precisely this conflation that came under attack.

Referring directly to the *Uses of the University*, Mario Savio, a prominent figure in the Berkeley Free Speech movement, accused Kerr of turning students into the "raw material" of a new "knowledge factory," an assembly line "where all the rough edges are taken off and smooth slick products come out."[40] Steeped in Frankfurt school humanism, Savio appealed to a "more traditional educational philosophy" that would no longer be "plugged into the military and the industrial" but would instead seek out "truth." Beyond these romantic denunciations of the knowledge factory, however, the student revolt also generated a more pointed critique of Johnson-era human capital theory. Johnson's inclusive higher education policy had unwittingly produced a generation of students who perfectly understood the connections between domestic race relations and anticommunism abroad and who refused the cozy relationship between the public research university and American imperialism. Students who took part in the Freedom Rides of 1964 brought the civil rights movement back to the North and promptly organized actions against local businesses that discriminated against blacks. Beginning in Wisconsin, students launched campaigns against Dow Chemical, the producer of napalm, and a host of other defense contractors who regularly recruited on American campuses, while antidraft actions targeted the many high-school students and graduates who would soon be eligible for conscription.[41] The civil rights and antiwar movements were connected in more ways than one: Not only did the former serve as a training ground for a new generation of activists, but the escalation of the war in Vietnam also reduced funding for domestic antipoverty programs and sent a disproportionate number of blacks to the frontlines of battle. At a time when third world anti-imperialism veered toward the left rather than the right and domestic dissent was casually classified as communist, the synergies between American race relations and imperialist geopolitics appeared transparent.

Yet student protest during this period also focused to a remarkable degree on the micropolitics of gender, race, and sexuality, as embodied in the peculiar tradition of *in loco parentis* rules on university campuses. The idea that college administrators were somehow endowed with the custodial powers of parents, and therefore authorized to act *in loco parentis*, was a very old one on American campuses, but it had been reinvigorated in the early twentieth century, when a court ruling gave colleges wide powers to expel students without due process.[42] Throughout the mid–twentieth century, *in loco parentis* rules transplanted the intimate normativity of the Fordist family into a wider institutional context, radiating its disciplines well beyond the confines of the family home into the liminal social space of the college campus, where students were considered neither complete adults nor children. *In loco parentis* allowed administrators and dorm officials to restrict the political activities of students, to regulate behavior, dress, and alcohol consumption, and to police sexuality. Controlled heteronormativity was the rule here. In an effort to "protect" women, contact between male and female students in college dorms was tightly regulated, while students could be expelled on the mere suspicion of homosexuality. The weight of surveillance bore down on female students in particular, who were subject to much stricter curfews and dress rules than their male counterparts and frequently scrutinized by both their peers and superiors. In the South, black students came to see *in loco parentis* as a form of institutionalized infantilism, a way of imposing norms of respectability and deference that were all too familiar as an expression of racial submission. Their mistrust was further reinforced when *in loco parentis* rules were invoked to suppress civil rights activism on Southern campuses.

The struggle against *in loco parentis* was a formative experience for the new student left and the various liberation movements that splintered off from it. These movements subjected the racial and sexual normativity of the Fordist family to relentless critique and explored the ways in which its intimate hierarchies pervaded the larger institutional space of the university. In his account of the epistemological revolution of the 1960s, Roderick Ferguson remarks that what in Europe took the form of a largely intellectual challenge to disciplinary norms—exemplified by the work of Michel Foucault—in North America, assumed the much more radical guise of comprehensive social insurrection.[43] The new student left, after all, emerged out of a historic shift in the demographics of the student population; and this shift was in turn reflected in the rise of movements demanding not simply inclusion in existing structures but a wholesale remaking of the institution itself. In campuses across the country, feminist students called for or initiated an immediate end to *in loco parentis* rules; affirmative action in admissions and hiring; information on birth control and abortion at student health centers; on-campus rape crisis centers; the creation of new women's studies programs, and the revision of the curriculum.[44] And beyond affirmative action, black, Native American, and Latino/a students called for a thorough overhaul of both the curriculum and pedagogical practice to better reflect the historical collusion between racism and capital in American history.[45] Without wanting to underplay the tensions between these various liberation movements, much less deny the normative and nationalist recuperations that occurred within them, together what they signaled was an effort to rethink the

entire institutional structure of the university—from its demographics to its curriculum and administrative structures—from the point of
view of Fordism's non-normative subjects.

These movements were both a product of the Fordist era democratization of higher education and radically in excess of its nationalist objectives. In one sense, it is obvious that they simply would not
have existed without Johnson's enormous infusion of public money
into higher education and the efforts of liberal administrators such
as UC President Kerr to maintain a free state university system. But
for the most part and with good reason, the student radicals of the
1960s saw these reformers as their enemies, enablers of the Cold War
military-industrial state who may have opened up higher education to
America's minorities but who had done so with the aim of further-
ing American imperialism and domestic anticommunism. Clark Kerr
in particular had demonstrated numerous times that he was all too
willing to compromise with the existing organization of American
capitalism. Although he valiantly withstood pressure from the House
Un-American Activities Committee to censor campus speakers, Kerr
was always prompt to offer concessions to the other side, insisting, for
instance, that left-wing speakers should be followed by anticommu-
nists as a demonstration of evenhandedness.[46] In an era of rising prosperity, it was perhaps difficult to imagine that within a few short years
the student critique of Fordist capitalism would be outflanked from
the right by a new class of political actor intent on undoing the public funding of education entirely. Thus, when Clark Kerr was finally
ousted from the University of California, it was with the blessing of
Ronald Reagan rather than the student protestors.

REAGAN AND THE BERKELEY STUDENT PROTESTS

More than a decade before his first budget as president of the United
States, Ronald Reagan had occasion to dress-rehearse his higher

education agenda when he came face to face with the nascent student protest movement in California. Indeed, many attribute Reagan's unexpected victory in the 1966 gubernatorial elections to his adroit handling of the Berkeley student movement, which he quickly managed to transform from a blip in the opinion polls into a wedge issue prizing white working-class Democrats from their traditional party allegiances.[47] Tuning in to white anxieties about the personal costs of affirmative action, Reagan organized his entire campaign rhetoric in opposition to Johnson's Great Society programs, which were at that very moment being rolled out across the country. Reagan was one of the first candidates to link the California property tax with excessive government spending and, by implication, racial inclusion, although his tax policies as governor were by no means consistent. He was also the first to successfully associate spending on higher education—which after all was inclusive of the white working class—with the dead weight of social welfare, exploiting the racial anxieties of white working-class voters to turn them against their own economic interests. As an alternative to Johnson's Great Society, Reagan came up with the idea of the "creative society," a precocious articulation of the so-called creative economy that extolled the virtues of public-private partnerships, entrepreneurial research, and intellectual property in the production of economic value.[48] Much like Richard Florida's later elaboration of the same idea, Reagan's creative society aspired to make full use of California's culturally and racially diverse human resources while at the same time neutralizing their most disruptive political claims.[49]

As early as 1965, Reagan set about stoking public resentment by denouncing the failure of the Democratic governor, Pat Brown, and Kerr to use force against the Berkeley radicals. Reagan remained in close contact with FBI agents throughout his campaign and on more than one occasion threatened to unleash a formal investigation against campus subversives.[50] But in his speeches at least, he toned down the Cold War rhetoric—deemed unnecessarily divisive by his advisors and likely to alienate alumni—and instead focused squarely on the issue of *in loco parentis* and its apparent decline.[51] Throughout the campaign, Reagan's aides plied him with memos outlining the numerous outrages of student radicals, who had allegedly moved on from free speech to free sex. According to these reports, students were holding naked parties where LSD was openly available and sex acts were performed in public; homosexuality was said to be rampant in campus dorms, bathrooms, even frat houses; female students were distributing pamphlets on birth control, sexually transmitted disease, and abortion; the list went on. Carefully avoiding any direct engagement with the students' political demands, Reagan's campaign rhetoric instead filtered campus unrest through the lens of a family drama, with Reagan himself cast in the redemptive role of the stern father.[52] If the postwar expansion of social welfare and public investment had enabled untold numbers of students to attend college, tuition-free, Reagan interpreted this as a form of parental indulgence—understandable, perhaps, but ultimately disastrous in its psychological consequences. In an address delivered to students at Eureka College, Illinois, he lamented the fact that parents of his generation had failed their children by dint of overgenerosity:

> We are the classic example of giving to you what we never had…from TV to Little League, but I am afraid we shortchanged you on responsibilities or the right to earn for yourselves.
>
> All too often, because we had to earn, we wanted to give. Our motives have been laudable, but our judgment has been bad. "No" was either a dirty word or dropped from our vocabulary.[53]

In another speech, he reflected that this was "an era not only of permissiveness, but of affluence" and went on to interrogate the relationship between rising prosperity and the criminality of the young:

> I cannot help but believe that goods and privileges carelessly given or lightly earned are lightly regarded….

Are we doing enough for our children by doing too much for them? Aren't they really better off if they are taught to accept responsibility and to learn that in the long run we all must earn what we get and that we usually get what we earn?[54]

Reagan was particularly concerned by the attitudes of left-wing faculty who he accused of deferring to student radicals and failing to act *in loco parentis*:

That educator is wrong who denies there are any absolutes—who sees no black and white or right or wrong, but just shades of gray in a world where discipline of any kind is an intolerable interference with the right of the individual. He rebels at the old fashioned idea of "loco parentis" and claims he is there to impart knowledge, not to substitute for absentee parents. But he cannot escape a responsibility for the students' development of character and maturity.... These institutions were created, and are presently maintained, to insure perpetuation of a social structure—a nation, if you will.[55]

In another speech, Reagan threatened to reinstate *in loco parentis* rules by imposing a code of conduct on faculty "that would force them to serve as examples of good behavior and decency for the young people in their charge."[56] Once elected, however, Reagan very conspicuously overruled the university's traditional forms of internal regulation and instead regularly called in police—and at one point the National Guard—to discipline students.

As governor, Reagan demonstrated an unusual interest in the internal affairs of the university. His position meant that he was considered an *ex officio* member of the Board of Regents of the University of California. Whereas previous governors had kept their distance, though, deferring to the university's long tradition of internal regulation, Reagan made full political use of the role, religiously attending each meeting and holding press conferences before and after in which he announced his intentions to the public and regents alike.[57] Reagan experienced an early, unexpected victory, at the January 21, 1967, meeting of the Board of Regents, the first he ever attended, when the regents voted 14–8 to dismiss Clark Kerr.[58] More than any other figure in California, Kerr had symbolized the hegemony of Theodore Schultz's theories in favor of free, publicly funded education. With Kerr out of the picture, Reagan was now free to push forward the competing ideas of Milton Friedman and the Chicago school.

A few short days after his swearing in as governor, Reagan's financial advisor unveiled sweeping plans to reform the UC and state university system. Having inherited a manufactured budget deficit from his predecessor, Reagan seized the opportunity to announce a 10 percent cut to the annual budget of the UC and state colleges and, more controversially, put forward a plan to introduce tuition fees as a way of covering the shortfall.[59] The action was widely perceived as a form of collective punishment and was spectacularly successful, in the short term, at uniting regents, students, and faculty against the new governor. Reagan's plan to introduce tuition fees was ultimately defeated by the regents in August 1967, although they did allow him to raise the revenue he wanted by increasing existing administrative charges.[60] In economic terms, the difference between Reagan's plan and the regents' eventual compromise solution was minimal. Yet, the idea of introducing tuition fees was understood as a devastating symbolic attack on the tradition of free college education. Once tuition was accepted in principle, how could one remain committed to the ideal of free education embodied in the California *Master Plan*? And what limits would be placed on annual increases?[61]

Certainly, Milton Friedman appreciated the symbolic importance of Reagan's stance on tuition. In his weekly column for *Newsweek* magazine, Friedman congratulated Reagan for validating his once marginal views on human capital investment. "Governor Reagan's proposal is long overdue and unduly modest," he wrote, "not only for the state of

California but for other states as well."[62] Turning the promise of public education on its head, Friedman caricatured the Berkeley protesters as middle-class rentiers living off the taxes of the decent hardworking poor, who ostensibly did not send their children to college:

> "Free" education is an ancient tradition in California, and this is one tradition that even the campus rebels are disposed to defend with all their might and main—after all, their pocketbooks are at stake.
>
> Unfortunately, low-income taxpayers and youngsters not in college are much less effective than students and professors in presenting their case to the public. 'Free' tuition is highly inequitable to them.[63]

Friedman's populist arguments ran directly counter to the evidence, which showed that free tuition, Pell grants and mentoring programs had enabled a growing number of lower income, female and minority students to attend college.[64] Yet, his rhetoric, like that of Reagan, was closely attuned to the grievances of white low- and middle-income taxpayers, who mistrusted the antipatriotism of campus radicals and resented their alliance with the civil rights movement.

At UCLA, the public choice economist James M. Buchanan (a former student of Milton Friedman) was even more outspoken in his defense of Reagan's tuition plans. "Why is free tuition such a sacred cow?" he asked: "Does Governor Reagan's proposal for charging tuition in California prove that he is out to destroy the institutions of higher learning? And why have academicians in California state universities and colleges so strongly resisted efforts to introduce even nominal tuition fees?"[65] The UCLA Economics Department was a stronghold of Chicago school neoliberalism and a special target of the campus student movement. In 1968, a bomb had been planted (but failed to detonate) outside the department head's office in protest against its failure to hire black professors.[66] Before returning to the University of Virginia in disgust, Buchanan, together with a colleague from the London School of Economics, published a book-length study that purported to explain the incentive structures driving student radicalism. Here they developed an elaborate theory of the relationship between public deficit spending and anti-authoritarianism, arguing that free tuition played a key role "in creating at least part of the chaos that we witness in our major universities."[67] The economics of campus "terror" could be explained as a rational response to the perverse incentives of free public education: "We reject the view that classifies these persons as deviants, as psychopaths, whose behavior is simply beyond the realm of rational explanation, economic or otherwise.... Although his hair might still be significantly longer, the hippie would himself have shorter hair if a tax on hair length should be levied."[68] By making college free, public investment desensitized students to the true price of education and led them to treat the university with contempt. By liberating students from their economic dependence on parents, free tuition allowed them to contest traditional authority at every level—within the family, the university, and the history of knowledge.[69] In short, it was the perverse incentive structures of public deficit spending that had generated the anarchic political movements of the 1960s. By contrast, a system of tuition fees and student loans would transform education from a public into a private investment and make students once again dependent on family.

As it developed throughout the 1970s, public choice economics was instrumental in challenging the intellectual hegemony of Musgravian public finance.[70] Virginia school economists such as Buchanan helped to discredit the key lesson of Keynesian economics that deficit spending for so-called productive investments was a necessary driver of economic growth and instead popularized the notion that budget deficits should be kept to a minimum as a matter of principle, even when fiscal discipline appeared inimical to economic growth. With the election of Ronald Reagan as president in 1980, balanced budgets and fiscal discipline became a constant refrain of government rhetoric— although bluntly contradicted by Reagan's exorbitant spending on defense and more often practiced by Democrats than Republicans. Buchanan's early work provides a valuable insight into the affective investments of public choice theory, suggesting that its arguments against public deficit spending were as much political as economic, motivated as much by the perceived collapse of the family as any overarching theory of macroeconomic rectitude. Buchanan saw no clear dividing line between the public economics of the state and the intimate economics of the family. By liberating a generation of children from the discipline of family obligation and filial debt, the expansion of public investment in higher education had served to finance a generalized revolt against authority. Only by rethinking the whole structure of public deficit spending could one hope to reverse this trend.

DEMOCRATIZING CREDIT: RESTORING FAMILY RESPONSIBILITY

After his landslide victory in the 1980 presidential elections, Reagan lost no time in pushing ahead with his education reforms. Inspired by a combination of monetarism and public choice economics, Reagan put forward an ambitious budget plan: Not only would he slash federal income taxes and cut public spending, but he would also balance the budget. As recognized by Reagan's budget advisor, David Stockman, the plan was inherently self-defeating, since Reagan had studiously exempted defense spending from his list of proposed cuts.[71] How did Reagan expect to balance the budget if he was simultaneously planning tax cuts and dramatic increases in military spending? The seeming impasse was exacerbated by the fact that the Volcker shock dried up tax receipts, forcing the government further into deficit, while dwindling inflation greatly magnified the burden of interest rates on existing public debt. In seeming contradiction with his campaign rhetoric, Reagan's fiscal policies ended up producing massive budget deficits, many times larger and significantly more costly than those of previous decades.[72] But if Reagan's budget plan contradicted the letter of public choice economics, it remained faithful to the spirit: The concern with budget deficits, after all, was never neutral with respect to where public money was being spent, and it was nurtured in a context where rising government expenditure on redistributive public services was held responsible for left-wing insurrection. During the 1970s, deficit spending on health, education, and welfare began for the first time to outpace spending on defense[73]—Reagan simply reversed this formula by relaunching the Cold War and implementing radical cuts in the health, education, and welfare budget.

Drawing on his experience in California, Reagan and his advisors fought hard to position free tuition as a burden on the taxpayer and a form of "perverse incentive" akin to public welfare. David Stockman denounced student aid as "one of those entitlements that we created in the 1970s that was excessive" and suggested "we could probably cut it a lot more."[74] Terrel Bell, secretary of education under the first Reagan administration, was instructed to "pull those leeches off the backs of decent, hardworking people."[75] His successor, the cultural conservative William Bennett, insisted that the costs of education (like those of welfare in general) should be primarily a family responsibility.[76] The aim was both to cut budget deficits and to revive respect for authority by restoring "the traditional role of parents and students in financing college costs."[77]

As part of this effort, Reagan's first budget proposed a 20 percent reduction in student aid spending comprising both grants and loans.[78] The budget called for set spending limits on Pell grants—a move that would immediately exclude many students who had qualified for help on paper. It also sought to reinstate the "dependent student" test for student loans, meaning that legally adult students would be expected to draw on parental support before they could qualify for credit. And it proposed the introduction of an onerous "origination fee" to be paid upfront by students at the time they took out a loan. These reforms were approved by Congress with remarkably little dissent and had almost immediate consequences: By 1985, the number of fresh-men participating in the Pell grant program had fallen by nearly a half, while the actual purchasing power of the grants began its long, steady descent.[79]

Although with each annual budget hearing Reagan proposed fur-ther drastic cuts to higher education, none were as successful as his opening salvo. Yet, as noted by Suzanne Mettler, Reagan's presidency was a turning point, signaling "the end of what had been a nearly forty-year effort, through higher education policy, to make college-going affordable to a broader cross section of the American public."[80] After Reagan's initial budget, this shift of agenda occurred as a result of "legislative deadlock" and "policy drift" rather than any system-atic ideological initiative.[81] Throughout the Reagan and George H. W. Bush administrations, congressional majorities blocked any attempt to expand the budget for student grants. And while Democrats routinely contested the size and necessity of proposed cutbacks, they could not prevent the value of federal grants from diminishing in real terms. Instead, Democrats and Republicans were able to reach a compromise by regularly agreeing to expand the student loan program, since this only required them to waive restrictions on who could borrow or to increase borrowing limits.[82]

The full significance of this "drift" becomes apparent if one con-siders the history of federally guaranteed student loans, once seen as secondary to student grants. With the passage of the Higher Education Act in 1965, President Johnson established both a generous system of grants for low-income students (later to be subsumed within the Pell grant system) and a guaranteed student loan program designed to fur-ther expand access for low- and middle-income students.[83] Rather than set up a direct federal lending program, it was considered cheaper and more efficient to provide private banks with incentives to issue stu-dent loans at below market interest rates. For each loan issued, the federal government not only compensated the banks for maintaining low-interest rates, it also agreed to pay all interest due throughout a student's period of enrollment and fully guaranteed the lender against the risk of default. Together these incentives transformed student lending into a virtually risk-free profit-making venture for private banks. In 1972, moreover, Congress created the government-sponsored entity known as the National Student Loan Marketing Association, or Sallie Mae, with the aim of further underwriting the risks of private lenders. Like Fannie Mae, its much older counterpart in the federal mortgage market, Sallie Mae provided lenders with a secondary market by purchasing their student loan portfolios. Banks that had originated loans would no longer have to retain them on their books and could instead sell on the liquidity risk to investors, thus freeing themselves up for further zero-risk lending. Despite these generous incentives to private lenders, however, the guaranteed loan program was intended to act as a mere supplement to the Pell grant system, which was considered the most important redistributive element of the Higher Education Act. As Michael Mumper explains, the logic of the HEA, particularly after its reauthorization in 1972, "was to shift a larger portion of the college costs from low-income students and their families to the federal government. In keeping with this spirit, the act sought to both increase the amount of aid available to low-income students and to lessen the volume of student borrowing and replace it with a system of direct grants."[84] For much of the 1970s, the student loan program did indeed play a secondary role with respect to grants, consuming a small proportion of the overall student aid budget and remaining more or less stable in terms of costs.

With Reagan's first budget, however, the prioritization of grants over student loans was reversed. As Democrats and Republicans repeatedly locked horns over the details of higher education spending and both parties ceded to the dogma of balanced budgets, the spending power of student grants steadily diminished relative to tuition. Democrats and Republicans routinely disagreed about how the student loan market should be organized, going so far as to completely reverse their respective positions on federal guarantees to private lenders between the 1980s and 1990s,[85] yet they found common ground in the idea that students should depend first and foremost on credit rather than direct grants to finance their education. By 1989, the real value of Pell grants had declined dramatically and loans had replaced grants as the largest source of federal funding for student aid.[86]

The true turning point occurred in the 1990s, when state governments began to feel the long-term effects of federal devolution on their budgets. Until this time, states had for the most part compensated for declines in federal funding by ratcheting up their contributions to public universities. By the 1990s, however, state governments (many of which had enacted spending limits in the wake of the 1970s tax revolts) increasingly had to triage between competing public spending priorities. For the most part, they prioritized Medicaid (whose costs had been partially devolved to the states by Reagan), K–12 education, and corrections over higher education.[87] Public universities such as Berkeley that had previously been tuition free had no other option than to increase fees—and refer students to the burgeoning student loan market—effectively implementing Milton Friedman's ideal funding formula for higher education.

Throughout the 1980s and '90s, Congress responded to the budget crisis in higher education by expanding the availability of credit. At various points in time, borrowing limits for student loans were raised, eligibility criteria were relaxed, and entirely new, high-risk lending solutions were created for students who had exhausted all other options. Students who had borrowed up to the maximum threshold on federally guaranteed student loans could now apply to take out unsubsidized federal loans on less favorable terms.[88] Increasingly, too, students were steered toward PLUS loans, an option created by President Carter in 1980 that allowed parents to sign up for federal loans on behalf of their children, although at higher interest rates than those reserved for standard student loans. Hitherto a last resort for students who had maxed out on their other sources of funding and could not obtain a private student loan, the PLUS program was expanded to include graduate and professional students in July 2006.[89] By the late 1990s, students could also apply for a loan from any one of the private lenders that had sprung up to cater to consumer demand (chief among them the newly privatized Sallie Mae, which quickly grew to dominate the market). These new private lenders did not receive federal guarantees or subsidies but were able to exploit insatiable investor appetite for asset-backed securities (including student-loan backed securities or SLABS) to offset their risks and make extraordinary profits.[90] Using variable loan structures and extortionate interest rates to price the default risks of "subprime" borrowers, and relying on securitization to divest themselves of long-term liquidity risk, private student lenders were able to include all students in their portfolios—at a price.[91]

With each round of debates on the student loan program and each reauthorization of the HEA, lenders were able to extract further concessions from Congress. Each time lenders won new ground, consumer protections for student borrowers were pared back, turning student debt into one of the most treacherous forms of household exposure by the end of the century. After its privatization in 1995, Sallie Mae persuaded Congress to approve the collection of extortionate fees and penalties from delinquent student borrowers, making it much more profitable for lenders to let students lapse into default rather than offer any refinancing or deferment options.[92] The landmark HEA reauthorization of 1998, passed with the final approval of Democrats, eliminated all statutes of limitations regulating the collection of student debt and exempted student debt from state usury laws. These amendments also abolished the existing amnesty period for bankrupt student borrowers.[93] Federal student loans were now no longer dischargeable in bankruptcy at all. In 2005, the Bankruptcy Abuse Prevention and Consumer Protection Act extended this provision to private loans also, making student loans the only category of debt in US history that could not be erased by filing bankruptcy. As the student loan program expanded then, risk was increasingly transferred from lenders to the state to students.

During the 1990s, the expansion of the student loan market came to be understood as part of a broader policy agenda, that of democratized finance. What had emerged as an ad hoc solution during the Reagan years, the result of legislative deadlock more than anything else, was now reformulated as a deliberate component of social policy. For Clinton's key economic advisors, Federal Reserve Chairman Alan Greenspan and Secretary of the Treasury Robert Rubin, the expansion of credit was the only credible and sustainable way of financing Clinton's Third Way policy agenda. Thus, where Reagan and George H. W. Bush had practiced an austere form of public choice economics, adhering rigidly to the idea that government spending on public goods such as education should be kept to a minimum whatever the costs, in the 1990s, Greenspan and Rubin developed a systematic argument for why limited public investment would in fact generate growth and how its inevitable social costs could be mitigated. Soon after his election, Greenspan and Rubin managed to convince Clinton that public investment must be restrained as far as possible in order to bring about low long-term interest rates, which would in turn generate an abundance of cheap credit and encourage borrowing on the part of interest-sensitive consumers.[94]

The sensibilities of bondholders played a critical role in their understanding of public economics. Investors in US Treasury bonds, it was argued, were suffering from a kind of posttraumatic stress disorder left over from the high inflation days of the 1970s. Bondholders were afraid that any decision to raise the level of public investment in education, health care, or infrastructure (all included in Clinton's campaign promises) would inflate wages and prices and undermine their returns on investment, much as it had in the 1970s.[95] More than a decade after the Volcker shock, bondholders were still demanding an inflation premium in the form of high long-term interest rates, a way of protecting themselves from the ever-present danger that the state might invest in its own citizenry.

Yet Greenspan believed he had a solution that would satisfy all parties. If bondholders could be persuaded that the government would not spend on public services and would not intervene to increase wages, they would be confident enough to let long-term interest rates fall. This would be of immediate benefit to workers because it would bring about a consumer credit boom that would compensate them for expensive education, soaring healthcare costs, and stagnant wages.[96] Instead of accessing services through higher wages and public investment, as they had in the 1960s, workers would accept precarious wages in order to access abundant credit. Instead of the government going into deficit to spend on public services, a scenario that was unwelcome to the holders of US government debt, the individual consumer would go into debt to purchase these same services. Greenspan envisaged the expansion of consumer credit as both a natural consequence of and solution to restrained public spending. Fiscal austerity and credit abundance went hand in hand; the one could not exist without the other. Clinton's Comptroller of the Currency, Eugene A. Ludwig, soon dubbed this strategy the "democratization of credit" and predicted that it would neutralize the simmering inequalities of American society.[97]

Monica Prasad has usefully enquired into the actual outcomes of this policy shift by investigating comparative data on household spending and debt. Building on a well-established body of literature that seeks to theorize the historical relationship between welfare states and consumer credit, Prasad finds that all things being equal, the countries that most consistently sought to cut back on social spending after 1980 were also those in which household indebtedness saw the greatest increases.[98] In the United States, she finds that household debt has clearly come to function as a substitute for public goods;

middle-income earners are using credit to finance college education and health care, not consumer luxuries. Ultimately, Prasad understands the democratization of credit as "an alternative form of redistribution" that differs from the Keynesian public investment model merely in its temporal logic.[99] We should be careful to avoid an overly teleological interpretation of the respective virtues of credit versus welfare, she warns, because "it is not obvious which of these methods—redistribution from the future versus redistribution in the present—would make the most sense."[100] Further, the "logic of the welfare state—that productive public investments will lead to growth and therefore pay for themselves—is not so different from the logic of credit" and proceeds from "the same insights about economic growth that fed Keynesianism."[101] In both models, deficit-spending fuels productive growth, only its locus is transferred from the public to the private and from the state to the household.[102]

Yet Prasad vastly underestimates the distributional differences between public and private deficit spending. Most obviously, credit, unlike a grant, is not an income transfer: it does not cancel out the personal costs of a college education, but merely postpones them to a later date. Credit comes at a higher price for the poor, too, even when it is subsidized by the government. Assuming the same initial burden of debt, a student with no assets or savings is more likely to have to defer, refinance, or default on a loan, accumulating a much longer temporal burden of interest payments than the student who can pay on schedule. The price that a low-income student must pay to get a college degree is much higher than the student who starts with family wealth. And contrary to the assumptions of Friedman's human capital theory, average earnings for female and minority graduates continue to lag behind those of their college cohorts, even correcting for work experience.[103] This means that they will be putting aside a higher portion of their monthly wages to pay back their student debt. In short, the generalization of student loans acts as a form of *regressive taxation*, placing a proportionately higher burden on lower-income students while paying lip service to the ideals of democratic inclusion.

Beyond this, however, the private debt model also serves to reassert the role of family wealth in determining the price of inclusion. Today, student debt is increasingly a family affair, keeping parents, children, and relatives enmeshed in webs of economic obligation for decades on end. Since there is no obvious source of collateral for student debt, private or unsecured federal loans transform the intimate dependencies of family into a form of substitute collateral—comparable to the forms of kinship-based collateral that anthropologists see at work in microfinance.[104] As more and more students turn to Parent PLUS loans, low-income, precariously waged parents are finding themselves saddled with nondischargeable student debt well into old age.[105] Most private loans also take the form of intergenerational debt, since they routinely require a parent or other relative to act as cosigners. Like other student loans, these debts are not dischargeable in bankruptcy and can be garnished from social security payments—an extraordinary burden for elderly parents who may have no other source of income. In many instances, it is only when a student goes into default that family members realize they are entirely responsible for the debt.[106] And it is only when a student dies prematurely that parents discover their debt is inheritable.[107] In short, where public investment in higher education once acted as an "inheritance tax" liberating students from their dependence on family wealth, the private debt model of college funding allows all students to attend college while simultaneously reinserting them in the economic obligations of family.

It is not the case then that we might undermine the debt obligations of high finance by valorizing our "debts...to our friends, families, and communities," as the Strike Debt movement advises us, since the global market in securitized household debt is entirely dependent on our intimate obligations to each other, particularly at the level of the family.[108] The fact that we are unwilling to abandon such obligations serves a highly useful anchoring role for the market in securitized credit, ensuring that consumer debtors will typically remain wedded to a contract much longer than professional market players. This expectation was made explicit in the wake of the subprime crisis, when investors in mortgage-backed securities began to fear that "underwater" homeowners might be tempted to walk away from their debts with the same equanimity typically displayed by professional investors. In the intense debate that followed, it became clear that the whole edifice of securitized household finance relied on the assumption that everyday consumer investors would in the long run behave differently from professional investors, even when they were encouraged to see themselves as fully fledged asset-holders. In the moment of crisis, and even as professional investors proceeded to liquidate all their long-term commitments, what was demanded of the personal debtor was a nonstrategic and in the last instance sentimental attachment to an illiquid asset of depreciating value (the home). While professional investors have always demonstrated a decided "liquidity preference" in favor of strategic default, the personal debtor alone is enjoined to treat the contractual investment as if it were a non-contractual familial obligation—"permanent and indissoluble, like marriage, except by reason of death," an option that Keynes briefly and facetiously entertained as a solution to the liquidity crises of modern financial markets.[109] The fact that student debt routinely takes the actual form of an intergenerational, familial debt and that student debt alone is excluded from consumer protections such as bankruptcy means that this logic is even more acutely operative here than it is in the mortgage market.

Clearly, the evolution of student financial aid has more than fulfilled William Bennett's call for greater "parental responsibility" in the financing of college education. The necessity of family responsibility applies at all levels of the class scale, but it bears down in particularly punitive ways on the poorest of students. For wealthy households, the costs of college education are now considered a routine family investment comparable to the down payment on a first home. These families have the cheaper option of paying for the costs of a college education upfront or taking out low-interest loans using housing equity as collateral. Low-income students, by contrast, have to borrow more and at a higher price to pay for the same education. A 2015 Demos report found that 84 percent of graduates who were poor enough to receive Pell grants graduated with debt, compared to 46 percent of those without grants.[110] Since class has a distinct racial profile in the United States, these figures correlate closely, although not perfectly, with figures comparing white students to African Americans and Hispanics. Hence, a 2013 study by the Urban Institute found that African Americans and Hispanics were almost twice as likely as whites to have student loan debt. Overall, 16 percent of whites held student loan debt, as compared to 34 percent of African Americans and 28 percent of Hispanics.[111] African Americans, moreover, were more likely to have taken out a private loan after exhausting their Pell grant and federal loan options and were also more likely to be charged higher interest rates on these loans.[112]

With each reauthorization of the Higher Education Act of 1965, successive governments since Reagan have utterly transformed the structures of college funding while never formally renouncing the democratic promise of the 1960s. Universities today loudly proclaim their commitment to diversity. But in the meantime, democratization through public investment has been replaced by democratization through consumer credit, effectively transferring the costs of diversity back to the individual student and her family. The beauty of securitized credit is that it excludes no one a priori. By abstracting from class stratification in the present, it can accommodate all differences preemptively simply by pricing them at variable rates and deferring repayment to some barely imaginable point in the future. In principle, we all have access to a college education, no matter how much we or our parents earn. Yet, private credit does not merely obscure the effects of class; it also actively exacerbates inequality by forcing those without income or collateral to pay higher rates for the same service. When the long-term costs of credit begin to materialize and accumulate, students are once again confronted with the intractable resistances of class, race, and gender stratification. The divisions of family wealth reassert themselves with all their historical force.

IN LOCO PARENTIS REDUX

As Chicago and Virginia school neoliberals struggled to respond to the challenge of the new student radicalism, the much younger neoconservative movement also cut its teeth on the student protests of the 1960s. Indeed, 1965 can be identified as one possible date for the birth of neoconservatism, the year in which the former Trotskyist professors Nathan Glazer and Seymour Martin Lipset went public with their reservations about the Berkeley Free Speech movement and the New Left counterculture.[113] Much of the very early writing of the neoconservatives was directed against the rise of an alleged new class, forged in the political and intellectual ferment of the late Fordist university. Viewed in objective terms, this new class closely resembled the up and coming generation of newly graduated knowledge workers, hailed by the likes of Clark Kerr as the future of postindustrial America. The neoconservatives, however, understood very quickly that this generation would be much less docile than their predecessors and much less willing to accept the social hierarchies of Fordist society than Kerr seemed to expect. They feared that this new class of knowledge workers, having received their education in the crucible of the New Left, were set to storm the centers of power of American political life, infiltrating the courts, schools, universities, and government bureaucracy with their incendiary ideas.

Throughout the following decades, neoconservatives concentrated their energies on attacking affirmative action—perceived as a threat to the American tradition of meritocracy—and the new, militant disciplines of women's studies, black studies and ethnic studies—denounced as a threat to the Western humanist tradition and its universal truths. These attacks were indefatigable, reaching new heights of political legitimacy in the 1980s, when Reagan's second secretary of education, William Bennett, published his report on the humanities in higher education, *To Reclaim a Legacy*.[114] Here he charged faculty and university administrators with a "collective loss of faith" in the Western tradition: instead of defending this tradition against the onslaughts of student activists, universities had allowed the curriculum to be desecrated and tribalized by the particularistic concerns of minority interest groups.[115]

Yet, if the neoconservatives and their fellow travellers achieved notable success in rolling back affirmative action in the 1990s, even Irving Kristol was forced to concede that the left had won the culture wars on the epistemic front.[116] Despite the best efforts of cultural conservatives to oust left-wing academics from their putative strongholds in the humanities, something had changed irreversibly in the structure of the disciplines that eluded the blunt force of neoconservative nostalgia. Ultimately, it seemed, the most enduring legacy of the student movements of the 1960s was the creation of the new minority disciplines that William Bennett so despised. These minoritarian epistemologies valiantly withstood the neoconservatives' full-frontal attack, although perhaps only because, in the meantime, they had proven useful to a new kind of academic capitalism. If "modes of power once disciplined difference in the universalizing names of canonicity, nationality, or economy," writes Roderick Ferguson, "other operations of power were emerging that would discipline through a seemingly alternative regard for difference and through a revision of the canon, national identity, and the market."[117]

As these epistemological experiments were incorporated into the new university curriculum, the economic conditions that had enabled minorities to challenge the institution in the first place were profoundly revised, leading not to the crude exclusion of times past but to highly conditional forms of private debt-based inclusion. What Ferguson calls the "interdisciplines" have survived—at times even thrived—on condition that they do not in any way upset the economic premises of expanded access to education.[118] Students may specialize in African American or ethnic studies even while the public investment strategies that allowed low-income minorities to attend college in the first place have been radically stripped back. Others may take a major in queer studies even while the institutional accreditation of this knowledge is utterly dependent on parental wealth and familial forms of economic obligation. In this context, it is hardly surprising that a certain kind of queer politics should see no contradiction between its claims to antinormative sexuality and the right to legally recognized forms of family life. The seemingly paradoxical articulation of marriage and queerness perfectly reflects the process by which capital has absorbed the antinormative critique of late Fordist liberation movements while recapturing their energies in the neoliberal/neoconservative imperative of private family responsibility. The neoconservatives may have lost the cultural wars on one front, in the long run conceding their failure to restore the normative epistemologies of the Fordist university, but in another respect they have triumphed. William Bennett was ultimately unable to reform the humanities curriculum, but he was much more successful in his attempts to restore parental responsibility as the condition of access to college. Together, neoliberals and neoconservatives won the war on that particular front.

In light of these trends, we should not be too surprised to learn that *in loco parentis* is making something of a comeback on college campuses, albeit in a strikingly different form. Having fallen into disuse at most institutions by the late 1960s, a new formulation of *in loco parentis* emerged in the 1980s, ironically at the behest of the very baby boomer generation that had been so instrumental in its demise.[119] Increasingly in this decade, the parents of college students began to bring private tort suits against colleges for failing to fulfill their duty to protect students from foreseeable dangers such as hazing incidents or on-campus rape. Drawing on the language of private liability, the plaintiffs demanded that colleges take reasonable precautionary steps to prevent incidents occurring, create safe spaces for the students who had paid for them, and give adequate warnings against the possible dangers that might confront students on campus. These lawsuits positioned parents as private investors in the future capital of their children, and colleges as standing in a trustee relationship to this investment—liable for damages if their charges were in any way harmed.

The extension of civil liability rules to colleges and universities marked a profound transformation of the norms of protection that had prevailed until the 1960s. For much of the twentieth century, *in loco parentis* rules accorded comprehensive powers of custodianship to universities, comparable to those of parents, and consequently virtually exempted them from civil liability. Just as the Fordist family enjoyed broad rights of tort immunity insulating parents from the threat of lawsuits brought by children, the university was also largely protected from litigation. Today, however, the presumption of tort immunity has retreated in accordance with changing understandings of the custodial relationship between parents and children, on the one hand, and college administrators and students on the other. What was once understood in legal terms as a paternalistic right to discipline and protect is now more readily perceived as a relationship of parental investment that should be subject to the same rules of civil liability as those that prevail in the business world.[120] *In loco parentis*, it seems, now speaks the language of personal injury rather than institutional paternalism and disciplinary norms.

The vernacular of campus minority politics is strikingly attuned to these shifts in the legal understanding of institutional liability. While not for the most part leading to actual litigation, a certain kind of left-wing politics appears to have wholly assimilated the imaginary of personal injury as defined by tort law, translating its guiding concepts into an elaborate vocabulary of safe spaces, microaggressions, and trigger warnings.[121] The demand that one be sufficiently apprised of reasonably foreseeable risks, after all, is a precise translation of the tort law innovation of informed consent, while the carefully signposted safe space is one very familiar way in which public and private authorities have sought to forestall the threat of tort litigation in recent years. More precisely, this is a politics that adopts and radicalizes the language of a particular kind of tort action, so-called torts of outrage, which foreground the intentional infliction of emotional rather than physical injury and appeal to measures of psychological trauma to establish the seriousness of any given act. A relatively recent innovation in tort law, and one that was hitherto restricted to the margins of civil litigation, torts of outrage are now increasingly common as stand-alone actions and appear also to be encroaching on territory once dominated by civil rights law.[122] The harms once attributed to the phenomena of "social discrimination" or "structural violence," that is, are now more readily perceived as private wrongs embedded in offensive words or images. Campus racism, misogyny, and other kinds of collective violence are here refigured as sources of psychic trauma that might depreciate the value of an expensive education, therefore warranting legal action or, at the very least, pure outrage against the institution that has allowed this to happen.

The politics of campus outrage has been subject to relentless caricature by the right-wing press. Indeed, right-wing commentators are among the first to have discerned a relationship between the rise of a culture of litigation in American society at large and what they perceive as a culture of grievance among today's college students. Both are signs, they allege, of the endemic infantilism of the left and a failure of personal responsibility amongst the young. Yet it would be difficult to deny that the university campus remains a site of intense sexual and racial inequalities, which routinely manifest in acts of extreme violence, and that these inequalities are the underside of a neoliberal diversity politics in which inclusion remains highly conditional on family wealth. As many have noted, the rise of tort litigation in neoliberal America is an understandable response to the retreat of social insurance and other forms of socialized risk protection—indeed, it represents one of the few forms of protection that one is authorized to demand in such an environment.[123] With the demise of affirmative action and the perceived failure of civil rights law to redress sexual and racial violence, tort litigation is one legal avenue that appears to offer at least some hope of redress. Its imaginary has subsequently become pervasive (although not quite all-pervasive) on the left.

Yet there is reason to question its political promise. To date, the most visible impact of the trigger warning phenomenon has been to shut down spaces of public, potentially injurious expression in much the same way that rising litigation claims on the part of underinsured citizens have forced municipal authorities to signpost public parks or restrict access to other spaces of hypothetical harm. These forms of preemptive censorship are most likely to hurt the left, since the moral authority of outrage has little impact on those outside its circles. The almost exclusive legitimation of emotional trauma as a currency of minority politics tends to foster a culture of internecine litigiousness on the left, where the voices of those who challenge consensus are readily perceived as traumatizing or abusive and promptly excommunicated. In the meantime, the role played by economic inequality in the distribution of gendered and racial violence is actively obscured. After all, the politics of outrage references a logic of litigation that cannot be activated in practice without considerable personal wealth. Civil litigation allows one to contest a seemingly endless menu of injuries, *except* those that derive from extreme poverty (thus class inequality can be registered, if at all, as "classism," as a threat to an essentialized working-class culture). Contrary to the denunciations of the right emotional outrage is wholly captured within the moral logic of personal responsibility, merely reversing its terms to focus on the fault of the perpetrator rather than that of the victim. In this respect, it speaks less to a rampant culture of grievance than a hyperrestriction of the space of dissent.

CHAPTER SEVEN

Theology of the Social:
The Rise of Faith-Based Welfare

Laws which violate the moral law are null and void
and must in conscience be disobeyed.
—Richard John Neuhaus, "The End of Democracy?"

Religious freedom is flourishing in American prisons. In the wake of
Charitable Choice legislation passed in 1996, more than a dozen states
have opened faith-based wings in correctional facilities, while several
others have created "faith and character" prisons entirely dedicated to
religious instruction. The first American faith-based prison program
was established near Houston, Texas, by then Governor George W.
Bush in 1997. Known as InnerChange Freedom Initiative (IFI), the
program was run by Prison Fellowship Ministries, a nonprofit set up
in 1976 by former Watergate felon Charles "Chuck" Colson, soon after
his conversion to evangelical Christianity.[1]

The IFI prison unit was just one of several church-state collaborations commissioned by Bush during his governorship of Texas, part of
his strategy to cut state budgets and inject moral purpose into social
policy by expanding faith-based welfare across the human services
sector.[2] The collaboration assigned the responsibility for shelter, food,
and basic security to the Texas Department of Criminal Justice while
leaving IFI to design, implement and fund inmate programs—a division of labor that was calculated to shield the program from the charge

of flouting church-state separation.[3] IFI describes itself as a "24-hour-a day, 7-day-a-week...revolutionary, Christ-centered, Bible-based prison program."[4] It is open to inmates who are up to two years away from release and is divided into three phases. The first phase, which lasts twelve months, initiates the prisoner into an intensive course of scripture and Christian theology, combined with "life skill" classes focused on anger management, job preparedness, and responsible fatherhood training.[5] In what amounts to a form of "testimonial politics," to borrow a term coined by Tanya Erzen, participants at this stage are expected to make a public profession of faith in which they acknowledge their sins and accept Jesus as their savior.[6] In the second phase of the program, inmates are required to undertake community service assignments working for Habitat for Humanity (a religious charity that builds houses for low-income people) or some other faith-based nonprofit. At this point, prisoners are also encouraged to make contact with the victims of their crimes and to seek their forgiveness—a process of "restorative justice" that is central to Chuck Colson's vision of Christian rehabilitation. The guidance offered by IFI follows the prisoner into the world after release, where he or she is assigned a Christian mentor to help with the practical tasks of finding a job and housing and the long-term goal of refraining from sin.

Participation in IFI is voluntary, yet it comes with distinct privileges.[7] Prisoners who transfer into the program have access to private cells with their own keys, their own bathrooms, and the right to receive family visits. Their participation guarantees a place in postrelease work assignments and is viewed favorably by parole boards. It is also one of the few "educational" programs now on offer in a state prison system that has dramatically reduced funding for all kinds of vocational and professional training. Bill Clinton summarily abolished the federal Pell grant system that once funded prisoners' access to higher education as part of his welfare reforms of the mid-1990s; most states soon followed suit with additional budget cuts.[8] As funding for higher education has dwindled, the federal government and states have invested almost exclusively in prison programs focused on healthy marriage, responsible fatherhood, and religion.[9] In the words of Erzen, "this form of incarceration expects men to transition from prison as religiously redeemed, rather than simply rehabilitated, subjects by becoming conversant in or strengthening already-existing religious identities. Faith-based prisons...reframe imprisonment as a moral issue of individual sin and personal redemption achieved through religious knowledge."[10]

During the same period, faith-based organizations have also become heavily involved in so-called prison diversion programs that channel drug users and other low-risk offenders into pedagogical or therapeutic alternatives to jail.[11] One such initiative, known as Project ROSE (Reaching Out on Sexual Exploitation), allows women arrested on prostitution charges to enter a faith-based rehabilitation program rather than doing time in prison.[12] The program is a collaboration between Catholic Charities Community Services, Arizona State University's School of Social Work, and Phoenix police. As part of the state of Arizona, Phoenix has some of the harshest penalties for solicitation in the country and allows police officers to arrest people who "manifest" intent to prostitute without having exchanged money (by for example, walking the streets, being dressed in a certain way, or engaging with passersby). The participants in Catholic Charities' diversion program are recruited twice a year when the Phoenix police carry out mass raids over the course of a weekend. The arrestees are brought in handcuffs to a facility donated by a local church and (as long as they have no prior convictions or outstanding warrants) given the choice of going to prison or undertaking a six-month course with Catholic Charities. Apart from offering health care, housing, and other support services to arrestees, Project ROSE enrolls them in a program of moral education designed to "give hope" and help them escape "the life."[13] Criminal charges are suspended until the arrestee completes the course.

The recent surge in faith-based programs in the American penal system bears witness to a renewed interest in the economic and social value of rehabilitation, after a long period in abeyance. Rehabilitative perspectives on crime flourished in the period following the New Deal, a symptom of the general optimism created by rising wages and an expanding social state. During this period, the dominance of socio-economic theories of crime helped sustain the notion that deviance was a product of social injustice and that at least some prisoners could be appropriately normalized through judicious investments in social work, counseling and education. By the mid-1970s, however, white middle-class anxieties about the rising costs of welfare and its association with black militancy propelled a "permanent tax revolt" against the expansionist policies of the Great Society social state.[14]

In this newly divisive context, the once-marginal "law and order" rhetoric of a Barry Goldwater became part of the political vernacular and public opinion turned abruptly against investments in prison rehabilitation. Influenced by a combination of neoliberal rational choice theories of crime and new paternalist visions of civic obligation, the new criminology argued in favor of deterrence-based and retributive forms of punishment, leading to the new normal of exploding prison populations and extraordinary rates of incarceration among America's former welfare classes.[15] Investments in prison education and other programming plummeted during this period, culminating in Clinton's decision to discontinue the allocation of Pell grants to prisoners.

In recent years, however, the enormous fiscal costs involved in sustaining prisons has persuaded states to reconsider the value of a purely retributive vision of crime. Conservative evangelicals have been at the forefront of a prison reform movement calling for a return to rehabilitation. Chuck Colson, for example, has spoken out against inflexible sentencing standards that send first-time drug offenders to jail or mandate long-term imprisonment after "three strikes." Along with other evangelicals, he has called for further expansion of the prison diversion and drug court system that channels low-risk offenders into alternative rehabilitation programs.[16] When evangelicals call for a return to rehabilitation, however, they understand something very different from the socioeconomic, psychotherapeutic, and ultimately (in the Foucauldian sense) normative vision of reform that prevailed in the postwar era. As explained by Chuck Colson and fellow prison evangelist, Pat Nolan:

> At its root, crime is a moral problem. Offenders make bad moral choices that result in harm to their victims. To break the cycle of crime, we must address this immoral behavior.... Job training and education alone will not transform an inmate from a criminal into a law-abiding citizen. For some inmates, such programs merely make them smarter, more sophisticated criminals. It is a changed heart that can transform a prisoner into a law-abiding citizen. Unfortunately, many prison programs ignore the moral aspect of crime and avoid all discussion of faith and morality. In doing so, they are missing a significant factor that has proven effective at changing criminals' behavior—faith.[17]

The current resurgence of faith-based prison units is reminiscent of a much older tradition of prison rehabilitation. Historian David Garland writes, "The religious influence upon prison reform and penal policy remained a powerful one throughout the nineteenth century.... Evangelicals were in the vanguard of reforming movements both in Britain and in the USA, helping to ameliorate conditions of captivity or to aid prisoners upon their release, and later developing alternatives to imprisonment such as probation, which began as a form of missionary work funded by church-based temperance societies."[18] As Garland reminds us, evangelical social reformers were almost alone in pushing for rehabilitation and prison alternatives in the first part of the nineteenth century, before they were superseded by social-scientific proponents of rehabilitation in the last decades of the century.

Alexis de Tocqueville and Gustave de Beaumont were fascinated by the reformative role played by religion in American prisons. Their 1833 treatise on the American penitentiary system includes a detailed account of Philadelphia's Walnut Street prison, where prisoners were subject to a minute discipline of biblical instruction and spiritual cleansing. "In Philadelphia," they remarked, "the moral situation in which the convicts are placed is eminently calculated to facilitate their regeneration"[19]—a choice of words that points to the historical indistinction between spiritual rebirth and rehabilitation. Tocqueville and Beaumont were particularly impressed by the way in which respect for religious freedom—enshrined in the First Amendment of the American Constitution—reinforced rather than weakened the persuasive force of the religious instruction delivered in these facilities.[20]

Tocqueville is a mandatory point of reference for today's proponents of faith-based welfare. His remarks on the importance of voluntary association and religious freedom in the Early Republic are endlessly cited as proof of the American genius for decentralized democracy. Yet Tocqueville's discussion of the Walnut Street prison reminds us that he also discerned an inescapable relationship between the American philosophy of religious freedom and the internalization of moral law. What Tocqueville so admired about the Puritans was their ability to combine civic freedom with a pervasive and inescapable respect for divine authority. This, he thought, was what prevented the decentralized administration of the American Republic from descending into utter chaos. Citing John Winthrop's distinction between natural and civil liberty, he noted that only the latter could "be termed moral, in reference to the covenant between God and man, in the moral law" because it made freedom contingent on respect for divine authority.[21] It was this close association between civic freedom and moral law, he believed, that defined the singularity of American democracy as against the godless republicanism of revolutionary France.

Today, Tocqueville's work affords a peculiar insight into contemporary struggles around the American public sphere, where the prohibitive force of moral law is routinely justified in the name of religious freedom and where the return of strong religion is more likely to appeal to freedom of speech than outright censorship (in interesting contrast to the resurgence of blasphemy laws in Catholic, Orthodox, and Muslim-majority countries). The very concept of religious freedom, as interpreted by Tocqueville, encapsulates the "double movement" of liberal and conservative tendencies within a certain strain of American republicanism, which sees political freedom as intimately subordinate to moral law.

The proliferation of religious programs in American prisons is symptomatic of a much wider transformation of the social services that has seen religious providers actively included in government contracts to provide homeless shelters, soup kitchens, group homes, substance-abuse treatment, welfare-to-work training, healthy marriage, and responsible fatherhood instruction, along with a whole host of other services for the poor. As central as it has been to recent transformations of the social, however, the rise of faith-based welfare has largely escaped investigation by the major theorists of the American welfare state, habituated no doubt to the more professionalized and technocratic forms of governance that we as social theorists have come to recognize as the conduits of modern power.[22] The selective silence of social theorists stands in stark contrast to a loquacious and now voluminous literature in postsecular theory that has dedicated itself, seemingly without self-reflection, to the task of wanly reproducing the demands of the religious right, variously calling for a greater deprivatization of religion, a new tolerance for the public expression of faith, and a retreat of something hubristic called secular liberalism.[23] This literature appears oblivious to the fact that some of the major theorists of postsecularism, Peter Berger for example, have themselves been key players in the project of faith-based welfare.

In the meantime, some of the most renowned figures in political philosophy have conceptualized the return of religion as a messianic, quasi-revolutionary event perhaps heralding the final overthrow of capitalism.[24] Instead, I see these literatures as expressions of the status quo and theorize the return of religion as a process of institutional transformation fully internal to the neoliberal-neoconservative state.

THE RISE OF FAITH-BASED WELFARE

The recent profusion of faith-based social services can be traced to Clinton's welfare reform of 1996, which contained an unassuming provision (section 104) exhorting federal and state government to contract with religious nonprofits without infringing on their rights to religious expression. The provision, known as Charitable Choice, was sponsored by the former Republican senator John Ashcroft and drafted by Carl Esbeck, a constitutional lawyer specializing in "religious freedom" cases. It largely escaped the intense congressional and public debate that accompanied the rest of Clinton's welfare reform.[25] Yet, it introduced profound changes to federal law concerning the relationship between church and state and represented a remarkable legislative victory for Christian right litigators who had been pursuing a similar agenda in the courts for more than a decade.

Overriding regulations established in the 1960s, the Charitable Choice provision allowed religious organizations, including churches, to contract directly with government agencies without having to form a separate nonprofit and without having to sacrifice the religious character of their services. Organizations that might once have been judged to be "pervasively sectarian"[26] were now free to express their religious mission in the act of service provision, short of attempting to convert their clients, while churches were no longer required to remove "religious art, icons, scripture, or other symbols" or "alter [their] form of internal governance" to receive federal funds.[27] Appealing to the higher cause of "religious freedom," the provision urged government to stop "discriminating" against religious organizations, while at the same time exempting these same organizations from the Civil Rights Act of 1964 with regard to their employment practices.[28] The shift was real, if subtle. A similar employment-based exemption had been enshrined in Title VII of the Civil Rights Act from the very beginning, but until the passage of Charitable Choice, it had not applied to religious organizations funded by public money.[29] By generalizing this particular exemption to federal and state welfare programs, Charitable Choice implicitly endorsed the notion—long championed by Christian litigators—that religious organizations alone should be untouched by antidiscrimination laws, an innovation whose full consequences are only now beginning to be felt.

The significance of Clinton's 1996 welfare reform for church-state relations went well beyond the Charitable Choice provision, however. The welfare reform act not only multiplied the number of social service contracts open to faith-based organizations, it also created entirely new programs that were uniquely suited to the sensibilities of conservative religious organizations. Under the funding rules of the old welfare program, AFDC, only some aspects of welfare provision could be contracted out to third-sector providers; under the terms of the new welfare program, TANF, which replaced AFDC, all aspects of welfare provision, from eligibility determination to child care, job services and counseling could be outsourced to third parties. While administrative and logistical services such as data management, electronic surveillance, and child support enforcement were contracted out to private companies such as Lockheed Martin, Maximus, and IBM, faith-based organizations assumed a prominent role in delivering the "soft skills" component of welfare provision, including job preparation, substance abuse services, and a whole host of new programs in moral instruction that had not previously been part of federal welfare policy.[30]

As we saw in Chapter 3, Clinton's welfare reform created dedicated federal budgets to fund "healthy marriage" programs and allocated millions of dollars in bonus funds to states that could demonstrate they had successfully reduced illegitimate births without increasing abortions.[31] Title V of PRWORA singled out abstinence-until-marriage as the only responsible form of sex education and provided a generous grant structure to finance such programs.[32] In 2000, Clinton used his executive powers to create the President's National Fatherhood Initiative, a program designed to reinstate the rights and responsibilities of fathers within the family.[33] These initiatives were all closely aligned with the moral politics of religious conservatives and therefore bound to attract such groups in the process of tendering welfare contracts.

The moral politics prescribed by PRWORA have been sustained, with remarkable continuity, across successive Democratic and Republican administrations.[34] George W. Bush continued to finance the marriage promotion, responsible fatherhood, and abstinence education programs initiated by Clinton, more than tripling the funding for such initiatives during his second term.[35] At the federal level, the various faith-based offices housed in government departments are closely involved in the administration of healthy marriage and responsible fatherhood programs. These programs have not disappeared under Obama, as some had predicted. Instead, Obama has shifted the focus from healthy marriage to responsible fatherhood programs, while doubling the funding for the latter and shifting the focus toward the black family.[36] And while Bush reached out to white evangelicals via the appointment of Wade Horn to a key position in the HHS, Barack Obama made similar outreach efforts to black churches that may be progressives with regard to economic justice but social conservatives when it comes to gender relations within the family.[37] Faith-based organizations have played an indispensable role in the on-the-ground implementation of this state-legislated moral politics.

If Clinton's Charitable Choice enacted a formal revolution in church-state relations, Bush fully exploited its institutional possibilities. Having failed to secure legislative authority to expand Charitable Choice during his first weeks in office, Bush fell back on his presidential executive powers to establish the White House Office of Faith-Based and Community Initiatives. He then went on to create satellite offices in the Department of Labor, HHS, Department of Housing and Urban Development, Department of Education, and Department of Justice, each endowed with a carefully selected director and staff.[38] These offices were instructed to facilitate collaborations between faith-based organizations and government by simplifying grant-writing procedures, organizing outreach efforts and offering logistical support. Lew Daly has underscored the extravagance of such a move.[39] No further executive orders were needed to establish the project of faith-based welfare; yet Bush's creation of faith-based offices internal to government departments ensured that religious nonprofits would not only be accepted into tenders for a greatly expanded range of government contracts, but openly favored and courted as preferred partners for certain kinds of contracts.

Having accomplished this first step, Bush then commissioned each satellite office to conduct a thorough audit of outreach methods, procurement practices, and internal regulations in their respective departments with the aim of identifying possible obstacles to the inclusion of faith-based welfare providers.[40] In late 2001, the White House published an excoriating report, *Unlevel Playing Field*, summarizing their findings. The report claimed to have uncovered a culture of pervasive "anti-religious" discrimination among federal bureaucrats and accused government agencies of adhering to an overly zealous interpretation of constitutional law. At a time when the Supreme Court and Congress were adopting a much more indulgent interpretation of church-state separation, the report claimed, public agencies went "well beyond constitutional restrictions" in their efforts to police faith-based welfare providers.

These agencies were in fact violating the civil rights of religious providers by infringing on their right to religious expression in public space. "It is not Congress, but these overly zealous Agency rules that are repressive, restrictive and which actively undermine the established civil rights of these groups."[41] The report also accused government agencies of favoring the "large and entrenched" charities that largely had lost their public religious character, to the detriment of smaller faith-based organizations whose religiosity was far more conspicuous. In conclusion, it urged federal administrators to take "affirmative" steps to actively welcome these smaller religious nonprofits among their routine partners. The report repeatedly described religious organizations as victims of systemic civil rights violations and deserving of affirmative action—a nod to the work of Christian litigators who had been perfecting a similar argument in the courts for well over a decade.

In response to these directives, each federal department duly revised its internal regulations to help encourage tenders by religious nonprofits and undertook major outreach efforts to help faith-based organizations navigate the logistics of large government contracts.[42] The Bush administration was especially assiduous in its efforts to solicit the participation of the smaller, less experienced but more conservative evangelical congregations in its faith-based contracts, even going so far as to exclude long-established charities such as Catholic Charities USA, Lutheran Social Services, and Jewish Family Services from its public relations events.[43] Although some of these older charities are themselves well versed in the arts of public moralism, clearly it was the "pervasively sectarian" and militant organizations of the new religious right, not those with long-term experience in the humdrum work of large-scale case management, that interested the Bush administration.

Bush's faith-based initiative marked a decisive breakthrough in the religious right's "long march through the institutions." Not only did it further expand the range of federal and state contracts open to faith-based organizations, but it also consolidated an elaborate infrastructure designed to entrench their position in the social services. "There has been nothing like it in the history of the White House or in American social welfare policy," observes Lew Daly, himself a sympathetic observer of faith-based welfare. "Taken together, the structural and administrative changes carried out by the faith-based initiative, coupled with state-level efforts and grant-seeking mobilizations, represent a massive political effort to reconstruct the social safety net around religious providers and their methods."[44]

The Charitable Choice provision of 1996, followed by the faith-based initiatives of George W. Bush and Obama, have facilitated a dramatic expansion of the number of religious organizations engaged in the provision of social services ranging from homeless shelters, prison and post-prison reentry programs, drug rehabilitation services, welfare-to-work training, disaster relief, and sex (abstinence) education, along with marriage and responsible fatherhood programs.[45] In the wake of welfare reform, the moral and economic obligations of work and family have been refashioned in the religious idiom of faith, conversion, and redemption.

THE GREAT SOCIETY AND ITS DISCONTENTS: A PREHISTORY OF FAITH-BASED WELFARE

The rhetoric surrounding faith-based welfare might lead one to assume that religious charities have only recently and grudgingly been welcomed into the arms of government welfare administrations. As several historians have pointed out, however, the practice of outsourcing social services to religious organizations was not an innovation of the Clinton presidency but was first implemented, albeit in more restrictive fashion, as part of Johnson's War on Poverty in the 1960s.[46] At the time, this represented a significant departure from existing welfare practice. Under the centralized model of welfare provision established by the New Deal, all major social programs were administered in-house by federal or state agencies, leaving very little space for partnerships between government and charitable organizations. President Johnson decisively broke with this tradition of bureaucratic centralism by allowing public agencies to subsidize certain kinds of nonprofit institution (hospitals, schools, and colleges) and to outsource key components of welfare programs to nonprofit contractors. Specifically, amendments to the Social Security act in 1967 dramatically altered the relationship between government and the nonprofit sector by encouraging states to enter into service contracts with voluntary agencies. Religious organizations were some of the major beneficiaries of this shift in the structure of welfare provision. Not only did they participate enthusiastically in the urban antipoverty programs created by the War on Poverty, but their denominational hospitals, schools, and universities also received enormous injections of funding from the creation of Medicaid and Medicare and expanding higher education budgets.[47] As noted by historian Axel Schäfer, these decentralized forms of church-state collaboration appealed to both Catholics, who had a long history of subsidiarist welfare provision dating back to the nineteenth century, and Protestants, who for much of the twentieth century had preached a strict form of church-state separation (largely directed against Catholics) but who now began to perceive the benefits of institutional expansion. During this period, even the most conservative and isolationist of Protestant denominations—fundamentalists, evangelicals, and Southern Baptists—took advantage of this new collaborative environment to build up their network of denominational schools and other institutions.[48]

Among the various denominations taking part in welfare programs, the mainline Protestant churches (comprising the Congregational Church, the Episcopal Church, the Evangelical Lutheran Church, the Presbyterian Church, the United Methodist Church, the American Baptist Convention, and the Disciples of Christ) were the most inclined to accommodate themselves to the terms of church-state collaboration, in large part because they were themselves heavily involved in the ongoing expansion of the welfare state. United under the banner of the National Council of Churches of Christ, these denominations were early supporters of Nixon's black family wage and held views on contraception and abortion that would appear surprisingly liberal in future decades.[49] They also favored strict ideological separation between church and state, even going so far as to support Supreme Court decisions banning prayer and Bible readings from public schools.[50] Conservative evangelicals and Catholics, by contrast, were always ambivalent about the compromises they were forced to make as providers of public welfare and, as the decade progressed, became increasingly ill at ease with the direction of federal law on issues pertaining to family, sexuality and religion. Moreover, as evangelicals became more confident about their role in social services, they became acutely aware of the difference between their particular vision of public theology and the social witness of the mainline churches.

The changing legal environment was real enough. Beginning in the 1950s, civil rights and civil liberties campaigners turned to the courts as a way of translating political change into legal reform. Finding a receptive audience in a Supreme Court presided over by Chief Justice Earl Warren (1953–69), progressive lawyers learnt to sidestep the conservative stranglehold over Congress by pushing through with highly experimental test case litigation and became increasingly expert at establishing precedents in critical areas of constitutional law. During this period, organizations such as the National Association for the Advancement of Colored People (NAACP) and the American Civil Liberties Union (ACLU), along with legal aid offices supported by the National Legal Services Corporation, won key victories in civil rights, criminal procedure, and sexual and religious freedom, using strategic challenges to constitutional law to override established state "police powers" with regards to racial segregation and the regulation of sexuality.[51]

The NAACP's Legal and Educational Defense Fund was one of the first organizations to perfect the strategy of public interest litigation. In what marked a turning point in civil rights law, *Brown v. Board of Education* (1954), the Supreme Court ruled that the segregation of public schools violated the Equal Protection clause of the Fourteenth Amendment and was therefore unconstitutional — a decision that outraged some (but by no means all) Southern Evangelicals and fundamentalists.[52] The Legal and Education Defense Fund went on to win a series of test cases challenging the segregation of public spaces such as parks, federally funded hospitals, and even restaurants. The civil litigators of the NAACP were also responsible for popularizing the use of "freedom of speech" and "freedom of association" arguments to defend civil rights activism — arguments that would soon be expanded to include "sexual expression."[53]

Building on the victories of the civil rights litigators and introducing key innovations of its own, the ACLU was instrumental in redefining the legal discourse around sexuality in the late twentieth century. In a series of test cases brought before the courts in the 1960s and '70s, the ACLU sought to establish the entirely unprecedented notion that sexual expression was a fundamental civil liberty and therefore deserving of constitutional protection under the free speech clause of the First Amendment. It was the ACLU that first seized on the idea that domestic privacy (a concept long established in state family law) might be reinterpreted to protect the right to sexual freedom in the bedroom.[54] Having been tested in a number of lawsuits throughout the 1950s, the argument finally bore fruit in the landmark *Griswold v. Connecticut* case (1965), overturning a state law criminalizing the sale of contraceptives, and even more emphatically in *Eisenstadt v. Baird* (1972), overriding the state's police power to limit the sale of contraceptives to married couples.[55] Handing down his opinion for the *Griswold v. Connecticut* case, Justice William O. Douglas argued that although a "right to privacy" could not be found in the text of the constitution, it was implied in "emanations" from the Bill of Rights. The "intimate relation of husband and wife," Douglas affirmed, was "a sacred precinct."[56] The idea of allowing the police to intrude here was "repulsive to notions of privacy surrounding the marital relationship." The Court went a step further in *Eisenstadt v. Baird* when it extended the right to privacy from the marital couple to the individual, whether married or unmarried. "What was new in that jurisprudence," explains legal scholar Jean L. Cohen, "was not the application of the concept of privacy to the marital relationship or to the family construed as an entity. Rather, the innovation lay in the Court's attempt to articulate constitutional grounds for directly protecting the personal privacy and decisional autonomy of individuals in relation to 'intimate' personal concerns, whether these arise in the family setting or outside."[57]

The litigation strategies developed by welfare rights lawyers were, if anything, even more ambitious than those of their predecessors. Drawing on the ACLU's jurisprudence of privacy, and combining it with the due process and equal protection arguments of the NAACP, lawyers associated with the National Welfare Rights Organization sought to override state police powers with regard to public assistance clients by bringing welfare administration within the confines of the federal constitution.[58] In the late 1960s, the Columbia Center for Social Welfare Policy, in collaboration with an affiliate of the ACLU, won a decisive victory when it accused the state of Alabama of violating the right of privacy, due process, and equal protection in its use of substitute father rules. In its ruling on the case, *King v. Smith* (1968), the Supreme Court declared that substitute father rules were in violation of the Social Security Act and were therefore unconstitutional.[59] In the wake of *King v. Smith*, a string of similar cases prohibited state welfare agencies from policing the sexual behavior of poor women, in the process extending the jurisprudence of sexual freedom beyond family law proper to include welfare law.[60] Going well beyond traditional notions of domestic privacy enshrined in state family law, the new jurisprudence extended the presumption of sexual freedom from the rich to the poor, from married to unmarried couples and from the family unit to the individual, and hence to women—a cumulative legal revolution that was devastating to moral conservatives, particularly in light of the restrictions that were simultaneously being placed on the public expression of religion.[61]

Here again, the litigation strategies of the ACLU proved transformative. In two key test cases, *Engel v. Vitale* (1962) and *Abington School District v. Schempp* (1963), ACLU lawyers convinced the Supreme Court that compulsory prayer and Bible reading in public schools was inconsistent with the First Amendment religion clause outlawing the state establishment of religion. These cases profoundly shifted the balance of constitutional interpretation in favor of strict separationism and continued to define the institutional relationship between church and state for the next two decades. Under the terms of the Economic Opportunity Act of 1964, religious nonprofits were free to deliver publicly funded welfare services in line with their religious mission but were theoretically barred from direct expression of their religious character via the display of scripture and iconography in publicly funded facilities. To conform with these rules, religious congregations and churches were obliged to form a separate nonprofit organization if they were to deliver government social services and could not tender for welfare contracts directly. And in the landmark *Lemon v. Kurtzman* case, handed down in 1971, the Supreme Court declared that "pervasively sectarian" organizations could not receive government funding. The decision is considered the high point of legal separationism.[62]

The extent to which such rules were actually enforced in practice is questionable. The *Lemon* decision applied unequivocally to the funding of public and private schools but was never explicitly extended to the numerous colleges, hospitals, and other welfare services funded under the War on Poverty. Moreover, historians have argued that even the most conservative of religious providers were given free rein to express their "pervasively sectarian" character during this period since the strict regulations governing church-state relations were rarely policed on the ground.[63] Yet in a context where the modernizing Protestant churches enjoyed broad cultural influence, evangelicals and Catholics perceived the *Engel v. Vitale* and *Abington* decisions as alarming portents of theological decline. The fact that the mainline churches publicly supported such decisions contributed to their sense of aggrieved isolation.[64]

In their retrospective accounts of American moral history, representatives of the religious right routinely identify the progressive Warren Court as the agent of America's spiritual decadence, holding it responsible for ills ranging from the liberalization of obscenity laws to the destruction of the family and the brutal expulsion of religion from public life.[65] But it was the *Roe v. Wade* decision of 1973, handed down by the Supreme Court under the rule of the conservative Chief Justice Burger, that proved decisive in precipitating the birth of the modern religious right. In *Roe v. Wade*, the Burger court built upon and radicalized the previous court's innovations in constitutional law by arguing that the "right of privacy" should be broad enough to "encompass a woman's decision whether or not to terminate a pregnancy."[66]

In subsequent years, feminist and queer theorists have detailed the profoundly limiting nature of this jurisprudence of privacy, pointing to the fact that it favors a gender-neutral understanding of sexual freedom and ignores the disabling effects of sexual inequality on women's sexual expression; that it exists in tension with laws seeking to limit domestic violence and indeed certain forms of abusive sexual freedom in the home; that it confines sexual freedom to the private sphere and thereby legitimates the further criminalization of (non-heterosexual or commercial) sex in public; and that it was perhaps in any case always meant to protect the sexual and reproductive freedom of heterosexuals only.[67] These critiques are compelling. Yet, for all its limitations, the courtroom sexual revolution of the 1960s and '70s undoubtedly played a galvanizing role in the formation of the religious right.

The *Roe v. Wade* decision, in particular, was the defining moment in the emergence of the religious right, propelling silent witnesses into action and leading to a coalition of forces that would have been unthinkable only a few years previously. This extension of sexual freedoms to include a woman's ability to control her own body was unthinkable for Catholics, who had barely emerged from a decade-long debate about the morality of "artificial birth-control"; but it also proved a step too far for fundamentalists and evangelicals and led, in the space of a few years, to a profound reshuffling of denominational alliances around the notion of a "right to life."

The National Conference of Catholic Bishops had remained silent in the face of Johnson's federally funded "family planning" clinics, despite misgivings, but it was no longer prepared to compromise on the issue of abortion.[68] In the wake of the decision, the bishops issued a call to civil disobedience and soon secured an official exemption excusing Catholic health workers from performing abortions or sterilizations, even in hospitals that were publicly funded.[69] This was the first of a series of "conscience clause" exemptions that religious conservatives would secure over the following decades.

The *Roe v. Wade* decision was no less significant for American Protestantism: Not only did it bring to light profound and irreparable differences between evangelical Protestants on the one hand and the mainline churches on the other, but it also gave rise to a new and unexpected alliance between evangelicals and Catholics. The alliance was unprecedented because American Protestants had traditionally held relatively liberal views on abortion (liberal, that is, by today's standards) and were unmoved by Catholic natural law doctrine attributing sanctity to "life itself." Up until the 1960s, even the most conservative of Protestant churches were in favor of legalizing abortion for "non-therapeutic" reasons within the first trimester of pregnancy.[70] As long as abortion was associated with the familialist, nationalist, and indeed eugenic politics of federal "family planning," and as long as it was performed for "non-therapeutic" reasons within the context of marriage, Protestants of all denominations were happy to express conditional support for the liberalization of abortion laws. Population control, after all, was more likely to apply to poor migrant Catholics and African Americans than white Protestants.

By the end of the 1960s, however, abortion had come to mean something very different. In the years leading up to *Roe v. Wade*, feminists had redefined abortion as a question of women's sexual liberation—from fathers, husbands, and the male-dominated medical profession—and had challenged the seemingly inevitable association between female sexuality and childbearing. Alongside feminists, *Playboy* magazine and the ACLU openly supported the decriminalization of abortion. In the space of a decade, the liberalization of abortion laws had come to represent everything evangelicals most feared, and consequently they adopted a new and increasingly intransigent position against abortion at any stage of pregnancy, eventually embracing the Catholic "right to life" doctrine as their own.[71] It is out of this alliance between evangelicals and Catholics that the modern religious right was born.

What the *Roe v. Wade* decision made manifest to all was the growing rift between evangelicals and the mainline Protestant churches. In the following years, evangelicals and fundamentalists refined their stance against abortion and found further reasons for aligning themselves with Catholics, while the mainline denominations continued to affirm and, in some cases, radicalize their positions in favor of legal abortion. Most disturbing to evangelicals was the fact that the mainline churches routinely grounded their support for abortion in the constitutional doctrine of "religious freedom," arguing in effect that personal freedom of conscience with respect to religion implied "privacy" with respect to sexuality. A year after the *Roe v. Wade* decision, an association led by Methodists formed the Religious Coalition for

Abortion Rights, an ecumenical group that justified its support for abortion rights by invoking the "constitutional guarantees of privacy and religious freedom." Although many mainline churches continued to place conditions on their support for legalized abortion, the United Church of Christ, a member of the Religious Coalition for Abortion Rights, recommended the "repeal of all legal prohibitions of physician performed abortions."[72] For evangelicals, these positions were intolerable. They had barely forgiven the mainline National Council of Churches for supporting Supreme Court decisions banning prayer and Bible reading from public schools, but the extension of this already privatized doctrine of religious freedom to encompass the private right to sexual pleasure represented an act of outright profanation.

These interdominational scissions occurred at time when evangelicals—on both the "left" and "right" of the spectrum[73]—were becoming increasingly aware of their power to affect the formal electoral process. The election of the publicly devout evangelical Jimmy Carter in 1976, along with the rise of the countercultural Jesus generation on university campuses, confirmed a growing intuition that the once unchallenged status of the mainline churches was coming under threat. Evangelicals now understood their power to instate and depose political leaders and the implications were not lost on their fellow Protestants. In his 1972 study *Why Conservative Churches Are Growing*, Methodist minister Dean Kelley warned the liberal churches that their cultural hegemony was likely to recede before the rising tide of once marginal sects.[74] Like other in-house critics of the National Council of Churches, Kelley wondered aloud whether the diluted religiosity of the modernizing churches was itself to blame for this state of affairs.

It was not clear in the early 1970s whether the future of the evangelical movement belonged to the "left" or "right": If anything, it was the social justice "left" that was most visible to the general public and the most active in inciting evangelicals to social action.[75] But evangelicals of all persuasions were disillusioned by Carter's failure to assert moral values in any but the most rhetorical of fashions. As the alliance between neoconservatives and neoliberals grew stronger throughout the decade, it was the evangelical right that was bound to reap the benefits. By the end of the decade, New Right political strategist Paul Weyrich made overtures to the fundamentalist minister Jerry Falwell, calculating that an ecumenical alliance of religious conservatives under Falwell's leadership could be readily recruited into the momentum of Reagan's election campaign. The creation of the Moral Majority marked the beginnings of an enduring alliance between religious conservatives and free-market neoliberals (together forming the so-called New Right), and between the New Right and the Republican Party. Not all religious conservatives were committed to free-market capitalism (certainly not the majority of Catholics) and not all neoliberals were religious (or indeed social) conservatives, but their alliance would come to dominate social policy reform over the following decades. What united them was a shared hostility to the new jurisprudence of privacy, which they understood as creating a positive constitutional right to sexual freedom.[76] Neoliberals and religious conservatives opposed this jurisprudence for different reasons: neoliberals because it appeared to justify the state subsidization of irresponsible life choices among the poor, and religious conservatives because it appeared to undermine the very moral foundations of the family. But while critics on the left have always (and with reason) lamented the restriction of sexual freedom to the private realm, neoliberals and religious conservatives have never been convinced that it would remain there. On the contrary, they feared that the right to sexual privacy would have dramatic transformative effects on the *public* life of the nation, and as such should be opposed at all costs.

The election of Ronald Reagan heralded the long-term decline of the mainline churches in terms of both numbers and political influence. Over the following decades, evangelicals and traditionalist Catholics would embark on a concerted campaign to wrest the discourse of "religious freedom" from the mainline churches and redefine it in much more muscular terms—as the right of deprivatized religion to impose moral law in the public realm. The National Council of Churches had been a vocal and articulate defender of church-state separation in the postwar years, but has barely contributed to recent legislative and judicial deliberations around religious freedom, effectively ceding the terrain to the religious right.[77] Although mainline religious organizations continue to be major players in the provision of welfare, their influence over the actual shape of social policy has steadily waned after the election of Reagan.[78] As Republicans and New Democrats hewed to the rhetoric of budget crisis and urgent welfare reform, and as mainline congregations began to express political opinions to the right of their leaders, the National Council of Churches found itself on the defensive. By contrast, the voice of the evangelical right resonated closely with the increasingly punitive and pedagogical turn in social welfare reform.

As early as 1965, the editor of the major evangelical journal *Christianity Today*, Carl F. H. Henry, urged his readers to exploit their growing presence in the social welfare arena to counter the modernizing influence of the mainline churches. Writing at a time when the National Council of Churches was still the dominant religious voice in social policy, Henry called on evangelicals to abandon their traditional aversion to politics and claim their true vocation as guardians of moral law. Henry's call to arms foreshadows arguments that would become omnipresent and increasingly strident over the following decades. Protestant liberals, he claimed, had diluted the historic mission of Christian theology by seeking to achieve the Kingdom of God on earth by sociological means. The "modernist dilution of historic Christian theology" in mainline Protestant circles "was largely responsible for compromising the message and power of institutional Christianity."[79] By excluding "supernatural redemptive facets of the Christian faith" from their social welfare work, the mainline religious organizations had "modified the proper content of the Christian ethic" and achieved social influence at the price of theological integrity.[80] In the face of this historical abdication, it fell to evangelicals to revive "scriptural theology" in social welfare. Beyond the material redistribution of wealth, true welfare resided in the distinctly "supernatural" experience of redemption (associated in the evangelical imagination with the experience of being born again). The work of redemption could be achieved only by restoring the family to its proper place within a Christian moral order. "The Evangelical Christian's social concern is first directed towards the family as the basic unit of society. He finds a hollow ring in the social passion for 'one world' that simultaneously lacks indignation over divorce, infidelity, and vagrancy in the home. Because liberalism fails to see society as a macrocosm of the family, it is bankrupt to build a new society."[81]

In the years following the election of Ronald Reagan, evangelicals strove to redefine the terms of collaboration between church and state, pushing to expand their presence in the social welfare arena while at the same time refusing the interpretation of privatized religious freedom that had been embraced by the mainline churches. Even as they railed against the sins of the Great Society welfare state then, evangelicals sought to imagine—and eventually implement—a form of welfare that would be faithful to the fundamental tenets of Christian morality. In his best-selling *Listen, America!* Jerry Falwell quoted liberally from Milton Friedman and called on conservative Christians to mount a united front against "left-wing, social-welfare bills," but even he admitted that welfare was "not always wrong," requiring reform not outright elimination.[82] The Moral Majority's chief strategist, the politically savvy Paul Weyrich, offers a more reliable insight into the long-term social policy agenda of the religious right. A study published by Weyrich's Institute for Cultural Conservatism in 1987 carefully explicated the religious conservative position on social welfare: "cultural conservatives" were emphatically not opposed to welfare as such but sought rather to implement a form of "cultural welfare" designed to inculcate traditional moral values amongst America's poor.[83] To achieve this, the state would need to incorporate churches and their affiliate organizations within the structures of welfare, preferably without infringing on their theological integrity. "Instead of leading the fight against welfare, conservatives will lead the fight for it."[84]

MEDIATING STRUCTURES: AN AGENDA FOR FAITH-BASED WELFARE

In 1977, the sociologist Peter Berger and the theologian Richard John Neuhaus collaborated on a slim book, *To Empower People*, that would go on to play a central role in the project of conservative welfare reform.[85] Published by the Enterprise Institute as the first in a series of studies on "mediating structures," the text rehearsed many of the familiar neoconservative grievances against the Great Society expansion of welfare but distinguished itself by according a central role to religion in any future reform of the welfare state. Reflecting back on the successes and failures of the War on Poverty, Berger and Neuhaus praised Johnson for bringing churches back into the fold of the welfare state while faulting federal agencies for suppressing the unique moral authority of religion. Johnson's experiment in decentralization, however laudable, had been implemented at the worst possible time—a moment in history when the Supreme Court and federal welfare agencies were overrun by progressive elites intent on regulating, from above, every aspect of welfare provision. The progressive orientation of federal welfare law had stripped the welfare state of its overarching legitimating function—that of sustaining civic virtue—and fatally undermined the natural moral structures of church, community, and family. "Without institutionally reliable processes of mediation, the political order becomes detached from the values and realities of individual life. Deprived of its moral foundation, the political order is 'delegitimated.' "[86]

The dominant religious charities, argued Berger and Neuhaus, were hardly less culpable. These institutions had lost any credibility they once had by failing to contest the increasingly hostile rulings of the Supreme Court and ceding to the secularizing imperatives of the state. "The loss of religious and cultural distinctiveness is abetted... by the dynamics of professionalization within the religious institutions and by the failure of the churches either to support their agencies or to insist that public policy respect their distinctiveness."[87] Large religious charities such as Lutheran Social Services were at risk of becoming "quasi-governmental agencies through the powers of funding, certification, licensing and the like."[88] Thus, even as religious charities had assumed a much greater public presence in the field of welfare services, religion as such had been progressively reprivatized and banished from the public square. In particular, Berger and Neuhaus denounced the mainline Protestant denominations for their complicity in this process: By touting a doctrine of "religious freedom" that negated the very possibility of public religiosity, the mainline churches had compromised their capacity to contribute anything of value in the social services arena. "American liberals are virtually faultless in their commitment to the religious liberty of individuals," they remarked, but "the liberty to be defended is always that of privatized religion."[89]

In a book published a few years later, *The Naked Public Square*, Neuhaus would formulate this critique in even more strident terms. The delegitimation of religious authority, he now asserted, was not primarily the fault of liberal bureaucratic elites or the anti-authoritarian New Left but of the mainline churches themselves. "The churches, then, cannot stand aloof from the gathering legitimation crisis in our public life. They are in large part responsible for it."[90] By accepting Supreme Court rulings banishing prayers from public schools and outlawing sectarianism in welfare services, by assenting to the new privacy jurisprudence around sexuality that culminated in the *Roe v.*

Wade decision, the mainline churches had ensured their own political irrelevance. "The public program of many mainline churches," Neuhaus commented acerbically, "is hardly distinguishable from the program of the Civil Liberties Union for the elimination of religious influence from American life."[91] Thus, while private rights to sexual freedom were now being wielded against the prerogatives of family and faith, religion itself was being deprived of its proper institutional freedoms.[92] Faced with what they understood as a wholesale crisis of legitimation, Berger and Neuhaus called for a radical new interpretation of constitutional law. "The wall of separation between church and state (Jefferson's phrase, not the constitution's) is a myth long overdue for thorough rethinking," they announced.[93] Although declaring themselves "deeply committed to the religious clauses of the First Amendment," they insisted that the prohibition against establishing a religion of state should not be understood as "requiring absolute separationism." Rather religious freedom should be interpreted as authorizing the "free exercise" of *all denominations* in the public square.

The enduring influence of Berger and Neuhaus's proposal for welfare reform can perhaps be attributed to the fact that it so expertly mediated between the neoliberal and neoconservative visions of the social. Like many neoliberal advocates of welfare devolution, Berger and Neuhaus were not prepared to abandon Johnson's experiment in political decentralization but argued instead that it had not been pursued far enough. In essence, what they called for was a more radical federalism and more comprehensive devolution of powers from the federal government to the states and from the states to civil society. At the same time, however, Berger and Neuhaus were adamant that "the devolution of government responsibilities" should not be "tantamount to dismantling the welfare state."[94] In this respect, their position converged with that of the neoconservatives, who remained attached to the fundamental principles of the New Deal welfare state even while they denounced the terrible moral failures of Johnson's Great Society:

"Partisan rhetoric aside, few people seriously envisage dismantling the welfare state. The serious debate is over how and to what extent it should be expanded."[95] Yet, they offered a much more creative institutional approach to the problem of welfare reform than the neoconservatives were able to come up with.

Berger and Neuhaus's specific contribution to this debate was to be found in the concept of "mediating structures." Welfare reform had most chance of success, they argued, if it were channeled through the "mediating structures" of civil society, defined as "those institutions standing between the individual in his private life and the large institutions of public life."[96] Rather than dictating the administrative form of welfare provision from on high, the federal government would be better advised to delegate its services to preexisting, quasi-natural institutions such as "neighborhood, family, church and voluntary association." And rather than enunciating laws from above, laws that too often had unintended and deleterious consequences, the government should authorize these institutions—in particular, religious institutions—to dictate their own forms of legitimacy. In this way, moral authority would not be lost but transferred downward and reinvested in the "mediating structures" of church, community, and family. Instead of diluting the moral purpose of welfare, decentralization would reinforce it by delegating authority to the most experienced enforcers of moral law.

It was clear from the very start that this reform agenda would necessitate an ambitious campaign of administrative and legal reform. Berger and Neuhaus were among the first to understand the importance of constitutional law to the project of implementing faith-based welfare; and Neuhaus was the first theologian to translate the public religiosity of the new Christian right into a comprehensive new doctrine of religious freedom, one that is fast becoming hegemonic in recent church-state jurisprudence. As early as *The Naked Public Square* (1984), Neuhaus called on religious organizations to refuse the prohibition against religious expression enunciated by recent Supreme Court decisions, urging them instead to openly embrace the "sectarian option."[97] Neuhaus's vision of religious freedom was radical, even insurrectionary: Ultimately, he saw religion as participating in an order of truth destined to override and annul the laws of the state whenever the latter came into conflict with moral law. "Very basic notions of religious freedom," he announced, "depend upon an understanding of religion as *the bearer of transcendent truth to which the nation is accountable.*"[98] Religious freedom, in this view, bestows the right to assert absolute moral law over and above federal law.

In key respects, the personal trajectories of Berger and Neuhaus bear witness to the historical vicissitudes of American Protestantism in its evolving relationship to the state. Former Lutherans who had been actively involved in the civil rights movement in the 1960s, both Neuhaus and Berger had by the 1970s turned against the countercultural New Left to embrace both a theological variant of neoconservatism and the antitax neoliberalism of the Reagan revolution. Neuhaus began his career as a Lutheran pastor in a predominantly black church located in the Bedford-Stuyvesant slum of New York. Alongside many of his fellow mainline clergy, Neuhaus was an active, even militant participant in the civil rights and antiwar movements. Together with Rabbi Abraham Joshua Heschel and Father Daniel Berrigan, he cofounded Clergy and Laymen Concerned about Vietnam (CALCAV) in 1965, an interdenominational group committed to prophetic protest and conscientious objection that later counted Martin Luther King among its members.[99] Berger, a Lutheran layman and self-described conservative, was also involved in the organization. By the late 1960s, however, Neuhaus and Berger were increasingly uncomfortable with the direction in which the left was heading. The civil rights movement was rapidly losing ground to militant Black Power, the antiwar movement was giving way to the countercultural New Left, and the New Left itself was splintering into various liberationist tendencies centered on sexuality and feminism. At his most militant, Neuhaus had endorsed the religious tradition of conscientious objection as an ethically justified response to the abuse of state power but he had never questioned the legitimacy of the nation itself, much less the family. The new social movements were doing precisely that: the antipatriotism of the Black Power and antiwar movements, the anti-authoritarianism of the new generation of student activists, and above all, the critique of family that was so central to the women's movement and gay liberation, convinced Berger and Neuhaus that they no longer had anything in common with the left.

As they turned against these new expressions of the left, Berger and Neuhaus were led, inevitably, to question the social activism of the mainline churches in which they themselves had been so heavily involved. Like many others who gravitated toward the new religious right around this time, Neuhaus's exit from the mainline National Council of Churches was galvanized by the *Roe v. Wade* decision of 1973 and a growing sense that the Supreme Court's recognition of a "right to privacy" authorized the liberation of women from the family. In an early reflection on the liberalization of abortion laws at the state level, Neuhaus drew an analogy between the rights of the unborn and the civil rights long denied to African Americans—an amalgam of fetal and civic states of victimhood that would soon become common sense on the religious right.[100] By the mid-1970s, Neuhaus officially withdrew from CALCAV and began to publicly distance himself from the mainline churches, whose social progressivism, however moderate, he saw as somehow complicit with the political and theological decline of the left in general. In 1975, Neuhaus and Berger brought together a group of prominent church leaders to pen the *Hartford Appeal for Theological Affirmation*, an antimodernist manifesto that viciously denounced the social gospel activism of the mainline churches.[101] At this point, Neuhaus began to consider himself a critical but sympathetic observer of the emerging Christian Right:

although he despaired of its populism, he also sought, through his writing and institutional work, to channel its eschatological, prophetic fervor into a more respectable, politically palatable form.[102]

By the late 1970s, Neuhaus had positioned himself as a mediator between the new Christian right and the neoconservative movement, on the one hand, and between conservative Catholics and evangelicals on the other.[103] In 1981, together with the Catholic neoconservative Michael Novak and the anticommunist social democrat Penn Kemble, he cofounded the Institute on Religion and Democracy. Espousing the cause of "religious freedom," the institute sought to undermine the influence of the National Council of Churches at home while also countering the alliance between Catholic liberation theology and communism in Central America.[104] Neuhaus went on to found the Institute on Religion and Public Life, dedicated to the cause of "religious freedom" in domestic politics, and its associated journal *First Things*, which published works by neoconservatives, conservative evangelicals, and Catholics.

Having abandoned the mainline Lutheran church and converted to Catholicism in 1990, Neuhaus was instrumental in consolidating the alliance between evangelicals and Catholics. Together with his friend Charles Colson, the director of Prison Fellowship Ministries, Neuhaus helped draft the ecumenical pledge, "Evangelicals and Catholics Together (1994)," setting out the terms of a shared political and legal agenda to restore moral law.[105] The document was notable for uniting Catholics and evangelicals around the twin causes of "religious freedom" (a concept endorsed by the Second Vatican Council but with deep roots in the American Protestant imagination) and the "right to life" (once unique to Catholics but now passionately embraced by evangelicals).[106] Religion, it announced, is "foundational in our legal order" but "Americans [were] drifting away from, [were] often explicitly defying, the constituting truths of this experiment in ordered liberty." The restoration of this originary constitutional order would require a vigorous campaign to defend "religious freedom" in all aspects of American life. The document went on to carefully explicate the mutually exclusive relationship between "religious freedom" and moral "tolerance": While the American Protestant tradition is defined by its tolerance for dissident faiths, religious freedom itself demands a radical *intolerance* vis-à-vis the non-normative, that is, immoral expression of sexuality. "Every effort must be made to cultivate the morality of honesty, law observance, work, caring, chastity, mutual respect between the sexes, and readiness for marriage, parenthood, and family," the authors proclaim; "We reject the claim that, in any or all of these areas, 'tolerance' requires the promotion of moral equivalence between the normative and the deviant."

Here we find a lucid articulation of the new politics of religious freedom and a clear acknowledgement of its prohibitive intent. Ultimately it is a shared respect for moral law—and a shared desire to outlaw certain expressions of sexuality—that allows evangelicals and Catholics to set aside their doctrinal differences and embark on a militant campaign to defend the place of religion in the public square. The normative language of deviance and pathology forged by the nineteenth- and twentieth-century medical and social sciences is here subsumed within an older vocabulary of religious law and deemed profane. Evangelicals are in fact moving closer to Catholics in their willingness to embrace a Thomist-Aristotelian theology of natural law that redefines sexual and gender deviance as a crime against a divine order of nature.[107] Promoted by the Vatican under John Paul II and weaponized as an instrument of legal casuistry by the so-called new natural law scholars, the Thomist philosophy of nature is presented as the most promising means of contesting the antinormative claims of "gender theory" in the public domain.[108] This it does not by engaging the debate on the terrain of normativity but by appealing to a higher order of natural, divine law, that tolerates no sin. Religious freedom, as defined by the new religious right, is not incidentally or marginally intolerant of sexual immorality. Rather, as Tocqueville intuited, it is defined by its absolute desire to annul such practices and sees itself as authorized by divine law to do so.[109]

Peter Berger, for his part, belonged to a generation of postwar sociologists who accepted Weber's theses on secularization as something close to historical fact. But Berger was also personally critical of the demoralizing influence of secularization on American society and privately nostalgic for a time when religion played a much more public and prohibitive role in social life.[110] In a 1971 address to the Consultation on Church Union, a coalition of liberal Protestant denominations formed several years previously with the aim of creating a single ecumenical church, Berger publicly qualified his early work, suggesting that he and his fellow sociologists may have been mistaken in too confidently projecting the secularization of modern society into the long-term future.[111] Rather than a continuation of historical trends, Berger suggested, what was becoming increasingly evident was a "widespread and deepening hunger for religious answers among people of many different sorts" pointing to a "possibly powerful reversal of the secularization process."[112] Whatever the outcome of these trends, Berger was doubtful that the mainline churches in their current form were capable of responding to the new desire for public religion. The beneficiaries of this shift were more likely to be the evangelical churches, which had never confused their mission with that of the secular state. "*If* there is going to be a renascence of religion, its bearers will *not* be the people who have been falling all over each other to be 'relevant to modern man'.... Ages of faith are not marked by dialogue but by *proclamation*."[113] Berger would spend the rest of his intellectual career revising his earlier work on secular pluralism and studying the political implications of resurgent evangelicalism. As director of the Institute of Culture, Religion and World Affairs (CURA) at Boston University, Berger worked on a revised version of Weber's Protestant ethic.[114] Pointing to the worldwide resurgence of Evangelical and

Pentecostal Protestantisms, Berger argued that born-again varieties of Christianity were uniquely attuned to the conditions of neoliberal economic reform in both the United States and the Global South. The Protestant ethic was on the march again, Berger insisted, but unlike the early modern Calvinism that informed Weber's analysis, the evangelical resurgence did not entail the progressive secularization of the world; rather, it was destined to play its role on the historical stage as an agent of profound desecularization.

Written at a time when the religious right was just beginning to flex its muscles, Berger and Neuhaus's *To Empower People* exerted an extraordinary influence over social policy debate throughout the following decades. Their intervention can be read as the blueprint for Charitable Choice not only in the obvious sense that it was repeatedly referenced by the architects of faith-based welfare but also because its concept of "mediating structures" lucidly prefigured the model of delegated service provision and outsourced moral authoritarianism that informed Clinton's welfare reform. The Christian libertarian Marvin Olasky may have reached a wider popular audience, but his prescriptions for a system of entirely private church charity were unrealistic in the extreme and much less predictive of future welfare reform.[115] Berger and Neuhaus's proposals had the advantage of appealing to both neoliberals and social conservatives. The Heritage Foundation fellow and neoliberal strategist Stuart Butler saw "mediating structures" as a way of achieving multiple pragmatic ends: The delegation of welfare to religious nonprofits would undercut the power of allegedly liberal federal welfare agencies; it would defund the left by diverting government contracts from left-wing to conservative nonprofits; combined with the use of vouchers, it would reconcile the church and the free market; and finally it would help to reduce welfare spending by contracting with religious charities that were already partly funded by private donations and could mobilize vast armies of unpaid labor.[116] The concept of "mediating structures" was equally appealing to religious conservatives such as Gary Bauer and Paul Weyrich, who saw it as a way of transforming, not defunding, the welfare state and infusing it with traditional moral values.[117] If both parties were forced to make concessions in the actual policy implementation process, the idea of "mediating structures" appeared to offer the perfect compromise.

A LONG MARCH THROUGH THE INSTITUTIONS

Religious organizations continued to build up their presence in the social service sector throughout the 1980s, but in a context that was very different from that of the previous decade. Whereas religious nonprofits had been actively included within the reach of an ever-expanding welfare state under Johnson's War on Poverty, they were now expected to *substitute* for services that were being eroded or starved of funding under the neoliberal policies of the Reagan administration. The austerity politics of welfare devolution now replaced Johnson's fully funded project in welfare decentralization as the guiding rationale for the growth of the nonprofit sector. In most instances, the budget cuts carried out by Reagan and his successors did not eradicate services to the poor altogether but simply transferred them to cheaper third-party providers. Religious nonprofits in particular were considered ideal partners of the state because of their reliance on unpaid volunteer labor and their access to alternative sources of funding.[118] For this reason, religious charities expanded greatly as a result of the selective dismantling of the welfare state, becoming fully integrated within the fabric of government social service contracts at a time when the old public welfare institutions were being disassembled.

The actual deinstitutionalization movement benefited religious nonprofits in a very direct way. When public health activists of the left called for the deinstitutionalization of the mentally ill and disabled throughout the 1960s, they did not for the most part consider the problem of building and maintaining alternative services in the long term.

It was assumed that mental health patients would end up in the "community," but few had really thought through the complexities of caring for the ill once they left the institutional environment of the asylum. Instead, conservative, denominational religious charities were some of the first to respond to the very obvious and urgent needs of those who were released from state institutions. When in 1975 the courts ordered the state of New York to close the infamous Willowbrook State School, a home for children with intellectual disabilities, it was at a loss what to do with former patients who had no relatives to return to and were incapable of caring for themselves. Having contacted the established Protestant foster-care agencies to no avail, the state ended up delegating the creation of group homes to Catholic and orthodox Jewish charities that saw care for the disabled as a logical consequence of their anti-abortion politics.[119] Without other viable options in sight, the state was prepared to overlook the "pervasively sectarian" nature of these homes. The experience was subsequently replicated across the country. In this way, notes historian Peter Dobkin Hall: "New York led the nation in creating community-based care and treatment for the dependent and disabled. Its system of nonprofit group homes—many of them faith-based—supported by variable mixes of federal, state and local funding, in many cases combined with traditional sources of private revenues (foundation grants and individual and corporate donations), would become a paradigm for the reorganization of social services throughout the country."[120] What looked like the deinstitutionalization of the disciplinary asylum, then, from another angle could be seen as the *reinstitutionalization of religion,* a process whereby religious charities resumed their once central role in the management of poverty but this time fully integrated into the contractual networks and budgetary calculations of the state.

During the same period, religious nonprofits responded to rising rates of homelessness by expanding or resuming traditional operations such as running homeless shelters and soup kitchens. In the first year of his administration, when the US was entering the worst recession since the Great Depression, Reagan convinced Congress to freeze social spending on the poor. The Omnibus Budget Reconciliation Act of 1981 suspended budget increases for Medicaid, unemployment compensation, and housing assistance, with substantial cuts to food stamps and child nutrition services. Implemented at a time when unemployment levels in once thriving industrial cities were reaching double digit figures, and deinstitutionalization had left many mentally ill people without shelter, the budget cuts brought a visible influx of newly homeless people onto the streets. Traditional charities, including many religious organizations, were some of the first to respond to the crisis, often at the behest of local authorities who were working with greatly reduced block grants from the federal government. Consequently, faith-based homeless shelters, food banks, and soup kitchens mushroomed across the country in the space of a few years.[121] The old evangelical rescue missions that had existed in almost every city center since the late nineteenth century found themselves overwhelmed by demand, while new missions sprang up around them. Established charities such as the Salvation Army and Catholic Charities multiplied their emergency shelter contracts with state and municipal authorities. Churches, convents, and synagogues opened their pews and basements to provide overnight shelter to the homeless during the winter.

When the federal government was finally roused to action, after several years of prevarication, it assigned religious charities an active role in the administration and provision of services. In 1983, Congress authorized an Emergency Food and Shelter Program to be administered by the Federal Emergency Management Agency (FEMA). The act simultaneously created a National Board composed of six charitable agencies, including the United Way of America, the American Red Cross, the Salvation Army, Catholic Charities USA, the Council of Jewish Federations, and the National Council of Churches, that were charged with the task of distributing funds to local service providers.[122] When the program was reauthorized under the McKinney Homeless Assistance Act of 1987, Reagan reiterated his "intention that charitable organizations, including those with religious affiliation, should continue to play a vital role in the delivery of services contemplated in this legislation."[123] The gradual institutionalization of this emergency response system has had the simultaneous although less noted effect of consolidating the role of religious charities in the provision of social services.

Collaborations of this kind were replicated at state and municipal levels. In New York City, Mayor Ed Koch appealed to religious charities to supplement the city's overcrowded shelter system in the early 1980s. The result was Partnership for the Homeless, an umbrella organization that mushroomed from three religious charities at its inception in 1982 to include 120 institutions by 2001, with a reported capacity of more than one thousand beds, most of them located in the basements of churches or synagogues.[124] Koch's call to religious charities was a calculated response to the interventions of a powerful urban reform movement that advocated for long-term, noncharitable solutions to urban poverty and had recently won notable successes in the courts. In 1979, Robert Hayes, an attorney who would go on to found the Coalition for the Homeless, brought a lawsuit against the Koch administration citing the inadequacies of its homeless shelter system. In his ruling on the case, *Callahan v. Carey* (1981), the State Supreme Court Justice concluded that the right to "adequate shelter" was inscribed in the New York State Constitution and ordered Koch to provide 750 more beds to homeless men.[125] The case was followed by countless other court orders to improve the shelter system. Rather than dip into municipal budgets to expand the existing shelter system or invest in public housing, Koch turned to religious nonprofits—a response that would be repeated across the country.[126]

National surveys conducted for the Urban Institute in 1995 and 1999 found that religious charities operated the majority of soup kitchens and over one third of homeless shelters, although some argue that these figures underestimate the size of the religious contribution.[127] These charities receive various levels of local, state, and federal aid, depending on their doctrinal and historical relationship to the state. The large religious charities such as the Salvation Army, Catholic Charities USA, and Lutheran Social Services have accepted federal aid since the 1960s or earlier and remain some of the largest nonprofit contractors with the state, although their private sources of funding often match or outweigh what they receive from the government.[128] Many other religious charities receive various kinds of assistance from the government, including direct financial aid or (in the case of most soup kitchens) surplus commodities donated by the Department of Agriculture.[129] Evangelical rescue missions remain the most independent of religious charities, for the most part refusing to receive government aid—except in the form of tax exemptions.[130] The presence of faith-based organizations varies as a function of urban and regional welfare histories. A city such as New York, which has the largest municipal shelter system in the country, is still largely dependent on the thousands of emergency beds offered by religious charities. In the South and Midwest, and in many medium and small cities across the country, faith-based organizations are often the only providers of emergency shelter.[131] Even in a city such as New York, faith-based shelters may dominate services for certain client groups such as the young.[132]

The resurgence of the religious factor in social welfare sits uneasily with the analytics of power we have inherited from such prominent theorists of the social as Michel Foucault and Erving Goffman. One investigator into the state of religious homeless shelters post-deinstitutionalization found a new kind of institution every bit as totalizing as Goffman's infamous asylum. This big city shelter for the homeless, run by a Catholic religious order, "reminded the author of the massive and regimented environment in institutions that she mistakenly believed no longer existed after the acclaimed 'deinstitutionalization' of America."[133] Although the shelter did not engage in direct religious instruction, its semi-permanent guests were subject to a close regime of curfews and petty sanctions, constantly serving to remind them of the conditional nature of the charity being offered. Another study speaks of the "hyperinstitutionalization" of long-term residents in an evangelical rescue mission whose exposure to continuous religious exhortation and limited contact with the outside world renders them fit for little else than missionary work in the shelter after their release. Evangelical missions practice overt forms of proselytization, holding their clients in an unspoken pact whereby food and shelter are exchanged for evangelism.[134] Gospel services are repeated before breakfast, lunch, and dinner as a condition of receiving care, and clients who do not express a devoted, or at least passive, attention may be summarily evicted from the premises. Somewhere between these two extremes lies the Salvation Army, a state-endorsed evangelical institution that is also one of the oldest and largest religious contractors in the country. Inspired by a nineteenth-century evangelical ethic eschewing the wealth gospel in favor of savings and hard work, the Salvation Army schools its homeless clients in a militaristic regime of self-discipline that implicitly attributes social failure to personal sin.[135]

Without completely displacing the normative disciplines of the social and human sciences, faith-based social services deploy a very different vocabulary of rule. These services do not seek to normalize or rehabilitate so much as redeem. They speak the language of sin rather than deviance or perversion. If they are undoubtedly reliant on practices of confession, this is in the overt Christian sense of religious witness. Theorists versed in the historical taxonomies of Foucault have trouble recognizing that contemporary power might speak the language of moral law, sin, and redemption as much if not more than normativity. Foucault's historiography tends to downplay the influence of religion in the formation of the modern social state, treating it as a residue of early modern forms of power or, in his later work, a horizon of ethical practice somehow impervious to the coercive machinations of the state or capital.[136] Yet, Christian practices of redemption were never alien to the poor-law tradition of poverty relief, which in its early nineteenth-century iteration was informed by both classical economic liberalism and evangelical theology.[137] Faith-based welfare translates the neoliberal ethic of family responsibility into the religious conservative idiom of personal sin, immorality, and redemption. If you are homeless, it is because you have failed before God. If you are in prison or unemployed, it is because you have negliected to assume your personal responsibilities as a father or have chosen the path of sin. Once one has accepted these premises, rehabilitation can be achieved only through a process of spiritual regeneration or rebirth, and this in turn demands intensive training in the practice of responsible family life. Faith-based welfare can be said to practice a form of power that is not so much normalizing or rehabilitative as intimately legislative and *orthopractic*, exhorting its clients to perform their deference to moral law even in the absence of any true change of heart. As Tocqueville and Beaumont noted of the religious prisons of early nineteenth-century America, evangelical instruction was not always able to instill a genuine respect for moral law among prisoners, yet it was almost always successful in eliciting moral habits—and this orthopractic effect was perhaps just as useful as an exercise of power.[138]

Although initially conceived as a temporary response to poverty, the emergency shelter and food system has progressively stabilized and now functions as a kind of para–welfare state supplementing the permanent budget shortfalls of local authorities. Federal programs that were enacted as emergency measures in the early 1980s have subsequently been reauthorized many times over, transforming them into permanent fixtures of the social service landscape. In an important sense, notes sociologist Janet Poppendieck, the ambitious antipoverty programs envisaged by the Great Society have been replaced by a system of domestic humanitarian relief designed to manage rather than eradicate the problems of homelessness and hunger. "The notion of a permanent emergency is certainly unattractive," she writes, "but a close look at the life-styles available to many poor people reveals what might be termed a state of chronic emergency—medical care from the emergency room because they are uninsured, a bed in the emergency shelter because they are without permanent residence, food from the emergency food provider on a regular basis."[139] This slow sedimentation of emergency relief structures has substantially reinvigorated the social role of charities, which now find themselves regularly factored into fiscal calculations as a cushion against predictable budget cuts. Religious charities that had once been peripheral to the welfare structures of the New Deal have now become indispensable components of federal and state antipoverty programs. What we are witnessing here is not a return to private charity as it existed before the New Deal, but rather the implementation of a form of structural charity—structural in the sense that it is fully aided and abetted by the state, but charitable in the sense that it retains the discretionary, unpredictable and ad-hoc nature of private philanthropy.

THE NEW RELIGIOUS FREEDOM:
CHRISTIAN PUBLIC INTEREST LITIGATION

As conservative religious organizations increased their presence in the social welfare field, the Christian right simultaneously adopted a new strategy of litigating church-state issues in the courts with a view to expanding its institutional freedoms. The 1990s saw a proliferation of conservative Christian law firms dedicated to reshaping church-state relations through the use of public interest litigation. These firms included the American Center for Law and Justice, founded by Pat Robertson in 1990, the Christian Legal Society's Center for Law and Religious Freedom, the Rutherford Institute, the Alliance Defense

Fund (now renamed the Alliance Defending Freedom), Liberty Counsel, and the Catholic-affiliated Becket Fund.[140] Together these organizations have used the courts to forge a new jurisprudence of "religious freedom" that has successfully challenged prevailing constitutional doctrine concerning church-state relations and progressively eroded the established prohibition against the public funding of "pervasively sectarian" welfare providers. The turn to litigation was an unexpected change in direction for the Christian right, which had traditionally eschewed the judiciary in favor of the electoral and legislative arenas and had long decried the left's disproportionate influence in the Supreme Court.

When Jerry Falwell founded the Moral Majority in 1978, he wanted to convey the idea that evangelicals were a majoritarian electoral bloc whose power had been usurped by a small group of liberal elites huddled in federal bureaucracies and the Supreme Court. Christian conservatives greeted the election of Ronald Reagan as a sign of imminent victory, fully expecting their representatives in Congress to push through with a comprehensive legislative agenda to restore religion in public schools and overturn *Roe v. Wade*. During this period, the Christian right focused its energies almost exclusively on the legislative and executive branches of government, engaging in elaborate campaigns to mobilize voting blocs and lobby members of Congress.[141] The tone was triumphalist: Christians were a majority reclaiming America from theological and social ruin at the hands of the Supreme Court. In its first few years, the Moral Majority did meet with some success: Not only did it push through the Hyde amendment limiting the public funding of abortions through Medicaid, but it also managed to paralyze federal action in the face of the AIDS epidemic for much of the 1980s. But this was far from the legislative counterrevolution that Christian conservatives had been hoping for, and the victories were coming at a much slower pace by the end of the decade.

By the 1990s, the Christian right was forced to adopt a more incremental, less triumphalist approach to political change. Falwell's influence was rapidly being eclipsed by new groups such as the Christian Coalition, created as a nonprofit organization shortly after Pat Robertson's failed bid for presidency in 1989. These new voices on the Christian right presented themselves in very different terms, as representatives of a persecuted minority rather than a majority claiming its rightful place in the seats of power.[142] Consciously adopting the language of the civil rights movement, the executive director of the Christian Coalition, Ralph Reed, likened the plight of Christians at the close of the twentieth century to that of African Americans at midcentury: Christians were systematically discriminated against in public life, denied equal protection of the law, and deprived of civil liberties such as freedom of religious expression; their collective condition was comparable to that of the unborn, the ultimate minority, who had been stripped of the most fundamental of civil rights, the right to life. These rhetorical moves not only managed to position Christians as victims of systemic discrimination, but they also served the strategic objective of neutralizing the all too recent history of racism among southern white Evangelicals. Under the direction of Ralph Reed, the Christian Coalition made concerted efforts to bring African Americans into the fold of the pro-life movement, at the same time urging white evangelicals to acknowledge and seek atonement for their complicity in the racial segregation of the American South.[143] Reed's efforts at building a transdenominational and interracial coalition around the "civil rights" of Christians heralded a new era in the strategizing of the religious right. Henceforth, Catholic and evangelical conservatives would seek to downplay racial and doctrinal differences in order to form a united bloc against sexual immorality; and as racial differences were muted, the language of civil rights would be arrogated by white Christians as a way of promoting the idea that Christians were subject to a universal condition of minoritization.

Beyond these coalitional and public relations strategies, however, the adoption of civil rights rhetoric signaled a real change in legal and political methods. Under the influence of the Christian Coalition, the religious right abandoned its exclusive focus on majoritarian institutions and instead turned to test case litigation in the courts—a method that had long been favored by the liberal and progressive left. In a book published in 1993, *The Turning Tide*, Pat Robertson called on Christians to borrow the weapons that had been used by the civil rights movement in the 1960s: civil disobedience and public interest litigation.[144] Christian conservatives had long decried the influence of groups such as the ACLU and NAACP in the Supreme Court, holding them responsible for the rampant secularization of American life in the 1960s. Without abandoning these grievances, the new Christian right has subsequently adopted the legal methods of the left almost wholesale, using amici curiae and judicial precedent to pave the way for future legislative reform. Beginning in the 1990s, notes Stephen Brown, litigating firms associated with the Christian right have "patterned both their courtroom and extracourtroom efforts after strategies pioneered by the ACLU, NAACP, [and] American Jewish Congress," artfully repurposing the precedents established by the liberal left to establish a "secular" jurisprudence of religious freedom.[145] For the most part, then, these firms have sought to expand the judicial accommodation of religion not by direct reference to the religion clauses of the First Amendment but by reworking the arguments around discrimination and freedom of expression once monopolized by their enemies. In a strange twist of history, the Equal Protection Clause of the Fourteenth Amendment that once helped dismantle segregation (much to the chagrin of white Southern fundamentalists) is now being invoked to defend the right to religious freedom, understood as the right of Christians to be free from discrimination. Stranger still, the right to freedom of expression established by the ACLU's landmark obscenity cases in the 1960s is now being invoked to defend the right to public expression of religion.[146] Not only have

Christian litigators borrowed the tools of their enemies, but they also have turned these tools against them—deploying religious freedom to annul the jurisprudence of sexual freedom and religious antidiscrimination laws to override the gender-based protections of a previous era.

Christian legal firms are now no longer content to maintain defensive positions. In the past few decades, their courtroom victories have steadily eroded the separationist doctrine of religious freedom that prevailed in the postwar period. In particular, Christian litigators have fought for and won ever-greater powers of public exemption for religious service providers by building on the precedent of conscience clause legislation, first granted to Catholic hospitals after the *Roe v. Wade* decision of 1973.[147] In different contexts, religious institutions and individual believers have been authorized to invoke "conscience clauses" allowing them to refuse to provide abortion, sterilization, or contraception or to deny service to homosexuals. Christian law firms have established precedents excusing religious organizations from employment discrimination laws, labor laws, workplace health insurance laws, and sexual discrimination laws. These exemptions are clearly oriented toward issues of sexual freedom; as noted by Martha Minow, religious organizations are emphatically not exempted from civil rights laws outlawing racial discrimination, but they have received notable exemptions with respect to discrimination based on gender and sexual orientation.[148] As redefined by the new Christian right, "religious freedom" has come to authorize very public expressions of "moral conscience" allowing faith-based providers of government-funded services to exempt themselves from federal laws whenever their religious sensibilities are offended. The moral exclusion zones established by such exemptions were bound to become ever more pervasive and claustrophobic as conservative religious providers increased their role in the provision of social services.

The case of abortion services is particularly alarming. Hospitals of all kinds have undergone a large number of consolidations in recent decades because of managed-care reforms in the health sector. Catholic hospitals have weathered these changes much better than other religious or nonprofit hospitals and over the past few years have sealed an unprecedented number of mergers. According to a report published in 2013, Catholic-sponsored hospitals accounted for one in nine beds across the country as of 2011, with much higher ratios in some states, including Washington, Wisconsin, and Iowa.[149] The largest Catholic health networks have continued to pursue an aggressive politics of expansion since the time of this report and are now likely to account for an even larger proportion of hospital beds. All Catholic hospitals in the United States, including most of the hospitals that have merged with them, are governed by the Ethical and Religious Directives issued by the US Conference of Catholic Bishops, a set of guidelines that ban elective abortion, sterilization, and contraception. These directives are sometimes interpreted to prohibit emergency contraception for women who have been raped and may limit the kinds of care available to women who have suffered miscarriages or ectopic pregnancies. Given the substantial levels of public funding that are allocated to these hospitals in the form of Medicare and Medicaid reimbursements, such practices must be understood as tacitly government-endorsed.

An equally alarming development is the growing number of homeless shelters run by conservative religious organizations. Faith-based shelters that receive federal funding are under no obligation to treat gender-nonconforming clients without discrimination—and yet these same organizations have gained increasingly robust rights to freedom of religious expression in recent years. This situation is of particular concern given that gay, bisexual, and gender nonconforming clients make up a high proportion of the homeless youth population.[150] The prohibitive and exclusive effects of religious freedom here become starkly obvious. As the state contracts out a growing number of essential social services to "pervasively sectarian" service providers, these same groups are empowered not merely to stigmatize or normalize but to banish certain practices and expressions of sexuality from the space of the social.

CHARITABLE CHOICE: FROM LITIGATION TO LEGISLATION

By the early 1990s, the slow and incremental work of test case litigation, relentlessly pursued by a handful of legal firms over the space of a decade, had created an environment conducive to spectacular legislative interventions. After successfully litigating a series of landmark test cases in favor of accommodation, the Christian Legal Society's Center for Law and Religious Freedom (CLRF) led a coalition of nearly sixty organizations from across the political spectrum (including groups as diverse as the ACLU and the National Association of Evangelicals) to support comprehensive new legislation on religious freedom.[151] The Religious Freedom and Restoration Act (or RFRA) received unanimous support from Congress and was signed into law by President Clinton in 1993. Responding to a recent test case that had placed limits on the free exercise clause, the RFRA reinstated a strong interpretation of religious freedom and outlined a statutory right to religious exemptions from all state and federal laws, subject to the compelling interest test.[152] According to its supporters, the act was designed simply to restore the legal status quo. In practice, the Supreme Court has interpreted it as a complete revolution in First Amendment case law, religious exemption from federal law that have never been accorded in the past.[153] In the wake of the notorious Hobby Lobby case, most commentators have focused on the fact that RFRA has legitimated the extension of religious exemptions from churches and faith-based nonprofits to corporations, but equally noteworthy is the fact that religion here authorizes an exemption from rules covering government-sponsored health insurance (in this case, the Affordable Care Act). Recent interpretation of RFRA signals an emerging consensus that moral law trumps federal law when it comes to the provision not only of direct social welfare services but also of social insurance.[154] RFRA can therefore be understood as a critical legislative step toward the implementation of faith-based welfare, even if it was not perceived as such at the time by many of its supporters.

Not incidentally, the very same organization that spearheaded RFRA—the Christian Legal Society's Center for Law and Religious Freedom (CLRF)—also played a leading role in the passage of Charitable Choice legislation, having first won a series of test cases in the Supreme Court. During the 1980s, lawyers associated with the CLRF managed to persuade an increasingly conservative Supreme Court to abandon the prevailing doctrine of strict church-state separation in favor of a philosophy of "positive neutrality" requiring equal protection of secular and religious organizations.[155] This trend accelerated under the Rehnquist Court (1986–2005), which in the *Bowen v. Kendrick* decision of 1988 approved federal legislation allowing religious organizations to provide government-funded pregnancy services and sex education under the terms of the Adolescent Family Life Act of 1981. The outcome of *Bowen v. Kendrick* was particularly encouraging to proponents of faith-based welfare because it was one of the first cases to take the constitutional issues of church-state separation out of the context of education into the social service sector as a whole.[156] Even more important, the case signaled a new willingness to endorse the teaching of Christian morality within federal welfare programs. In *Bowen v. Kendrick*, the "Court allowed religious organizations to provide government-funded services in an area that implicated matters of fundamental religious significance. These were programs that, presumably, could easily blur the lines between the religious, moral, and secular dimensions of teen pregnancy and sexual activity."[157] In the wake of *Bowen v. Kendrick*, it appeared that the Supreme Court was ready to countenance the funding of "pervasively sectarian" organizations in the provision of welfare services.

Building on the precedent set by *Bowen v. Kendrick* and buoyed by the success of RFRA legislation, the CLRF made the bold decision to propose a new set of religious provisions as part of Clinton's promised welfare reforms. Charitable Choice legislation was drafted by the University of Missouri law professor Carl Esbeck, a longtime associate of the Center for Law and Religious Freedom, and sponsored by then Senator John Ashcroft.[158] The provision utterly transformed the role of religion within public welfare, affording faith-based organizations much greater institutional freedoms than had been allowed under the terms of Johnson's War on Poverty. Charitable Choice, in fact, responded point by point to the checklist of demands voiced by religious conservatives since the 1970s. It instructed government contractors to cease their alleged discrimination against religious organizations and to include faith-based providers within all tenders, while at the same time exempting religious organizations themselves from antidiscrimination laws in hiring. It overruled administrative regulations established by Johnson's Office of Economic Opportunity by allowing churches to display icons, scripture, and other signs of religious affiliation, and invalidated the distinction between "pervasively sectarian" and secular institutions.

Most important, perhaps, Charitable Choice legislation was inserted into a comprehensive welfare reform project that was itself focused on the promotion of moral values in the family, bringing federal welfare policy into close conversation with the most conservative religious organizations for the first time in many years. In the 1970s, religious conservatives were outraged when the Supreme Court and federal government overturned the traditional police powers of states to regulate the morality of welfare recipients; with the passage of PRWORA, the federal government arrogated these police powers to itself and now instructed states to make moral education a central focus of their welfare programs.[159] Marriage promotion, abstinence education, and faith-based responsible fatherhood programs are now all integral components of federal welfare policy. As the conservative commentator Leslie Lenkowsky observed of Bush's implementation of Charitable Choice: "What is distinctive about the President's plan is not its reliance on proxies to provide the federal government's social services—this, as not a few worried conservatives have observed, was a key innovation of the Great Society. What is distinctive, rather, is its unabashedly moral tone. That tone is a throwback to an era when the nation's charities were concerned not just about the material circumstances of those they helped but about their character and behavior as well."[160] With the passage of Charitable Choice, religious service providers were set to play a critical role in translating the coercive imperatives of welfare reform into a comprehensive program of moral and subjective reeducation. This, however, was less a throwback to a previous era of private charity than a selective implementation of moral law by the state.

Conclusion

In a remarkable essay published in 1960, "Why I Am Not a Conservative," Friedrich Hayek offers a sustained reflection on the complex historical relationship between classical liberalism and the modern conservative tradition. Here he takes issue with the charge of "conservatism" that is commonly leveled against the modern inheritors of classical economic liberalism.[1] If conservatives and neoliberals are united in their aversion to socialism, he concedes, their orientations are nevertheless radically divergent, since only conservatism is exclusively defined by its desire to arrest change. Economic liberalism, by contrast, "has never been a backward-looking doctrine."[2] By its nature, it is oriented to the new: "There never has been a time when liberal ideals were fully realized and when liberalism did not look forward to further improvement of institutions."[3] This future orientation can be described as speculative in the sense that it appeals to no prior distribution of historical probabilities and thus makes no claims to prediction: If "one of the fundamental traits of the conservative attitude is a fear of change, a timid distrust of the new as such...the liberal position is based on courage and confidence, on a preparedness to let change run its course even if we cannot predict where it will lead."[4]

So ingrained is this orientation toward the new, Hayek insists, that neoliberals are prepared to entrust the future to "uncontrolled social forces," even when these forces emanate from a direction they do not like. "Without preferring the new merely because it is new, the liberal is aware that it is of the essence of human achievement that it produces something new; and he is prepared to come to terms with new knowledge, whether he likes its immediate effects or not."[5] Hayek's political philosophy of neoliberalism could usefully be described as preemptive in the sense that its first instinct is to accommodate the future, whether in the form of new knowledge or new social realities. Yet Hayek is equally clear that the neoliberal will to adapt exists side by side with an unwavering deference to historical selection—the social conventions of religion, family, and inherited wealth that are thrown up as if by chance but subsequently validated by the weight of social norms.[6] If neoliberalism is prepared to accommodate the new of "uncontrolled social forces," then, it is only in order to channel them into the constantly reinvented form of private wealth and familial inheritance.[7]

Thus, Hayek combines a speculative orientation toward the future with an unshakeable respect for the traditions that are periodically validated or, in his words, selected in the process of spontaneous social evolution. His entire philosophy, in fact, could be read as an uncritical expression of the capitalist double movement: poised between the self-revolutionizing orientation of credit-based temporality and the imperative of sustaining tradition via the private distribution of wealth.

This preemptive orientation is less often associated with neoconservatism. But Irving Kristol was clear on this point. If there was something that distinguished the neoconservatives from the American paleoconservatives or traditionalists, it was their willingness to accommodate and respond to change: "What is 'neo' ('new') about this conservatism is that it is resolutely free of nostalgia. It, too, claims the future—and it is this claim, more than anything else, that drives its critics on the Left into something approaching a frenzy of denunciation."[8] Where paleoconservatives and traditionalists held steadfast in their opposition to the New Deal and its aftermath, neoconservatives were willing to confront and to some degree incorporate the changes wrought by the democratic movements of the postwar era. As children of the same democratic expansion (most of them were the sons or daughters of Jewish migrants), neoconservatives remained committed to the New Deal welfare state, the civil rights movement, and even some of the interventions carried out under Johnson's Great Society. If they balked at the antinormative liberation movements of the New Left and its derivatives, they also sought to neutralize their demands through the reorientation — rather than the outright dismissal — of the New Deal welfare state.

In contrast to traditionalist conservatism, then, both neoliberalism and neoconservatism can be defined by their preemptive orientation toward the political future. Brought together by their confrontation with the liberation movements of the 1960s, neoliberals and neoconservatives sought to contain the antinormative and redistributive promise of these movements by capturing them within the horizon of reinvented tradition. Looking backward, they sought to revive an older poor-law tradition of private family responsibility; looking forward, they sought to reinvent this tradition using the administrative legacy of the welfare state itself; and to democratize its reach by the targeted expansion of consumer credit markets. In a somewhat paradoxical fashion, private family responsibility would become the guiding principle of social policy, and its boundaries would be stretched to include the non-normative subjects who were once radically excluded from the Fordist family wage.

The neoconservative Nathan Glazer wrote that the "creation and building of new traditions, or new versions of old traditions, must be taken more seriously as a requirement of social policy itself."[9] The tradition he had in mind was one that had already undergone multiple reinventions throughout American history. At various moments, the colonial poor-law tradition of family responsibility was adapted to deal with the emancipation of slaves, rising divorce rates, family dissolution among the white urban poor, and unmarried mothers seeking welfare. The neoconservatives and their fellow travelers sought to revive the poor law tradition once again by adapting it to what they saw as the excesses of the late Fordist welfare state. Unlike paleoconservatives and traditionalist conservatives, they were willing to work with the institutional legacy of the postwar welfare state to achieve this goal, seeking not to destroy the welfare state as such but to repurpose it as the enforcer of traditional family values. "In economic and social policy," noted Irving Kristol, neoconservatism "feels no lingering hostility to the welfare state, nor does it accept it resignedly, as a necessary evil. Instead, it seeks not to dismantle the welfare state in the name of free-market economics but rather to reshape it so as to attach it to the conservative predispositions of the people."[10]

Neoliberalism, for its part, can be defined as "neo" in the simple sense that it comes after the twentieth-century welfare state and is therefore confronted with the task of either overcoming its structures or adapting them to new ends. While individual neoliberal scholars have repeatedly called for the extreme reduction of the welfare state or the privatization of its most generous social insurance programs (Social Security, for instance), in practice their policy reforms have tended to repurpose rather that dismantle the institutional legacy of the twentieth-century welfare state. Most striking here is the way in which neoliberal social reformers have adopted the institutional innovations of Johnson's Great Society—which sought to decentralize, devolve, and outsource social service provision while simultaneously reinforcing federal authority over the general direction of welfare programs. The salient difference is that where Johnson-era federalization was designed to impose more progressive rules on the states with the aim of expunging the last vestiges of the poor-law tradition from state welfare practice, neoliberal welfare legislation has done the exact opposite. In fact, it has federalized the poor-law tradition of public relief for the first time in American history and now imposes it on the states as the only viable model of welfare provision. At the same time, the micropolitical implementation of these laws has been relayed downward and delegated to a multiplicity of private, nonprofit, and faith-based actors now charged with the task of enforcing personal and family responsibility in the service of the state. Neoliberals and neoconservatives are able to resolve their differences through the mobilization of these so-called mediating structures — non-state organizations that perform the work of de facto privatization while also enforcing the moral virtues prescribed by federal welfare law.

Unlike neoconservatives, however, neoliberal scholars recognized that if the poor-law tradition were to be reactivated in any sustainable way, it would need to defer to and incorporate the antinormativity of the late Fordist liberation movements. The imperative of private family responsibility could not be successfully revived unless it was somehow reconciled with the cultural and social revolution of the 1960s. Very early on, Milton Friedman and Gary Becker intuitively understood that such a project could be achieved via an enormous expansion of consumer credit, although the details of this policy solution would be worked out only in practice, in the tumultuous economic cauldron of the following decades. After the Volcker shock of 1979, Democratic and Republican administrations from Reagan to Clinton discovered that the lingering claims of the late Fordist social revolution could be effectively neutralized by democratizing consumer credit and stimulating asset inflation. If the wage and welfare inflation of the 1970s had appeared to detach people from the private family and to encourage the proliferation of non-normative lifestyles, asset appreciation, with its ties to private home ownership, was understood as a means of disciplining these demands within the logic of inheritance. And if the late Fordist revolution in family life could not be simply reversed, it would be domesticated, and made profitable, by translating the non-normative lifestyle choice into the idiom of democratized credit. The curious temporal logic of credit—its ability to materialize the future in the present—was here harnessed as a means of recapturing non-normative desire in the inherently regressive form of private familial debt.

Acknowledgments

I am indebted to the many people who have made this book possible. First, I would like to thank Michel Feher and Wendy Brown for bravely commissioning a book that was still only an idea and somehow trusting it would happen. Their faith in this project, along with the expert editorial support of Meighan Gale, have made this an unusually smooth experience. The book would not have been possible without the continuous conversations that have taken place in the context of the Social Studies of Finance group at the University of Sydney. Several of the chapters developed here were first presented in these workshops and benefited from the close critical feedback of the many local and international scholars who took part. I am particularly grateful to Dick Bryan and Martijn Konings for their incisive critiques and generous feedback. I also owe much to the participants of the second Roads from Mont-Pèlerin workshop, which took place at the Wissenschaftszentrum Berlin für Sozialforschung in March 2016. Their individual presentations and feedback on my paper provided much needed impetus for the last phase of revisions and led to a much stronger manuscript. In particular, I am indebted to Philip Mirowski and Dieter Plehwe, for their generous invitation, and to Eddie Nik-Khah for his invaluable help with the details of economic history. Lucette Cysique saw the book take shape from beginning to end and unfailingly asked the most disarming questions at the right time. In different ways, Catherine Waldby, Miguel Vatter, Nadine Ehlers, Anne Pollock, Melissa McAdams, and Ari Larissa Heinrich have all been important interlocutors throughout the writing of this book. I would like to thank Rachel Rowe and Regrette Etcetera for their reflections on housing inflation, welfare, and family in Sydney and for energizing me in the final stages of the writing process. Finally, I am grateful to the students in my Economic Sociology and Contemporary Social Theory courses, who have grappled with many of the ideas presented here and have been a constant source of intellectual inspiration.

Notes

CHAPTER ONE: BETWEEN NEOLIBERALISM
AND THE NEW SOCIAL CONSERVATISM

1. On this and the following points, see Judith Stacey, *In the Name of the Family: Rethinking Family Values in the Postmodern Age* (Boston: Beacon Press, 1996).

2. Daniel Patrick Moynihan, "The Moynihan Report: The Negro Family: The Case for National Action," in Lee Rainwater and William L. Yancey (eds.), *The Moynihan Report and the Politics of Controversy* (Cambridge, MA: MIT Press, 1967 [1965]), p. 93. On the alleged crisis of the white middle-class family, see Barbara Dafoe Whitehead, "Dan Quayle Was Right," *Atlantic Monthly* (April 1993), writing from the communitarian "left," and Charles Murray, "The Coming White Underclass," *Wall Street Journal* (October 29, 1993), from the conservative-libertarian "right."

3. On the "marriage gap" among lower-income white Americans, see Charles A. Murray, *Coming Apart: The State of White America, 1960–2010* (New York: Crown Forum, 2012). For a social-progressive but nevertheless communitarian perspective on the marriage gap, see Andrew J. Cherlin, *Labor's Love Lost: The Rise and Fall of the Working Class Family in America* (New York: Russell Sage Foundation, 2014).

4. Gary S. Becker, *Treatise on the Family* (Chicago: University of Chicago Press, 1981), p. 1.

5. Gary S. Becker and Guity Nashat Becker, *The Economics of Life: From*

Baseball to Affirmative Action to Immigration, How Real-World Issues Affect Our Everyday Life (New York: McGraw-Hill, 1996), p. 93.

6. *Ibid.*, pp. 95–102.

7. Antony Giddens, *The Transformation of Intimacy* (Cambridge: Polity Press, 1992); Ulrich Beck and Elizabeth Beck-Gernsheim, *The Normal Chaos of Love* (Cambridge: Polity Press, 2995); Zygmunt Bauman, *Liquid Modernity* (Cambridge: Polity Press, 2000), pp. 89–90; Eva Illouz, *Consuming the Romantic Utopia: Love and the Cultural Contradictions of Capitalism* (Berkeley: University of California Press, 1997). The tone ranges from optimistic in the work of Giddens and the Becks to frankly nostalgic in the work of Bauman and Illouz.

8. Wolfgang Streeck, "Flexible Employment, Flexible Families, and the Socialization of Reproduction" in Florian Coulmas and Ralph Lützeler (eds.), *Imploding Populations in Japan and Germany: A Comparison* (Leiden: Brill, 2011), pp. 63–96.

9. *Ibid.*, p. 72.

10. *Ibid.*, p. 76.

11. *Ibid.*, pp. 76–77. For a pointed reminder of the continuity of women's economic precariousness under Fordist and post-Fordist labor regimes, see Angela Mitropoulos, "Precari-us?" in *Mute: Precarious Reader* (London: Mute Publishing, 2005), pp. 12–19.

12. Luc Boltanski and Eve Chiapello, *The New Spirit of Capitalism* (New York: Verso, 2007), p. 190.

13. *Ibid.*, p. xl.

14. Nancy Fraser, "From Redistribution to Recognition? Dilemmas of Justice in a 'Post-Socialist' Age," *New Left Review* 212 (1995), pp. 68–93.

15. Nancy Fraser, *Fortunes of Feminism: From Women's Liberation to Identity Politics to Anti-Capitalism* (New York: Verso, 2013), p. 218.

16. *Ibid.*, p. 220.

17. *Ibid.*, pp. 134–35.

18. The debt is sometimes explicit. See for example, Wolfgang Streeck, *Re-forming Capitalism: Institutional Change in the German Political Economy*

(Oxford: Oxford University Press, 2008), pp. 247–63 and 266–67; Nancy
Fraser, "A Triple Movement: Parsing the Politics of Crisis after Polanyi?"
New Left Review 81 (2013), pp. 119–32.

19. However, see Angela Mitropoulos and Martijn Konings for critiques
of Karl Polanyi that are germane to the one I am offering here. Angela Mitropoulos, *Contract and Contagion: From Biopolitics to Oikonomia* (New York:
Minor Compositions, 2012), pp. 158–66; Martijn Konings, *The Emotional
Logic of Capitalism: What Progressives Have Missed* (Stanford, CA: Stanford
University Press, 2015), pp. 1–19. Both of these theorists lean toward a Marxian
critique in envisaging the "double movement" as fully internal to and constitutive of capital's dynamics. See also Miranda Joseph, *Against the Romance
of Community* (Minneapolis: University of Minnesota Press, 2002), for an
account of contemporary neoliberalism that attends to the coconstitution
of capitalism and community; and Andrea Muehlebach, *The Moral Neoliberal:
Welfare and Citizenship in Italy* (Chicago: University of Chicago Press, 2012),
who examines the coexistence of neoliberal and new Catholic conservative
philosophies of welfare in contemporary Italy.

20. Karl Polanyi, *The Great Transformation: The Political and Economic
Origins of our Time* (Boston: Beacon Press, 1944 [2001]).

21. The reference to Aristotle's household economy or *oikonomia* is implicit
in *The Great Transformation* but discussed at length in Polanyi's philosophical
work "Aristotle Discovers the Economy," in George Dalton (ed.), *Primitive,
Archaic and Modern Economies: Essays of Karl Polanyi* (New York: Anchor Books,
1968), pp. 78–115. With its references to the anthropology of Henry Sumner
Maine and Ferdinand Tönnies, the conservative underpinnings of Polanyi's
thought become explicit here. See my "The Living and the Dead: Variations
on de Anima," *Angelaki: Journal of the Theoretical Humanities* 7. 3 (2002),
pp. 81–104, for an analysis of Marx's more ambivalent references to Aristotle
and the critique of chrematistics.

22. Polanyi, *The Great Transformation*, p. 139.

23. *Ibid.*, pp. 30–32, 245–56.

24. With its reference to limits and curves, Marx's *Grundrisse* is evidently

grappling with the problem of change in time as exemplified in the language of the differential calculus. His primary philosophical reference point is Hegel's *Science of Logic*—itself a reflection on the differential calculus. Yet, several readers of Marx have suggested that although Marx was inhabiting the language of Hegel in the *Grundrisse*, he was simultaneously struggling to define a different kind of mathematics of change or curvature. Francine Markovits pursues this argument from a philosophical and philological perspective, arguing that Marx was attempting to escape (not simply reverse) the Hegelian dialectic as early as his doctoral thesis on Epicurean philosophy. See Francine Markovits, *Marx dans le jardin d'Epicure* (Paris: Éditions de Minuit, 1974). Daniel Bensaïd similarly suggests that Marx saw the calculation project of capital in terms similar to those of fractal mathematics or nonlinear complex systems theory in physics. Basing his argument on a close reading of Marx's letters to Engels, he asserts that "Marx never gave up on the hope of finding a nonlinear mathematics 'of irregular curves' that would allow him to discover order in chaos" (p. 50, my translation). According to Bensaïd, Marx was stopped short in this endeavor only by the limitations of contemporary mathematics. If we read Marx as working with an Epicurean or fractal understanding of change, this implies that difference, curvature, or change-in-time must be understood as ontologically primary with respect to presence and hence never reducible to the Hegelian concept of negativity. Whatever the value of these arguments with respect to Marx's real intentions, it seems to me that this is the most interesting and enabling way of reading Marx today. Daniel Bensaïd, *La discordance des temps: Essais sur les crises, les classes, l'histoire* (Paris: Éditions de la Passion, 1995), p. 50.

25. In the *Grundrisse*, Marx writes that "as representative of the general form of wealth—money—capital is the endless and limitless drive to go beyond its limiting barrier. Every boundary [*Grenze*] is and has to be a barrier [*Schranke*] for it. Else it would cease to be capital—money as self-reproductive. If ever it perceived a certain boundary not as a barrier, but became comfortable within it as a boundary, it would have itself declined from exchange value to use value, from the general form of wealth to a specific, substantial mode of the same."

And yet the "universality towards which it irresistibly strives encounters barriers in its own nature." Karl Marx, *Grundrisse: Foundations of the Critique of Political Economy (Rough Draft)*, trans. Martin Nicolaus (London: Penguin, 1993), pp. 334 and 410.

26. Marx, *Grundrisse*, p. 410.

27. In the *Grundrisse*, Marx defines capital's "internal limit" in the most abstract terms as the necessity of capturing surplus value within the form of private property (pp. 415–16). For Marx, this limit must be understood as internal to capital—not external and transcendent—because it is not a natural limit to growth but a limit that is imposed by the specifically privatized form of wealth creation under capitalism. In *Capital*, Marx offers a much more detailed account of the various limits which capital imposes upon its own self-valorization. On the gold standard and landed property as barriers, see Karl Marx, *Capital Volume 3* (London: Penguin, 1981), pp. 706–708 and 882–907. On the legal appropriation of land and vagrancy laws as barriers, see Karl Marx, *Capital Volume 1* (London: Penguin, 1976), pp. 873–904.

28. Marx, *Grundrisse*, p. 410.

29. Marx's unwillingness to extend the critique of fundamental value to the question of sexual politics is far from accidental. Although Marx and Engels call for the abolition of private inheritance in *The Communist Manifesto*, in his various other writings, Marx revealed himself to be ambivalent about such a project. Despite their searing critique of the bourgeois family, Marx and Engels remained committed to the male breadwinner wage as the foundational institution of working-class politics. Indeed, the very notion of a unified working class appears to depend on the sexual division of labor. This division is simply assumed in Marx's work but in fact involved the forcible expulsion of women from the factories in the early part of the nineteenth century. On Marx's ambivalence with respect to the question of inheritance, see Jacqueline Stevens, *Reproducing the State* (Princeton, NJ: Princeton University Press, 1999), pp. 27–36. On Marx's support for the male breadwinner wage, see Melinda Cooper, "Reproduktion neu denken. Leihmutterschaft zwischen Vertrag und Familie," in Melinda Cooper, Catherine Waldby, Felicita Reuschling and

Susanne Schultz, *Sie nennen es Leben, wir nennen es Arbeit: Biotechnologie,*
Reproduktion und Familie im 21. Jahrhundert (Berlin: Edition Assemblage, 2015),
pp. 49–77.

30. Reva B. Siegel, " 'The Rule of Love': Wife-Beating as Prerogative and
Privacy," *Yale Law Journal* 105 (1996), p. 2119.

31. Eric Hobsbawm, "Introduction — Inventing Traditions," in Eric
Hobsbawm and Terence Ranger (eds.), *The Invention of Tradition* (Cambridge:
Cambridge University Press, 1983), pp. 1–14. For an extended reflection
on the reinvention of tradition (as idea and practice) in nineteenth-century
England, see Stephen Prickett, *Modernity and the Reinvention of Tradition:*
Backing into the Future (Cambridge: Cambridge University Press, 2009).

32. Peter Osborne, *The Politics of Time: Modernity and the Avant-Garde*
(London: Verso, 1995), p. 164.

33. Wendy Brown, "American Nightmare: Neoliberalism, Neoconservatism,
and De-Democratization," *Political Theory* 34. 6 (2006), pp. 690–714.

34. Roger D. Congleton, "Buchanan and the Virginia School," in Geoffrey
Brennan, Hartmut Kliemt, and Robert D. Tollison (eds.), *Methods and Morals in*
Constitutional Economics: Essays in Honor of James M. Buchanan (New York:
Springer, 2002), pp. 22–38; S. M. Amadae, *Rationalizing Capitalist Democracy:*
The Cold War Origins of Rational Choice Liberalism (Chicago: Chicago Univer-
sity Press, 2003); Monica Prasad, *The Politics of Free Markets: The Rise of Neo-*
liberal Economic Policies in Britain, France, Germany, and the United States
(Chicago: University of Chicago Press, 2006); Philip Mirowski and Dieter
Plehwe (eds.), *The Road from Mont Pèlerin: The Making of the Neoliberal Thought*
Collective (Cambridge, MA: Harvard University Press, 2009); Ross B. Emmett,
(ed.), *The Elgar Companion to the Chicago School of Economics* (Northampton,
MA: Edward Elgar, 2010); Jamie Peck, *Constructions of Neoliberal Reason*
(Oxford: Oxford University Press, 2010); Serge Audier, *Néo-libéralisme(s):*
Une archéologie intellectuelle (Paris: Grasset, 2012); Angus Burgin, *The Great*
Persuasion: Reinventing Free Markets since the Depression (Cambridge, MA:
Harvard University Press, 2012); Pierre Dardot and Christian Laval, *The New*
Way of the World: On Neoliberal Society, trans. Gregory Elliott (New York: Verso,

2013); Robert van Horn, Philip Mirowski, and Thomas A. Stapleford, (eds.), *Building Chicago Economics: New Perspectives on the History of America's Most Powerful Economics Program* (Cambridge: Cambridge University Press, 2013); Daniel Stedman Jones, *Masters of the Universe: Hayek, Friedman, and the Birth of Neoliberal Politics* (Princeton, NJ: Princeton University Press, 2014). Beyond these essential references, there exists a much larger critical and philosophical literature on neoliberalism that I am unable to reference in its entirety.

35. The economist Melvin Reder reflected that if "the vitality of the [Chicago] tradition is threatened," it was more a result of the "growing acceptance of many of its key ideas than [due to] resistance to them." Quoted in Peck, *Constructions of Neoliberal Reason*, p. 116.

36. Russell Kirk, *The Conservative Mind: From Burke to Santayana* (Washington, DC: Regnery Press, 1953).

37. On this alliance, its connections to and difference from the emergent neoconservative-neoliberal alliance, see Robert B. Horwitz, *America's Right: Anti-Establishment Conservatism from Goldwater to the Tea Party* (London: Polity, 2013), pp. 23–62. Phyllis Schlafly, a leading Catholic figure in the new religious right, was a supporter of Barry Goldwater's presidential campaign in 1964. Goldwater himself remained a committed libertarian and was subsequently critical of the Republican Party's concessions to the religious right.

38. *Ibid.*, pp. 63–111.

39. *Ibid.*, pp. 112–56.

40. Stacey, *In the Name of the Family*, pp. 54–55, 95.

41. R. Kent Weaver, *Ending Welfare as We Know It* (Washington, DC: Brookings Institution Press, 2000), pp. 117–20.

42. I do not mean to imply that such efforts ended in the 1980s. In recent years, we have seen a notable resurgence of political practices that refuse to separate the question of sexual politics from that of economic justice. See Dean Spade, *Normal Life: Administrative Violence, Critical Trans Politics and the Limits of Law* (Boston: South End Press, 2011). See also the following theoretical reflections on the articulation of sexual politics and political economy; Rosemary Hennessy, *Profit and Pleasure: Sexual Identities in Late Capitalism*

(London: Routledge, 2000); Lisa Duggan, *The Twilight of Equality? Neoliberalism, Cultural Politics, and the Attack on Equality* (Boston: South End Press, 2004); Kevin Floyd, *The Reification of Desire: Toward a Queer Marxism* (Minnesota: University of Minnesota Press, 2009); Silvia Federici, *Revolution at Point Zero: Housework, Reproduction and Feminist Struggle* (New York: Autonomedia, 2012); Mitropoulos, *Contract and Contagion*; Nikita Dhawan, Antke Engel, Christoph F. E. Holzhey, and Volker Woltersdorff (eds.), *Global Justice and Desire: Queering Economy* (London: Routledge, 2015).

43. Thomas Frank, *What's the Matter with Kansas? How Conservatives Won the Heart of America* (New York: Henry Holt, 2004); Paul Krugman, *The Conscience of a Liberal* (New York: Norton, 2007), pp. 173–97.

44. For a now classic critique of these distinctions, see Judith Butler, "Merely Cultural," *Social Text* 52/53 (1997), pp. 265–77, and, in response, Nancy Fraser, "Heterosexism, Misrecognition, and Capitalism: A Response to Judith Butler," *Social Text* 52/53 (1997), pp. 279–89. I will return to a discussion of these texts in Chapter 4.

45. G. R. Searle, *Morality and the Market in Victorian Britain* (Clarendon Press: Oxford, 1998), pp. 134–66.

46. Thomas Piketty, *Capital in the Twenty-First Century* (Cambridge, MA: Harvard Belknap, 2014).

CHAPTER TWO: THE MORAL CRISIS OF INFLATION

1. I am drawing here on the accounts of William Greider in *Secrets of the Temple: How the Federal Reserve Runs the Country* (New York: Simon & Schuster, 1989); Iwan Morgan, *Deficit Government: Taxing and Spending in Modern America* (Chicago: Ivan R. Dee, 1995); Robert L. Hetzel, "Arthur Burns and Inflation," *Federal Reserve Bank of Richmond Economic Quarterly* 84. 1 (1998), pp. 21–44; Allan H. Meltzer, *A History of the Federal Reserve, Volume 2, Book 2* (Chicago: University of Chicago Press, 2009); Iwan Morgan, "Monetary Metamorphosis: The Volcker Fed and Inflation," *The Journal of Policy History* 24. 4 (2012), pp. 545–71.

2. See on this point Morgan, *Deficit Government*, pp. 108–15.

3. *Ibid.*, pp. 116–17.

4. *Ibid.*, p. 116.

5. Greta R. Krippner, *Capitalizing on Crisis: The Political Origins of the Rise of Finance* (Cambridge, MA: Harvard University Press, 2011), p. 64.

6. Edward N. Wolff, "The Distributional Effects of the 1969–75 Inflation on the Holdings of Household Wealth in the United States," *Review of Income and Wealth* 25. 2 (1979), p. 207.

7. Greider, *Secrets of the Temple*, p. 41.

8. Joseph J. Minarik, "The Distributional Effects of Inflation and Their Implications," in *Stagflation: The Causes, Effects and Solutions* (Washington, DC: Joint Economic Committee, U.S. Congress, 1980), pp. 225–77.

9. Greider, *Secrets of the Temple*, pp. 16–17, 44, 104; Morgan, "Monetary Metamorphosis," p. 554.

10. Greider, *Secrets of the Temple*, pp. 40–42.

11. Rose and Milton Friedman had this to say about the rise of antigovernment populism in the 1970s: "The first reaction is resentment; the second is to attempt to get around obstacles by legal means; finally, there comes a decline in respect for law in general. This final consequence is deplorable but inevitable." Milton Friedman and Rose Friedman, *Free to Choose: A Personal Statement* (New York: Harcourt Brace Jovanovich, 1980), p. 289.

12. Milton Friedman, "Nobel Prize Lecture: Inflation and Unemployment," *Journal of Political Economy* 85. 3 (1977), p. 454.

13. See on this point Leo Panitch and Sam Gindin, *The Making of Global Capitalism: The Political Economy of American Empire* (New York: Verso, 2012), pp. 164–72, and Edwin Dickens, "The Federal Reserve's Low Interest Rate Policy of 1970–72: Determinants and Constraints," *Review of Radical Political Economics* 28. 33 (1996), pp. 115–25.

14. Interview with Paul Volcker, Transcript from *Commanding Heights*, PBS, available online at http://www.pbs.org/wgbh/commandingheights/shared/minitext/int_paulvolcker.html (last accessed December 1, 2015). William L. Silber traces Volcker's abiding mistrust of inflation to the influence of Friedrich Hayek, his "favorite author as an undergraduate at Princeton."

William S. Silber, *Volcker: The Triumph of Persistence* (New York: Bloomsbury Press, 2012), p. 33. According to Volcker, "Hayek's words forever linked inflation and deception deep inside my head. And that connection, which undermines trust in government, is the greatest evil of inflation" (*ibid*). At Princeton, Volcker was also heavily influenced by the anti-inflationary views of his economics professor, Friedrich Lutz, who was close to both the Austrian and Ordoliberal schools of neoliberalism.

15. Friedman and Friedman, *Free to Choose*, p. 266. "Monetizing the debt" occurs when the Federal Reserve holds Treasury bonds and returns any money earned on these bonds back to the Treasury. Thus, the Treasury is able to borrow money without actually paying it back. Milton Friedman saw this kind of "money printing" as the primary cause of inflation.

16. *Ibid.*, pp. 102–27.

17. James M. Buchanan and Richard E. Wagner, *Democracy in Deficit: The Political Legacy of Lord Keynes* (New York: Academic Press, 1977), pp. 16–20.

18. *Ibid.*, pp. 64–65.

19. Henry Hazlitt, *The Inflation Crisis and How to Resolve It* (New York: Arlington House, 1978), p. 138.

20. For a comprehensive analysis of the diverse currents feeding into the "neoliberal thought collective," see Philip Mirowski and Dieter Plehwe (eds.), *The Road from Mont Pèlerin: The Making of the Neoliberal Thought Collective* (Cambridge, MA: Harvard University Press, 2009).

21. Daniel Bell, *The Cultural Contradictions of Capitalism: Twentieth Anniversary Edition* (New York: Basic Books, 1978 [1996]).

22. Marisa Chappell, *The War on Welfare: Family, Poverty and Politics in Modern America* (Philadelphia: University of Pennsylvania Press, 2010).

23. Suzanne Mettler, *Dividing Citizens: Gender and Federalism in New Deal Public Policy* (Ithaca, NY: Cornell University Press, 1998). Daniel Patrick Moynihan, "A Family Policy for the Nation," in Lee Rainwater and William L. Yancey (eds.), *The Moynihan Report and the Politics of Controversy* (Cambridge, MA: MIT Press, 1967 [1966]), pp. 387–88.

24. Mettler, *Dividing Citizens*, p. 54.

25. *Ibid.*, pp. 143 and 213.

26. *Ibid*, p. 142. Gwendolyn Mink, *Welfare's End* (Ithaca, NY: Cornell University Press, 1998), p. 48.

27. Mink, *Welfare's End*, p. 46.

28. Mettler, *Dividing Citizens*, p. 167; Mink, *Welfare's End*, p. 46.

29. Mettler, *Dividing Citizens*, p. 169; Mink, *Welfare's End*, p. 48.

30. Premilla Nadesan, *Welfare Warriors: The Welfare Rights Movement in the United States* (London: Routledge, 2005), pp. 7–8.

31. *Ibid.*, p. 7. See also Mettler, *Dividing Citizens*, p. 169.

32. Mettler, *Dividing Citizens*, pp. 171–74. Nadesan, *Welfare Warriors*, p. 6.

33. Felicia Kornbluh, *The Battle for Welfare Rights* (Philadelphia: University of Pennsylvania Press, 2007), pp. 67–68. On the specific role of state administrative law and so-called police powers in American law, see William J. Novak, *The People's Welfare: Law and Regulation in Nineteenth-Century America* (Chapel Hill: University of North Carolina Press, 1996). In American constitutional law, the state's police power—that is, its power to regulate everything from public hygiene to infrastructure to morality, as long as it does not conflict with federal law—is authorized under the Tenth Amendment.

34. Kornbluh, *The Battle for Welfare Rights*, pp. 67–68; Mink, *Welfare's End*, p. 50.

35. President Lyndon B. Johnson, "The Howard University Address," in Lee Rainwater and William L. Yancey (eds.), *The Moynihan Report and the Politics of Controversy* (Cambridge, MA: MIT Press, 1967), p. 130.

36. Daniel Patrick Moynihan, "The Moynihan Report: The Negro Family: The Case for National Action," in *ibid.*, p. 93.

37. *Ibid.*, p. 60.

38. Irving Kristol, "Preface" in *Reflections of a Neoconservative: Looking Back, Looking Ahead* (New York: Basic Books, 1983), p. x.

39. On the relationship between an American Catholic social philosophy and the New Deal, see Kenneth J. Heineman, *A Catholic New Deal: Religion and Reform in Depression Pittsburgh* (University Park: Penn State University Press, 1999).

40. Moynihan, "A Family Policy for the Nation," pp. 387–88 and 391.

41. *Ibid.*, p. 393.

42. Marisa Chappell, *The War on Welfare*, p. 37.

43. *Ibid.*, p. 39. Peter Steinfels, *The Neoconservatives: The Origins of a Movement* (New York: Simon & Schuster, 2013 [1979]), p. 137.

44. David M. Lewis-Colman, *Race Against Liberalism: Black Workers and the UAW in Detroit* (Champaign: University of Illinois Press, 2008), pp. 97–105.

45. On Richard Cloward's role in the National Welfare Rights Organization, see Chappell, *The War on Welfare*, p. 46; Nadesan, *Welfare Warriors*, p. 143; Kornbluh, *The Battle for Welfare Rights*, pp. 36–38.

46. Richard A. Cloward and Frances Fox Piven, "The Weight of the Poor: A Strategy to End Poverty," *The Nation* 202 (May 2, 1966), pp. 510 and 513–14.

47. *Ibid.*, p. 35.

48. See, on this point, Kornbluh, *The Battle for Welfare Rights*, pp. 99–100, 168–69. Kornbluh is particularly illuminating on the political positions held by African American women activists such as Beulah Sanders who were opposed *both* to workfare requirements (on the grounds that it would push them back into domestic service) *and* the role of unpaid housewife advocated by the leaders of the National Welfare Rights Organization.

49. For a general history of the Family Assistance Plan, see Brian Steensland, *The Failed Welfare Revolution: America's Struggle Over Guaranteed Income Policy* (Princeton, NJ: Princeton University Press, 2008). This history, however, has very little to say about the welfare rights movement, much less the tensions within it.

50. Felicia Ann Kornbluh elucidates the gendered politics of the Family Assistance Plan as follows: "The Nixon administration made two gendered arguments in favor of FAP. The first was that AFDC and, by extension, the whole New Deal state system, discriminated against men. Its purpose was therefore to undo the 'blatant unfairness' in public assistance, and 'the inequitable treatment of male-headed families as opposed to those headed by a female.' The single greatest innovation in the legislation was its extension of federal public assistance to men and two-parent working couples. The target

population for the FAP was the 'working poor,' defined by Secretary Finch as 'families in poverty headed by men working full time.' The second argument was that AFDC broke otherwise workable nuclear families asunder.... FAP was designed to undo the damage by allowing low earning men to stay with their wives (or girlfriends) and children without endangering the family's access to aid. The Nixon administration went so far as to hope that FAP would promote cohabitation or marriage." Kornbluh, *The Battle for Welfare Rights*, p. 148.

51. Milton Friedman and Rose Friedman, *Capitalism and Freedom* (Chicago: University of Chicago Press, 1962), pp. 192–95.

52. Friedman and Friedman, *Free to Choose*, pp. 120, 123.

53. Moynihan, "A Family Policy for the Nation," p. 386. Looking back on the early years of the Nixon administration, Moynihan recalled that the question of cost barely entered into debates surrounding the Family Assistance Plan. Daniel Patrick Moynihan, "How the Great Society 'Destroyed the American Family,'" *The Public Interest* 108 (Summer 1992), p. 60.

54. Milton Friedman to Patrick Buchanan, 25 October 1973, Box 22, Folder 11, Friedman Papers. Cited in Angus Burgin, *The Great Persuasion: Reinventing Free Markets since the Depression* (Cambridge, MA: Harvard University Press, 2012), p. 197. Burgin here makes the perceptive comment that "Friedman was a radical idealist who constructed his public policy proposals with a deep and perceptive attention to strategy. Few public figures in modern history have matched a utopian social philosophy with such close attention to the maintenance of practical goals."

55. Chappell, *The War on Welfare*, pp. 90–91.

56. William Ruger, *Milton Friedman* (London: Bloomsbury Academic, 2011), pp. 120–21.

57. Nixon's change of tack on the black family wage presaged a more general turn to the right within his administration. See Kornbluh, *The Battle for Welfare Rights*, pp. 148–50.

58. Jill Quadagno, *The Color of Welfare: How Racism Undermined the War on Poverty* (Oxford: Oxford University Press, 1994), p. 158.

59. For a careful reading of Moynihan's trajectory, see Steinfels, *The Neo-conservatives*, pp. 113–69. Steinfels locates Moynihan's neoconservative turn in his decision to advise Nixon. I place it later, after the defeat of the Family Assistance Plan.

60. Daniel Patrick Moynihan, *The Politics of a Guaranteed Income: The Nixon Administration and the Family Assistance Plan* (New York: Random House, 1973), p. 14.

61. Moynihan, "How the Great Society 'Destroyed the American Family,'" p. 59.

62. Moynihan was the architect of the 1988 Family Support Act under Reagan, the first major reform to AFDC but one that was disappointing for many on the right. On Moynihan's changing politics, see Chappell, *The War on Welfare*, p. 229.

63. Milton Friedman and Rose D. Friedman, *Two Lucky People* (Chicago: University of Chicago Press, 1998), pp. 381–82.

64. Milton Friedman, *Commanding Heights Interview*, 1980, available online at http://www.pbs.org/wgbh/commandingheights/shared/minitext /int_milton-friedman.html#1 (last accessed December 1, 2015).

65. Friedman and Friedman, *Free to Choose*, p. 127.

66. Ruger, *Milton Friedman*, pp. 96 and 122, and Lanny Ebenstein, "The Increasingly Libertarian Milton Friedman: An Ideological Profile," *Econ Journal Watch* 11. 1 (2014), pp. 81–96.

67. Milton Friedman quoted in "The Economy: We Are All Keynesians Now," *Time Magazine* 86. 27 (1965), p. 79. In a letter to the editor, Friedman qualified his words: "Sir: You quote me [Dec. 31] as saying: 'We are all Keynesians now.' The quotation is correct, but taken out of context. As best I can recall it, the context was: 'In one sense, we are all Keynesians now; in another, nobody is any longer a Keynesian.' The second half is at least as important as the first." Milton Friedman, "Letter to the Editor," *Time Magazine* 87. 5 (1966), p. 13.

68. The historian Justin Vaïsse identifies three distinct phases to the neo-conservative movement. The first phase—which I focus on here—was almost

exclusively concerned with social welfare and defined itself in opposition to the New Left. He associates the second phase with the rise of the "Scoop Jackson Democrats" who opposed the drift toward the left within the Democratic Party, were associated with the established labor unions, and supported welfare state policies at home and anticommunism abroad. If the first two phases of neo-conservatism arose out of the Democratic party in opposition to the New Left, the third generation was unambiguously associated with the Republican right, had no commitment to New Deal welfare whatsoever, and was defined by the idea that America had a unique imperial role to play in the international world order. Justin Vaïsse, *Neoconservatism: The Biography of a Movement* (Cambridge, MA: Harvard University Press, 2010), pp. 6–18. It is significant that the first book-length study of the neoconservatives, published in 1979, is almost exclusively focused on the question of social policy. Steinfels, *The Neoconservatives.*

69. Kristol, "Preface," p. x.

70. Nathan Glazer, *The Limits of Social Policy* (Cambridge, MA: Harvard University Press, 1988), pp. 1–2.

71. *Ibid.,* p. 3.

72. Irving Kristol, "Countercultures," in *Neoconservatism: The Auto-biography of an Idea* (New York: Free Press, 1995 [1994]), pp. 141–42.

73. Vaïsse, *Neoconservatism,* pp. 42–43.

74. Panitch and Gindin, *The Making of Global Capitalism,* pp. 135–36.

75. Samuel p. Huntington, "The United States" in Michel Crozier, Samuel p. Huntington, and Joji Watanuki (eds.), *The Crisis of Democracy: Report on the Governability of Democracies to the Trilateral Commission* (New York: New York University Press, 1975), pp. 59–118.

76. Irving Kristol identified the New Class as white-collar elites who typically graduated from the student counterculture to join the ranks of bloated welfare bureaucracies, where they formed a parasitic administrative caste catering to the needs of the equally parasitic nonworking poor. He contrasted this white-collar elite to the blue-collar working class, whose interests it supposedly despised. For an excellent discussion of the neoconservative understanding of the New Class, see Robert B. Horwitz, *America's Right: Anti-Establishment*

Conservatism from Goldwater to the Tea Party (Cambridge: Polity Press, 2013), pp. 120–23. The equation between the lumpenproletariat and the rentier class has a long history on the left also. Marx's reflections on the question of surplus population, for example, wavered between the registers of the analytic and the moralizing.

77. On this point again, see Greider, *Secrets of the Temple*, pp. 15–17, 44, 104. Greider comments on the popular perception that inflation had allowed "working girls" to buy fancy jewelry, an interesting expression of the idea that poor women were engaging in speculative consumption. Greider, *Secrets of the Temple*, pp. 15–16.

78. Huntington, "The United States," pp. 65–74.

79. For a critique of the idea of a causal relationship between public deficits and inflation and a theory of just why "balanced budgets" have come to exert such a strong emotional influence on American politics in the late twentieth century, see James D. Savage, *Balanced Budgets and American Politics* (Ithaca, NY: Cornell University Press, 1988). The idea of a causal relationship between public deficits and inflation was rejected even by Milton Friedman.

80. Friedman, "Nobel Prize Lecture: Inflation and Unemployment," pp. 451–72.

81. Huntington, "The United States," pp. 74–75.

82. Bell, *Cultural Contradictions of Capitalism.*

83. The thrust of this argument is outlined in Chapter 6 of Bell's *Cultural Contradictions of Capitalism,* "The Public Household: On 'Fiscal Sociology' and the Liberal Society." *Ibid.,* pp. 220–82. Daniel Bell's argument compresses references to the fiscal sociology of Richard Musgrave and his theory of the "public household" (which we will explore in greater detail in Chapter 6), Max Weber's theory of the Protestant ethic, and Aristotle's distinction between the household economy and chrematistics.

84. *Ibid.,* p. 75.

85. The reference is to Richard A. Musgrave, *The Theory of Public Finance* (New York: McGraw-Hill, 1959).

86. Glazer, *The Limits of Social Policy,* pp. 9–10.

87. *Ibid.*, p. 9.

88. For an illuminating reading of this speech and what it reveals about the tensions between neoliberalism and neoconservatism, see Burgin, *The Great Persuasion*, pp. 186–213. Friedman was elected president of the Mont Pèlerin Society at a time when it had lost much of its early pluralism and was dominated by free-market economists of the kind who now populated the Chicago and Virginia schools.

89. Kristol later republished the speech in essay form. See Irving Kristol, "Capitalism, Socialism, and Nihilism," in *Neoconservatism: The Autobiography of an Idea* (New York: Free Press, [1972/1973] 1995), pp. 92–105.

90. *Ibid.*, p. 102.

91. See for example, Margaret Jane Radin, *Contested Commodities* (Cambridge, MA: Harvard University Press, 1996), and Michael J. Sandel, *What Money Can't Buy: The Moral Limits of Markets* (New York: Farrar, Straus and Giroux, 2012). These left critiques of neoliberalism are very close to Amitai Etzioni's Third Way communitarianism. For Etzioni's most extended critique of Chicago school neoliberalism, see Amitai Etzioni, *The Moral Dimension: Toward a New Economics* (New York: Simon & Schuster, 1998).

92. Gary S. Becker, "Altruism in the Family," in *A Treatise on the Family, Enlarged Edition* (Cambridge, MA: Harvard University Press, 1993 [1981]), pp. 277–306.

93. The point is made most overtly and forcefully by Richard A. Epstein, when he writes that certain "biological constants . . . lie at the root of family behavior, and demarcate the zone of voluntary market exchange from that of the non-price, nonexchange economy of the family. Every legal system must draw some distinction between those within the family and those outsiders who deal with the family at—to use the instructive legal phrase—'arm's length.'" Richard Epstein, *Principles for a Free Society* (New York: Basic Books, 1998), pp. 22–23.

94. Wendy Brown, "Liberalism's Family Values," in *States of Injury: Power and Freedom in Late Modernity* (Princeton, NJ: Princeton University Press, 1995), pp. 135–65. Brown here seeks to conceptualize the "persistent legal and

political tension between the individual and the family in liberalism," a tension we also find in neoliberalism. Ultimately, she argues, the tension and its elision can be explained only by the naturalization of women's subordination within classical liberal and neoliberal economic thought.

95. See on this point, Martijn Konings, "State of Speculation: Contingency, Measure, and the Politics of Plastic Value," *South Atlantic Quarterly* 114.2 (2015), p. 252.

96. Friedman and Friedman, *Free to Choose*, p. 106.

97. Milton Friedman, *Milton Friedman Speaks: Lecture 1—What is America?* (New York: Harcourt Brace Jovanovich, 1978). Video. 1:07:14–1:09:09. Available online at http://www.freetochoose.tv/program.php?id=mfs_1&series=mfs (last accessed December 1, 2015).

98. Gary S. Becker, *A Treatise on the Family*, p. 1.

99. Becker, "The Evolution of the Family," in *A Treatise on the Family*, p. 357.

100. On the family as a natural insurance mechanism, see Becker, "Altruism in the Family," pp. 281–82.

101. "Both the welfare state and economic activity have grown much more slowly in advanced countries since the early 1970s.... If economic development continues to slow down and the expansion of the welfare state continues to moderate, the analysis in this chapter predicts much less steep declines in fertility and less rapid increases in divorce, labor force participation of married women, illegitimacy, and female-headed households.... Indeed, a sufficient slowing of the pace of development could eventually raise fertility and also reverse the trends in other aspects of family behavior." Gary S. Becker, "The Evolution of the Family," in *A Treatise on the Family*, p. 360.

102. Gary S. Becker and Guity Nashat Becker, *The Economics of Life: From Baseball to Affirmative Action to Immigration, How Real-World Issues Affect Our Everyday Life* (New York: McGraw-Hill, 1996), p. 95.

103. Irving Kristol, *Reflections of a Neoconservative: Looking Back, Looking Ahead* (New York: Basic Books, 1983), p. vii.

104. Irving Kristol, "Social Reform: Gains and Losses," in *Neoconservatism: The Autobiography of an Idea* (New York: Free Press, 1995 [1973]), pp. 200–204.

105. Lawrence M. Mead, *Beyond Entitlement: The Social Obligations of Citizenship* (New York: Free Press, 1986). Here Mead argues that the contract of free labor depends ultimately on the obligation of unfree labor—and this is an obligation that the state must impose by force when necessary. "The solution must lie in public authority. Low-wage work apparently must be mandated, just as a draft has sometimes been necessary to staff the military" (p. 84). See Lawrence M. Mead and Christopher Beem (eds.), *Welfare Reform and Political Theory* (New York: Russell Sage Foundation, 2005), for a collection of essays that examine this thesis with respect to both work and family-based policies.

106. According to Glazer, the "creation and building of new traditions, or new versions of old traditions, must be taken more seriously as a requirement of social policy itself." Glazer, *The Limits of Social Policy*, p. 8.

107. Sanford Schram, "Neoliberalizing the Welfare State: Marketizing Social Policy, Disciplining Clients," in Damien Cahill, Martijn Konings, and Melinda Cooper (eds.), *Handbook of Neoliberalism* (London: Sage Publications, 2018).

108. Pat O'Malley offers a sustained reflection on the role of the incentive in neoliberal thought, with a particular focus on the law and economics school. Pat O'Malley, *The Currency of Justice: Fines and Damages in Consumer Societies* (New York: Routledge-Cavendish, 2009). However, he does not inquire into the limits of the incentive as a mode of control.

109. Gary S. Becker, "Revamp Welfare to Put Children First (1992)," in Becker and Becker, *The Economics of Life*, pp. 100–102. The sanction system has now become an integral part of welfare governance, at the limit serving to cut welfare recipients off the rolls completely when they fail to comply with the minimal conditions of welfare payment. For an analysis of the performance-linked incentive in social policy, see Jamie Peck and Nik Theodore, "Recombinant Workfare, Across the Americas: Transnationalizing 'Fast' Social Policy," *Geoforum* 41. 2, pp. 195–208.

110. Alice O'Connor, *Social Science for What? Philanthropy and the Social Question in a World Turned Rightside Up* (New York: Russell Sage Foundation, 2007), pp. 104–15.

111. Chappell, *The War on Welfare*, p. 202.

112. *Ibid.*

CHAPTER THREE: THE ETHIC OF FAMILY RESPONSIBILITY

1. I am indebted to Brenda Cossman's reading of PRWORA on this point. See her "Contesting Conservatisms: Family Feuds and the Privatization of Dependency," *American University Journal of Gender, Social Policy and Law* 13 (2005), pp. 415–509. Cossman speaks of the "hybrid nature of the PRWORA, which seeks to promote both a fiscal conservative [neoliberal] privatization of the once public costs of supporting families and a social conservative vision of the traditional family by reducing the number of births outside of marriage and promoting marriage" (p. 454). Cossman notes that both neoliberals and social conservatives "agreed on the objective of promoting personal responsibility" but for neoliberals "personal responsibility was cast primarily in financial terms, while for social conservatives it was also cast in moral terms." What I would add to Cossman's argument is the proposition that the slippage between personal and family responsibility within (neo)liberal discourse is what allows neoliberals to forge an alliance with social conservatives.

2. Governor of California (Ronald Reagan), *California's Blueprint for National Welfare Reform: Proposals for the Nation's Food Stamp and Aid to Families with Dependent Children Programs* (Sacramento, CA: Office of the Governor, 1974), p. 2.

3. Ronald Reagan, "Remarks at the Annual Meeting of the National Alliance of Business, September 14, 1987," *Public Papers of the Presidents of the United States: Ronald Reagan, 1987, Book 2* (Washington, DC: Office of the Federal Register, 1989), p. 1032.

4. M. A. Crowther, "Family Responsibility and State Responsibility in Britain before the Welfare State," *The Historical Journal* 25. 1 (1982), p. 135. Crowther is referring specifically to the English New Poor Law of 1834, which inspired America's post–Civil War system of public relief.

5. Stuart Butler and Anna Kondratas (both associated with the Heritage Foundation) place "family responsibility" at the heart of their agenda for

"conservative" welfare reform and seamlessly weave together neoliberal and social conservative concerns about the role of the family. Stuart Butler and Anna Kondratas, *Out of the Poverty Trap: A Conservative Strategy of Welfare Reform* (New York: Free Press, 1987), pp. 148–59.

6. This venture is by no means peculiar to the United States. The political philosopher Robert E. Goodin sees the revival of family responsibility provisions as characteristic of neoliberal welfare reform in the United States, Britain, Australia, New Zealand, and Canada. Robert E. Goodin, *Reasons for Welfare: The Political Theory of the Welfare State* (Princeton, NJ: Princeton University Press, 1998), pp. 332–59. See Wendy Larner, "Post-Welfare State Governance: Towards a Code of Social and Family Responsibility," *Social Politics* 7. 2 (2000), pp. 244–65, for an analysis of the New Zealand government's very deliberate attempt to incorporate the poor law within social welfare policy.

7. See Marvin Olasky, *The Tragedy of American Compassion* (Washington, DC: Regnery Publishing. 1992), and Gertrude Himmelfarb, *The Demoralization of Society: From Victorian Virtues to Modern Society* (New York: Vintage Books, 1994). The historian Stephen Pimpare addresses the actual and imagined affinities between Gilded Age and late twentieth-century American welfare policy in his *The New Victorians: Poverty, Politics and Propaganda in Two Gilded Ages* (New York: New Press, 2004). "The Poor Law–influenced ideas espoused by Gilded Age reform leaders and the policies they helped enact would ... serve as models for Marvin Olasky, Newt Gingrich, Charles Murray, and other leaders of the more recent reform movement; among our modern anti-welfare moralists, only historian Gertrude Himmelfarb would find occasion to draw explicitly on English policy. It is from these American Victorians that we have gained our current thinking about poor relief policy; it is from this Gilded Age experience that our New Victorians have borrowed, often quite consciously" (p. 17). There now exists an abundant literature tracing the historical affinities between Gilded Age American economic liberalism and neoliberal economic policy. See, for example, Larry M. Bartels, *Unequal Democracy: The Political Economy of the New Gilded Age* (Princeton, NJ: Princeton University Press, 2008). However, few critical studies of the Gilded Age pay attention

to the confluence of classical liberal and social conservative ideas during this period.

8. Jacob S. Hacker, *The Great Risk Shift: The New Economic Insecurity and the Decline of the American Dream* (Oxford: Oxford University Press, 2006).

9. Wendy Brown, *States of Injury: Power and Freedom in Late Modernity* (Princeton, NJ: Princeton University Press, 1995), pp. 149–50.

10. Milton and Rose Friedman, *Tyranny of the Status Quo* (Harmondsworth, UK: Penguin Books, 1985), p. 132. My italics.

11. Gary L. Bauer, *The Family: Preserving America's Future: A Report to the President from the White House Working Group on the Family* (Washington, DC: Domestic Policy Council, 1986), p. 17.

12. 43 Eliz. 1, ch.2, § VI (1601) (as amended).

13. Daniel R. Mandelker, "Family Responsibility under the American Poor Laws I," *Michigan Law Review* 54. 4 (1956), p. 500; Mary Ann Mason, *From Father's Property to Children's Rights: The History of Child Custody in the United States* (New York: Columbia University Press, 1994), p. 25.

14. Edith Abbott, "Poor Law Provision for Family Responsibility," *Social Service Review* 12. 4 (1938), p. 600.

15. Walter I. Trattner, *From Poor Law to Welfare State: A History of Social Welfare in America*, 6th ed. (New York: Simon & Schuster, 2007), p. 17

16. Mason, *From Father's Property to Children's Rights*, p. 27.

17. Abbott, "Poor Law Provision for Family Responsibility," p. 599.

18. Drew D. Hansen, "The American Invention of Child Support: Dependency and Punishment in Early American Child Support," *Yale Law Journal* 108. 5 (1999), pp. 1123–53.

19. Poor Law Commissioners, *Poor Law Commissioners' Report of 1834* (London: Darling and Son, 1905), pp. 95–96.

20. Crowther, "Family Responsibility and State Responsibility in Britain before the Welfare State," pp. 131–37.

21. Specifically, Malthus combined classical liberal tenets with a form of economic theology shaped by evangelical Christianity. See, on this point,

Michael C. Waterman, *Revolution, Economics and Religion: Christian Political Economy, 1798–1833* (Cambridge: Cambridge University Press, 1991). For an extensive discussion of Malthus' influence on the New Poor Law, see Joseph Persky, "Classical Family Values: Ending the Poor Laws as They Knew Them," *Journal of Economic Perspectives* 11. 1 (1997), pp. 185–87. Persky notes that "Malthus's patriarchal views on the family were widely shared by both liberals and conservatives of his time" (p. 185).

22. Trattner, *From Poor Law to Welfare State*, p. 83.

23. Amy Dru Stanley, *From Bondage to Contract: Wage Labor, Marriage, and the Market in the Age of Slave Emancipation* (Cambridge: Cambridge University Press, 1998), pp. 138–47.

24. Angela Onwuachi-Willig, "The Return of the Ring: Welfare Reform's Marriage Cure as the Revival of Post-Bellum Control," *California Law Review* 93. 6 (2005), pp. 1654–55.

25. Priscilla Yamin, *American Marriage: A Political Institution* (Philadelphia: University of Pennsylvania Press, 2012), p. 32.

26. Donna L. Franklin, *Ensuring Inequality: The Structural Transformation of the African American Family* (Oxford: Oxford University Press, 1997), p. 31.

27. Yamin, *American Marriage*, p. 33.

28. Katherine Franke, "Becoming a Citizen: Reconstruction Era Regulation of African American Marriages," *Yale Journal of Law and the Humanities* 11 (1999), pp. 277–78.

29. *Ibid.*, pp. 282 and 289–90.

30. *Ibid.*, pp. 302–303; Onwuachi-Willig, "The Return of the Ring," pp. 1658–61.

31. Franke, "Becoming a Citizen," p. 303.

32. On convict labor, see Alex Lichtenstein, *Twice the Work of Free Labor: The Political Economy of Convict Labor in the New South* (New York: Verso Press, 1996). On domestic service as a regime of servitude, see Cecilia Rio, " 'A Treadmill Life': Class and African American Women's Paid Domestic Service in the Postbellum South, 1863–1920," *Rethinking Marxism* 20. 1 (2008), pp. 91–106. However, it should be remembered that many women were also

subject to convict labor. See Talitha LeFouria, *Black Women and Convict Labor in the New South* (Chapel Hill: University of North Carolina Press, 2015).

33. Franklin, *Ensuring Inequality*, pp. 31–32; Eric Foner, *Forever Free: The Story of Emancipation and Reconstruction* (New York: Knopf Doubleday, 2013), pp. 84–85. Donna Franklin notes that complaints of domestic violence became increasingly common once the Bureau began enforcing women's legal subordination in marriage and labor contracts (pp. 31–32).

34. Martin A. Berger, *Man Made: Thomas Eakins and the Construction of Gilded Age Manhood* (Berkeley: University of California Press, 2000), p. 38.

35. Samuel Mencher, *Poor Law to Poverty Program: Economic Security Policy in Britain and the United States* (Pittsburgh: University of Pittsburgh Press, 1967), pp. 241–66. Mencher remarks that despite their differences, "American Romantics and social Darwinists were on common ground in their praise of self-reliance" (p. 245).

36. Leon Fink, *The Long Gilded Age: American Capitalism and the Lessons of a New World Order* (Philadelphia: University of Pennsylvania Press, 2015), pp. 1–33.

37. The historian, Martha Branscombe, notes that "during the period following the Civil War...the poor law principle of the liability of relatives within certain degrees of kinship, which had been developed to supplement common law responsibilities, was more vigorously urged as a means of repressing poverty." Martha Branscombe, *The Courts and the Poor Laws in New York State 1784–1929* (Chicago: University of Chicago Press, 1943), p. 249.

38. Brown, *States of Injury*, pp. 135–65.

39. Pimpare, *The New Victorians*, p. 15.

40. William J. Novak, *The People's Welfare: Law and Regulation in Nineteenth-Century America* (Chapel Hill: University of North Carolina Press, 1996).

41. On the history of the Charity Organization Societies, see Pimpare, *The New Victorians*, pp. 47–54 and 70–75. The first citywide American COS was founded in Buffalo, New York, in 1877, closely modeled on its English namesake; before the end of the nineteenth century, several hundred chapters would be established across the United States.

42. Crowther, "Family Responsibility and State Responsibility in Britain," pp. 134–35.

43. Charles Stewart Loch, *The Prevention and Relief of Distress* (London: P. S. King and Son: 1931 [1883]), p. 31.

44. Mary E. Richmond, *Friendly Visiting Among the Poor: A Handbook for Charity Workers* (New York: Macmillan, 1899), p. 149.

45. Elizabeth N. Agnew, *From Charity to Social Work: Mary E. Richmond and the Creation of an American Profession* (Champaign: University of Illinois Press, 2004), p. 100.

46. Hansen, "The American Invention of Child Support," p. 1142.

47. *Ibid.*, p. 1147; Jocelyn Elise Crowley, *The Politics of Child Support in America* (Cambridge: Cambridge University Press, 2003), pp. 58–63.

48. Hansen, "The American Invention of Child Support," p. 1149.

49. Michael Grossberg, *Governing the Hearth: Law and Family in Nineteenth-Century America* (Chapel Hill: University of North Carolina Press, 1988), pp. 9–12.

50. David Wagner, *Ordinary People: In and Out of Poverty in the Gilded Age* (Boulder, CO: Paradigm Publishers, 2008), p. 122.

51. Quoted in Grossberg, *Governing the Hearth*, p. 21.

52. It is at this historical turning point in the understanding of domestic relations—around 1870—that Janet Halley locates the origins of modern family law, as opposed to the older law of domestic relations. See Janet Halley, "What Is Family Law? A Genealogy (Part I)," *Yale Journal of Law and the Humanities* 23. 1 (2011), pp. 1–109. At a time when the contract-at-will was being proposed as the ideal, if not empirical, legal framework for governing the exchange of free wage-labor in the world of commerce, relationships within the family were increasingly defined in opposition to the market. It was not that domestic relations were considered wholly alien to the laws of contract. Marriage continued to be defined as a "civil contract," as it had been in the late eighteenth century commentaries of William Blackstone. But as the will theory of individual contract took precedence over earlier theories of the social or public contract, marriage came to be understood as a special kind of transaction, one that could not be breached at will.

53. Emile Durkheim, *The Division of Labor in Society* (Glencoe, IL: Free Press, 1933), p. 214.

54. Grossberg, *Governing the Hearth*, pp. 83–86; Stephanie Coontz, *The Way We Never Were: American Families and the Nostalgia Trap* (New York: Basic Books, 2000), p. 131; Joanna L. Grossman and Lawrence M. Friedman, *Inside the Castle: Law and the Family in Twentieth Century America* (Princeton, NJ: Princeton University Press, 2011), pp. 9 and 85.

55. See Coontz, *The Way We Never Were*, pp. 130–33 for an illuminating discussion of the mutual dependence between laissez-faire classical liberalism and social conservatism. She notes, astutely, that the "subjugation of families to public authority did not stem from a socialist or collectivist agenda but from an attempt to build individualistic definitions of private responsibility" (p. 133).

56. For an unparalleled intellectual history of the European welfare state, focusing on France in particular, see François Ewald, *Histoire de l'État Providence* (Paris: Grasset, 1996). For a comparative account of social insurance in Bismarck's Germany, other European states, and the United States, see John Fabian Witt, *The Accidental Republic: Crippled Workingmen, Destitute Widows, and the Remaking of American Law* (Cambridge, MA: Harvard University Press, 2004), pp. 71–102.

57. F. Spencer Baldwin, "Old Age Pension Schemes: A Criticism and a Program," *The Quarterly Journal of Economics* 24. 4 (1910), pp. 727–28. Spencer Baldwin was president of the Massachusetts Commission for old age pensions.

58. *Ibid.*

59. Alice Kessler-Harris, *In Pursuit of Equity: Women, Men, and the Quest for Economic Citizenship in Twentieth-Century America* (Oxford: Oxford University Press, 2001), pp. 64–116.

60. Isaac Max Rubinow, *Social Insurance: With Special Reference to American Conditions* (New York: Holt, 1913), pp. 314–16; Abbott, "Poor Law Provision for Family Responsibility," p. 610.

61. Alvin Louis Schorr, *Filial Responsibility in the Modern American Family. U.S. 96. Department of Health, Education and Welfare, Division of Program Research* (Washington, DC: US Government Printing Office, 1960), p. 23;

R. Shep Melnick, *Between the Lines: Interpreting Welfare Rights* (Washington, DC: Brookings Institution Press, 1994), pp. 67–68. Having fought unsuccessfully to persuade Congress to overhaul state welfare programs through legislative action, federal administrators ended up relying on sympathetic professionals in state welfare agencies to restrict the use of the old poor-law provisions.

62. Schorr, p. 23; Melnick, *Between the Lines*, pp. 69–70.

63. Daniel R. Mandelker, "Family Responsibility under the American Poor Laws II," *Michigan Law Review* 54. 5 (1956), p. 626.

64. Abbott, "Poor Law Provision for Family Responsibility," p. 617; Schorr, *Filial Responsibility in the Modern American Family*, pp. 25–26.

65. Jacobus tenBroek, "California's Dual System of Family Law: Its Origin, Development, and Present Status: Part III," *Stanford Law Review* 17. 4 (1965), pp. 634–36.

66. *Ibid.*, pp. 638–39. Governor Reagan was enraged by this decision. In a speech on California's welfare system delivered on March 21, 1968, he complained that "the legislature has virtually repealed responsibility of sons and daughters to contribute to the support of their parents.... In this anomalous situation, we still permit these relatives who have been absolved of filial responsibility to inherit the estates of the recipients." Quoted in Amos Kiewe and Davis W. Houck, *A Shining City on a Hill: Ronald Reagan's Economic Rhetoric, 1951–1989* (New York: Praeger, 1991), p. 47.

67. Quoted in Terrance A. Kline, "A Rational Role for Filial Responsibility Laws in Modern Society?" *Family Law Quarterly* 26. 3 (1992), p. 199.

68. Melnick, *Between the Lines*, p. 96.

69. *Ibid.*, pp. 73–76; Martha F. Davis, *Brutal Need: Lawyers and the Welfare Rights Movement, 1960–1973* (New Haven, CT: Yale University Press, 1993); Mark Neal Aaronson, "Representing the Poor: Legal Advocacy and Welfare Reform during Reagan's Gubernatorial Years," *Hastings Law Journal* 64 (2013), p. 992.

70. Jana B. Singer, "The Privatization of Family Law," *Wisconsin Law Review* 5 (1992), pp. 1443–1568.

71. Jacobus tenBroek, "California's Dual System of Family Law: Its Origin, Development, and Present Status: Part I," *Stanford Law Review* 16. 2 (1964), pp. 257–84.

72. These arguments are lucidly outlined by Yale law professor Charles A. Reich in "Individual Rights and Social Welfare: The Emerging Legal Issues," *Yale Law Journal* 74. 7 (1965), pp. 1245–57, and "Social Welfare in the Public-Private State," *University of Pennsylvania Law Review* 114. 4 (1966), pp. 487–93.

73. Melnick, *Between the Lines*, pp. 96 and 79.

74. *Ibid.*, p. 81.

75. *Ibid.*, p. 84.

76. *Ibid.*, p. 103.

77. *Ibid.*, p. 96. For a list of the relevant decisions, see Judith B. Stouder, "Child Support Enforcement and Establishment of Paternity as Tools of Welfare Reform," *Washington Law Review* 52 (1976), pp. 180–81.

78. Governor of California, *California's Blueprint for National Welfare Reform*, p. vii.

79. Aaronson, "Representing the Poor," p. 1002.

80. As white married women reentered the paid workforce in the 1960s, refusing the unpaid reproductive labor of the Fordist household, African American women were abandoning paid domestic labor in droves to pursue higher paying service or clerical work outside the home. See Enobong Hannah Branch, *Opportunity Denied: Limiting Black Women to Devalued Work* (New Brunswick, NJ: Rutgers University Press, 2011), pp. 127–53.

81. Coontz, *The Way We Never Were*, p. 59.

82. Bauer, *The Family: Preserving America's Future*, p. 19.

83. Alice O'Connor, *Social Science for What? Philanthropy and the Social Question in a World Turned Rightside Up* (New York: Russell Sage Foundation, 2007), pp. 107–108.

84. Aaronson, "Representing the Poor," pp. 1011–12.

85. O'Connor, *Social Science for What*, p. 107. Mark Neal Aaronson makes

a similar argument, observing that Reagan's state welfare reform "represented a return to and reinvigoration of longstanding seventeenth-century English principles of public relief." Aaronson, "Representing the Poor," p. 1028.

86. Ronald A. Zumbrun, Raymond M. Momboisse, and John H. Findley, "Welfare Reform: California Meets the Challenge," *Pacific Law Journal* 4 (1973), p. 769.

87. *Ibid.*

88. Governor of California, *California's Blueprint for National Welfare Reform*, p. 55.

89. Jyl J. Josephson, *Gender, Families and State: Child Support Policy in the United States* (Lanham, MD: Rowman & Littlefield, 1997), pp. 34–37. The 1974 amendment was "directed at the goal of achieving or maintaining economic self-support to prevent, reduce, or eliminate dependency' (P.L. 93-647, Part A, Sec. 2001)" (quoted in Josephson, p. 35).

90. For a full account of these various laws, see Brenda Cossman, "Contesting Conservatisms," pp. 447–48.

91. Personal Responsibility and Work Opportunity Reconciliation Act of 1996, H.R. 3734 104th Cong. (1995–1996).

92. Jamie Peck, *Workfare States* (New York: Guilford Press, 2001).

93. Jane L. Collins and Victoria Mayer, *Both Hands Tied: Welfare Reform and the Race to the Bottom in the Low-Wage Labor Market* (Chicago: University of Chicago Press, 2010), p. 6.

94. On the narrowing of the pay gap between black and white women, which endured up until the early 1990s, see Branch, *Opportunity Denied*.

95. Evelyn Nakano Glenn, "From Servitude to Service Work: Historical Continuities in the Racial Division of Reproductive Labor," *Signs: Journal of Women in Culture and Society* 18. 1 (1992), p. 22.

96. For readings of Clinton's welfare reform that point to the historical provenance of "workfare" in the American poor-law tradition, see Gertrude Schaffner Goldberg and Sheila D. Collins, *Washington's New Poor Law: Welfare "Reform" and the Roads not Taken, 1935 to the Present* (New York: Council on International and Public Affairs, 2001), and Desmond King, *In the Name*

of Liberalism: Illiberal Social Policy in the USA and Britain (Oxford: Oxford University Press, 1999), pp. 259–86.

97. See Onwuachi-Willig, "The Return of the Ring," for a full account of these parallels.

98. Laura W. Morgan, "Family Law at 2000: Private and Public Support of the Family: From Welfare State to Poor Law," *Family Law Quarterly* 33. 3 (1999), pp. 710–12.

99. Gwendolyn Mink, *Welfare's End* (Ithaca, NY: Cornell University Press, 1998), p. 73; Anna Marie Smith, *Welfare Reform and Sexual Regulation* (New York: Cambridge University Press, 2007), p. 118.

100. Mink, *Welfare's End*, p. 74; Smith, *Welfare Reform and Sexual Regulation*, p. 129.

101. Harry D. Krause, "Child Support Reassessed: Limits of Private Responsibility and the Public Interest," *Family Law Quarterly* 24. 1 (1990), p. 4.

102. Mink, *Welfare's End*, pp. 74, 87–88, 91.

103. Indeed, it is well documented that the close forms of family dependence created by PRWORA have made it very difficult for women on welfare to escape situations of domestic abuse. See Dána-Ain Davis, *Battered Black Women and Welfare Reform: Between a Rock and a Hard Place* (Albany: SUNY Press, 2006).

104. The novelty of the situation is highlighted by the family law scholar Patrick Parkinson, who notes that "economic fatherhood [now] created artificial families where none had existed before. These families were not born out of mutual intention and consent, other than the consent to sexual intercourse, but were formed at the behest of the state to ensure that children had adequate means of support" (p. 215). Parkinson notes that the increasing involvement of the state in legislating and enforcing nonconsensual legal relations of parenthood has served to counteract the growing liberalization of divorce law. For a brief moment in the 1970s, no-fault divorce signaled the end of a marital relationship and often the end of legal parentage (typically between the father and his children). In response, the federal government moved to strengthen parental ties as a means of maintaining the legal obligations of family support.

What to many social conservative critics appears as an unrelenting liberalization of family law, then, is simply a transfer of state coercion from the marital to the parental relationship. Again in Parkinson's words, the "state is no less involved in seeking to preserve family relationships through law than a century ago, but the focus of its involvement has shifted. Whereas once the state played a role in maintaining the indissolubility of marriage by forbidding or severely restricting divorce, now it has largely abandoned that role. Instead, the state's emerging role in the regulation of family life is to maintain the indissolubility of biological parenthood, with limited recognition being given to other quasi-parental relationships" (p. 14). Patrick Parkinson, *Family Law and the Indissolubility of Parenthood* (Cambridge: Cambridge University Press, 2011).

105. On the high administrative costs of child support enforcement, see Robert I. Lerman and Elaine Sorensen, "Child Support: Interaction between Private and Public Transfers" in Robert A. Moffitt (ed.), *Means-Tested Transfer Programs in the United States* (Chicago: University of Chicago Press, 2007), pp. 609–11.

106. According to Gwendolyn Mink, the average annual amount collected for each welfare applicant was $1,889 in 1989. Mink, *Welfare's End*, p. 85.

107. Morgan, "Family Law at 2000," p. 706. Laura Morgan presents the most extensive case in favor of the idea that PRWORA is inspired by the poor-law tradition of family responsibility.

108. Mark Neal Aaronson, "Scapegoating the Poor: Welfare Reform All Over Again and the Undermining of Democratic Citizenship," *Hastings Women's Law Journal* 7. 2 (1996), p. 225.

109. Gary S. Becker, "The Best Reason to Get People off the Dole (1995)," in Gary S. Becker and Guity Nashat Becker, *The Economics of Life: From Baseball to Affirmative Action to Immigration, How Real-World Issues Affect Our Everyday Life* (New York: McGraw-Hill, 1996), pp. 95–96.

110. Gary S. Becker, "Altruism in the Family," in *A Treatise on the Family, Enlarged Edition* (Cambridge, MA: Harvard University Press, 1993 [1981]), pp. 277–306.

111. Cossman, "Contesting Conservatisms," p. 442. See also Anna Marie

Smith, who notes that PRWORA "expresses a remarkable hybrid discourse: it appropriates both the religious right's moralistic emphasis on patriarchal and heterosexist 'family values' and the neoconservative [neoliberal] emphasis on downsizing government and exposing the impoverished individual to the corrective rigors of the market." Anna Marie Smith, "The Politicization of Marriage in Contemporary American Public Policy: The Defense of Marriage Act and the Personal Responsibility Act," *Citizenship Studies* 5. 3 (2001), p. 315. I will argue that the success of Clinton's social conservative/neoliberal alliance hinged on his ability to widen the appeal of social conservative discourse beyond the religious and Republican right to include New Democrats.

112. Personal Responsibility and Work Opportunity Reconciliation Act of 1996, H.R. 3734 104th Cong. (1995–1996), preamble.

113. Title IX, Section 905 (a)(1–2).

114. Dorit Geva, "Not Just Maternalism: Marriage and Fatherhood in American Welfare Policy," *Social Politics: International Studies in Gender, State and Society* 18. 1 (2011), p. 25.

115. The idea that family law has experienced a process of ongoing liberalization since the 1960s is well established in the family law literature. See in particular Singer, "The Privatization of Family Law." Others speak of a "dejuridification" or "deregulation" of family law. See Mary Ann Glendon, *The Transformation of Family Law: State, Law, and Family in the United States and Western Europe* (Chicago: University of Chicago Press, 1989), p. 293, and Milton C. Regan, *Family Law and the Pursuit of Intimacy* (New York: New York University Press, 1993). Reflecting on this literature, Nancy Cott notes that both the Defense of Marriage Act and PRWORA can be read as a "reestablishment" or "rejuridification" of family law. See Nancy F. Cott, *Public Vows: A History of Marriage and the Nation* (Cambridge, MA: Harvard University Press, 2000), pp. 200–27.

116. Tonya L. Brito, "The Welfarization of Family Law," *University of Kansas Law Review* 48. 2 (2000), pp. 229–83.

117. A number of scholars have examined the pervasive recourse to notions of legitimacy in same-sex marriage jurisprudence. As Nancy D. Polikoff (2012)

explains, recent legal decisions around lesbian parenthood have awarded parental rights on the basis of a preexisting legal relationship (civil union or marriage) between the two mothers, citing this relationship as a proof of "legitimate" connection to the child. No similar jurisprudence has extended parental rights to lesbian mothers who are unmarried or not in a civil union, despite the fact that the notion of legitimacy has long been considered void in similar cases relating to heterosexual parents. See Nancy D. Polikoff, "The New Illegitimacy: Winning Backward in the Protection of the Children of Lesbian Couples," *Journal of Gender, Social Policy and the Law* 20. 3 (2012), pp. 721–40. Marriage equality proponents have subsequently extended the argument from legitimacy to same-sex marriage jurisprudence in its entirety, identifying the illegitimacy of children born to gay couples as one of the most pernicious of wrongs associated with the federal prohibition of gay marriage. Melissa Murray, "What's so New about the New Illegitimacy?" *Journal of Gender, Social Policy and the Law* 20. 3 (2012), pp. 387–436. In so doing, they have resuscitated the legal pertinence of legitimate childbearing some three decades after the notion of illegitimacy was officially discredited by family law jurisprudence. They have done so at precisely the historical moment when federal and state welfare laws have sought to revive the punitive consequences of illegitimate childbearing for poor single mothers.

118. On Reagan's Family Support Act of 1988, see Brenda Cossman, "Contesting Conservatisms," pp. 466–68.

119. R. Kent Weaver, *Ending Welfare as We Know It* (Washington, DC: Brookings Institution Press, 2000), p. 206. For a thorough discussion of the Democratic Leadership Council and its influence on Clinton's welfare policy, see Brendon O'Connor, *A Political History of the American Welfare System: When Ideas Have Consequences* (Lanham, MD: Rowman & Littlefield, 2004), pp. 185–203. To confuse terminology somewhat, New Democrats often refer to themselves as "neoliberals," by which they mean new liberal progressives. For obvious reasons, I will not be following this terminology here.

120. Weaver, *Ending Welfare as We Know It*, p. 117; Steven M. Teles, *Whose Welfare? AFDC and Elite Politics* (Lawrence: University Press of Kansas, 1998),

p. 148. Known as a "big government" conservative, Lawrence Mead was briefly courted by the Republicans in the late 1980s before being abandoned in favor of libertarian anti-welfare theorists such as Charles Murray and Marvin Olasky.

121. Judith Stacey, *In the Name of the Family: Rethinking Family Values in the Postmodern Age* (Boston: Beacon Press, 1996), pp. 53–56. The Institute for American Values was founded in 1987 shortly after the creation of the Democratic Leadership Council. Most of its members identify themselves as New Democrats. For an account of the communitarian influence on the Democratic Leadership Council and Clinton in particular, see Amitai Etzioni, *My Brother's Keeper: A Memoir and a Message* (Lanham, MD: Rowman & Littlefield, 2003), pp. 259–68.

122. Melanie Heath, *One Marriage Under God: The Campaign to Promote Marriage in America* (New York: New York University Press, 2012), pp. 1–2.

123. Anna Gavanas, *Fatherhood Politics in the United States: Masculinity, Sexuality, Race and Marriage* (Urbana: University of Illinois Press, 2004), pp. 23–24, 26, 41.

124. Stacey, *In the Name of the Family*, pp. 52–82. Gavanas, *Fatherhood Politics in the United States*, p. 41. Following Dan Quayle's speech, the social historian Barbara Dafoe Whitehead (at the time, vice president of the Institute for American Values) published an article in the liberal-progressive *Atlantic Monthly* corroborating Quayle's fears and using social science statistics to argue that the white family was indeed in crisis. See Barbara Dafoe Whitehead, "Dan Quayle Was Right," *Atlantic Monthly* (April 1993). Charles Murray followed up with an article asserting that white family disintegration had replaced black family crisis as the defining problem of the times. See Charles Murray, "The Coming White Underclass," *Wall Street Journal* (October 29, 1993).

125. My account of the difference between the National Fatherhood Initiative and the fragile families project is indebted to Gavanas, *Fatherhood Politics in the United States*, pp. 24 and 30–31.

126. Indeed, they can be seen as part of a wider community of scholars who are positioned on the center-left but are broadly sympathetic to Moynihan's findings. See, for example, the articles collected in "The Moynihan Report

Revisited: Lessons and Reflections after Four Decades," *The Annals of the American Academy of Political and Social Science* 621. 1 (2009).

127. For an overview of this literature, see Obie Clayton, Ronald B. Mincy, and David Blankenhorn (eds.), *Black Fathers in Contemporary Society: Strengths, Weaknesses and Strategies for Change* (New York: Russell Sage Foundation, 2003).

128. See the essays collected in Timothy M. Smeeding, Irwin Garfinkel, and Ronald B. Mincy (eds.), "Young Disadvantaged Men: Fathers, Families, Poverty, and Policy," *The Annals of the American Academy of Political and Social Science* 635. 1 (2011).

129. Jean Hardisty, *Pushed to the Altar: The Right Wing Roots of Marriage Promotion* (Somerville, MA: Political Research Associates/Women of Color Resource Center, 2008), pp. 5 and 8; Shirley Anne Warshaw, *The Co-Presidency of Bush and Cheney* (Stanford, CA: Stanford University Press, 2009), p. 95; Jessica Dixon Weaver, "The First Father: Perspectives on the President's Fatherhood Initiative," *Family Court Review* 50. 2 (2012), p. 299; Sarah Olson, "Marriage Promotion, Reproductive Injustice, and the War against Poor Women of Color," *Dollars and Sense* January/February (2005), available online at http://www.dollarsandsense.org/archives/2005/0105olson.html (last accessed October 1, 2015).

130. Weaver, "The First Father," p. 299; Monica Potts, "Daddy Issues: Is Promoting Responsible Fatherhood Really the Best Way to Lift Families out of Poverty?" *The American Prospect* (April 2010), p. 23.

131. Barack Obama, *The Audacity of Hope: Thoughts on Reclaiming the American Dream* (New York: Crown Publishers, 2006), p. 254. Obama writes that "in private—around kitchen tables, in barbershops, and after church—black folks can often be heard bemoaning the eroding work ethic, inadequate parenting, and declining social mores with a fervor that would make the Heritage Foundation proud."

132. *Ibid.*, p. 255.

133. *Ibid.*, pp. 214–15.

134. Glendon, *The Transformation of Family Law*; Milton C. Regan, "Postmodern Family Law: Toward a New Model of Status," in David Popenoe, Jean

Bethke Elshtain, and David Blankenhorn (eds.), *Promises to Keep: Decline and Renewal of Marriage in America* (Lanham, MD: Rowman & Littlefield, 1996), pp. 157–86; Carl E. Schneider, "The Law and the Stability of Marriage: The Family as a Social Institution," in *ibid.*, pp. 187–244; Margaret F. Brinig, *From Contract to Covenant: Beyond the Law and Economics of the Family* (Cambridge, MA: Harvard University Press, 2000).

135. See, for example, the communitarian critique of Becker and Posner in Don S. Browning, "Egos without Selves: A Critique of the Family Theory of the Chicago School of Economics," in *Equality and the Family: A Fundamental, Practical Theology of Children, Mothers, and Fathers in Modern Societies* (Grand Rapids, MI: William B. Eerdmans, 2007), pp. 263–82. Communitarian perspectives on law and economics are inspired by Amitai Etzioni's classic critique *The Moral Dimension: Toward a New Economics* (New York: Simon & Schuster, 1998).

136. Richard A. Posner, *Sex and Reason* (Cambridge, MA: Harvard University Press, 1992), pp. 181–89, and Gary S. Becker, "Finding Fault with No-Fault Divorce (1992)," in Becker and Becker, *The Economics of Life*, pp. 98–100.

137. This assumption is widespread in the critical literature on neoliberalism. See, for instance, Anne Alstott, "Neoliberalism in U.S. Family Law: Negative Liberty and Laissez-Faire Markets in the Minimal State," *Law and Contemporary Problems* 77. 4 (2014), pp. 25–42. For a detailed rebuttal of this position with respect to Richard Posner, see Jean L. Cohen, *Regulating Intimacy: A New Legal Paradigm* (Princeton, NJ: Princeton University Press, 2004), pp. 77–124.

138. In Posner's words, the "Supreme Court's decision on sexual privacy are not only poorly reasoned but poorly informed." *Sex and Reason*, p. 7. For a comparable critique of the jurisprudence of sexual privacy from the communitarian point of view, see Mary Ann Glendon, *Rights Talk: The Impoverishment of Political Discourse* (New York: Macmillan, 1991).

139. See Brinig, *From Contract to Covenant*, for her effort to reconcile these perspectives.

140. Richard Epstein, *Principles for a Free Society* (New York: Basic Books,

1998), p. 23. Thus a landmark decision by the Illinois Supreme Court, *People v. James W. Hill* (1896), defended the state's poor-law provisions by proclaiming that the purpose of such laws was "to protect the public from loss occasioned by the neglect of a moral or natural duty imposed on individuals, and to do this by transforming the imperfect moral duty into a statutory and legal liability" (*People v. James W. Hill*, 163 Ill. 186 [1896]).

CHAPTER FOUR: THE RETURN OF INHERITED WEALTH

1. Mary Ann Glendon, "The New Family and the New Property," *Tulane Law Review* 53. 3 (1979), p. 705.

2. Charles A. Reich, "The New Property," *The Yale Law Journal* 73. 5 (1964), pp. 733–87.

3. Robert Lynn, "Estate Planning: Goodbye to Wills, Trusts and Future Interests," *Ohio State Law General* 39. 4 (1978), pp. 717–35. Lynn writes for a more specialist audience, but he makes the same connection between the law of private wealth transmission and family as Glendon. He notes that the "conventional law on the devolution of private wealth—the law of property, trusts, wills, future interests, and administration of estates—presupposes acquisition of property (through work, gifts, inheritance, theft or chance) and its accumulation, conservation, taxation, and transmission from generation to generation, almost exclusively within the family" (p. 717). He goes on to note that the combined effects of inflation and social welfare have undermined the importance of these traditional forms of family wealth transmission, such that "significant segments of the population who previously used the law of wills, trusts, and future interests, are unlikely to use it appreciably hereafter" (p. 730). Like Glendon, he concludes that the "transmission of wealth by the middle class has been deeply affected by the changing nature of the family, by the desire to avoid probate, and by the sharing of the burdens of dependency and disability … [made possible] by disagreeable taxation and controversial income transfers" (p. 734).

4. Martin Feldstein, "Social Security and the Distribution of Wealth," *Journal of the American Statistical Association* 71. 356 (1976), pp. 800–807. It is

interesting, to say the least, that Martin Feldstein should have produced this article, given his later role in pushing for the privatization of Social Security.

5. She would later refer to this process as the "dejuridification" of the relationship between the family and the state. Mary Ann Glendon, *The Transformation of Family Law: State, Law, and Family in the United States and Western Europe* (Chicago: University of Chicago Press, 1989), p. 293.

6. Abraham Epstein, *Insecurity: A Challenge to America—A Study of Social Insurance in the United States and Abroad* (New York: H. Smith and R. Haas, 1933), p. 101.

7. Jill Quadagno, *The Color of Welfare: How Racism Undermined the War on Poverty* (Oxford: Oxford University Press, 1994), p. 158.

8. *Ibid.*, p. 159.

9. Much like the federal government's private home ownership programs, analyzed below, public housing policy privileged married couples with children and placed single people at the bottom of waiting lists. *Public Health and Welfare Act* § 1437b [3]. In 1977, the HUD decided to open public housing lists to unmarried couples living together and to homosexual couples, providing the latter could demonstrate a "stable family relationship." This revision of federal housing policy seems to have been introduced at the personal initiative of a HUD housing program administrator, Priscilla Banks. See "H.U.D. Will Accept Unmarried Couples for Public Housing," *New York Times* (May 29, 1977), p. 22. The revision was extremely short-lived, however, and was reversed by Congress barely three weeks later.

10. Thomas Piketty, *Capital in the Twenty-First Century* (Cambridge, MA: Harvard Belknap, 2014).

11. *Ibid.*, p. 22. Piketty proposes a "U-shaped curve" that sees income and wealth inequality decline in the postwar era up until the late 1970s, when it rises precipitously. He observes that "inequality was not eradicated in the three decades after World War II, but it was viewed primarily from the optimistic angle of wage inequalities"; in other words, the importance of wealth inequality and hence inheritance was attenuated by rising incomes (p. 409). He goes on to note that those born in the 1970s and after have had a markedly different expe-

rience of rising wealth and income inequality and "have already experienced…
the important role that inheritance will once again play in their lives" (p. 381).

12. June Carbone and Naomi Kahn, *Marriage Markets: How Inequality Is Remaking the American Family* (Oxford: Oxford University Press, 2014).

13. Piketty's eye for the empirical trajectories of economic inequality is impressive. His ability to analyze what drives these trajectories is much blunter. When called upon to explain *why* the rate of return on capital has so precipitously outrun that of labor, Piketty relies on bioeconomic laws that equate economic and demographic growth and attribute rising inequality to a slowing of these growth rates. Aging populations signify low growth; high birth rates mean high economic growth and a reduction in inequality. As Williams and Engelen point out, Piketty is much closer to the classical political economy of Malthus, with his bioeconomic laws of population growth, than to Marx, whose theory of surplus population utterly refutes the demographic reading of capital. See Karel Williams and Ewald Engelen, "Just the Facts: On the Success of Piketty's *Capital*," *Environment and Planning A* 46. 8 (2014), pp. 1771–77. Having accepted the existence of economic laws, Piketty can account for change only by resorting to an essentially accidental and anecdotal concept of history. Thus, he attributes the redistributive trends of the postwar era to the "accident" of war and its demographic effects, wholly neglecting the impact of political process (the New Deal) or political struggle (the trade union movement) on productivity and wages. Where he recognizes historical variation in labor's share of national income, he attributes these to external contingencies such as war or recession that appear as so many natural catastrophes or "shocks" interrupting the implacable progress of economic laws. The labor movement, feminism, the minority and anticolonial struggles that so profoundly destabilized the Fordist model of growth in the 1970s, all fade into the most distant background. To be fair, Piketty does recognize the role of regressive tax reform in exacerbating the rising inequality of the last four decades. He therefore accords a central role to progressive tax reform, over and above population growth, in any effort to reverse these trends. See, on this point, the journalistic writings collected in Thomas Piketty, *Why Save the*

Bankers? And Other Essays on Our Economic and Political Crisis, trans. Seth Ackerman (Boston: Houghton Mifflin Harcourt, 2015). However, a history of taxation alone cannot account for the steady appreciation of financial assets in the period after 1980. We need also to understand the role of central bank policy in generating rising asset prices and returns to capital during this period.

14. Gerald F. Davis, *Managed by the Markets: How Finance Re-shaped America* (Oxford: Oxford University Press, 2009), p. 193.

15. Michel Feher, "Self-appreciation; or, The Aspirations of Human Capital," *Public Culture* 21. 1 (2009), p. 27.

16. With respect to the correlation between ownership of financial assets and family wealth transfers, Elmelech notes: "family transfers in the form of gifts and inheritance are strongly and positively associated with investment in financial assets...receipt of inheritance and gifts enhances financial assets." See Yuval Elmelech, *Transmitting Inequality: Wealth and the American Family* (New York: Rowman & Littlefield, 2008), p. 61. Elmelech goes on to argue that the appreciation of financial assets over wages means that economists need to integrate an understanding of the family into their analysis of class: "both marriage and intergenerational transfers need to be studied as an integral part of class formation. In contrast to production-based classes, the unit of analysis in wealth-based typology includes households and individuals as members of households" (p. 63). Of course, Elmelech's perspective does not imply that the wages and professional status of parents do not have any impact on the reproduction of class, simply that assets are directly inheritable in a way that wages and education are not.

17. Jan Toporowski, *Why the World Economy Needs a Financial Crash and Other Critical Essays on Finance and Financial Economics* (London: Anthem Press, 2010), pp. 89–96. Angela Mitropoulos goes so far as to argue that the inheritability of assets is implicit in the original theory of human capital. See Angela Mitropoulos, *Contract and Contagion: From Biopolitics to Oikonomia* (New York: Minor Compositions, 2012), p. 200.

18. This chapter distinguishes between "wealth" and "income" according

to commonly accepted usage in the economic literature. Edward N. Wolff, for example, explains that "wealth refers to the net value of assets (e.g. ownership of stock, bonds, real estate, etc) less debt held at the same time, whereas income refers to a flow of dollars (e.g. wages and salaries, interest received etc) over a set period." Edward N. Wolff, "The Rich Get Increasingly Richer," Economic Policy Institute Briefing Paper (Washington, DC: Economic Policy Institute, 1993), p. 2. The use of the term "income" is complicated by the fact that it can refer to flows of money from both wages *and* financial assets (for example, dividends, interest and rents). The distributional and class features of these income flows are very different: I therefore distinguish carefully between the two in the text. Financial assets can also generate price appreciation or "capital gains," which are not strictly classified as a form of income. Yuval Elmelech draws a useful distinction between "functional" and "financial" assets. A "functional" asset is one that generates no significant income and does not appreciate in value. A "financial" asset is one that generates income in the form of rent or capital gains in the form of price appreciation. The one form of property—for example, a house—can sometimes be classified as a functional asset, sometimes a financial one. See Elmelech, *Transmitting Inequality*, p. 60. Thomas Piketty conflates the two kinds of "asset" under his general definition of wealth. See Piketty, *Capital in the Twenty-First Century*, p. 48. In this chapter I distinguish between the two kinds of assets; unless otherwise specified, I use the general term "assets" to refer to "financial assets."

19. Joseph J. Minarik, "The Distributional Effects of Inflation and Their Implications," in *Stagflation: The Causes, Effects and Solutions* (Washington, DC: Joint Economic Committee, U.S. Congress, 1980), pp. 225–77.

20. *Ibid.*, p. 228.

21. *Ibid.*, p. 226.

22. *Ibid.*, p. 228.

23. William Greider, *Secrets of the Temple: How the Federal Reserve Runs the Country* (New York: Simon & Schuster, 1989), p. 40.

24. George Gilder, *Wealth and Poverty* (New York: Basic Books, 1981), pp. 19, 101.

25. Wolff, "The Rich Get Increasingly Richer," p. 9.

26. Edward N. Wolff, "The Distributional Effects of the 1969–75 Inflation on the Holdings of Household Wealth in the United States," *Review of Income and Wealth* 25. 2 (1979), p. 207.

27. Kenneth L. Hirsch, "Inflation and the Law of Trusts," *Real Property, Probate and Trust Journal* 18. 4 (1983), p. 601.

28. Lynn, "Estate Planning," p. 729.

29. Gilder, *Wealth and Poverty*, p. 100.

30. For a detailed discussion of George McGovern and the neoliberal campaign against the estate tax, see Jens Beckert, *Inherited Wealth* (Princeton, NJ: Princeton University Press, 2008), pp. 193–200.

31. Gordon Tullock, "Inheritance Justified," *Journal of Law and Economics* 14. 2 (1971), pp. 465–74; Richard E. Wagner, *Inheritance and the State* (Washington, DC: American Enterprise Institute, 1977).

32. Milton Friedman and Rose Friedman, *Free to Choose: A Personal Statement* (New York: Harcourt Brace Jovanovich, 1980), p. 136.

33. Milton Friedman, *Milton Friedman Speaks: Lecture 1— What is America?* (New York: Harcourt Brace Jovanovich, 1978). Video. 1:07:14–1:09:09. Available online at http://www.freetochoose.tv/program.php?id=mfs_1&series=mfs (last accessed December 1, 2015).

34. Henry C. Simons, *Economic Policy for a Free Society* (Chicago: University of Chicago Press, 1948), pp. 165–248.

35. Kevin Phillips, *The Politics of Rich and Poor* (New York: HarperCollins, 1990), p. 67. The contortions of Gilder's argument in *Wealth and Poverty* are fascinating. While purporting to celebrate the creativity of entrepreneurial risk-taking, Gilder nevertheless insists that the "the most catalytic wealth in America is unearned income" and rails against the injustice of inheritance taxes (p. 60).

36. For an illuminating history of these multiple origins, see William Martin, *The Permanent Tax Revolt: How the Property Tax Transformed American Politics* (Stanford, CA: Stanford University Press, 2008). The "tax revolt" was originally embraced by activists in the welfare rights movement, who sought to undo the unfair tax benefits privileging the white middle class and business

owners. A sign of the very different sense of political possibility that reigned in the 1970s, the Marxist political economist, James O'Connor was confident that the "tax revolt" would come from the left. See James O'Connor, *The Fiscal Crisis of the State* (New York: St. Martin's Press, 1973).

37. John Ehrenberg and Mike Davis are illuminating on the racial politics of the tax revolts. See John Ehrenberg, *Servants of Wealth: The Right's Assault on Economic Justice* (Lanham, MD: Rowman & Littlefield, 2006), pp. 8–9, and Mike Davis, *City of Quartz: Excavating the Future in Los Angeles* (New York: Verso, 1990), pp. 180–86.

38. Byron L. Dorgan, "The American Estate Tax: A Death Penalty," in Dean C. Tipps and Lee Webb (eds.), *State and Local Tax Revolt: New Directions for the 80's* (Washington, DC: Transaction Publishers, 1980), p. 216.

39. Greta R. Krippner, *Capitalizing on Crisis: The Political Origins of the Rise of Finance* (Cambridge, MA: Harvard University Press, 2011), pp. 114–20, and Martijn Konings, "State of Speculation: Contingency, Measure, and the Politics of Plastic Value," *South Atlantic Quarterly* 114. 2 (2015), pp. 265–67.

40. Public Law 79-304, 79th Congress, S. 380. Section 2.

41. The shift is highlighted by Greta Krippner when she writes that the result of the Volcker shock was "to transfer inflation from the nonfinancial to the financial economy—where it was not visible (or conceptualized) as such." Krippner, *Capitalizing on Crisis*, p. 103. However, Krippner offers little insight into the political struggles that propelled the shift from wage to asset inflation. These struggles are the focus of E. Ray Canterbery's account of central bank policy in *Wall Street Capitalism: The Theory of the Bondholding Class* (River Edge, NJ: World Scientific, 2000). Compelling accounts of asset price inflation as a central objective (and more recently Achilles heel) of neoliberal monetary policy can be found in Thomas Palley, *From Financial Crisis to Stagnation: The Destruction of Shared Prosperity and the Role of Economics* (Cambridge: Cambridge University Press, 2012), pp. 32–56, and Toporowski, *Why the World Economy Needs a Financial Crash*. The question of whether or not central banks should also target asset inflation has only recently become a subject of policy debate. See Charles Goodhart, "What Weight Should Be Given to Asset Prices

in the Measurement of Inflation?" *The Economic Journal* III. 472 (2001), pp. 335–56.

42. Canterbery, *Wall Street Capitalism*, p. 28; William Greider, *Secrets of the Temple: How the Federal Reserve Runs the Country* (New York: Simon & Schuster, 1989), pp. 695–705.

43. Gerald A. Epstein and Arjun Jayadev, "The Rise of Rentier Incomes in OECD Countries: Financialization, Central Bank Policy and Labor Solidarity," in Gerald A. Epstein (ed.), *Financialization and the World Economy* (Cheltenham, UK: Edward Elgar, 2005), p. 54. Epstein and Jayadev define "rentier income" as "profits earned by firms engaged in financial activities plus interest income realized by all nonfinancial non-government resident units, i.e. the rest of the private economy." Their definition does not include capital gains (p. 50).

44. Beckert, *Inherited Wealth*, pp. 201–204. Middle-class opposition to estate taxes in the 1970s can be considered a prelude to the vigorous anti– "death tax" movement that would emerge in the 1990s.

45. Phillips, *The Politics of Rich and Poor*, pp. 76–78.

46. *Ibid.*, p. 80.

47. *Ibid.*, p. 82.

48. Gary Burtless and Christopher Jencks, "American Inequality and its Consequences," in Henry J. Aaron, James M. Lindsay and Pietro S. Nivola (eds.), *Agenda for the Nation* (Washington, DC: Brookings Institution Press, 2003), p. 70.

49. Ian Dew-Becker and Robert J. Gordon, "Where Did the Productivity Growth Go?" *NBER Working Paper* No. 11842 (Washington, DC: National Bureau of Economic Research, 2005).

50. Wolff, "The Rich Get Increasingly Richer," p. 10.

51. *Ibid.*, p. 9.

52. Edward N. Wolff, "Household Wealth Trends in the United States, 1983–2010," *Oxford Review of Economic Policy* 30. 1 (2014), p. 25.

53. All of the major specialists in wealth inequality note that different kinds of assets are distributed unequally among households, with certain asset- classes concentrated in the hands of the rich. Edward N. Wolff reports that in

1989, "the super rich (the top one half of one percent of owners of wealth) held 29 percent of all outstanding stock owned by households, 41 percent of bonds, almost half the value of unincorporated business, and about one-third of non-home real estate. The top 10 percent of households accounted for over 80 percent of stock shares and non-home real estate, and close to 90 percent of bonds, trusts and business equity." Wolff, "The Rich Get Increasingly Richer," p. 24. These patterns of asset distribution have subsequently shifted as a result of policies promoting popular shareholding, home ownership, and other forms of "asset-based welfare" discussed later in the chapter. However, the long-term distribution of wealth does not seem to have been positively affected by these policy interventions. Yuval Elmelech offers an illuminating taxonomy of class distinctions based on different kinds of asset ownership. Elmelech, *Transmitting Inequality*, pp. 62–66.

54. Wolff, "The Rich Get Increasingly Richer," p. 28.

55. The estate law specialist John H. Langbein observes that inter vivos transfers of wealth from living parents to children became increasingly common in the 1980s, reflecting the ongoing need of young adults for the financial support of their parents. John H. Langbein, "The Twentieth-Century Revolution in Family Wealth Transmission," *Michigan Law Review* 86. 4 (1988), pp. 722–51.

56. Brooke Harrington, "From Trustees to Wealth Managers," in Guido Erreygers and John Cunliffe (eds.), *Inherited Wealth: Justice and Equality* (London: Routledge, 2012), pp. 190–209.

57. Piketty, *Capital in the Twenty-First Century*, p. 22.

58. On the importance of household debt in the dynamics of neoliberal financialization, see Dick Bryan, Randy Martin and Michael Rafferty, "Financialization and Marx: Giving Labor and Capital a Financial Makeover," *Review of Radical Political Economics* 41. 04 (2009), pp. 458–72. See Colin Crouch, *The Strange Non-Death of Neoliberalism* (Cambridge: Polity Press, 2011), pp. 97–124, on "privatized Keynesianism."

59. "Constrained in what they could get from their labor for two decades, and dependent on debt for consumption, working class families were drawn into the logic of asset inflation not only through the investments of their

pension funds, but also through the one major asset they held in their own hands (or could reasonably aspire to hold) in their own hands—their family home." Leo Panitch and Sam Gindin, *The Making of Global Capitalism* (New York: Verso, 2012), p. 306.

60. An overview of this tradition, with special focus on Rawls, can be found in Martin O'Neill and Thad Williamson (eds.), *Property-Owning Democracy: Rawls and Beyond* (New York: Wiley, 2012).

61. See Ben Jackson, "Property-Owning Democracy: A Short History," in *ibid.*, pp. 33–52.

62. Peter Drucker, *The Unseen Revolution: How Pension Fund Socialism Came to America* (London: Heinemann, 1976); Bruce Ackerman and Anne Alstott, *The Stakeholder Society* (New Haven, CT: Yale University Press, 1999); Michael Sherraden, *Assets and the Poor: A New American Welfare Policy* (New York: M. E. Sharpe, 1991); Stuart M. Butler (ed.), *Agenda for Empowerment: Readings in American Government and the Policy Process* (Washington, DC: Heritage Foundation, 1990). On Bush's ownership society, see Davis, *Managed by the Markets*, pp. 208–22.

63. In the words of Peter Ferrara and Michael Tanner, two prominent advocates of Social Security privatization based at the libertarian Cato Institute: "An important side benefit of Social Security privatization is that it would allow every American—including poor Americans—an opportunity to participate in the American economy by owning a part of that economy. In effect, privatizing Social Security will act as a nationwide employee stock option plan, allowing even the poorest workers to become capitalists. Through Social Security privatization, workers would become stock holders themselves. The artificial and destructive division between labor and capital would be broken down." Peter J. Ferrara and Michael Tanner, *A New Deal for Social Security* (Washington, DC: Cato Institute, 1998), p. 107.

64. Gokhale and Kotlikoff lament that Social Security has deprived low-income workers of the benefits of family wealth transmission and identify their exclusion from inheritable wealth as the very cause of their disadvantage. Jagadeesh Gokhale and Laurence J. Kotlikoff, "The Impact of Social Security

and Other Factors on the Distribution of Wealth," in Martin Feldstein and
Jeffrey B. Liebman (eds.), *The Distributional Aspects of Social Security and Social
Security Reform* (Chicago: University of Chicago Press, 2002), p. 106. Ferrara
and Tanner explain how the privatization of Social Security would simultaneously rehabilitate the economic function of the family: "a private system would
keep retirement funds within the family and under its control. This would
greatly enhance the power of family members to help one another, drawing
the family closer together as an economic unit.... With Social Security, by
contrast, the money flows out of the family to the government. This helps pull
the family apart as members look to the government for support and assistance
rather than to each other. The family breakup that results is analogous to the
family dissolution that occurs when welfare replaces the family as a source
of support." Ferrara and Tanner, *A New Deal for Social Security*, p. 106. They
conclude that the "privatization of Social Security would be one of the most
pro-family reforms that could be adopted" (p. 107).

65. Peter Saunders, *A Nation of Home Owners* (London: Unwin Hyman,
1990). On "familial accumulation," see p. 163.

66. *Ibid.*

67. The founding text on asset-based welfare is Sherraden's *Assets and
the Poor*. Throughout the 1980s, the asset-based perspective on welfare was
associated almost exclusively with the Republican right. During this period,
neoliberals and libertarians affiliated with right-wing think tanks such as
the Heritage Foundation, the American Enterprise Institute, and the Cato
Institute assiduously promoted the idea that the poor should be "empowered"
to take part in asset accumulation via the privatization of formerly public
services. In the late 1980s, however, new arguments in favor of "asset-based
welfare" emerged from the center left, with Michael Sherraden as its most
prominent spokesperson. The exponents of "asset-based welfare" reiterated
much of the neoliberal right's critique of government income transfers.
However, they were never in favor of dismantling traditional forms of welfare
entirely and always saw asset-based approaches as a supplement not a substitute for income transfers.

68. The Ford Foundation adopted asset-based welfare as a template for its domestic and global poverty program in 1996 and has since become one of the major driving forces behind a new global empowerment paradigm promoting microfinance and asset ownership as the solution to poverty. Together, the Ford Foundation and the Center for Social Development at Washington University in St. Louis, headed by Michael Sherraden, serve as headquarters for the dissemination of asset-based welfare policy in the United States. Their influence has extended across the political spectrum, from Bill Clinton to George W. Bush. In the UK, the Institute for Public Policy Research or IPPR, associated with New Labour, has been an important conduit for social policy experiments in asset-based welfare. On the relationship between asset-based welfare and the Democratic Leadership Council, see Andrew Karch, *Domestic Laboratories: Policy Diffusion among the American States* (Ann Arbor: University of Michigan Press, 2007), p. 85.

69. The White House, *The National Homeownership Strategy: Partners in the American Dream*, Department of Housing and Urban Development (May 2, 1995).

70. Henry G. Cisneros, *Renewing America's Communities from the Ground Up: The Plan to Complete the Transformation of HUD* (Washington, DC: Diane Publishing, 1996), p. 11.

71. William J. Clinton, "Remarks on the National Homeownership Strategy," June 5, 1995. Available online at http://www.presidency.ucsb.edu/ws/?pid=51448 (last accessed October 1, 2015).

72. Michael B. Katz, *The Price of Citizenship: Redefining the American Welfare State* (Philadelphia: University of Pennsylvania Press, 2008), pp. 124–26.

73. On the internal reform of the HUD, see Alyssa Katz, *Our Lot: How Real Estate Came to Own Us* (New York: Bloomsbury, 2009), p. 32.

74. These data are presented and analyzed in Department of Housing and Urban Development, *U.S. Housing Market Conditions* (Washington, DC: US Government Printing Office, 1996).

75. Mechele Dickerson, *Homeownership and America's Financial Underclass: Flawed Promises, Broken Promises, New Prescriptions* (New York: Cambridge

University Press, 2014), pp. 23, 183–84. See also Herman Schwartz, "Finance and the State in the Housing Bubble," in Manuel B. Aalbers (ed.), *Subprime Cities: The Political Economy of Mortgage Markets* (Oxford: Blackwell-Wiley, 2012), pp. 53–73.

76. Bob Woodward, *The Agenda: Inside the Clinton White House* (New York: Simon & Schuster, 1994), pp. 69–70 and pp. 228–29.

77. *Ibid.*, p. 70.

78. Greenspan repeatedly referred to the "wealth effect" of asset appreciation in the stock and housing markets. The "wealth effect" could be seen when the mere expectation of rising asset prices led to an actual increase in consumption and investment in the present. See Alan Greenspan, *Issues for Monetary Policy*, December 19 (Washington, DC: Federal Reserve Board, 2002).

79. Eugene A. Ludwig, "The Democratization of Credit and the Future of Community Development," NR 96-21. Speech before the Community Development Conference, Arlington, Virginia. February 23 (1996).

80. Kenneth T. Jackson, *The Crabgrass Frontier: The Suburbanization of the United States* (Oxford: Oxford University Press, 1985), pp. 195–96; Martha Poon, "From New Deal Institutions to Capital Markets: Commercial Consumer Risk Scores and the Making of Subprime Mortgage Finance," *Accounting, Organizations and Society* 35. 5 (2009), pp. 654–74; Louis Hyman, *Debtor Nation: The History of America in Red Ink* (Princeton, NJ: Princeton University Press, 2011), pp. 49–72.

81. Jackson, *The Crabgrass Frontier*, pp. 215–16.

82. Adam Gordon, "The Creation of Homeownership: How New Deal Changes in Banking Regulation Simultaneously Made Homeownership Accessible to Whites and Out of Reach for Blacks," *Yale Law Journal* 115. 1 (2005), p. 207.

83. Thomas M. Shapiro and Melvin L. Oliver have explored in detail the long-term effects of postwar housing policy on wealth inequality among whites and blacks. See Thomas M. Shapiro and Melvin L. Oliver, *Black Wealth, White Wealth: A New Perspective on Racial Inequality*, 2nd ed. (New York: Routledge,

2006), and Thomas M. Shapiro, *The Hidden Costs of Being African American: How Wealth Perpetuates Inequality* (Oxford: Oxford University Press, 2004).

84. Ira Katznelson, *When Affirmative Action Was White: An Untold History of Racial Inequality in Twentieth-Century America* (New York: Norton, 2005).

85. Christopher Howard, *The Welfare State Nobody Knows: Debunking Myths about U.S. Social Policy* (Princeton, NJ: Princeton University Press, 2007).

86. Clayton Howard, "Building a 'Family-Friendly' Metropolis: Sexuality, the State, and Postwar Housing Policy," *Journal of Urban History* 39. 5 (2013), pp. 933–55.

87. Quoted in Howard, "Building a 'Family-Friendly' Metropolis," p. 938.

88. *Ibid.*

89. *Ibid.*, pp. 936 and 938.

90. *Ibid.*, p. 935.

91. *Ibid.*, p. 934.

92. For a comparative account of the civil rights and feminist campaigns to democratize access to consumer credit, see Hyman, *Debtor Nation*, pp. 173–219. Jaffe and Lautin report that in 1971, members of the Gay Activists Alliance stormed the offices of the Household Finance Corporation on Park Avenue to protest its discrimination against gay customers. See Stephen H. Jaffe and Jessica Lautin, *Capital of Capital: Money, Banking, and Power in New York City, 1784–2012* (New York: Columbia University Press, 2014), p. 228.

93. Hyman, *Debtor Nation*, pp. 215–17.

94. The following section is adapted from my article "The Strategy of Default—Liquid Foundations in the House of Finance," *Polygraph: An International Journal of Culture and Politics* 23/24 (2013), pp. 79–96.

95. Sarah Quinn, "Lemon Socialism and Securitization," *Trajectories: Newsletter of the ASA Comparative and Historical Sociology Section* 20. 2 (2009), pp. 3–6. Although Fannie Mae had provided a secondary market for mortgages since its creation in the 1930s, the modern market for mortgage-backed securities was created much later with the passage of the Housing and Urban Development (HUD) Act of 1968. The Act was passed with the intention of responding to a short-term credit crunch in the housing market. But because

the federal government was already in deficit because of the Vietnam War, it was considered expedient to remove Fannie Mae from the balance sheets while retaining it as a "government sponsored entity" whose claims were implicitly backed by the full faith and credit of the US government. The HUD Act simultaneously created the GSE Freddie Mac to act as a private competitor for Fannie Mae and authorized both to create and sell bonds (securities) out of the mortgages they underwrote.

96. Poon, "From New Deal Institutions to Capital Markets," p. 656.

97. *Ibid.*, pp. 656–57.

98. Herman Schwartz, *Subprime Nation: American Power, Global Capital, and the Housing Bubble* (Princeton, NJ: Princeton University Press, 2009), p. 185.

99. Gary Dymski, "Racial Exclusion and the Political Economy of the Subprime Crisis," *Historical Materialism* 17. 2 (2009), pp. 160–61.

100. Gary Dymski, Jesus Hernandez, and Lisa Mohanty, "Race, Gender, Power, and the US Subprime Mortgage and Foreclosure Crisis: A Meso Analysis," *Feminist Economics* 19. 3 (2013), pp. 124–51.

101. Jens Beckert, "Are We Still Modern? Inheritance Law and the Broken Promise of the Enlightenment," in Guido Erreygers and John Cunliffe (eds.), *Inherited Wealth, Justice and Equality* (London: Routledge, 2013), pp. 70–80.

102. Launched in 2005, but retroactive to 2002, the Child Trust Fund endowed every newborn child with a sum of £250 (£500 for lower-income households), which parents were then free to invest in a number of government-endorsed private sector funds. The trust fund could be topped up by parents to a maximum of £1,200 every year and received two successive government contributions before being made available to the child at the age of eighteen. It appears that Michael Sherraden directly inspired the idea of the Child Trust Fund, after the Institute for Public Policy Research (IPPR) invited him to present before Tony Blair and the British Labour Party in 2001. See Michael Sherraden, "Assets and Public Policy," in Michael Sherraden (ed.), *Inclusion in the American Dream: Assets, Poverty, and Public Policy* (Oxford: Oxford University Press, 2005), p. 16 n. 10.

103. Tony Blair, "The Saving Grace of the Baby Bond: The Child Trust Fund

Will Turn Hope into Realistic Ambition," *The Guardian* (April 10, 2003). Blair's promise that the British would soon become a democracy of inheritors was not in itself new but had been promoted by Conservative advocates of private home ownership in the 1980s and 1990s. Chris Hamnett quotes from Nigel Lawson, Chancellor of the Exchequer, who in 1988, stated that "Britain is about to become a Nation of Inheritors. Inheritance, which used to be the preserve of the few, will become a fact of life for the many. People will be inheriting houses and possibly also stocks and shares." Chris Hamnett, *Winners and Losers: Home Ownership in Modern Britain* (London: UCL Press, 1999), p. 125.

104. Bruce Ackerman and Anne Alstott, "Inherit the Windfall: Funding Baby Bonds with Tax on Private Inheritance Is Both Fair and Just," *The Guardian* (October 11, 2007). The article is critical of Labor's failure to combine the Child Trust Fund with a progressive estate tax.

105. Alan Finlayson, " 'What Will Yours Grow Into': Governmentality, Governance, Social Science and the Child Trust Fund," *Policy and Politics* 39. 4 (2011), pp. 547–48.

106. Support for progressive taxation on inherited wealth appears to be the one unambiguous point of differentiation between Third Way advocates of asset-based welfare and right-wing supporters of the ownership society and related initiatives.

107. Department of Housing and Urban Development, *Blueprint for the American Dream*, October (Washington, DC: HUD, 2002). Available online at http://archives.hud.gov/initiatives/blueprint/blueprint.pdf (last accessed October 1, 2015).

108. E. Ray Canterbery, *Alan Greenspan: The Oracle Behind the Curtain* (Singapore: World Scientific, 2006), pp. 126–28.

109. Edmund L. Andrews, *Busted: Life Inside the Great Mortgage Crunch* (New York: Norton, 2009), pp. 36–37.

110. Michael J. Graetz and Ian Shapiro, *Death by a Thousand Cuts: The Fight over Taxing Inherited Wealth* (Princeton, NJ: Princeton University Press, 2005), p. 73.

111. With the passage of the Economic Growth and Tax Relief Reconciliation

Act of 2001, Bush gradually increased the exemption threshold to $3.5 million and eliminated the estate tax entirely by the year 2010. However, subsequent legislation passed in 2010 and 2012 reintroduced the tax with a higher threshold of exemption.

112. Quoted in Graetz and Shapiro, *Death by a Thousand Cuts*, p. 69.

113. Luntz Research Companies Memorandum, "The Death Tax and Gay and Lesbian Americans," April 24 (2001). Available online at http://www .center4studytax.com/pub.htm#gaysurvey. Quoted in Graetz and Shapiro, *Death by a Thousand Cuts*, p. 73.

114. Edward N. Wolff, "Household Wealth Trends in the United States." E. Ray Canterbery finds similar results for the stock market boom of the 1990s. See Canterbery, *Wall Street Capitalism*, pp. 9–10, 210–11.

115. In an exchange with Nancy Fraser, Butler argues that the distribution and inheritance of property rests inescapably on the social structures of kinship, sexual reproduction, and normative gender identities. Contrary to Fraser, then, Butler concludes that the politics of "redistribution" cannot be usefully separated from the politics of "recognition" or status. Butler's argument focuses in particular on those instances in which "lesbians and gays are rigorously excluded from state-sanctioned notions of the family (which is, according to both tax and property law, an economic unit); are stopped at the border; are deemed inadmissible to citizenship...; are denied the right, as members of the military, to speak their desires; or are deauthorized by the law to make emergency medical decisions about dying lovers, or to receive the property of dead lovers" (p. 273). She goes on to ask, "Is it really possible to say that gay people do not constitute a differential 'class,' considering how the profit-driven organization of health care and pharmaceuticals impose differential burdens on those who live with HIV and AIDS? How are we to understand the production of the HIV population as a class of permanent debtors? Do poverty rates among lesbians not deserve to be thought of in relation to the normative heterosexuality of the economy?" (*ibid.*). The article is fascinating as an effort to think sexuality and political economy together. However, the preemptive subsumption of non-normative sexuality within the category of "class" serves

to obscure the fact that queerness is precisely in excess of class, because distributed across all classes. See Judith Butler, "Merely Cultural," *Social Text* 52/53 (1997), pp. 265–77, and Nancy Fraser, "Heterosexism, Misrecognition, and Capitalism: A Response to Judith Butler," *ibid.*, pp. 279–89.

116. There exist a number of interesting accounts of the interactions between queer politics and consumerism during this period. For the most part, however, these accounts remain within the framework of commodity fetishism and do not analyze the specific dynamics of securitized consumer credit. Alexandra Chasin, *Selling Out: The Gay and Lesbian Movement Goes to Market* (New York: Macmillan, 2000); Eric O'Clarke, *Virtuous Vice: Homoeroticism and the Public Sphere* (Durham, NC: Duke University Press, 2000); Katherine Sender, *Business, Not Politics: The Making of the Gay Market* (New York: Columbia University Press, 2004).

117. M. V. Lee Badgett, "Beyond Biased Samples: Challenging the Myths of the Economic Status of Lesbians and Gay Men," in Amy Gluckman and Betsy Reed (eds.), *Homo Economics: Capitalism, Community, and Lesbian and Gay Life* (New York: Routledge, 1997), pp. 65–71.

118. For a sympathetic reading of Queer Nation, see Lauren Berlant and Elizabeth Freeman, "Queer Nationality" in Michael Warner (ed.), *Fear of a Queer Planet: Queer Politics and Social Theory* (Minneapolis: University of Minnesota Press, 1993), pp. 193–229.

119. Judith Butler, *Gender Trouble: Feminism and the Subversion of Identity* (London: Routledge, 1990) and *Bodies That Matter: On the Discursive Limits of Sex* (London: Routledge, 1993). The preface to Butler's *Bodies that Matter* outlines her misgivings concerning the "voluntarist" reading of *Gender Trouble* (pp. viii–x).

120. Robert J. Shiller, *Macro Markets: Creating Institutions for Managing Society's Largest Economic Risks* (Oxford: Clarendon, 1993), and *The New Financial Order: Risk in the 21st Century* (Princeton, NJ: Princeton University Press, 2003).

121. "It's not about the mainstream, profit-margins, patriotism, patriarchy or being assimilated. It's not about executive directors, privilege and elitism.

It's about being on the margins, defining ourselves; it's about gender-fuck and secrets, what's beneath the belt and deep inside the heart; it's about the night." *Queers Read This: A Leaflet Distributed at Pride March in New York* (June 1990). Available online at http://www.qrd.org/qrd/misc/text/queers.read.this (last accessed June 10, 2015).

122. See, for example, Rosemary Hennessy, *Profit and Pleasure: Sexual Identities in Late Capitalism* (London: Routledge, 2000), pp. 126–29; Peter Drucker, *Warped: Gay Normality and Queer Anti-Capitalism* (Leiden: Brill, 2015), pp. 300–304.

123. A classic explication of this dynamic can be found in the work of Irving Fisher, "The Debt-Deflation Theory of Great Depressions," *Econometrica* 1. 4 (1933), pp. 337–57.

124. As Jan Toporowski notes, there exists a real difference between those who take investment risks using already secured assets as collateral and those who own assets only on credit. The indebted owner depends on the continual appreciation of assets to transcend the limits of earned income and write-off debt, and is always vulnerable to sudden depreciations in asset value. In Toporowski's words, the "asset-rich have their financing and income hedged by assets, and a hedged risk is no risk at all, or a purely subjectively perceived risk. The biggest risks are undertaken by the asset-poor because their financing and income are not hedged by assets and an unhedged risk is a real one." Toporowski, *Why the World Economy Needs a Financial Crash*, p. 96.

125. Nancy D. Polikoff, "The New Illegitimacy: Winning Backward in the Protection of the Children of Lesbian Couples," *Journal of Gender, Social Policy and the Law* 20. 3 (2012), pp. 721–40; and Melissa Murray, "What's so New about the New Illegitimacy?" *Journal of Gender, Social Policy and the Law* 20. 3 (2012), pp. 387–436.

126. Inheritance law has remained stubbornly resistant to reform and, particularly in cases where someone dies intestate (without a will), reverts to notions of legitimate family relationships that have been overturned in other areas of family law. See Frances H. Foster, "The Family Paradigm of Inheritance Law," *North Carolina Law Review* 80 (2001), pp. 199–273; Ralph

C. Brashier, *Inheritance Law and the Evolving Family* (Philadelphia: Temple University Press, 2004).

127. The case in question is *United States v. Windsor*, 570 U.S. (2013) (Docket No. 12-307). The case was brought by Edie Windsor, whose partner, Thea Spyer, died in 2007. Upon Thea's death, the federal government refused to recognize their marriage and taxed Edie's inheritance from Thea as though they were unrelated, in keeping with the so-called marital deduction, which applies only to legally married couples. In June 2013, the Supreme Court ruled that section three of the "Defense of Marriage Act" or DOMA was unconstitutional and that the federal government no longer had the right to discriminate against married same-sex couples for the purposes of deciding federal benefits and protections.

128. Lisa Bennett and Gary G. Gates, *The Cost of Marriage Inequality to Gay, Lesbian and Bisexual Seniors: A Human Rights Campaign Foundation Report* (Washington, DC: Human Rights Campaign, 2004). Available online at http://tpcprod.urban.org/UploadedPDF/410939_cost_of_marriage_inequality.pdf (last accessed December 1, 2015); William D. Steinberger, *Federal Estate Tax Disadvantages for Same-Sex Couples* (Los Angeles: Williams Institute, UCLA, 2009). Available online at http://williamsinstitute.law.ucla.edu/wp-content/uploads/Steinberger-Federal-Estate-Tax-Nov-2009.pdf (last accessed December 1, 2015).

129. Foucault observed that in the work of Gary Becker, deviations from the norm are no longer categorized under the rubric of the pathological but appear instead as an expanding horizon of market opportunities to be included, as far as possible, within the terms of contract. Michel Foucault, *The Birth of Biopolitics: Lectures at the Collège de France, 1978–1979*, ed. Frédéric Gros (New York: Palgrave Macmillan, 2008), pp. 259–60.

130. Lisa Duggan defines the new homonormativity as a neoliberal sexual politics that "does not contest dominant heteronormative assumptions and institutions, but upholds and sustains them, while promising the possibility of a demobilized gay constituency and a privatized, depoliticized gay culture anchored in domesticity and consumption." *The Twilight of Equality? Neoliberalism, Cultural Politics, and the Attack on Democracy* (Boston: Beacon Press, 2003),

p. 50. Duggan's highly influential definition relies on a distinction between queer politics on the one hand and a "homonormative" gay and lesbian politics on the other. However, it seems to me that the push toward new forms of legitimation was not initiated by the "old" gay and lesbian politics, where we find a much stronger critique of marriage and family, but rather by the "new" antinormative, anti-assimilationist queer politics represented by groups such as Queer Nation, where we are much more likely to find the notion that institutions such as marriage or gender difference can be performatively resignified. Although certainly not comparable to the strident conservatism of the gay Republicans, it is arguable that Queer Nation's performativity politics already embodied a form of latent conservatism—that is, its performance of inclusion actively worked to liquidate the question of economic inequality in its relationship to gender, race, and sexuality.

CHAPTER FIVE: THE PRICE OF PROMISCUITY

1. Tomas J. Philipson and Richard A. Posner, *Private Choices and Public Health: The AIDS Epidemic in an Economic Perspective* (Cambridge, MA: Harvard University Press, 1993). Richard A. Posner is considered one of the founders of the law and economics movement. Tomas Philipson was a post-doctoral student of Gary Becker's at the University of Chicago in the 1990s who later specialized in health economics. See Johan Van Overtveldt, *The Chicago School: How the University of Chicago Assembled the Thinkers who Revolutionized Economics and Business* (Chicago: Agate, 2007), pp. 148–49.

2. For an institutional and intellectual history of the law and economics movement, see Steven G. Medema, *The Hesitant Hand: Taming Self-Interest in the History of Economic Ideas* (Princeton, NJ: Princeton University Press, 2009), pp. 160–96. The Coase article referred to is Ronald H. Coase, "The Problem of Social Cost," *The Journal of Law and Economics* 3. 1 (1960), pp. 1–44. For a reflection on the "economics imperialism" of the Chicago school and its modus operandi, see Edward Nik-Khah and Robert Van Horn, "Inland Empire: Economics Imperialism as an Imperative of Chicago Neoliberalism," *Journal of Economic Methodology* 19. 3 (2012), pp. 258–82.

3. Philipson and Posner, *Private Choices and Public Health*, p. 6.

4. *Ibid.*, p. 5.

5. *Ibid.*, p. 6.

6. *Ibid.*, p. viii.

7. C. Everett Koop, "Surgeon General's Report on Acquired Immune Deficiency Syndrome," (1986), available online at http://profiles.nlm.nih.gov/ NN/B/B/V/N/ (last accessed May 1, 2015); Presidential Commission on the Human Immunodeficiency Virus Epidemic, *Report of the Presidential Commission on the Human Immunodeficiency Virus Epidemic, June 24* (Washington, DC: US Government Printing Office, 1988), available online at http://eric.ed.gov/ ?id=ED299531 (last accessed May 1, 2015).

8. Philipson and Posner account for their position so: "Unlike many conservatives, who are libertarian when it comes to economic markets (narrowly defined) but turn interventionist when issues of morality are at stake, we do not take a stand on the political and ethical issues that ultimately determine the choice of public policies. A number of proposals that we criticize — including mandatory testing for the AIDS virus and quarantining persons who test positive — come from conservatives. And our analysis provides support for such quintessentially 'liberal' policies as recognizing rights to abortion and to homosexual marriage. But liberals will be disappointed by our failure to discover a compelling economic case for publicly subsidizing AIDS research and education as heavily as it is being done today." Philipson and Posner, *Private Choices and Public Health*, p. ix.

9. Michel Foucault, *The Birth of Biopolitics: Lectures at the Collège de France, 1978–1979*, ed. Frédéric Gros (New York: Palgrave Macmillan, 2008), pp. 259–60.

10. Philipson and Posner, *Private Choices and Public Health*, pp. ix, 14, 118, 124.

11. *Ibid.*, p. 118.

12. *Ibid.*, p. vii.

13. *Ibid.*, p. 13.

14. *Ibid.*

15. *Ibid.*, p. 73.

16. Interestingly then, while law and economics scholars reject normative ideas about perversion when it comes to individual behavior, the notion that incentives themselves can be perverse is ubiquitous in their work. *Ibid.*, pp. viii, 13, 148, 187, 199. Thus, there are no perverts, only a perverse welfare state. On the essential rationality of preferences within the law and economics perspective, see George J. Stigler and Gary S. Becker, "De Gustibus Non Est Disputandum," *American Economic Review* 67. 2 (1977), pp. 76–90. I am grateful to Miguel Vatter for clarifying this point.

17. *Ibid.*, p. 175.

18. *Ibid.*

19. *Ibid.*, p. 179.

20. Richard A. Posner, *The Economics of Justice* (Cambridge, MA: Harvard University Press, 1981), p. 190. A similar argument concerning the insurance function of the family is made by Gary Becker, "Altruism in the Family," in *A Treatise on the Family, Enlarged Edition* (Cambridge, MA: Harvard University Press, 1993 [1981]), pp. 281–82.

21. Richard A. Posner, *Sex and Reason* (Cambridge, MA: Harvard University Press, 1992), pp. 3, 182. In this book, Posner spends a considerable amount of time reflecting on the forms of sexual regulation that are justified within a libertarian framework. Thus, the "focus will be on what regulations are appropriate under a laissez-faire approach to sex—an approach that, by treating sex as morally indifferent, would limit sexual freedom only to the extent required by economic or other utilitarian considerations" (p. 181). Posner is particularly interested in the question of whether or not no-fault divorce and nonmarried childbearing should be permitted and under what conditions, since these are forms of sexual freedom that may ultimately cost the state a considerable amount of money in the form of welfare payments. Referring to Foucault's *Use of Pleasure*, Posner notes that "eating is guided by aesthetic and prudential considerations" and so "would sex be in a society in which it was a morally indifferent subject" (p. 182). See Michel Foucault, *The History of Sexuality Vol. 2: The Use of Pleasure*, trans. Robert Hurley (London: Penguin, 1992 [1984]).

22. For an account of neoclassical welfare economics, focusing on A. C. Pigou, see Medema, *The Hesitant Hand*, pp. 54–76. For an account of the transition from the welfare economics of A. C. Pigou to the postwar neo-Keynesian arguments of Kenneth Arrow and Paul Samuelson, see Philip Mirowski, *Science-Mart: Privatizing American Science* (Cambridge, MA: Harvard University Press, 2011), p. 57.

23. Mirowski, *Science-Mart*, p. 57.

24. Kenneth J. Arrow, "Uncertainty and the Welfare Economics of Medical Care," *The American Economic Review* 53. 5 (1963), p. 961.

25. *Ibid.*, p. 960.

26. For an institutional and intellectual history of this counteroffensive, see Medema, *The Hesitant Hand*, pp. 101–99. For an intellectual history of this counteroffensive that focuses on the Chicago school of law and economics and explores its relationship to nineteenth-century tort and contract law, see Pat O'Malley, *The Currency of Justice: Fines and Damages in Consumer Societies* (New York: Routledge-Cavendish, 2009). Ronald Coase's 1960 article "The Problem of Social Cost" is considered the seminal text in this counteroffensive; it reversed Pigou's argument that market failure called for government intervention by proposing instead that government was the problem. The problem of externalities could be dealt with much more efficiently if competitive free markets in the contested "good" or "harm" were established: market actors would then be free to bargain for their rights to cause or be free from harm and would thereby establish the most efficient market price for the externality in question. The Coase theorem underlies many of the most successful policy initiatives of the neoliberal era, including that of carbon trading. A number of accounts have explored the institutional and political effects of the neoliberal counteroffensive in the diverse areas of enterprise liability and safety regulation, antidiscrimination and employment law, and health care respectively. See Thomas O. McGarity, *Freedom to Harm: The Lasting Legacy of the Laissez Faire Revival* (New Haven, CT: Yale University Press, 2013); Ruth Colker, *American Law in the Age of Hypercapitalism: The Worker, The Family, and the State* (New York: NYU Press, 1998); Kimberly J. Morgan and Andrea Louise Camp-

bell, *The Delegated Welfare State: Medicare, Markets, and the Governance of Social Policy* (Oxford: Oxford University Press, 2011); and Timothy Stolftzfus Jost, *Health Care at Risk: A Critique of the Consumer-Driven Movement* (Durham, NC: Duke University Press, 2007). The Chicago and Virginia school share a common urtext in Coase's "The Problem of Social Cost."

27. O'Malley, *The Currency of Justice*, p. 153.

28. Mark V. Pauly, "The Economics of Moral Hazard: Comment," *The American Economic Review* 58. 3 (1968), pp. 531–37. For extended analyses of the debate between Pauly and Arrow and its influence on healthcare reform in the following decades, see Jacob S. Hacker, *The Great Risk Shift: The New Economic Insecurity and the Decline of the American Dream* (Oxford: Oxford University Press, 2006), pp. 48–49, and Jost, *Health Care at Risk*, pp. 70–85.

29. Tom Baker provides a now classic assessment of the role played by "moral hazard" in the law and economics literature. Tom Baker, "A Genealogy of Moral Hazard," *Texas Law Review* 75. 2 (1996), pp. 237–92. The conventional lesson taken from the economics of moral hazard, observes Baker, "is that 'less is more': Less welfare means more Americans out of poverty; less products liability means safer homes; less workers' compensation means safer workplaces; less disability insurance means more people without disabilities; and less health insurance means more healthy people" (p. 238).

30. Richard A. Posner, "Book Review: Guido Calabresi, The Cost of Accidents: A Legal and Economic Analysis (1970)," *University of Chicago Law Review* 37 (1970), pp. 636–48. Mark V. Pauly and Martin S. Feldstein make similar arguments about the psychological aspects of "moral hazard" in the following articles: Martin S. Feldstein, "The Welfare Loss of Excess Health Insurance," *The Journal of Political Economy* 18. 2 (1973), p. 256; Mark V. Pauly, "Overinsurance and Public Provision of Insurance: The Roles of Moral Hazard and Adverse Selection," *The Quarterly Journal of Economics* 88. 1 (1974), p. 54.

31. Pauly, "Overinsurance and Public Provision of Insurance"; Martin S. Feldstein, "The Welfare Loss of Excess Health Insurance," *The Journal of Political Economy* 18. 2 (1973), pp. 251–80.

32. Pauly, "The Economics of Moral Hazard: Comment," p. 532.

33. Mark V. Pauly, "The Welfare Economics of Community Rating," *The Journal of Risk and Insurance* 37. 3 (1970), pp. 407–18.

34. Mark V. Pauly, "Risk Variation and Fallback Insurers in Universal Coverage Insurance Plans," *Inquiry* 29. 2 (1992), pp. 137–47.

35. Pauly, "The Economics of Moral Hazard: Comment," pp. 531, 535.

36. On the moral philosophy inherent in nineteenth-century tort law notions of responsibility and fault, see François Ewald, *Histoire de l'État Providence* (Paris: Grasset, 1996), pp. 150–51. Ewald points out that the shift toward social insurance in the late nineteenth and early twentieth century made the question of fault irrelevant and was therefore widely perceived as an assault on the ethic of personal responsibility.

37. Joel Feinberg offers a philosophical account of the doctrine of *volenti non fit injuria* in *The Moral Limits of the Criminal Law Volume 1: Harm to Others* (Oxford: Oxford University Press, 1987), pp. 115–17. Richard Posner formulates the principle of *volenti* in the following terms: "It is my contention that a person who buys a lottery ticket and then loses the lottery has 'consented' to the loss so long as there is no question of fraud or duress; at least he has waived any objection to the outcome, assuming there was no fraud in the lottery. Many of the involuntary, and seemingly uncompensated, losses experienced in the market or tolerated by the institutions that take the place of the market where the market cannot be made to work efficiently are fully compensated ex ante and hence are consented to in the above sense." Posner, *The Economics of Justice*, p. 94. For illuminating accounts of the revival of the *volenti* doctrine in contemporary neoliberal and libertarian philosophy, see Robert E. Goodin, "Volenti Goes to Market," *The Journal of Ethics* 10. 1–2 (2006), pp. 53–74, with respect to the work of the libertarian philosopher Robert Nozick; Robin West, "Authority, Autonomy and Choice: The Role of Consent in the Moral and Political Visions of Franz Kafka and Richard Posner," *Harvard Law Review*, 99. 2 (1985), pp. 384–428; and O'Malley, *The Currency of Justice*, pp. 116–25 and 152–53, with specific reference to the history of *volenti* in nineteenth-century

labor law and its importance to the Chicago school law and economics movement.

38. Philipson and Posner, *Private Choices and Public Health*, p. 184.

39. *Ibid.*, pp. 119–20.

40. Daniel M. Fox was one of the first and most perceptive commentators on the convergence between the AIDS epidemic and neoliberal healthcare reform. See Daniel M. Fox, "AIDS and the American Health Polity: The History and Prospects of a Crisis of Authority," *The Milbank Quarterly* 83. 4 (2005 [1986]), pp. 1–26.

41. Paul Starr, *The Social Transformation of American Medicine* (New York: Basic Books, 1982), pp. 382, 394–97.

42. I borrow the term "rearguard action" from Paul Starr, who usefully analyzes Nixon's relationship to the left as follows: "In the early years, 1969 to 1971, the Nixon administration fought a rearguard action against the social programs of the Great Society, but the political climate was still predominantly liberal." *Ibid.*, p. 394.

43. Alice Sardell, *The U.S. Experiment in Social Medicine: The Community Health Center Program, 1965–1986* (Pittsburgh: University of Pittsburgh Press, 1998), p. 3.

44. Alondra Nelson, *Body and Soul: The Black Panther Party and the Fight against Medical Discrimination* (Minneapolis: University of Minnesota Press, 2013), pp. 55–105.

45. *Ibid.*, pp. 105–106.

46. *Ibid.*, p. 113.

47. The Black Panthers, along with Black Muslims and nationalists, were overwhelmingly opposed to abortion, which they equated with eugenics and genocide. See Donald T. Critchlow, *Intended Consequences: Birth Control, Abortion, and the Federal Government in Modern America* (Oxford: Oxford University Press, 1999), pp. 142–44.

48. Sandra Morgen, *Into Our Own Hands: The Women's Health Movement in the United States, 1969–1980* (New Brunswick, NJ: Rutgers University Press, 2002).

49. Starr, *The Social Transformation of American Medicine*, p. 391.

50. Jennifer Brier, *Infectious Ideas: U.S. Political Responses to the AIDS Crisis* (Chapel Hill: University of North Carolina Press, 2009), pp. 16–17.

51. Erving Goffman, *Asylums: Essays on the Social Situation of Mental Patients and Other Inmates* (Chicago: Aldine, 1962) and Michel Foucault, *Discipline and Punish: The Birth of the Prison*, trans. Alan Sheridan (New York: Vintage Books, 1995 [1975]). In the Anglophone world, theoretical perspectives on the history of "variance" or "abnormality" are very much skewed by Foucault's European-focused work. But for a comparable history of the construction of normal sexuality and race in America, see Julian B. Carter, *The Heart of Whiteness: Normal Sexuality and Race in America, 1880–1940* (Durham, NC: Duke University Press, 2007).

52. The gay liberation movement emerged in the wake of the Stonewall riots, in New York, and similar actions against police harassment in San Francisco. It was closely informed by the militancy of the New Left and rejected the accommodationist civil rights tactics of the early homophile movement. Beginning in 1970, gay liberation activists disrupted panel sessions at meetings of the American Medical Association, the Behavior Modification Conference, and the American Psychiatric Association (APA), eventually persuading the APA to declassify homosexuality in 1973. Despite the earlier conservatism of its positions, however, the homophile movement also adopted a radical position against the pathologization of homosexuality around 1965. See Henry L. Minton, *Departing from Deviance: A History of Homosexual Rights and Emancipatory Science in America* (Chicago: University of Chicago Press, 2002), pp. 219–64.

53. On this point, see Starr, *The Social Transformation of American Medicine*, p. 392.

54. On this point, these movements were at odds with the later Foucault, who appears to confound the critique of Fordist sexual normativity with the rejection of social insurance tout court. See Michel Foucault "Social Security: Interview" in *Politics, Philosophy, Culture: Interviews and Other Writings, 1977–1984*, ed. Lawrence D. Kritzman (London: Routledge, 1988), pp. 159–77. The

sociologist Daniel Zamora recently generated some controversy when he used this text as evidence of Foucault's late turn toward neoliberalism. See "Foucault, les exclus et le dépérissement néolibéral de l'État," in Daniel Zamora (ed.), *Critiquer Foucault: Les années 1980 et la tentation néolibérale* (Brussels: Éditions Aden, 2014), pp. 87–113. Without claiming to resolve this debate here, it seems to me irrefutable that in this particular text, Foucault is deploying a fairly standard neoliberal critique of social insurance, replete with the familiar jargon of "perverse effects."

55. Starr, *The Social Transformation of American Medicine*, p. 406; Robert Crawford, "You Are Dangerous to Your Health: The Ideology and Politics of Victim Blaming," *International Journal of Health Services* 7. 4 (1977), pp. 665–66.

56. Task Force on Health Promotion and Consumer Health Education, *Preventive Medicine USA: Task Force Reports* (New York: Prodist, 1976), p. 88.

57. Leon Kass, "Regarding the End of Medicine and the Pursuit of Health," *Public Interest* Summer 40 (1975), p. 41.

58. Starr, *The Social Transformation of American Medicine*, pp. 393–96.

59. John H. Knowles, "The Responsibility of the Individual," *Daedalus* 106. 1 (1977), p. 59.

60. In the words of public health theorists, Anne and Herman Somers: "Since most individual behavior is culturally conditioned, is it possible to counteract the overpowering forces in American culture, such as commercial advertising and the prevailing hedonistic lifestyle? What, specifically, can be done in a democracy about these deeply ingrained risk-factors? What evidence is there to justify faith in, or support for, a new thrust in this direction?" Anne R. Somers and Herman M. Somers, "A Proposed Framework for Health and Health Care Policies," *Inquiry* 14. 2 (1977), p. 130. In an earlier article, Anne Somers remarked that "most of the nation's major health problems—including automobile accidents, all forms of drug addiction including alcoholism, venereal disease, many cancers, most heart disease, and most infant mortality—are primarily attributable not to shortcomings on the part of the providers but to the living conditions, ignorance or irresponsibility of the patient" (p. 161). The

issue, she predicted, "will become even more complex as we further socialize the costs of health care. The non-smoking taxpayer is likely to ask with increasing frequency why he should be taxed to finance medical care for a smoker while the latter dies a lingering, expensive death from lung cancer or emphysema" (p. 162). Anne R. Somers, "The Nation's Health: Issues for the Future," *Annals of the American Academy of Political and Social Science* 399. 1 (1972), pp. 160–74.

61. Mark Lalonde, *A New Perspective on the Health of Canadians: A Working Document* (Ottawa: Report of the Government of Canada, 1974); Department of Health and Social Services (UK), *Prevention and Health: Everybody's Business* (London: HMSO, 1976); Surgeon General of the United States, *Healthy People: Report on Health Promotion and Disease Prevention* (Washington, DC: US Government Printing Office, 1979).

62. Daniel Wikler, "Personal and Social Responsibility for Health," in Sudhir Anand, Fabienne Peter, and Amartya Sen (eds.), *Public Health, Ethics, and Equity* (Oxford: Clarendon, 2005), p. 109.

63. Beatrix Hoffman, *Health Care for Some: Rights and Rationing in the United States since 1930* (Chicago: University of Chicago Press, 2012), p. 169.

64. Jennifer A. Parks, *No Place Like Home? Feminist Ethics and Home Health Care* (Bloomington: Indiana University Press, 2003), pp. 9–14; Sandra R. Levitsky, *Caring for Our Own: Why There is No Political Demand for New American Welfare Rights* (Oxford: Oxford University Press, 2014), pp. 46–47.

65. Eileen Boris and Jennifer Klein, *Caring for America: Home Health Workers in the Shadow of the Welfare State* (Oxford: Oxford University Press, 2012).

66. Evelyn Nakano Glenn, *Forced to Care: Coercion and Caregiving in America* (Cambridge, MA: Harvard University Press, 2010), pp. 154–55.

67. Ronald Reagan, "Proclamation 5812 — National Family Week, 1988, November 19," in *Public Papers of the Presidents: Ronald Reagan 1988–1989* (Washington, DC: US Government Printing Office, 1990), pp. 1563–1564; Ronald Reagan, "Proclamation 5913 — National Home Care Week, 1988, November 19," in *ibid.*, p. 1564.

68. Ronald Reagan, "Remarks at the Annual Meeting of the National Alliance

of Business, October 5, 1981," in *Public Papers of the Presidents: Ronald Reagan 1981* (Washington, DC: US Government Printing Office, 1982), pp. 883 and 886.

69. Lowell S. Levin and Ellen L. Idler, *The Hidden Health Care System: Mediating Structures and Medicine* (Washington, DC: Ballinger [American Enterprise Institute for Policy Research], 1981). Lowell S. Levin had been an early champion of New Left healthcare experiments. See Lowell S. Levin, Alfred Hyman Katz, and Erik Holst, *Self-Care: Lay Initiatives in Health* (London: Croom Helm, 1977). For a subtle analysis of the trajectory of self-care, from New Left counterpractice to neoliberal prescription, see Christopher Ziguras, *Self-Care: Embodiment, Personal Autonomy and the Shaping of Health Consciousness* (London: Routledge, 2004).

70. Charles Perrow and Mauro F. Guillén, *The AIDS Disaster: The Failure of Organizations in New York and the Nation* (New Haven, CT: Yale University Press, 1990), p. 68.

71. Kim Moody, *From Welfare State to Real Estate: Regime Change in New York City, 1974 to the Present* (New York: New Press, 2007), pp. 9–92.

72. Perrow and Guillén, *The AIDS Disaster*, p. 71.

73. *Ibid.*, pp. 71–72.

74. *Ibid.*, p. 107.

75. In his political memoir of Gay Men's Health Crisis, Philip Kayal is bluntly honest about the convergence between early AIDS activism and Reagan-era voluntarism. GMHC, he writes, "was shaped by two undeniable social facts: homophobic disinterest and the rebirth of American volunteer ideology under President Ronald Reagan" (p. 5). While noting the actual marginalization of gay men from American political life in the early 1980s, Kayal's sense of the potential future alliances between gay activism and American patriotism is remarkably prescient: "The linkage of volunteerism to the religious imagery of patriotism and nationalism is now considered by many to be part of our civil religion and is central to understanding of gay/AIDS volunteerism. Ironically, gays' taking the initiative to serve others in need reflects a value emphasized by all American religions and complements the country's Protestant and capitalistic character. Gay volunteers adhere, albeit

unknowingly, to conservative and republican views of where responsibility for problem solving lies, while the growing AIDS industry demands more public support" (p. 72). See Philip M. Kayal, *Bearing Witness: Gay Men's Health Crisis and the Politics of AIDS* (Boulder, CO: Westview Press, 1993). Cindy Patton is equally incisive. She writes: "Ironically, this approach [the turn to voluntary grassroots organization], dovetailed with the Reagan plan to shift virtually all government services into communities under the guise of Christian charity and volunteerism.... The common perception that government inaction was the result of straightforward, conscious homophobia—that the government failed to act because it was gay men who were most identified with AIDS— obscured the broader convergences of patterns of discrimination caused by Reaganite disfunding strategies. The homophobia argument focused on patterns of funding to the private sector—largely gay-community-based groups—with little analysis of the failure to fund drug and poverty programs with AIDS components, programs which Reagan was gutting precisely at the moment when AIDS began exacerbating these longstanding problems" (pp. 16–17). Cindy Patton, *Inventing AIDS* (New York: Routledge, 1990).

76. On this context, see Patton, *Inventing AIDS*, pp. 15–19.

77. Lester M. Salamon, "Non-Profit Organizations: The Lost Opportunity," in John L. Palmer and Isabel V. Sawhill (eds.), *The Reagan Record: An Assessment of America's Changing Domestic Priorities* (Washington, DC: The Urban Institute, 1984), p. 272.

78. George E. Peterson, "Federalism and the States: An Experiment in Decentralization," in *ibid.*, pp. 227–34.

79. According to Lester Salamon, "it was the 'Great Society' agencies that seem to have suffered most under the Reagan Administration." Salamon, "Non-Profit Organizations," p. 280. Sandra Morgen also notes that many women's healthcare clinics closed under the impact of Reagan's budget cuts. Morgen, *Into Our Own Hands*, p. 184.

80. American Federation of State County and Municipal Employees (AFSCME), *The State, the People and the Reagan Years* (Washington, DC: AFSCME, 1984), p. 15.

81. Reagan's budget advisor, the fiscal conservative David Stockman, was particularly alarmed by Reagan's exorbitant spending on defense. David Stockman, *The Triumph of Politics* (London: Coronet, 1987), pp. 245–87.

82. Salamon, "Non-Profit Organizations," p. 274.

83. Martha Davis, *Brutal Need: Lawyers and the Welfare Rights Movement, 1960–1973* (New Haven, CT: Yale University Press, 1993).

84. Peter Lewis Allen, *The Wages of Sin: Sex and Disease, Past and Present* (Chicago: University of Chicago Press, 2000), pp. 134–36. Lisa Duggan and Nan D. Hunter see the Helms amendment as part of a wider strategy to insert "no promo homo" clauses in public funding bills to restrict the uses of public money. See Lisa Duggan and Nan D. Hunter, *Sex Wars: Sexual Dissent and Political Culture* (London: Routledge, 2006), pp. 129–33.

85. Allen, *The Wages of Sin*, p. 137.

86. "A History of the Ban on Federal Funding for Syringe Exchange Programs," Smart Global Health Blog, The CSIS Global Health Policy Center, available online at http://www.smartglobalhealth.org/blog/entry/a-history-of-the-ban-on-federal-funding-for-syringe-exchange-programs/ (last accessed February 2, 2015); "Gag Rule" in Jeffrey D. Schultz and Laura A. Van Assendelft (eds.), *Encyclopedia of Women in American Politics* (Phoenix, AZ: Oryx Press, 1999), p. 90.

87. Allen, *The Wages of Sin*, pp. 144–45.

88. Parks, *No Place Like Home*, p. 11.

89. The legislation in question was passed in 1983. See State Medicaid Manual, HCFA Pub. 45-3. 3812, Transfer Binder paragraph 32 457, February (1983). For a reading of this legislation, see Daniel Callahan, "What Do Children Owe Elderly Parents?" in Gail Henderson (ed.), *The Social Medicine Reader* (Durham, NC: Duke University Press, 1997), pp. 175–84.

90. For an account of this action see Tamar W. Carroll, *Mobilizing New York: AIDS, Antipoverty, and Feminist Action* (Chapel Hill: University of North Carolina Press, 2015), pp. 155–59, and Allen, *The Wages of Sin*, pp. 142–44. Allen is also illuminating on the New York Catholic Churches' incipient involvement in "faith-based welfare." See *ibid.*, pp. 144–45.

91. The controversy is captured in the documentary film, Jim Hubbard, *United in Anger: A History of Act UP* (New York: United in Anger Inc., 2012).

92. Perrow and Guillén, *The AIDS Disaster*, p. 166.

93. Patton, *Inventing AIDS*, p. 20.

94. On the ACT UP housing committee, see Brier, *Infectious Ideas*, pp. 177–79.

95. Theda Skocpol, *Boomerang: Health Care Reform and the Turn against Government* (New York: Norton, 1996), pp. 22–23.

96. Hacker, *The Great Risk Shift*, pp. 144–46.

97. Skocpol, *Boomerang*, pp. 22–23.

98. Dorothy Porter, *Health, Civilization and the State: A History of Public Health from Ancient to Modern Times* (London: Routledge, 2005), p. 263.

99. Centers for Disease Control, "Epidemiologic Aspects of the Current Outbreak of Kaposi's Sarcoma and Opportunistic Infections," *New England Journal of Medicine*, 306. 4 (1982), pp. 248–52.

100. Hoffman, *Health Care for Some*, pp. 177–78; Peter Baldwin, *Disease and Democracy: The Industrialized World Faces AIDS* (Berkeley: University of California Press, 2005), p. 128; Deborah Stone, "AIDS and the Moral Economy of Insurance," *The American Prospect* (December 4, 2000), available online at http://prospect.org/article/aids-and-moral-economy-insurance (last accessed January 20, 2015).

101. Hoffman, *Health Care for Some*, p. 177.

102. *Ibid.*

103. Patton, *Inventing AIDS*, p. 128.

104. Cathy J. Cohen, *The Boundaries of Blackness: AIDS and the Breakdown of Black Politics* (Chicago: University of Chicago Press, 1999), p. 123.

105. Jon C. Des Jarlais, Samuel R. Friedman, and Jo L. Sotheran, "The First City: HIV among Intravenous Drug Users in New York City," in Elizabeth Fee and Daniel M. Fox (eds.), *AIDS: The Making of a Chronic Disease* (Berkeley: University of California Press, 1992), pp. 279–95.

106. Cohen, *The Boundaries of Blackness*, p. 129.

107. For example, AIDS in men often expressed itself in the form of Kaposi's

sarcoma, but women with full-blown AIDS more often suffered from pelvic inflammatory disease, cervical cancer, or bacterial pneumonia. Risa Denenberg, "Unique Aspects of HIV Infection in Women," in the ACT UP/New York Women and AIDS Book Group (eds.), *Women, AIDS, and Activism* (Boston: South End Press, 1990), pp. 31–44; Kimberly Christensen, "Vessels, Vectors, and Vulnerability: Women in the U.S. HIV/AIDS Epidemic," in Karen L. Baird, Dána-Ain Davis, and Kimberly Christensen (eds.), *Beyond Reproduction: Women's Health, Activism and Public Policy* (Madison, NJ: Fairleigh Dickinson University Press, 2009), pp. 58–61; Brier, *Infectious Ideas*, pp. 172–73.

108. Chris Norwood, "Alarming Rise in Deaths: Are Women Showing New 'AIDS' Symptoms?" *Ms.* (July 1988), pp. 65–67. For an analysis of these findings, see Christensen, "Vessels, Vectors, and Vulnerability," p. 56.

109. Sarah Schulman, "Interview with Karin Timour," April 5, 2003, Transcript, *ACT UP Oral History Project*, p. 14. Available online at http://www. actuporalhistory.org/interviews/images/timour.pdf (last accessed October 1, 2014).

110. Schulman, "Interview with Karin Timour," pp. 15–16.

111. Hoffman, *Health Care for Some*, p. 179.

112. Christensen, "Vessels, Vectors, and Vulnerability," pp. 64–65.

113. *Ibid.*, pp. 65–66.

114. Brier, *Infectious Ideas*, p. 175.

115. Christensen, "Vessels, Vectors, and Vulnerability," pp. 66–67.

116. Peter F. Cohen, *Love and Anger: Essays on AIDS, Activism and Policy* (London: Routledge, 2014), pp. 67–68.

117. *Ibid.*

118. For an illuminating discussion of the political splits within ACT UP, see Brier, *Infectious Ideas*, pp. 170–71, 179, 183.

119. To my knowledge, the only theorist to have extensively analyzed this aspect of the campaign for same-sex marriage is Jaye Cee Whitehead, in *The Nuptial Deal: Same-Sex Marriage and Neo-Liberal Governance* (Chicago: University of Chicago Press, 2012), pp. 35–50, 59–72. According to Whitehead, leading players in the same-sex marriage campaign such as the Williams Institute

based at UCLA, "appeal to the state's interest in marriage as a model of care that reduces state expenditures and increases revenues—the same logic that brought marriage promotion programs to the forefront of welfare reform. This model of care comes with an ethic of self-sufficiency characteristic of calls for reductions in state-funded care structures. Many proponents of same-sex marriage do not directly appeal to state economization efforts; however, they appear to ardently believe in the same ethic of self-sufficiency that tends to mask privilege and stigmatize universal care structures as 'state dependency'" (pp. 43–44). In the same-sex marriage campaign, she notes, marriage is conceived as "the ultimate form of insurance" (p. 71). The analysis developed in this section is indebted to Whitehead's work.

120. M. V. Lee Badgett, *Money, Myths, and Change: The Economic Lives of Lesbians and Gay Men* (Chicago: University of Chicago Press, 2001), p. 143. The quotation is from Robert A. Pollak, "A Transaction Cost Approach to Families and Households," *Journal of Economic Literature* 23. 2 (1985), p. 585. Pollak is a (sometimes critical) exponent of Gary Becker's "new household economics."

121. Badgett, *Money, Myths, and Change*, p. 203.

122. William N. Eskridge Jr., *The Case for Same-Sex Marriage: From Sexual Liberty to Civilized Commitment* (New York: Free Press, 1996), p. 68.

123. Whitehead, *The Nuptial Deal*, pp. 40–43.

124. Marriage Cases, S1479999, 43 Cal. 4th 757 (76 Cal. Reptr. 3rd 683 p. 3d. 384) (2008), p. 11. Quoted in Whitehead, *The Nuptial Deal*, p. 37.

125. Eskridge, *The Case for Same-Sex Marriage*, p. 74.

126. Jonathan Rauch, "Not Whether but How: Gay Marriage and the Revival of Burkean Conservatism," *Southern Texas Law Review* 50. 1 (2008), p. 8.

CHAPTER SIX: *IN LOCO PARENTIS*

1. Richard Fry, *A Record 21.6 Million in 2012: A Rising Share of Young Adults Live in Their Parents' Home, August 1* (Washington, DC: Pew Research Center, 2013), available online at http://www.pewsocialtrends.org/files/2013/07/ SDT-millennials-living-with-parents-07-2013.pdf (last accessed October 30, 2015); Zachary Bleemer, Meta Brown, Donghoon Lee, and Wilbert van der

Klaauw, *Debt, Jobs, or Housing: What's Keeping Millennials at Home? Federal Reserve Bank of New York Staff Reports, 1 November* (New York: Federal Reserve Bank of New York, 2014), available online at https://www.newyorkfed.org/research/staff_reports/sr700.html (last accessed October 30, 2015).

2. Meta Brown, Andrew Haughwout, Donghoon Lee, Joelle Scally, and Wilbert van der Klaauw, "Measuring Student Debt and its Performance," in Brad Hershbein and Kevin M. Hollenbeck (eds.), *Student Loans and the Dynamics of Debt* (Kalamazoo, MI: W. E. Upjohn Institute for Employment Research, 2015), p. 39.

3. *Ibid.*, p. 40.

4. Andrew Ross, *Creditocracy and the Case for Debt Refusal* (New York: OR Books, 2013), pp. 107–10.

5. According to Richard Fry, 1960 was the year in which young adults under twenty-five were most likely to live independently of family. See Richard Fry, "Record Share of Young Women are Living with Their Parents, Relatives," *Pew Research Center, FactTank News* in the Numbers, available online at http://www.pewresearch.org/fact-tank/2015/11/11/record-share-of-young-women-are-living-with-their-parents-relatives (last accessed October 30, 2015).

6. Samuel p. Huntington, "The United States," in Michel Crozier, Samuel p. Huntington, and Joji Watanuki (eds.), *The Crisis of Democracy: Report on the Governability of Democracies to the Trilateral Commission* (New York: New York University Press, 1975), pp. 74–75.

7. *Ibid.*, p. 110.

8. See Foucault's discussion of Gary Becker's theory of human capital in Michel Foucault, *The Birth of Biopolitics: Lectures at the Collège de France, 1978–1979*, ed. Frédéric Gros (London: Palgrave Macmillan, 2008), pp. 215–37.

9. For a nuanced discussion of the different strands within human capital theory and their variable policy impact, see Simon Marginson, *Human Capital Theory and Education Policy. Discussion Paper No. 3*. November (Kensington, NSW: Public Sector Research Centre, University of New South Wales, 1989), and Simon Marginson, "Human Capital Theory," in *Education and Public Policy in Australia* (Cambridge: Cambridge University Press, 1993), pp. 31–54.

10. Robert M. Solow, "Technical Change and the Aggregate Production Function," *The Review of Economics and Statistics* 39 (1957), pp. 312–20, and Robert M. Solow, "Technical Progress, Capital Formation, and Economic Growth," *The American Economic Review* 52 (1962), pp. 76–86.

11. Theodore W. Schultz, "Investment in Human Capital," *The American Economic Review* 51. 1 (1961), p. 6.

12. Schultz, "Investment in Human Capital," pp. 13–14; Theodore W. Schultz, "Woman's New Economic Commandments," *Bulletin of the Atomic Scientists* XXVIII. 2 (1972), pp. 29–32.

13. Schultz, "Investment in Human Capital," p. 15.

14. For a full account of Walter Heller's influence in translating Schultz's ideas into government policy, see Jeff Biddle and Laura Holden, "Walter Heller and the Introduction of Human Capital Theory into Education Policy," unpublished paper, November 2014, available online at https://www.utexas.edu/cola/_files/ms37643/Holden-Biddle_for_Hamerama.pdf (last accessed October 1, 2015).

15. Walter W. Heller, "Economics and the Applied Theory of Public Expenditure," in Joint Economic Committee, *Federal Expenditure for Economic Growth and Stability: Papers Submitted by Panelists Appearing Before the Subcommittee on Economic Policy* (Washington: USGPO, 1957), pp. 98–107. The paper is discussed in Biddle and Holden, "Walter Heller and the Introduction of Human Capital Theory into Education Policy," p. 34.

16. Richard A. Musgrave, "Higher Education and the Federal Budget," *Review of Economics and Statistics* 42. 3 (1960), p. 96.

17. Musgrave, "Higher Education and the Federal Budget," pp. 99–100.

18. Christopher p. Loss, *Between Citizens and the State: The Politics of Higher Education in the Twentieth Century* (Princeton, NJ: Princeton University Press, 2007), pp. 168–78; Suzanne Mettler, *Degrees of Inequality: How the Politics of Higher Education Sabotaged the American Dream* (New York: Basic Books, 2014), pp. 51–59.

19. Schultz, "Investment in Human Capital," p. 15.

20. Mettler, *Degrees of Inequality*, p. 53.

21. Milton Friedman and Simon Kuznets, *Income from Independent Professional Practice* (New York: National Bureau of Economic Research, 1945). My reading of Friedman and Kuznets is indebted to that of Simon Marginson in *Human Capital Theory and Higher Education Policy*.

22. Friedman and Kuznets, *Income from Independent Professional Practice*, p. vi.

23. *Ibid.*, p. 90.

24. Most student loans are now financed by debt rather than equity finance (i.e., stock investment). However, there exists at least one private company, Lumni, that uses equity finance to fund investment in students' college education. See http://www.lumni.net/about/ (last accessed December 1, 2015). The cofounder of the fund, Miguel Palacios, outlines his theory of equity-based human-capital investment in *Investing in Human Capital: A Capital Markets Approach to Student Funding* (Cambridge: Cambridge University Press, 2004). Palacios acknowledges his debt to the work of Milton Friedman.

25. Milton Friedman and Rose Friedman, *Capitalism and Freedom* (Chicago: University of Chicago Press, 1962), pp. 100–101.

26. *Ibid.*, p. 107.

27. *Ibid.*, pp. 102–105. Friedman's vision of a federally administered student loan program tied to the tax system was formalized as the "income-contingent loan" and implemented in Australia in 1989. Although its effects are regressive due to the accumulation of interest on outstanding loans, it is now sometimes presented as a pleasant alternative to the non-income-contingent student loan system that has developed in the United States.

28. In fact, the first federal student loan program was created on the advice of Milton Friedman and consisted of direct loans funded by the US Treasury. These loans were included in the National Defense Education Act of 1958. When Congress decided to expand this program under the Higher Education Act of 1965, it followed Friedman's alternative and preferred solution of guaranteeing private bank loans. See "History of Federal Student Loan Programs," July 8 (2015), available online at http://atlas.newamerica.org/federal-student-loan-programs-history (last accessed October 1, 2015).

29. Gary S. Becker, "Inequality and Intergenerational Mobility," in *A Treatise on the Family, Enlarged Edition* (Cambridge, MA: Harvard University Press, 1993 [1981]), p. 222. Other than this, Becker shared Milton Friedman's skepticism with regard to the idea that free education generated social returns. See Gary S. Becker, *Human Capital: A Theoretical and Empirical Analysis with Special Reference to Education* (New York: Columbia University Press, 1964).

30. In Becker's words, "a progressive income tax system not only reduces efficiency by discouraging investment but may also widen the equilibrium inequality in disposable incomes. By contrast, policies that improve access of poor families to the capital market to finance their investments in human capital reduce inequality while raising efficiency," in Becker, "Inequality and Intergenerational Mobility," p. 222.

31. *Ibid.*

32. Marginson, *Human Capital Theory and Higher Education Policy*, pp. 16–17.

33. Richard B. Freeman, *The Overeducated American* (New York: Academic Press, 1976).

34. Marginson, *Human Capital Theory and Higher Education Policy*, p. 17.

35. Kerr's most extensive discussion of human capital theory can be found in *Marshall, Marx and Modern Times: The Multidimensional Society* (Cambridge: Cambridge University Press, 1969), where he cites Theodore Schultz but relies most heavily on Alfred Marshall's work. I refer to this as Schultzian human capital theory to distinguish it from the theory of private investment in human capital championed by Becker and Friedman.

36. The Master Plan Survey Team, *A Master Plan for Higher Education in California, 1960–1975: Prepared for the Liaison Committee of the State Board of Education and the Regents of the University of California* (Sacramento: California State Department of Education, 1960).

37. Paddy Riley, "Clark Kerr: From the Industrial to the Knowledge Economy," in Nelson Lichtenstein (ed.), *American Capitalism: Social Thought and Political Economy in the Twentieth Century* (Philadelphia: University of Pennsylvania Press, 2011), p. 79.

38. In conversation with David Riesman and others, Clark Kerr commented: "I can just see, having done arbitration in the industrial scene, that the employers will love this generation, that they are not going to press very many grievances, there won't be much trouble, they are going to do their jobs, they are going to be easy to handle. There aren't going to be riots. There aren't going to be revolutions. There aren't going to be many strikes." This conversation is reported in Margaret L. Habein, ed., *Spotlight on the College Student: A Discussion by the Problems and Policies Committee of the American Council on Education led by David Riesman, Philip E. Jacob and Nevitt Sanford* (Washington, DC: American Council on Education, 1959), pp. 40–41.

39. Clark Kerr, *The Uses of the University, with a Postscript (1972)* (New York: Harper and Row, 1972 [1963]), pp. 86–88.

40. Cited in Parker Donham, "Savio Blasts Kerr's 'Knowledge Factory,'" *The Harvard Crimson* (December 12, 1964).

41. Terry H. Anderson, *The Movement and the Sixties* (Oxford: Oxford University Press, 1996), p. 161.

42. In *Gott v. Berea College*, 1913, the Kentucky Court of Appeals ruled that college authorities "stand *in loco parentis* concerning the physical and moral welfare, and mental training of the pupils, and we are unable to see why to that end they may not make any rule or regulation for the government or betterment of their pupils that a parent could for the same purposes." Quoted in Britton White, "Student Rights: From In Loco Parentis to Sine Parentibus and Back Again? Understanding the Family Educational Rights and Privacy Act in Higher Education," *B.Y.U Education and Law Journal* 2 (2007), p. 324. There exists a vast literature on *in loco parentis* rules and their catalytic role in the student revolts of the 1960s. For general discussions, see Anderson, *The Movement and the Sixties*, pp. 97–101 and 112–13; Loss, *Between Citizens and the State*, pp. 182–87 and 203–11. On the connections between feminism, civil rights, and *in loco parentis* in the South, see Renee Nicole Lansley, "College Women or College Girls? Gender, Sexuality, and in loco parentis on Campus," PhD dissertation, Ohio State University, History (2004), available online at http://rave.ohiolink.edu/etdc/view?acc_num=osu1101681526 (last accessed

October 1, 2015). On the connections between gay liberation and *in loco parentis*, see "The Challenge to In Loco Parentis, Campus Masculinity, and Administrative Anxiety (1960–1970)," Oberlin College LGBT Community History Project, available online at http://www.oberlinlgbt.org/behind-the-masks/1960s/1960s-3 (last accessed October 1, 2015).

43. Roderick Ferguson, *The Reorder of Things: The University and its Pedagogy of Minority Differences* (Minneapolis: University of Minnesota Press, 2012), pp. 45–49. Ferguson's book offers a highly nuanced account of these movements and the role they have played in the remaking of academic capital.

44. See, for example, the account of the feminist and lesbian movement at Berkeley in Kate Adams, "Built out of Books: Lesbian Energy and Feminist Ideology in Alternative Publishing," in Sonya L. Jones (ed.), *Gay and Lesbian Literature since World War II: History and Memory* (London: Routledge, 2014), pp. 119–20.

45. Ferguson, *The Reorder of Things*.

46. David Burner, *Making Peace with the 60s* (Princeton, NJ: Princeton University Press, 1996), p. 137.

47. Christopher Newfield, *Unmaking the Public University: The Forty-Year Assault on the Middle Class* (Cambridge, MA: Harvard University Press, 2008) p. 52; Michelle Reeves, " 'Obey the Rules or Get Out': Ronald Reagan's 1966 Gubernatorial Campaign and the 'Trouble in Berkeley,' *Southern California Quarterly* 92. 3 (2010), pp. 275–305; Gerard J. De Groot, "Ronald Reagan and the Student Unrest in California, 1966–1970," *Pacific Historical Review* 65. 1 (1996), pp. 107–29. Aaron Bady and Mike Konczal go further and see Reagan's attack on the University of California system as a forewarning: "It is important to remember this chapter in California history because it may, in retrospect, have signaled the beginning of the end of public higher education in the United States as we'd known it." Aaron Bady and Mike Konczal, "From Master Plan to No Plan: The Slow Death of Public Higher Education," *Dissent* Fall (2012), available online at https://www.dissentmagazine.org/article/from-master-plan-to-no-plan-the-slow-death-of-public-higher-education (last accessed October 1, 2015). Certainly Reagan's state-level experiments in welfare and

education reform were subsequently incorporated into his presidential agenda and extended by his successors.

48. Ronald Reagan, "The Creative Society," in *The Creative Society: Some Comments on Problems Facing America* (New York: Devin-Adair Company, 1968), pp. 1–9, and "The Perils of Government-Sponsored Higher Education" in *Ibid.*, pp. 109–17.

49. On the parallels between Reagan's creative society and the work of Richard Florida, see Toby Miller, "The Children of Reagan's Hippies," *R/evolutions* 1. 1 (2013), pp. 70–83.

50. Seth Rosenfeld, *The FBI's War on Student Radicals and Reagan's Rise to Power* (New York: Farrar, Straus and Giroux, 2012), pp. 291–488.

51. Matthew Dallek, *The Right Moment: Ronald Reagan's First Victory and the Decisive Turning Point in American Politics* (Oxford: Oxford University Press, 2000), p. 191.

52. This aspect of Reagan's rhetoric is convincingly brought to light by Jeffrey Dudas in "Subversives All! Ronald Reagan and the Paternal Roots of 'Law and Order' at Home and Abroad," *Law, Culture and the Humanities* 8. 1 (2012), pp. 119–52. Seth Rosenfeld reports that in the early 1960s Reagan had employed FBI agents to investigate the sex life of his own daughter, so the parallels between his political and family life were quite real. See Rosenfeld, *The FBI's War on Student Radicals and Reagan's Rise to Power*, pp. 148–49.

53. Reagan, "The Generation Gap," in *The Creative Society*, p. 63.

54. Reagan, "Crime—1968," in *ibid.*, pp. 25–26.

55. Reagan, "What Is Academic Freedom," in *ibid.*, p. 120.

56. Reagan, "The Morality Gap at Berkeley," in *ibid.*, p. 127.

57. De Groot, "Ronald Reagan and the Student Unrest in California," pp. 118, 124.

58. Lou Cannon, *Reagan* (New York: G. p. Putnam's Sons, 1982), p. 149. According to Cannon, Reagan had long-term plans to dismiss Kerr but was pleasantly surprised when the Board of Regents preempted him at this first meeting.

59. Ray Zeman, "Reagan Pledges to Squeeze, Cut and Trim State Spending:

Reagan Pledges Strict Government Economy," *Los Angeles Times* (January 6, 1967), pp. 1 and 20; Art Berman, "Tuition Storm: Educators Blast Reagan Plans UC Regents' Emergency," *Los Angeles Times* (January 6, 1967), pp. 1 and 24. The UC budget for 1967–68 was eventually cut by $20 million.

60. Gladwin Hill, "Reagan Defeated on Tuition Plans: Regents Vote, 14–7, to Bar Fees at the University," *New York Times* (September 1, 1967), p. 13. The existing administrative fees were minimal and could be spent on noninstructional expenses only, such as administration, health services, and counseling.

61. As it turned out, once the Board of Regents conceded to an increase in administrative (as opposed to tuition) fees, these were raised every year anyhow until by the end of the decade the idea of free college education existed in name only. See Robert Lindsey, "California Weighs End of Free College Education," *New York Times* (December 28, 1982).

62. Milton Friedman, " 'Free' Education," *Newsweek* (February 14, 1967), p. 86.

63. *Ibid.* Elsewhere, Friedman railed against the "intolerant radicals who are seeking to destroy all universities." Milton Friedman, "Police on Campus," *Newsweek* (April 14, 1969), p. 87.

64. Patricia J. Gumport, Maria Iannozzi, Susan Shaman, and Robert Zemsky, *Trends in Higher State Education from Massification to Post Massification* (Stanford, CA: National Center for Postsecondary Improvement, 1997), pp. 5–6.

65. James M. Buchanan and Nicos E. Devletoglou, *Academia in Anarchy: An Economic Diagnosis* (New York: Basic Books, 1970), p. 23. Other prominent neoliberal figures in the UCLA Economics Department also expressed their support for Reagan's tuition plans in a letter to the editor of the *Los Angeles Times*. See Armen A. Alchian, Jack Hirshleifer, and Roland McKearn, "The Tuition Proposal: 'Good,' Say 3 Professors," *Los Angeles Times* (January 4, 1967), p. B4. Armen Alchian and colleagues also published work on the economic structures of student violence. Armen A. Alchian, "The Economic and Social Impact of Free Tuition," *New Individualist Review* 5. 1 (1968), pp. 42–58; Armen A. Alchian and William R. Allen, "What Price Zero Tuition?" *Michigan Quarterly Review* 7. 4 (1968), pp. 269–72.

66. On the history of the UCLA Economics Department, its connection with the Chicago school of economics, and the failed bomb attack, see William R. Allen, "A Life Among the Econ, Particularly at UCLA (William R. Allen Interviewed by Daniel B. Klein)," *Econ Journal Watch* 7. 3 (2010), pp. 205–34. Milton Friedman recounts a visit to the UCLA Department of Economics in the winter of 1967, where he was introduced to Reagan and debated students on the question of Reagan's proposed tuition fees. See Milton Friedman and Rose D. Friedman, *Two Lucky People* (Chicago: University of Chicago Press, 1998), pp. 209–10.

67. Buchanan and Devletoglou, *Academia in Anarchy*, p. 27.

68. *Ibid.*, p. 121.

69. *Ibid.*, p. 77.

70. For an illuminating analysis of what was at stake in the shift from public finance to public choice economics, see Wolfgang Streeck, *Buying Time: The Delayed Crisis of Democratic Capitalism* (New York: Verso, 2014), pp. 70–75. However, Streeck fails to attend to the familial dimensions of this shift. For an interesting insight into the conflict between the two currents, from the point of view of the practitioners, see James M. Buchanan and Richard A. Musgrave (eds.), *Public Finance and Public Choice: Two Contrasting Visions of the State* (Cambridge, MA: MIT Press, 1999).

71. David Stockman, *The Triumph of Politics* (London: Coronet, 1987), pp. 245–87.

72. As many have noted, the rise of "balanced budget conservatism" — exemplified most eloquently by public choice economics — has paradoxically coincided with a period of chronic budget deficits and previously unheard of levels of public debt, interrupted only by a brief period of budget surpluses under Clinton. For illuminating political readings of this seeming paradox, see Sidney Plotkin and William E. Scheuerman, *Private Interest, Public Spending: Balanced Budget Conservatism and the Fiscal Crisis* (Boston, MA: South End Press, 1994); Robert Heilbroner and Peter Bernstein, *The Debt and the Deficit: False Alarms/Real Possibilities* (New York: Norton, 1989).

73. Leo Panitch and Sam Gindin, *The Making of Global Capitalism: The Political Economy of American Empire* (New York: Verso, 2012), p. 128.

74. "A Chat With Dave Stockman," *Columbia Daily Spectator* 146 (October 1981), pp. 1 and 3.

75. Terrel H. Bell, *The Thirteenth Man: A Reagan Cabinet Memoir* (New York: Free Press, 1988), p. 75.

76. United States Congress, *Senate Committee on Labor and Human Resources, Nomination: Hearing Before the Committee on Labor and Human Resources, United States Senate, Ninety-ninth Congress, First Session, on William J. Bennett, of North Carolina, to be Secretary, Department of Education*, January 28 (Washington, DC: US Government Printing Office, 1985), p. 162.

77. William Bennett to Terry Branstad, White House Office of Records Management, Ronald Reagan Library, July 3 (1985). Cited in Devin Fergus, "Financial Fracking in the Land of the Fee, 1980–2008," in Reid Cramer and Trina R. Williams Shanks (eds.), *The Assets Perspective: The Rise of Asset Building and Its Impact on Social Policy* (New York: Palgrave Macmillan, 2014), p. 78.

78. Michael Mumper, *Removing College Price Barriers: What Government Has Done and Why It Hasn't Worked* (Albany: SUNY Press, 1996), p. 94; Mettler, *Degrees of Inequality*, p. 66.

79. Fergus, "Financial Fracking," p. 77.

80. Mettler, *Degrees of Inequality*, p. 96.

81. Michael Mumper speaks of "legislative deadlock and programmatic drift" in *Removing College Price*, p. 96. Mettler speaks of "policy drift" in *Degrees of Inequality*, p. 67.

82. Mettler, *Degrees of Inequality*, p. 67.

83. Mumper, *Removing College Price Barriers*, pp. 78–80.

84. *Ibid.*, p. 84.

85. Mettler, *Degrees of Inequality*, p. 76.

86. *Ibid.*, p. 53.

87. *Ibid.*, pp. 120–27.

88. Up until 1992, all federal student loans were subsidized, meaning that the government paid the interest on the loan while the student was still enrolled. In 1992, Congress approved the creation of an unsubsidized loan

program that is available to a larger cross-section of students but does not cover the costs of interest before graduation. Richard Fossey and Mark Bateman (eds.), *Condemning Students to Debt: College Loans and Public Policy* (New York: Teachers College Press, 1998), p. 11.

89. Rachel Fishman, *The Parent Trap: Parent PLUS Loans and Intergenerational Borrowing. Policy Paper, January 08* (Washington, DC: New America/ Education Policy Program, 2014). Until recently, there were no fixed borrowing limits to the PLUS loan program and minimal efforts were made to check the credit history of borrowers. Changes were made to tighten the credit check in 2011, as it became clear how many parents were being burdened with intolerable amounts of student debt that could not be discharged in bankruptcy.

90. During its first eight years of existence, Sallie Mae sold debt securities composed of student loans on secondary markets. With the passage of the HEA amendments of 1980, it was allowed to securitize its financial assets, that is, to issue synthetic securities blending different borrower profiles into risk-classified tranches. See Susanne Soederberg, "Student Loans, Debtfare and the Commodification of Debt: The Politics of Securitization and the Displacement of Risk," *Critical Sociology* 40. 5 (2014), p. 696. Like other asset-backed securities, sales of SLABS really took off only after 1993, escalating steeply by the end of the decade, as Greenspan's Federal Reserve policies spurred a consumer credit boom. See the chart tracking SLABS sales in Chadwick Matlin, "Student Loan Bubble Babble," *The Great Debate Blog*, Reuters US edition, March 7 (2013), available online at http://blogs.reuters.com/great-debate/2013/03/07/ student-loan-bubble-babble/ (last accessed November 10, 2015). When Sallie Mae was privatized in 1995, it came to dominate the market in student loan backed securities, issuing securities backed by both private and federal loans.

91. In 2012, a group of investors filed a class action suit against Sallie Mae, claiming that at the height of the consumer credit boom in 2006–2007, it had relaxed its lending standards to bolster its portfolio of high-interest earning "subprime" loans. While Sallie Mae offered a settlement to the investors, no compensation was offered to the "subprime" borrowers. Andrew Leonard, "Selling Out Students," *Salon*, June 8 (2012), available online at http://www.

salon.com/2012/06/08/selling_out_students/ (last accessed November 10, 2015).

92. Alan Michael Collinge, *The Student Loan Scam: The Most Oppressive Debt in US History—and How We Can Fight Back* (Boston, MA: Beacon Press, 2009), p. 14.

93. Congress passed a law declaring student loans nondischargeable in bankruptcy as early as 1976, but it provided for an amnesty period of five years (later extended to seven). See Collinge, *The Student Loan Scam*, pp. 14–15.

94. Douglas W. Elmendorf, Jeffrey B. Liebman, and David W. Wilcox, "Fiscal Policy and Social Security Policy during the 1990s," in Jeffrey Frankel and Peter Orszag (eds.), *American Economic Policy in the 1990s* (Cambridge, MA: MIT Press, 2002), pp. 61–119; Robert Rubin, "Comments: Fiscal Policy and Social Security Policy during the 1990s," in *ibid.*, pp. 130–35. During his campaign, Clinton promised to reduce the budget deficit and increase public investment in "human capital." Rubin and Greenspan soon persuaded him to concentrate on his deficit reduction strategy.

95. Bob Woodward, *The Agenda: Inside the Clinton White House* (New York: Simon & Schuster, 1994), pp. 69–70; Bob Woodward, *Greenspan's Fed and the American Boom* (New York: Simon & Schuster, 2000), p. 96.

96. *Ibid.*

97. Eugene A. Ludwig, "The Democratization of Credit and the Future of Community Development," NR 96–21. Speech before the Community Development Conference, Arlington, Virginia (February 23, 1996).

98. Monica Prasad, *The Land of Too Much: American Abundance and the Paradox of Poverty* (Cambridge, MA: Harvard University Press, 2012), pp. 227–45. These findings hold even when countries have seen comparable levels of financial deregulation.

99. *Ibid.*, p. 239.

100. *Ibid.*

101. *Ibid.*

102. This observation has led others to characterize this new financial

regime as a form of "privatized Keynesianism." See Colin Crouch, *The Strange Non-Death of Neoliberalism* (Cambridge: Polity Press, 2011), pp. 97–124. Crouch observes that "instead of governments taking on debt to stimulate the economy, individuals and families did so, including some rather poor ones" (p. 114). Crouch's account of this new financial regime is illuminating and more attentive to the distributional effects than is usually the case. However, I prefer to avoid the term "privatized Keynesianism," since it seems to suggest a simple displacement of Keynesian methods and discourages further enquiry into the salient differences.

103. Mumper, *Removing College Price Barriers*, p. 132. Andrew Ross provides updated figures on expected returns on investment that confirm these findings. See Ross, *Creditocracy and the Case for Debt Refusal*, pp. 140–41.

104. Caroline E. Schuster, *Social Collateral: Women and Microfinance in Paraguay's Smuggling Economy* (Berkeley: University of California Press, 2015).

105. Marian Wang, Beckie Supiano, and Andrea Fuller, "No Income? No Problem! How the Government is Saddling Parents with College Loans They Can't Afford," *Propublica* (October 4, 2012), available online at http://www.propublica.org/article/how-the-govt-is-saddling-parents-with-college-loans-they-cant-afford (last accessed November 10, 2015).

106. Tara Siegel Bernard, "The Many Pitfalls of Private Student Loans," *New York Times* (September 4, 2015), available online at http://www.nytimes.com/2015/09/05/your-money/student-loans/the-many-pitfalls-of-private-student-loans.html?_r=0 (last accessed November 10, 2015).

107. Parents whose child has passed away discover that they are still liable for the costs of the child's education. Blake Ellis, "Grieving Parents Hit with $200,000 in Student Loans," *CNN Money* (July 28, 2014), http://money.cnn.com/2014/07/28/pf/parents-student-loans/ (last accessed November 10, 2015).

108. "We want an economy where our debts are to our friends, families, and communities—and not to the 1%." Available online at http://strikedebt.org/ (last accessed April 13, 2016).

109. John Maynard Keynes, *The General Theory of Employment, Interest*

and Money (London: Macmillan, 1936), p. 160. See my article "The Strategy of Default—Liquid Foundations in the House of Finance," *Polygraph: An International Journal of Culture and Politics* 23/24 (2013), pp. 79–96, for a more detailed analysis of this debate.

110. Mark Huelsman, *The Debt Divide: The Racial and Class Bias Behind the "New Normal" of Student Borrowing* (New York: Demos, 2015), p. 2.

111. Caroline Ratcliffe and Signe-Mary McKernan, *Forever in Your Debt: Who Has Student Loan Debt, and Who's Worried?* (Washington, DC: The Urban Institute, 2013), p. 2.

112. Consumer Financial Protection Bureau, *Private Student Loans* (Washington, DC: Department of Education, 2012), p. 41; Mekela Panditharatne, "What Color Is Your Student Loan?" *Huffington Post* (January 17, 2015), available online at http://www.huffingtonpost.com/mekela-panditharatne/what-color-is-your-studen_b_6485452.html?ir=Australia (last accessed November 10, 2015).

113. Justin Vaïsse, *Neoconservatism: The Biography of a Movement* (Cambridge, MA: Harvard University Press, 2010), p. 73. Glazer and Lipset both published collections of their various writings on the student protests. See Nathan Glazer, *Remembering the Answers: Essays on the American Student Revolt* (New York: Basic Books, 1970), and Seymour Martin Lipset, *Rebellion in the University: A History of Student Activism in America* (London: Routledge and Kegan Paul, 1972). For a complete account of the neoconservative and cultural conservative "war" on left academia, see Andrew Hartman, *A War for the Soul of America: A History of the Culture Wars* (Chicago: University of Chicago Press, 2015), pp. 38–69, 222–52.

114. William J. Bennett, *To Reclaim a Legacy: A Report on the Humanities in Higher Education* (Washington, DC: National Endowment for the Humanities, 1984).

115. *Ibid.*, p. 19.

116. For an account of the assault on affirmative action and its victories in the 1990s, see Newfield, *Unmaking the Public University*, pp. 92–106.

For Kristol's admission of defeat, see Irving Kristol, "Faith a la Carte," *Times Literary Supplement* (May 26, 2000), p. 14.

117. Ferguson, *The Reorder of Things*, p. 6.

118. *Ibid.*, pp. 19–40.

119. On the revival of *in loco parentis*, see James J. Szablewicz and Annette Gibbs, "Colleges' Increasing Exposure to Liability: The New *In Loco Parentis*," *Journal of Law and Education* 16. 4 (1987), pp. 453–65.

120. Some legal scholars reject the argument that the rise of tort litigation against colleges and universities should be understood as a transformation of *in loco parentis*. See for example, Peter F. Lake, "Rise of Duty and the Fall of *In Loco Parentis* and Other Protective Tort Doctrines in Higher Education Law," *Missouri Law Review* 64. 1 (1999), pp. 1–28. Lake points to the fact that *in loco parentis* rules traditionally did not allow for tort litigation to argue that the new understanding of institutional civil liability has nothing to do with this older tradition. However, what this critique misses is the parallel shift in the understanding of the parent-child relationship, which suggests that the rise of tort litigation against colleges should indeed be understood as a transformation of *in loco parentis*.

121. Wendy Brown's study of injury remains pertinent to an understanding of identity politics today. See Wendy Brown, *States of Injury: Power and Freedom in Late Modernity* (Princeton, NJ: Princeton University Press, 1995). For a perspective on the peculiar forms of injury defined by private tort law and the culture of litigation, see Sarah S. Lochlann Jain, *Injury: The Politics of Product Design and Safety Law in the United States* (Princeton, NJ: Princeton University Press, 2006), and Martha Chamallas and Jennifer B. Wriggins, *The Measure of Injury: Race, Gender and Tort Law* (New York: New York University Press, 2010).

122. Martha Chamallas, "Discrimination and Outrage: The Migration from Civil Rights to Tort Law," *William and Mary Law Review* 48. 6 (2007), pp. 2115–87.

123. Thomas Frederick Burke, *Lawyers, Lawsuits, and Legal Rights: The Battle over Litigation in American Society* (Berkeley: University of California Press, 2002).

1. Kendrick Oliver, "Attica, Watergate, and the Origin of Evangelical Prison Ministry, 1969–1975," in Axel Schäfer (ed.), *American Evangelicals and the 1960s* (Madison: University of Wisconsin Press, 2013), pp. 121–38.

2. For an account of Bush's faith-based initiative in Texas, see Texas Freedom Network, *The Texas Faith-Based Initiative at Five Years: Warning Signs as President Bush Expands Texas-Style Program at National Level* (Austin: Texas Freedom Network, 2002).

3. This is not to say that faith-based prisons have entirely escaped constitutional challenge. See Winnifred Fallers Sullivan, *Prison Religion: Faith-Based Reform and the Constitution* (Princeton, NJ: Princeton University Press, 2009).

4. Cited in Jonathan Burnside, "Preparing Evangelists: InnerChange Freedom Initiative (IFI)," in Jonathan Burnside, Nancy Loucks, Joanna R. Adler, and Gerry Rose (eds.), *My Brother's Keeper: Faith-Based Units in Prison* (Portland, OR: Willan Publishing, 2005), p. 246.

5. The following description of IFI programming is based on material in Burnside, "Preparing Evangelists," and Tanya Erzen, "Testimonial Politics: The Christian Right's Faith-Based Approach to Marriage and Imprisonment," *American Quarterly* 59. 3 (2007), pp. 991–1015.

6. Erzen, "Testimonial Politics."

7. *Ibid.*, p. 1008.

8. Tanya Erzen, "In the Prison of New Beginnings," *Guernica Magazine*, October 15, 2014, available online at https://www.guernicamag.com/features/in-the-prison-of-new-beginnings (last accessed May 1, 2015).

9. Funding for faith-based instruction, responsible fatherhood, and healthy marriage classes is often combined, and faith-based organizations are often responsible for delivering the latter programs.

10. Tanya Erzen, "Religious Literacy in the Faith-Based Prison," *MLA* 123. 3 (2008), p. 660.

11. Faith-based organizations such as the evangelical Teen Challenge are major players in the prison diversion system for drug offenders. For insight

into faith-based substance abuse treatment, see Christopher M. Meissner, "Prayer or Prison: The Unconstitutionality of Mandatory Faith-Based Substance Abuse Treatment," *Cleveland State Law Review* 54 (2006), pp. 671–712, and Timoteo Rodriguez, " 'Bio-Pistis': Conversion of Heroin Addicts in Prisons, on Medicine, and with God," in Julie Adkins, Laurie Occhipinti, and Tara Hefferan (eds.), *Not by Faith Alone: Social Services, Social Justice, and Faith-Based Organizations in the United States* (Lanham, MD: Lexington Books, 2012).

12. Jordan Flaherty, "Arizona's Tenacious Laws against Sex Workers: US State's Initiative that Aimed to Improve Prostitutes' Lives has Brought 'No Real Reform' as Harsh Penalties Persist," *Al Jazeera America*, November 14, 2013, available online at http://www.swopphoenix.org/arizonas-tenacious-laws-against-sex-workers; Sarah Hoye, "How a Controversial Arizona Program Tries to Keep Sex Workers out of Jail," *Al Jazeera America*, November 14, 2013, available online at http://america.aljazeera.com/watch/shows/america-tonight/america-tonight-blog/2013/11/14/project-rose-prostitutesjail.html; SWOP Phoenix, "Support Monica Jones and De-fund Project ROSE," *SWOP Phoenix* Website (2015), available online at http://www.swopphoenix.org/monica/ (last accessed May 1, 2015).

13. Details on the DIGNITY program are provided on the homepage of Catholic Charities Community Services: https://www.catholiccharitiesaz.org/diversion/000018. See also Ambria Hammel, "A Life Reclaimed: DIGNITY Program Transforms Women Who See themselves as 'Throwaway,' " *The Catholic Sun*, March 20, 2014, available online at http://www.catholicsun.org/2014/03/20/a-life-reclaimed-dignity-program-transforms-women-who-see-selves-as-throwaway/ (last accessed May 1, 2015).

14. I borrow the term from Isaac William Martin, *The Permanent Tax Revolt: How the Property Tax Transformed American Politics* (Stanford, CA: Stanford University Press, 2008).

15. See Ruth Wilson Gilmore, *Golden Gulag: Prisons, Surplus, Crisis, and Opposition in Globalizing California* (Berkeley: University of California Press, 2007), and Loïc Wacquant, *Punishing the Poor: The Neoliberal Government of Social Insecurity* (Durham, NC: Duke University Press, 2009), for political

histories of this period. See Bernard Harcourt, *The Illusion of Free Markets: Punishment and the Myth of Natural Order* (Cambridge, MA: Harvard University Press, 2011), for a theoretical analysis of the neoliberal perspective on crime and punishment and the apparent contradiction of expanding prison populations in neoliberal times.

16. Erzen, "Testimonial Politics."

17. Chuck Colson and Pat Nolan, "Prescription for Safer Communities," *Notre Dame Journal of Law, Ethics and Public Policy* 18. 2 (2004), p. 392.

18. David Garland, *Punishment and Modern Society* (Chicago: University of Chicago Press, 1990), p. 204. For further details on the prison work of evangelicals, see Michael Ignatieff, *A Just Measure of Pain* (London: Macmillan, 1978), pp. 143–73.

19. Gustave de Beaumont and Alexis de Tocqueville, *On the Penitentiary System in the United States and Its Application in France* (Philadelphia: Carey, Lea and Blanchard, 1833), pp. 82–83.

20. "These schools are voluntary. Though no convict is obliged to join them, they consider it as a favor to be admitted.... The free choice left to the prisoners to join or not the school, makes those who enter it thus voluntarily, much more zealous and docile.... The minister who administers this service, accompanies it almost always with a sermon, in which he abstains from every dogmatical discussion, and treats only of religious morals; so that the instruction of the minister is as fit for the Catholic as for the Protestant, for the Unitarian as for the Presbyterian..." *Ibid.*, p. 37.

21. Alexis de Tocqueville, *Democracy in America*, Volume 1, trans. Henry Reeve, Esq., 3rd ed. (Cambridge, MA: Sever and Francis, 1863), p. 53. For an illuminating discussion of the reciprocal relationship between civic freedom and moral law in Tocqueville, see Arthur Kaledin, *Tocqueville and His America: A Darker Horizon* (New Haven, CT: Yale University Press, 2011), pp. 265–66.

22. For example, the otherwise powerful overviews recently published by Michael B. Katz and Joe Soss, Richard C. Fording, and Sanford F. Schram barely mention the project of faith-based welfare. Michael B. Katz, *The Undeserving Poor: America's Enduring Confrontation with Poverty*, 2nd ed.

(Oxford: Oxford University Press, 2013); Joe Soss, Richard C. Fording, and Sanford F. Schram, *Disciplining the Poor: Neoliberal Paternalism and the Persistent Power of Race* (Chicago: University of Chicago Press, 2011).

23. Jürgen Habermas and Joseph Ratzinger, *The Dialectics of Secularization: On Reason and Religion* (San Francisco: Ignatius Press, 2007), Jürgen Habermas, *What is Missing: Faith and Reason in a Post-Secular Age* (London: Polity, 2010), Craig Calhoun, "Secularism, Citizenship and the Public Sphere," in Craig Calhoun, Mark Juergensmeyer, and Jonathan Vanantwerpen (eds.), *Rethinking Secularism* (Oxford: Oxford University Press, 2011), pp. 75–91.

24. Giorgio Agamben, *The Time That Remains: A Commentary on the Letter to the Romans*, trans. Patricia Dailey (Stanford, CA: Stanford University Press, 2005); Alain Badiou, *Saint Paul: The Foundation of Universalism*, trans. R. Brassier (Stanford, CA: Stanford University Press, 2003); Slavoj Žižek, "Paul and the Truth Event," in J. Milbank, S. Žižek, C. Davis and C. Pickstock (eds.), *Paul's New Moment: Continental Philosophy and the Future of Christian Theology* (Grand Rapids, MI: Brazos Press, 2010), pp. 74–99.

25. Amy Black, Douglas Koopman, and David Ryden, *Of Little Faith: The Politics of George W. Bush's Faith-Based Initiatives* (Washington, DC: Georgetown University Press, 2004), pp. 52–53.

26. The term "pervasively sectarian" was popularized by the *Lemon v. Kurtzman* case of 1971, which set strict limits on the government funding of such organizations in the educational sector. See Black, Koopman, and Ryden, *Of Little Faith*, pp. 41–42.

27. Personal Responsibility and Work Opportunity Reconciliation Act of 1996, H.R. 3734 104th Cong. 2nd Session, P.L. 104-193 (1995–1996), Section 104 d. 2. A. and B.

28. *Ibid.*, Section 104 c, d and f.

29. Martha Minow, "Should Religious Groups Be Exempt from Civil Rights Laws?" *Boston College Law Review* 48. 2 (2007), p. 789.

30. On the outsourcing of welfare to private contractors, see Mark Carl Rom, "From Welfare State to Opportunity, Inc: Public-Private Partnerships in Welfare Reform," in Pauline Vaillancourt Rosenau (ed.), *Public-Private*

Policy Partnerships (Cambridge, MA: MIT Press, 2000), pp. 161–82. On the outsourcing of "soft skills" to faith-based organizations, see Steven K. Green, "In 'Bad Faith': The Corruption of Charitable Choice," in Marci A. Hamilton and Mark J. Rozell (eds.), *Fundamentalism, Politics, and the Law* (New York: Palgrave Macmillan, 2011), p. 117.

31. Dorit Geva, "Not Just Maternalism: Marriage and Fatherhood in American Welfare Policy," *Social Politics: International Studies in Gender, State and Society* 18. 1 (2011), pp. 39–40.

32. PRWORA required states receiving federal funding for sex education to follow all eight points of the program outlined in Title V. To gain a sense of the comprehensive moral politics implied in abstinence education (which pointedly excludes homosexual relationships from the "expected standard of sexual relationships" and prescribes abstinence as the best response to sexually transmitted diseases such as HIV/AIDS), it is worth quoting the full text of Title V: "the term 'abstinence education' means an educational or motivational program which: A. has as its exclusive purpose teaching the social, psychological, and health gains to be realized by abstaining from sexual activity; B. teaches abstinence from sexual activity outside marriage as the expected standard for all school-age children; C. teaches that abstinence from sexual activity is the only certain way to avoid out-of-wedlock pregnancy, sexually transmitted diseases, and other associated health problems; D. teaches that a mutually faithful monogamous relationship in the context of marriage is the expected standard of sexual activity; E. teaches that sexual activity outside of the context of marriage is likely to have harmful psychological and physical effects; F. teaches that bearing children out-of-wedlock is likely to have harmful consequences for the child, the child's parents, and society; G. teaches young people how to reject sexual advances and how alcohol and drug use increase vulnerability to sexual advances; and H. teaches the importance of attaining self-sufficiency before engaging in sexual activity." Personal Responsibility and Work Opportunity Reconciliation Act of 1996, H.R. 3734 104th Cong. (1995–1996).

33. Jessica Dixon Weaver, "The First Father: Perspectives on the President's Fatherhood Initiative," *Family Court Review* 50. 2 (2012), p. 298.

34. Jean V. Hardisty, *Pushed to the Altar: The Right Wing Roots of Marriage Promotion* (Somerville, MA: Political Research Associated and Women of Color Resource Center, 2008).

35. Weaver, "The First Father," p. 299.

36. Monica Potts, "Daddy Issues: Is Promoting Responsible Fatherhood Really the Best Way to Lift Families out of Poverty?" *The American Prospect* (April 2010), pp. 21–24; Weaver, "The First Father," p. 299. It is largely thanks to Obama that responsible fatherhood programs have become so pervasive in prison and postrelease programs.

37. On Bush and Wade Horn, see Shirley Anne Warshaw, *The Co-Presidency of Bush and Cheney* (Stanford, CA: Stanford University Press, 2009), p. 95. On black churches' involvement in faith-based welfare under Obama, see David K. Ryden, "The Obama Administration, Faith-based Policy, and Religious Groups' Hiring Rights," in R. Drew Smith (ed.), *From Every Mountainside: Black Churches and the Broad Terrain of Civil Rights* (Albany: SUNY Press, 2013), pp. 167–88.

38. Anne Farris, Richard P. Nathan, and David J. Wright, *The Expanding Administrative Presidency: George W. Bush and the Faith-Based Initiative (The Roundtable on Religion and Social Welfare Policy)* (New York: The Rockefeller Institute of Government and The Pew Charitable Trusts, 2004), p. ii.

39. Lew Daly, *God and the Welfare State* (Cambridge, MA: Boston Review, 2006), p. 34.

40. Green, "In 'Bad Faith,'" p. 111.

41. White House (President George W. Bush), *Unlevel Playing Field: Barriers to Participation by Faith-Based and Community Organizations in Federal Social Service Programs, January 29* (Washington, DC: The White House, 2001).

42. Green, "In 'Bad Faith,'" p. 112.

43. *Ibid.*, p. 116; Farris, Nathan, and Wright, *The Expanding Administrative Presidency*, pp. 14, 17; Bob Wineburg, *Faith-Based Inefficiency: The Follies of Bush's Initiatives* (Westport, CT: Praeger, 2007), p. 57. Wineburg points out that Catholic Charities USA, Lutheran Social Services, and Jewish Family Services were conspicuously not invited to the launch of the Faith-Based Initiative in early 2001. Along with the Salvation Army, these are some of

the largest religious charities in the United States and some of the largest recipients of government funds. The Salvation Army, with its reputation for sectarianism, was invited to the event.

44. Daly, *God and the Welfare State*, p. 42.

45. John P. Bartkowski and Helen A. Regis, *Charitable Choices: Religion, Race and Poverty in the Post-Welfare Era* (New York: New York University Press, 2003); Judith Goode, "Faith-Based Organizations in Philadelphia: Neoliberal Ideology and the Decline of Political Activism," *Urban Anthropology* 35. 2–3 (2006), pp. 203–36; Jason Hackworth, *Faith-Based: The Politics of Religious Neoliberalism in the United States* (Athens: University of Georgia Press, 2012); Vincanne Adams, *Markets of Sorrow, Labors of Faith* (Durham, NC: Duke University Press, 2013).

46. Andrew J. Morris, *The Limits of Voluntarism: Charity and Welfare from the New Deal to the Great Society* (Cambridge: Cambridge University Press, 2009), p. 222; Axel Schäfer, *Piety and Public Funding: Evangelicals and the State in Modern America* (Philadelphia: University of Pennsylvania Press, 2012), pp. 1–18.

47. Schäfer, *Piety and Public Funding*; Frank Adloff, "Religion and Social-Political Action: The Catholic Church, Catholic Charities, and the American Welfare State," *International Review of Sociology/Revue Internationale de Sociologie* 16. 1 (2006), pp. 16–17.

48. Schäfer, *Piety and Public Funding*, pp. 13–14.

49. The mainline churches supported the welfare rights movement as long as it was construed as family-friendly. Their support did not extend to those activists within the welfare rights movement who contested the very rationale of the male breadwinner wage. See Guida West, *The National Welfare Rights Movement: The Social Protest of Poor Women* (New York: Praeger, 1981), pp. 147–71; Brian Steensland, "The Hydra and the Swords: Social Welfare and Mainline Advocacy, 1964–2000," in Robert Wuthnow and John H. Evans (eds.), *The Quiet Hand of God: Faith-Based Activism and the Public Role of Mainline Protestantism* (Berkeley: University of California Press, 2002), p. 218.

50. Derek H. Davis, "From Engagement to Retrenchment: An Examination

of First Amendment Activism by America's Mainline Churches, 1980–2000," in Wuthnow and Evans, *The Quiet Hand of God*, pp. 317–42.

51. Steven Michael Teles, *The Rise of the Conservative Legal Movement: The Battle for Control of the Law* (Princeton, NJ: Princeton University Press, 2008), pp. 22–60.

52. Mark V. Tushnet, *Making Civil Rights Law: Thurgood Marshall and the Supreme Court, 1930–1961* (Oxford: Oxford University Press, 1996). Southern Evangelicals and fundamentalists were divided on the outcome of *Brown v. Board of Education*, with prominent organizations such as the Southern Baptist Convention endorsing the decision. See on this point Rick Perlstein, *Before the Storm: Barry Goldwater and the Unmaking of the American Consensus* (New York: Nation Books, 2009), p. 125.

53. Maimon Schwarzchild, "Civil Rights Laws and Freedom of Speech," in Paul Finkelman (ed.), *Encyclopedia of American Civil Liberties* (London: Routledge, 2013), pp. 302–305.

54. Leigh Ann Wheeler, *How Sex Became a Civil Liberty* (Oxford: Oxford University Press, 2013).

55. On the relationship between these Supreme Court rulings on sexual privacy and traditional state police powers, see Joanna L. Grossman and Lawrence M. Friedman, *Inside the Castle: Law and the Family in Twentieth Century America* (Princeton, NJ: Princeton University Press, 2011), pp. 109–41.

56. Cited in Grossman and Friedman, *Inside the Castle*, p. 113.

57. Jean L. Cohen, *Regulating Intimacy: A New Legal Paradigm* (Princeton, NJ: Princeton University Press, 2004), p. 6.

58. Martha Davis, *Brutal Need: Lawyers and the Welfare Rights Movement, 1960–1973* (New Haven, CT: Yale University Press, 1993).

59. Premilla Nadesan, *Welfare Warriors: The Welfare Rights Movement in the United States* (London: Routledge, 2005), pp. 59–60.

60. Gwendolyn Mink, *Welfare's End* (Ithaca, NY: Cornell University Press, 1998), pp. 50–61.

61. In his report to the President on the state of the American family, Gary Bauer, one of a handful of religious conservative advisors to President Reagan,

vividly conveys the sense of horror engendered by this legal revolution in family and welfare law. "It was not predictable—indeed, it was a shocking surprise... that the Supreme Court...would hand down a series of decisions which would abruptly strip the family of its legal protections and pose the question of whether this most fundamental of American institutions retains any constitutional standing.... In *King v. Smith, New Jersey Welfare Rights Organization v. Cahill*, and *USDA v. Moreno*, the Court gutted attempts to enforce the moral order of the family as the basis for public assistance.... The Court has struck down State attempts to protect the life of children in utero, to protect paternal interest in the life of the child before birth, and to respect parental authority over minor children in abortion decisions." Gary L. Bauer, *The Family: Preserving America's Future—A Report to the President from the White House Working Group on the Family* (Washington, DC: Domestic Policy Council, 1986), p. 11.

62. Black, Koopman, and Ryden, *Of Little Faith*, p. 41.

63. Schäfer, *Piety and Public Funding*, pp. 6, 18, 145–47.

64. Davis, "From Engagement to Retrenchment," p. 328.

65. Jerry Falwell, *Listen, America!* (New York: Doubleday, 1980), p. 222.

66. Quoted in Wheeler, *How Sex Became a Civil Liberty*, p. 138.

67. Catherine MacKinnon, "Privacy v. Equality: Beyond *Roe v. Wade*," in *Feminism Unmodified: Discourses on Life and Law* (Cambridge, MA: Harvard University Press, 1983); Martha Albertson Fineman, "Intimacy Outside of the Natural Family: The Limits of Privacy," *Connecticut Law Review* 23 (1991), pp. 955–72; Craig Willse and Dean Spade, "Freedom in a Regulatory State? Lawrence, Marriage and Biopolitics," *Widener Law Review* 11 (2005), pp. 309–29; Marc Stein, *Sexual Injustice: Supreme Court Decisions from Griswold to Roe* (Chapel Hill: University of North Carolina Press, 2010).

68. Donald T. Critchlow, *Intended Consequences: Birth Control, Abortion, and the Federal Government in Modern America* (Oxford: Oxford University Press, 1999), pp. 118–19.

69. The so-called Church Amendments (42 U.S.C § 300a-7) exempting religious hospitals from performing abortions were included in the Public

Health Service Act immediately after the *Roe v. Wade* ruling. By the end of the decade, almost every state had passed similar legislation allowing health workers to refuse treatments at odds with their religious conscience. Karina Eileraas, " 'Freedom of Conscience' Legislation," in Mary Zeiss Stange, Carol K. Oyster, and Jane E. Sloan (eds.), *Encyclopedia of Women in Today's World Volume 1* (London: Sage, 2011), p. 588.

70. Daniel K. Williams, "Sex and the Evangelicals: Gender Issues, the Sexual Revolution, and Abortion in the 1960s," in Axel Schäfer (ed.), *American Evangelicals and the 1960s* (Madison: University of Wisconsin Press, 2013), pp. 111–12.

71. *Ibid.*, pp. 112–13.

72. Davis, "From Engagement to Retrenchment," p. 334.

73. I use the terms "left" and "right" advisedly here, since they fail to convey a nuanced sense of actual political affiliations. Left-wing evangelicals such as Ronald Sider and Jim Wallis favor historically progressive social policies such as welfare redistribution and environmentalism, while right-wing evangelicals espouse the virtues of the free market and individual enterprise. However, evangelicals of the left and right are equally committed to a conservative moral politics. They are in general opposed to abortion and homosexuality, although the evangelical left attempts to promote a wider politics of life that would include opposition to the death penalty, gun control, and environmentalism alongside opposition to abortion. The shared moral politics is one reason why the influence of the evangelical left could be so rapidly eclipsed by the right in the 1970s; since the religious right spent most of its time vocalizing its support for moral values, the left was outmaneuvered and had little leeway with which to contest its economic politics.

74. Dean M. Kelley, *Why Conservative Churches Are Growing: A Study in Sociology of Religion* (New York: Harper & Row, 1972).

75. Stephen P. Miller, *The Age of Evangelicalism: America's Born-Again Years* (Oxford: Oxford University Press, 2014), pp. 34–40.

76. As I indicated in Chapter 3, there is a common misconception that

the right to sexual privacy is informed by neoliberal legal thinking, while in fact neoliberal legal scholars have always been loudly opposed to this innovation.

77. Davis, "From Engagement to Retrenchment," p. 317.

78. Steensland, "The Hydra and the Swords," pp. 214–22.

79. Carl F. H. Henry, "Evangelicals in the Social Struggle," *Christianity Today* 10 (October 8, 1965), p. 4.

80. *Ibid.*

81. *Ibid.*, p. 9.

82. Falwell, *Listen, America!*, pp. 18, 258.

83. Institute for Cultural Conservatism, *Cultural Conservatism: A National Agenda* (Lanham, MD: Free Congress Research and Education Foundation, 1987), pp. 83–84.

84. *Ibid.*, p. 85.

85. Peter L. Berger and Richard John Neuhaus, "To Empower People: From State to Civil Society," in Michael Novak (ed.), *To Empower People* (Washington, DC: American Enterprise Institute Press, [1977] 1996), pp. 157–214.

86. *Ibid.*, p. 159.

87. *Ibid.*, pp. 187–88.

88. *Ibid.*, p. 187.

89. *Ibid.*, p. 161.

90. Richard John Neuhaus, *The Naked Public Square: Religion and Democracy in America*, 2nd ed. (Grand Rapids, MI: Eerdmans, 1986 [1984]), p. 142.

91. *Ibid.*, p. 137.

92. Berger and Neuhaus, "To Empower People," p. 161.

93. *Ibid.*, p. 188.

94. *Ibid.*, p. 163.

95. *Ibid.*, p. 157.

96. *Ibid.*, p. 158.

97. Neuhaus, *The Naked Public Square*, p. 118.

98. *Ibid.*, p. 142. My italics.

99. Damon Linker, *The Theocons: Secular America Under Siege* (New York: Anchor Books, 2007), pp. 18–19; Randy Boyagada, *Richard John Neuhaus: A Life in the Public Square* (New York: Random House, 2015), pp. 131–34.

100. Boyagada, *Richard John Neuhaus*, pp. 160–63.

101. Peter Berger and Richard John Neuhaus (eds.), *Against the World for the World: The Hartford Appeal and the Future of American Religion* (New York: Seabury Press, 1976); Linker, *The Theocons*, p. 48; Boyagada, *Richard John Neuhaus*, pp. 179–85.

102. Robert B. Horwitz offers the following insightful comments on Neuhaus's relationship to the religious right: "*The Naked Public Square* essentially put in more moderate, acceptably scholarly form the arguments proffered by new Christian right stalwarts Jerry Falwell and Tim LaHaye. A seemingly reasonable, quiet extremism was Neuhaus's particular talent." Robert B. Horwitz, *America's Right: Anti-Establishment Conservatism from Goldwater to the Tea Party* (London: Polity, 2013), p. 126.

103. Horwitz, *America's Right*, p. 125.

104. Boyagada, *Richard John Neuhaus*, pp. 223–26.

105. "Evangelicals and Catholics Together: The Christian Mission in the Third Millennium," *First Things* (May 1994).

106. The signatories to the pledge included the natural law scholars Robert P. George and Mary Ann Glendon, who would go on to become powerful Catholic voices in favor of religious freedom.

107. Because of their commitment to the nonmediated experience of grace, Evangelicals and Protestants have often been quite reluctant to embrace the scholastic philosophy of natural law. However, this scepticism has receded markedly in recent years, perhaps because of the greater willingness of Evangelicals to make legal claims. See Jesse Covington, Bryan T. McGraw and Micah Watson (eds.), *Natural Law and Evangelical Political Thought* (Lanham, MD: Lexington Books, 2012).

108. On the political mobilization of natural law theory by the Vatican, see Mary Anne Case, "After Gender the Destruction of Man? The Vatican's Nightmare Vision of the 'Gender Agenda' for Law," *Pace Law Review* 31. 3

(2011), pp. 802–17. On the new natural law philosophers and their influence on constitutional law, see Nicholas C. Bamforth and David A. J. Richards, *Patriarchal Religion, Sexuality and Gender: A Critique of New Natural Law* (Cambridge: Cambridge University Press, 2008).

109. Postsecular theorists who seek to fashion some harmonious compromise between an antinormative sexual ethics and the claims of public faith seriously misconstrue the new politics of religious freedom and are ill prepared to address its legislative and prohibitive ambitions. Jackobsen and Pellegrini make a valiant attempt to do just this by proposing an alternative notion of "religious freedom" that is stripped of all reference to "moral law." However, the fusion between "religious freedom" and "moral law" is the defining innovation of the new religious right and cannot be simply wished away. Janet R. Jakobsen and Ann Pellegrini, *Love the Sin: Sexual Regulation and the Limits of Tolerance* (New York: New York University Press, 2003).

110. Steve Bruce, "The Curious Case of Unnecessary Recantation: Berger and Secularization," in Linda Woodhead, Paul Heelas, and David Martin (eds.), *Peter Berger and the Study of Religion* (London: Routledge, 2001), pp. 87–100; Miller, *The Age of Evangelicalism*, pp. 14–15.

111. Peter L. Berger, "A Call for Authority in the Christian Community," *Christian Century* October no. 27 (1971), pp. 1257–63.

112. *Ibid.*, p. 1261.

113. *Ibid.*, p. 1262.

114. Bernice Martin, "Interpretations of Latin American Protestantism: 1960s to the Present," in Calvin Smith (ed.), *Pentecostal Power: Expressions, Impact and Faith of Latin American Pentecostalism* (Leiden: Brill, 2011), pp. 116–17.

115. Marvin Olasky, *The Tragedy of American Compassion* (Washington, DC: Regnery, 1994).

116. Stuart M. Butler, *Privatizing Federal Spending: A Strategy to Eliminate the Deficit* (New York: Universe Books, 1985), pp. 113–14; Stuart M. Butler and Anna Kondratas, *Out of the Poverty Trap: A Conservative Strategy for Welfare Reform* (New York: Free Press, 1987), pp. 102–36.

117. Bauer, *The Family*, p. 5; Institute for Cultural Conservatism, *Cultural Conservatism*, pp. 81–84.

118. Much of the nonprofessional labor that runs these institutions is provided in-house by former guests whose rehabilitation prepares them for little else, or by court-ordered "volunteers" who carry out their community service orders in religious organizations.

119. Sheila M. Rothman and David J. Rothman, *The Willowbrook Wars: Bringing the Mentally Disabled into the Community* (New York: Harper & Row, 1984), pp. 159–71, 191–95; Peter Dobkin Hall, "Historical Perspectives on Religion, Government and Social Welfare in America," in Andrew Walsh (ed.), *Can Charitable Choice Work?* (Hartford, CT: Trinity College Center for the Study of Religion in Public Life, 2001), pp. 100–106.

120. Hall, "Historical Perspectives on Religion," p. 103.

121. Janet Poppendieck, *Sweet Charity? Emergency Food and the End of Entitlement* (New York: Penguin Books, 1998), pp. 81–106; Teresa Gowan, *Hobos, Hustlers, and Backsliders: Homeless in San Francisco* (Minneapolis: University of Minnesota Press, 2010), pp. 47–48.

122. Poppendieck, *Sweet Charity*, p. 103.

123. Ronald Reagan, "Statement on Signing the Stewart B. McKinney Homeless Assistance Act," July 22, 1987. Available online at http://www.presidency.ucsb.edu/ws/?pid=34591 (last accessed May 1, 2015).

124. Robert S. Ogilvie, *Voluntarism, Community Life, and the American Ethic* (Bloomington: Indiana University Press, 2004), p. 2.

125. Jonathon M. Soffer, *Ed Koch and the Rebuilding of New York City* (New York: Columbia University Press, 2013), p. 281.

126. Ogilvie, *Voluntarism, Community Life, and the American Ethic*.

127. Laudan Y. Aron and Patrick T. Sharkey, *The 1996 National Survey of Homeless Assistance Providers and Clients: A Comparison of Faith-Based and Secular Non-Profit Programs* (Washington, DC: Office of the Assistant Secretary for Planning and Evaluation, US Department of Health and Human Services, 2002). Available online at http://aspe.hhs.gov/hsp/homelessness/nshapco2/index.htm (last accessed May 1, 2015).

According to Aron and Sharkey, 60 percent of soup kitchens and food pantries are run by religious nonprofits and 25 percent of homeless shelters, with notable differences depending on the region. Janet Poppendieck cites a figure of 70 percent for religious charities involved in running soup kitchens although she adds that the figure is probably an underestimation because it excludes religiously inflected activities that are not affiliated with a particular church. Poppendieck, *Sweet Charity*, p. 188. A follow up report on homeless shelters published by the Urban Institute in 1999, found that the number of faith-based homeless shelters had risen from 25 percent in 1996 to 34 percent in 1999. See Martha R. Burt, Laudan Y. Aron, Toby Douglas, Jesse Valente, Edgar Lee, and Britta Iwen, *Homelessness: Programs and the People They Serve. Summary Report. Findings of the National Survey of Homeless Assistance Providers and Clients* (Washington, DC: The Urban Institute, 1999), p. 60.

128. For example, in 1993 the Salvation Army derived nearly half of its $68 million budget from government contracts but also received more private donations than any other charity in the United States. Rebecca Anne Allahyari, *Visions of Charity: Volunteer Workers and Moral Community* (Berkeley: University of California Press, 2000), p. 216.

129. Poppendieck, *Sweet Charity*, pp. 102, 121.

130. Hackworth, *Faith Based*, pp. 88–113.

131. Julie Adkins, "Bricks without Straw: Faith-Based Responses to Homelessness in the Hostile City," in Julie Adkins, Laurie Occhipinti, and Tara Hefferan (eds.), *Not by Faith Alone: Social Services, Social Justice, and Faith-Based Organizations in the United States* (Lanham, MD: Lexington Books, 2012), pp. 91–106; Mary L. Mapes, *A Public Charity: Religion and Social Welfare in Indianapolis, 1929–2002* (Bloomington: Indiana University Press, 2004); Mary A. Cooper, "The Role of Religious and Nonprofit Organizations in Combating Homelessness," in R. D. Bingham, Roy E. Green, and Sammis B. White (eds.), *The Homeless in Contemporary Society* (Newbury Park, CA: Sage, 1987); Michael Robertson, "Piety and Poverty: The Religious Response to the Homeless in Albuquerque, New Mexico," in Anna Lou Dehavenon (ed.), *There's No Place Like*

Home: Anthropological Perspectives on Housing and Homelessness in the United States (Westport, CT: Bergin and Garvey, 1996), pp. 105–19.

132. Kristina Gibson reports that as of 2006, 270 of the 300 emergency shelter beds for homeless youth in New York City were provided by the notorious Covenant House, a religious charity noted for its hostility to queer and transgender clients. Kristina E. Gibson, *Street Kids: Homeless Youth, Outreach, and Policing New York's Streets* (New York: New York University Press, 2011), pp. 68–69, citing James Bolas, ed. *State of the City's Homeless Youth Report, 2006. New York City Association of Homeless and Street-Involved Youth Organizations* (New York: Empire State Coalition of Youth and Family Services, 2006).

133. Sharon M. Keigher, "Rediscovering the Asylum," *Journal of Sociology and Social Welfare* 177. 1 (1992), p. 177.

134. Mark Mulder, "Faith-Based Homeless Shelters and 'Hyper-Institutionalization': A Case Study," *Michigan Sociological Review* 18 (Fall 2004), pp. 143–49; Poppendieck, *Sweet Charity*, pp. 188–93; Gowan, *Hobos, Hustlers, and Backsliders*, pp. 47–48.

135. Allahyari, *Visions of Charity*.

136. In both *Discipline and Punish* and *The History of Sexuality Volume 1*, Foucault traces the process whereby classical conceptions of sexual and political crime were displaced by modern, normative, and disciplinary understandings of deviance beginning in the late eighteenth century. In both instances, a legalistic, sovereign, and religious understanding of crime is understood as giving way to a set of secular, normalizing and statistical knowledges and practices. Michel Foucault, *Discipline and Punish: The Birth of the Prison*, trans. Alan Sheridan (New York: Vintage Books, 1995 [1975]) and Michel Foucault, *The History of Sexuality Volume 1: An Introduction*, trans. Robert Hurley (New York: Pantheon Books, 1978 [1976]). In Foucault's late lectures at the Collège de France, we find an attempt to rethink early Christian practices of asceticism in terms of a positive ethical horizon residing beyond normativity. See Michel Foucault, *On the Government of the Living: Lectures at the Collège de France, 1979–1980*, trans. Graham Burchell (New York: Picador, 2016).

137. Malthus, who had an enormous influence on the New Poor Law of 1834, combined classical liberal tenets with a form of economic theology shaped by evangelical Christianity. See on this point Michael C. Waterman, *Revolution, Economics and Religion: Christian Political Economy, 1798–1833* (Cambridge: Cambridge University Press, 1991).

138. "Perhaps, leaving the prison he is not an honest man; but he has contracted honest habits." Beaumont and Tocqueville, *On the Penitentiary System in the United States*, p. 58.

139. Poppendieck, *Sweet Charity*, p. 141.

140. Steven P. Brown, *Trumping Religion: The New Christian Right, the Free Speech Clause, and the Courts* (Tuscaloosa: University of Alabama Press, 2002); Hans J. Hacker, *The Culture of Conservative Christian Litigation* (Lanham, MD: Rowman & Littlefield, 2005); Rogers M. Smith, "An Almost-Christian Nation? Constitutional Consequences and the Rise of the Religious Right," in Steve Brint and Jean Reith Schroedel (eds.), *Evangelicals and Democracy in America Volume 1* (New York: Russell Sage Foundation, 2009), pp. 329–56; Jay Michaelson, *Redefining Religious Liberty: The Covert Campaign against Civil Rights* (Somerville, MA: Political Research Associates, 2013).

141. Hacker, *The Culture of Conservative Christian Litigation*, pp. 6–9. See also Elizabeth A. Castelli, "Persecution Complexes: Identity Politics and the 'War on Christians,'" *Differences: A Journal of Feminist Cultural Studies* 18. 3 (2007), pp. 152–80.

142. David John Marley, "Riding in the Back of the Bus: The Christian Right's Adoption of Civil Rights Movement Rhetoric," in Renée Christine Romano and Leigh Raiford (eds.), *The Civil Rights Movement in American Memory* (Athens: University of Georgia Press, 2006), p. 348.

143. Nancy D. Wadsworth, *Ambivalent Miracles: Evangelicals and the Politics of Racial Healing* (Charlottesville: University of Virginia Press, 2014), pp. 81–116; Ralph Reed, *Active Faith: How Christians Are Changing the Soul of American Politics* (New York: Free Press, 1996), pp. 55–69.

144. Pat Robertson, *The Turning Tide: The Fall of Liberalism and the Return of Common Sense* (Dallas: Word Publishing, 1993), p. 125. Cited in Marley,

"Riding in the Back of the Bus," p. 351. In 1990, Robertson founded his own Christian litigation firm, the American Center for Law and Justice, with the express aim of countering the American Civil Liberties Union on church-state and religious freedom issues.

145. Brown, *Trumping Religion*, p. 132.

146. *Ibid.*, pp. 139–40.

147. Karina Eileraas, " 'Freedom of Conscience' Legislation"; Martha S. Swartz, "'Conscience Clauses' or 'Unconscionable Clauses': Personal Beliefs Versus Professional Responsibilities," *Yale Journal of Health Policy, Law, and Ethics* 6. 2 (2006), pp. 269–350; Claire Marshall, "The Spread of Conscience Clause Legislation," *Human Rights Magazine* 39. 2 (2013).

148. Minow, "Should Religious Groups be Exempt from Civil Rights Laws?," p. 782.

149. Lois Uttley and Sheila Reynertson, *Miscarriage of Medicine: The Growth of Catholic Hospitals and the Threat to Reproductive Health Care* (New York: ACLU and MergerWatch, 2013).

150. Gibson, *Street Kids*, pp. 68–69; Nicholas Ray, *Lesbian, Gay, Bisexual and Transgender Youth: An Epidemic of Homelessness* (Washington, DC: National Gay and Lesbian Task Force Policy Institute and National Coalition for the Homeless, 2006); David Wagner, "Issue Brief on Gay and Transgender Youth Homelessness," *Center for American Progress* August 10 (2010), available online at https://www.americanprogress.org/issues/lgbt/report/2010/08/10/8224/nowhere-to-go (last accessed May 1, 2015). Wagner notes that federal funding "is currently being awarded to shelters without any requirement that they not discriminate against homeless gay and transgender youth."

151. Smith, "An Almost-Christian Nation," p. 343.

152. The case in question was *Employment Division v. Smith* (1990), in which the Supreme Court upheld a federal law banning the use of peyote in religious ceremonies. In this case, the Court decided that government has the right to limit certain religious practices by upholding laws that are applicable to the general population.

153. Micah Schwartzman, Richard Schragger, and Nelson Tebbe, "The

New Law of Religion: Hobby Lobby Rewrites Religious-Freedom Law in Ways that Ignore Everything That Came Before," *Slate* (July 2014), available online at http://www.slate.com/articles/news_and_politics/jurisprudence/2014/07/after_hobby_lobby_there_is_only_rfra_and_that_s_all_you_need.html (last accessed May 1, 2015). The Supreme Court invalidated the RFRA in the *City of Boerne v. Flores* decision of 1997. However, it continues to apply to the federal government, and many states have passed RFRAs that are applicable to state and local levels of government.

154. I borrow the expression from Katherine Franke, who is quoted in Nina Martin, "To Say 'My Religious Law Trumps Your Secular Law' Is a Radical Idea," *Salon* (March 19, 2014), available online at http://www.salon.com/2014/03/19/to_say_my_religious_law_trumps_your_secular_law_is_a_radical_idea_partner/ (last accessed July 1, 2015).

155. Daly, *God and the Welfare State*, pp. 28–29, 68; Black, Koopman, and Ryden, *Of Little Faith*, pp. 43–44.

156. Black, Koopman, and Ryden, *Of Little Faith*, pp. 44–45, 225–26.

157. *Ibid.*, p. 45.

158. *Ibid.*, p. 47; Smith, "An Almost-Christian Nation," p. 348.

159. Interestingly, religious conservatives have a long history of attempting to federalize state police powers governing morality. See Gaines M. Foster, *Moral Reconstruction: Christian Lobbyists and the Federal Legislation of Morality, 1865–1920* (Chapel Hill: University of North Carolina Press, 2002).

160. Leslie Lenkowsky, "Funding the Faithful: Why Bush Is Right," *Commentary* 111. 6 (2001), p. 24.

CONCLUSION

1. Friedrich von Hayek, "Why I Am Not a Conservative," in *The Constitution of Liberty* (London: Routledge, 1960), pp. 343–55.

2. *Ibid.*, p. 345.

3. *Ibid.*

4. *Ibid.*

5. *Ibid.*, pp. 346 and 349.

6. *Ibid.*, p. 345. On the necessity of tradition and morality more generally, see F. A. Hayek, *The Fatal Conceit: The Errors of Socialism* (Chicago: University of Chicago Press, 1988). It is in this work that Hayek most clearly outlines his evolutionary theory of moral tradition.

7. Like the Chicago and Virginia school neoliberals, Hayek's position on inherited wealth changed dramatically over time. Hayek expressed limited support for inheritance taxes in *Individualism and Economic Order*, published in 1949. Yet, by 1960, he saw no incompatibility between the free market and unearned wealth. See Friedrich Hayek, *Individualism and Economic Order* (London: Routledge and Kegan Paul, 1949), p. 118, and *The Constitution of Liberty*, pp. 78–80. In the latter text, Hayek presents the family and inherited wealth as historically validated social conventions.

8. Irving Kristol, *Reflections of a Neoconservative: Looking Back, Looking Ahead* (New York: Basic Books, 1983), p. xii.

9. Nathan Glazer, *The Limits of Social Policy* (Cambridge, MA: Harvard University Press, 1988), p. 8.

10. Kristol, *Reflections of a Neoconservative*, p. vii.

Index

Brown, Pat, 233.

Brown, Wendy, 18, 58, 71, 83, 335–36 n.94, 405 n.121.

Brown v. Board of Education, 274, 413 n.52.

Buchanan, James M., 18, 30, 225, 237–39.

Buckley, William F., Jr., 20.

Burger, Warren, 277.

Burns, Arthur, 29, 127, 132.

Bush, George H. W., 141, 169, 192, 241, 245.

Bush, George W., 68, 112, 124, 134, 138–39, 154–56, 259, 268–71, 310, 366 n.68, 371 n.111.

Butler, Judith, 158, 163.

Butler, Stuart, 293.

CALABRESI, GUIDO, 178.

CALCAV. *See* Clergy and Laymen Concerned about Vietnam (CALCAV).

California, 92, 97–98.

California Proposition 13, 130.

California's Blueprint for National Welfare Reform, 64–65, 100.

California State Supreme Court, 92, 95, 213.

Callahan v. Carey, 297.

Capitalism: free-market and counter-movements, 13–15, 18; industrial, 14–15, 17, 75; laissez-faire, 13–14; Marxist conception of, 16–17; modern, 13, 15–17.

Capitalism and Freedom (Friedman and Friedman), 224.

Carter, Jimmy, 19, 243, 280–81.

Catholic Charities Community Services, 261.

Catholic Charities USA, 270, 296, 298, 411 n.43.

Catholic liberation theology, 290.

Catholics, 272, 278–79, 281, 290–91.

Cato Institute, 66.

CDC. *See* Centers for Disease Control (CDC).

Center for Law and Religious Freedom, 301–302, 307–309.

Center for Social Development, Washington University, St. Louis, 366 n.68.

Centers for Disease Control (CDC), 195, 204–208.

Central bank, 19, 124, 133, 215, 358 n.13, 361 n.41.

Chappell, Marisa, 32, 40, 65.

Charitable Choice, 196, 266–69, 271, 293, 308–10.

Charity Organization Societies (COS), 84–87.

Chiapello, Eve, 11–12.

Chicago school of economics, 8, 31, 48, 57, 129, 167–68, 170, 175–76, 218–19, 225–26, 236–37.

Chicago Women's Liberation Union, 183.

Children, illegitimate, 68, 73–74, 84, 86, 94–96, 108–10, 115, 120, 163, 268, 351 n.117.

Child support, 67–68, 75, 81, 86, 96, 100–101, 103–105, 110, 112, 115, 267.

Child Support Act, 101.

Child Trust Fund, 153–54, 369 n.102.

Chrematistics, 13, 55, 334 n.83.

Christian Coalition, 303–304.

Christianity Today, 282.

Christian Legal Society, 301, 307.

Church and state, relationship between, 266, 272–73, 283, 286, 302, 308.

Cisneros, Henry, 141.

City of Boerne v. Flores, 424 n.153.

Civil Rights Act of 1964, 267.

Civil rights law, 255–56, 273–74, 305.

Civil rights movement, 18, 36–37,

Falwell, Jerry, 281, 283, 302–303.
Familial obligation, bonds of, 59–60,
    68–69, 75–77, 85, 90–92, 95, 138.
Family Assistance Plan, 43, 45–46,
    45–47, 47, 330 n.50, 331 n.53.
Family law, 10, 65, 94–96, 104–105,
    108–109, 114–15, 119–21, 274–76,
    343 n.52, 349 n.104, 350 n.115,
    351 n.117. *See also* Same-sex marriage;
    Welfare reform.
Family responsibility, 82, 197–98;
    charity-centered, 70–71, 84–86, 89;
    higher education, 240, 249, 253;
    male wage, 8, 33, 37, 41–42, 55, 80,
    90–91, 121–22, 323 n.29, 412 n.49;
    and modern social welfare, 89–93,
    100–101, 106, 197; in neoliberal-
    neoconservative discourse, 21–22,
    64, 68–73, 97, 99–100, 114, 210–11,
    218, 253, 300, 313–15, 338 n.1,
    338 n.5, 339 n.6, 345 n.66; and
    poor-law tradition, 15, 21, 64,
    69–70, 73–77, 81, 84–87, 91, 99,
    103, 106, 137, 141, 197, 212, 214,
    313–15, 349 n.107; same-sex
    marriage, 211–14. *See also* Child
    support; Welfare reform.
Family wage, 12–13, 40, 42, 46; break-
    down of, 8; and feminism, 12;
    New Deal, 40, 111, 121; redistributive
    policies of, 23, 32.
Fannie Mae, 142, 144, 149, 242,
    368–69 n.95.
Fascism, 15.
Fatal Conceit: The Errors of Socialism,
    The (Hayek), 425 n.6.
Fatherhood, responsible, 68, 86, 104,
    107, 111–14, 260–61, 265, 268,
    271, 309, 406 n.9, 411 n.36.
Fatherlessness. *See* Single-parent
    households.

FBI. *See* Federal Bureau of Investigation
    (FBI).
Federal Bureau of Investigation (FBI),
    182, 233, 297 n.52.
Federal Emergency Management Agency
    (FEMA), 296.
Federal Fatherhood Initiative, 113.
Federal Housing Administration (FHA),
    144, 146–47.
Federal National Mortgage Association
    (FNMA). *See* Fannie Mae.
Federal Reserve, 28, 58, 124, 127, 132–34,
    136, 142, 215–17, 328 n.15, 401 n.90.
    See also Burns, Arthur; Greenspan,
    Alan; Volcker, Paul.
Feher, Michel, 124.
Female-headed households. *See*
    Mothers, single.
Feminism, 11–12, 21, 39, 44, 59, 87, 121,
    148, 160, 182–83, 231, 277, 279, 289,
    357 n.13.
Ferguson, Roderick, 231, 252–53.
Ferrara, Peter, 365 n.64.
FHA. *See* Federal Housing Admin-
    istration (FHA).
Finch, Robert, 45, 331 n.50.
First Amendment, to US Constitution,
    264.
First Things, 290.
Florida, Richard, 233.
Ford, Gerald, 185.
Ford Foundation, 111, 138, 140, 157,
    176, 227, 366 n.68.
Fordist family wage, 8, 10, 12–13, 15, 23,
    29, 32, 34–36, 42, 46–48, 55, 79, 111,
    114, 121–22, 144, 148–49, 184, 193,
    211; efforts to expand, 21, 32, 35,
    39–40, 43–47, 51, 63–64, 69, 98–99,
    114, 273; normativities of, 8, 21, 121,
    149, 159, 164, 210, 313.
Foucault, Michel, 8, 164, 170, 174–75,

Labor, "natural" price of, 83.
Labour Party, 138.
Labor relations, flexible, and family
  formation, 9.
Labor unions. *See* Trade unions.
Lake, Peter F., 405 n.120.
League of Revolutionary Black
  Workers, 40.
Lee Badgett, M. V., 212–13.
Lemon v. Kurtzman, 276, 409 n.26.
Lenkowsky, Leslie, 310.
Levin, Lowell S., 190, 385 n.69.
LGBT movement, 211.
Liberation movements, 21, 51–52, 55.
Liberty Counsel, 302.
Lipset, Seymour Martin, 251.
Listen, America! (Falwell), 283.
Loch, Charles Stewart, 85.
Lockheed Martin, 267.
Ludwig, Eugene, 143, 246.
Lumni, 393 n.24.
Lutheran Social Services, 270, 285,
  298, 411 n.43.
Lynn, Robert, 355 n.3.

MAINE, HENRY SUMNER, 22.
Malthus, Thomas Robert, 76, 357 n.13,
  422 n.137.
Managed Care movement, 189.
Manhattan Institute, 66.
Marginson, Simon, 226.
Marriage: as civil contract, 343 n.52;
  contractual nature of, 88; destabili-
  zation of, 10; as marker of class, 7,
  123; as social insurance, 174, 212–14.
Marriage promotion, 173, 291. *See also*
  Freedmen's Bureau; Same-sex
  marriage; Welfare reform
Marx, Karl, 16–18, 152, 321–23 nn.24–25,
  334 n.76.
Mason, Mary Ann, 74.

*Master Plan for Higher Education in
  California*, 227, 236.
Maximus, 267.
Mayer, Victoria, 102.
McCarthyism, 50.
McGovern, George, 128–29.
McGovern, Terry, 208.
McKinney Homeless Assistance Act
  of 1987, 297.
Mead, Lawrence, 19–20, 62, 65, 110,
  337 n.105.
Medicaid, 93, 126, 170, 173, 176, 179–80,
  189, 194, 197, 202–203, 206–207,
  243, 272, 296, 302, 306.
Medicare, 65, 126, 176, 179–80, 189,
  197, 208, 272, 306.
Mentally ill, support of, 92, 183, 194,
  199, 294–96.
Mettler, Suzanne, 241.
Military spending, 26, 54.
Minarik, Joseph J., 27, 126–27.
Mincy, Ronald B., 111.
Minow, Martha, 305.
Mises, Ludwig von, 31.
Mont Pèlerin Society, 56, 138, 335 n.88.
Moral hazard, 379 n.29; healthcare sub-
  sidies, 172, 177–79, 185, 202; same-
  sex marriage, 214; social insurance,
  178–79; work subsidies, 43.
Moral Majority, 281, 283, 302.
Morgan, Iwan, 26–27.
Morgan, Laura, 105.
Morgen, Sandra, 386 n.79.
Mortgages, 249; access to, 138–39, 142;
  exclusionary lending practices,
  144–51; high-risk and marginalized
  borrowers, 150–51, 155; maximizing
  lender profits, 142–43; private
  brokers, 142–43, 150–51, 154–55, 158–
  60; subprime loans, 150–51, 155, 159,
  244, 401 n.91; vanilla mortgages,

New religious right, 19.
New Right, 191, 281.
New social conservatism: defined,
    19–20; ties with neoliberalism,
    20–21, 33, 49, 63.
New Spirit of Capitalism (Boltanski
    and Chiapello), 11–12.
New York City, 189, 191–92, 196,
    198–99, 206–207, 288, 297–98,
    382 n.52, 421 n.132.
New York Federal Reserve, 215–16.
New York Trump Tower, 200.
Nixon, Richard, 19, 43–48, 51, 64, 69,
    98–99, 121, 126, 180, 185, 273,
    330 n.50, 331 n.57; and black family
    wage, 43.
Nolan, Pat, 263.
Nonprofit sector, and government,
    181–82, 192–98, 272. *See also*
    Faith-based organizations.
Novak, Michael, 290.
Novak, William, 84.

OBAMA, BARACK, 68, 112–14, 268,
    271, 411 n.36.
O'Connor, Alice, 99.
O'Connor, John, 198.
Office of Child Support Enforcement,
    101.
Office of Economic Opportunity, 94,
    181, 194, 309.
Office of Faith-Based and Community
    Initiatives, 269.
Oil embargoes of 1973 and 1979, 26.
Olasky, Marvin, 70–71, 293.
Old Age Insurance (OAI), 35.
Old Poor Law. *See* Elizabethan Poor
    Law.
Omnibus Budget Reconciliation Act
    of 1981 (OBRA), 65, 188–89,
    194, 296.

Osborne, Peter, 17.
Outdoor relief, 83–85.

PAINE, THOMAS, 137.
Panitch, Leo, 29.
Parents, family responsibilities to,
    58, 73, 84, 90, 100.
Parkinson, Patrick, 348–49 n.104.
Parks, Jennifer, 197.
Partnership for the Homeless, 297.
Paternity obligations, 67–68, 103–104.
Patton, Cindy, 204.
Pauly, Mark, 177–79.
Pell, Claiborne, 223.
Pellegrini, Ann, 418 n.109.
Pell grants, 223, 237, 240–43, 250,
    260, 262.
Pension accounts, 138.
People v. James W. Hill, 355 n.140.
Perrow, Charles, 191, 199.
Personal Responsibility and Work
    Opportunity Reconciliation Act
    (PRWORA), 67, 101–104, 106–108,
    268, 309, 350 n.115, 410 n.32.
Pew Center, 215.
Philipson, Tomas, 167–75, 179–80,
    203, 214.
Phillips, Kevin, 129.
Phillips curve, 28, 54.
Pigou, A. C., 175.
Piketty, Thomas, 23, 123, 137, 356–
    57 n.11, 357 n.13.
Pimpare, Stephen, 84.
Piven, Frances, 41–42.
PLUS loans, 216, 243–44, 248, 401 n.89.
Podhoretz, Norman, 49.
Polanyi, Karl, 13–18, 61, 321 n.21.
Pollak, Robert A., 212.
Poon, Martha, 150.
Poor laws. *See* Family responsibility.
Popenoe, David, 110.

University of California at Los Angeles (UCLA), 18, 204, 237.
University of Chicago, 18.
University of Virginia, 18.
Unlevel Playing Field, 269.
Urban Institute, 298, 420 n.127.
US Conference of Catholic Bishops, 306.
US Congress, 78, 93, 98, 101, 109, 112–13, 134, 148, 195, 223, 240–44, 266, 269–70, 273, 296, 302, 307, 345 n.61, 356 n.9, 393 n.28, 401 n.88, 402 n.93.
US Court of Appeals for the Seventh Circuit, 168.
USDA v. Moreno, 414 n.61.
Use of Pleasure (Foucault), 175, 377 n.21.
Uses of the University (Kerr), 228–29.
US Hispanic Chamber of Commerce, 155.
US Pan Asian American Chamber of Commerce, 155–56.
US Supreme Court, 94–95, 269, 275–76, 304, 308, 374 n.127, 414 n.61; and federal welfare law, 36–37.
US Treasury, 127, 245, 328 n.15, 393 n.28.

VAÏSSE, JUSTIN, 52, 332–33 n.68.
Vietnam War, 26, 54, 229–30, 369 n.95.
Virginia Polytechnic University, 18.
Virginia school: economists, 18–19, 30–32, 225, 238, 335 n.88, 379 n.26; neoliberals, 32, 128, 251.
Virginia school of public choice theory, 30–31, 176–77, 218.
Volcker, Paul, 25, 29, 124, 132–35, 327–28 n.14.
Volcker recession, 200.
Volcker shock, 25, 29, 64, 132–33, 138, 188, 191, 239, 246, 315, 361 n.41.

Volenti non fit injuria, 179, 202, 207, 380 n.37.

WAGNER, RICHARD, 18, 30, 128.
Wallis, Jim, 415 n.73.
Walnut Street Prison, Philadelphia, PA, 264.
War on Poverty, 100, 121, 181–82, 229, 271–72, 277, 284, 294, 309.
Warren, Earl, 95–96, 273.
Watkins, James D., 169.
Wealth, redistribution of, 15, 17, 27; Fordist family wage, 23. *See also* Welfare reform.
Wealth and Poverty (Gilder), 128.
Weber, Max, 55, 292–93.
"Weight of the Poor: A Strategy to End Poverty" (Cloward and Piven), 41.
Welfare. *See* Outdoor relief.
Welfare, as redistributive system, 15, 21, 32–33, 44, 46–49, 51, 62–64, 70, 130–31, 139–40, 143, 283, 415 n.73.
Welfare, asset-based, 138–41, 146, 152–57, 363 n.53, 365–66 n.67, 366 n.68, 370 n.106.
Welfare block grants, 101–102, 108, 194, 296.
Welfare devolution, 286–87, 294.
Welfare law, 36–37, 41, 69, 71, 94–97, 104–105, 108, 120, 276, 284, 315, 351 n.117, 413–14 n.61. *See also* Family law; Family responsibility.
Welfare recipients: morality of, 36, 94–95, 122; "queens," 46, 53; racial minorities, 7; single mothers, 7, 109.
Welfare reform, 33, 41–42; abstinence education, 309, 410 n.32; and family formation, 9, 43–45, 47, 103, 122–23; family wage, 40, 42; healthy marriage programs, 68, 261, 265, 267–68, 406 n.9; marriage promotion,

ZONE BOOKS *NEAR FUTURES* SERIES
Edited by Wendy Brown and Michel Feher

The turn of the 1980s marked the beginning of a new era in the Euro-Atlantic world: Inspired by the work of neoliberal economists and legal scholars, the "conservative revolutionaries" who came to power during these pivotal years used their offices to undermine the thinking and dismantle the institutional framework upon which welfare capitalism had rested. In their view, the role of the government was not to protect vulnerable segments of the population from the potential violence of market relations but, instead, to shelter the allegedly fragile mechanisms of the market from stifling rules and the disabling influence of so-called "special interests" which ranged from organized labor to protectors of the environment. They also believed that, once markets were properly shielded, their domain could be extended beyond the traditional borders of the private sector.

Eager to blunt the resistance raised by their agenda, neoliberal reformers initiated a series of deregulations, regarding capital flow and asset creation, that were meant to replace social protection and guaranteed employment with abundant and accessible credit—thereby endowing all economic agents with entrepreneurial ambitions and discipline. Yet, under the guise of diffusing the ethos of the self-reliant entrepreneur throughout the entire population, their reforms eventually enabled the speculative logic of financial markets to preside over the allocation of resources on a global scale. Thus, far from restoring thrift and frugality as the virtuous paths to personal independence and lasting profit, the reign of deregulated finance defined success as leverage, understood as the ability to invest with borrowed funds, and compelled the less fortunate to stake their livelihood on perennial indebtedness.

Much more than a mood swing, whereby the advocates of freer markets would temporarily prevail over the harbingers of a more protective State, the policies instigated under Ronald Reagan and Margaret Thatcher, and further refined by their "Third Way" successors, have successively transformed everything from corporate management to statecraft, household economics to personal relations. In the world shaped by these transformations—a world where the securitization of risks and liabilities greatly widens the realm of potentially appreciable assets—even the criteria according to which individuals are incited to evaluate themselves no longer match the civic, business, and family values respectively distinctive of political, economic, and cultural liberalism.

Along the way, the purchase of markets and "market solutions" has expanded to a range of domains hitherto associated with public services or common goods—from education to military intelligence to environmental stewardship. Simultaneously, the number and purview of democratically debatable issues has been drastically reduced by the sway of "good governance" and "best practices"—two notions originating in a corporate culture devoted to the creation of shareholder value but later co-opted by public officials whose main concern is the standing of the national debt in bondholders' eyes.

For a long time, many critics on the left hoped that the changes they were witnessing might be transient. As the unconstrained quest for short-term capital gain would bear its bitter fruits, the thinking went, gaping inequalities and the prospect of an environmental catastrophe would induce elected officials to change course or, if they failed to do so, expose them to a massive popular upheaval. However, neither the steady deterioration of labor conditions nor the increasingly alarming damages caused to the environment has acted as the anticipated wake up call. To the contrary, the aftermath of the Great Recession has demonstrated the remarkable resilience of a mode of government, disseminated across public and private institutions, that gives precedence to the gambles on tomorrow's presumptive profits over the mending of today's social woes and the prevention of after-tomorrow's ecological disaster.

Once filled with the hopes and apprehensions of radical change, the near future has been taken over by speculations on investors' tastes. As such, it mandates the sacrifice of the present and the deferral of any serious grappling with long-term sustainability. Yet, for those who wish to uncover alternative trajectories, the ultimate purpose of exposing the current dominance of speculators and the nefarious effects of their short-termism is not to forego the near future but to find ways of reclaiming it.

Reckoning with the epochal nature of the turn that capitalism has taken in the last three decades, the editors of *Near Futures* seek to assemble a series of books that will illuminate its manifold implications—with regard to the production of value and values, the missions or disorientations of social and political institutions, the yearnings, reasoning, and conduct expected of individuals. However, the purpose of this project is not only to take stock of what neoliberal reforms and the dictates of finance have wrought: insofar as every mode of government generates resistances specific to its premises and practices, *Near Futures* also purports to chart some of the new conflicts and forms of activism elicited by the advent of our brave new world.

Near Futures series design by Julie Fry
Typesetting by Meighan Gale
Printed and bound by Maple Press